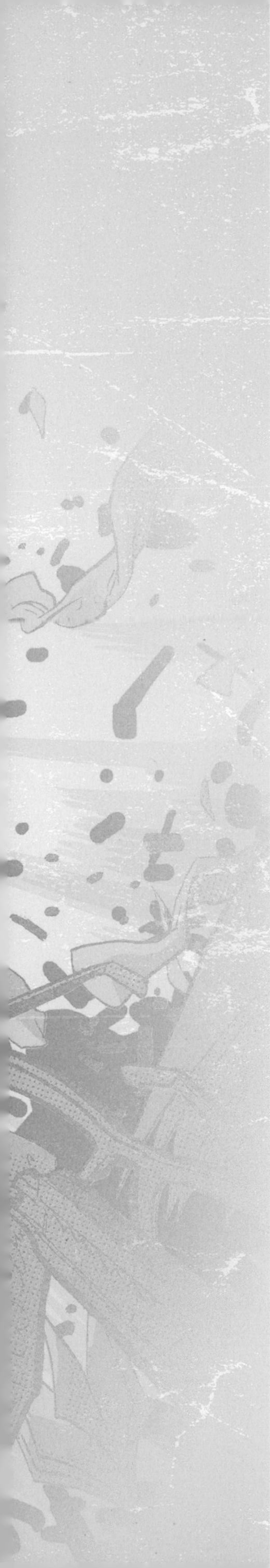

COLLAPSER

MIKEY WAY
SHAUN SIMON
writers

ILIAS KYRIAZIS
artist

CRIS PETER
colorist

SIMON BOWLAND
letterer

ILIAS KYRIAZIS
series and collection cover artist

COLLAPSER created by **MIKEY WAY, SHAUN SIMON,** and **ILIAS KYRIAZIS**

DC'S YOUNG ANIMAL curated by **GERARD WAY**

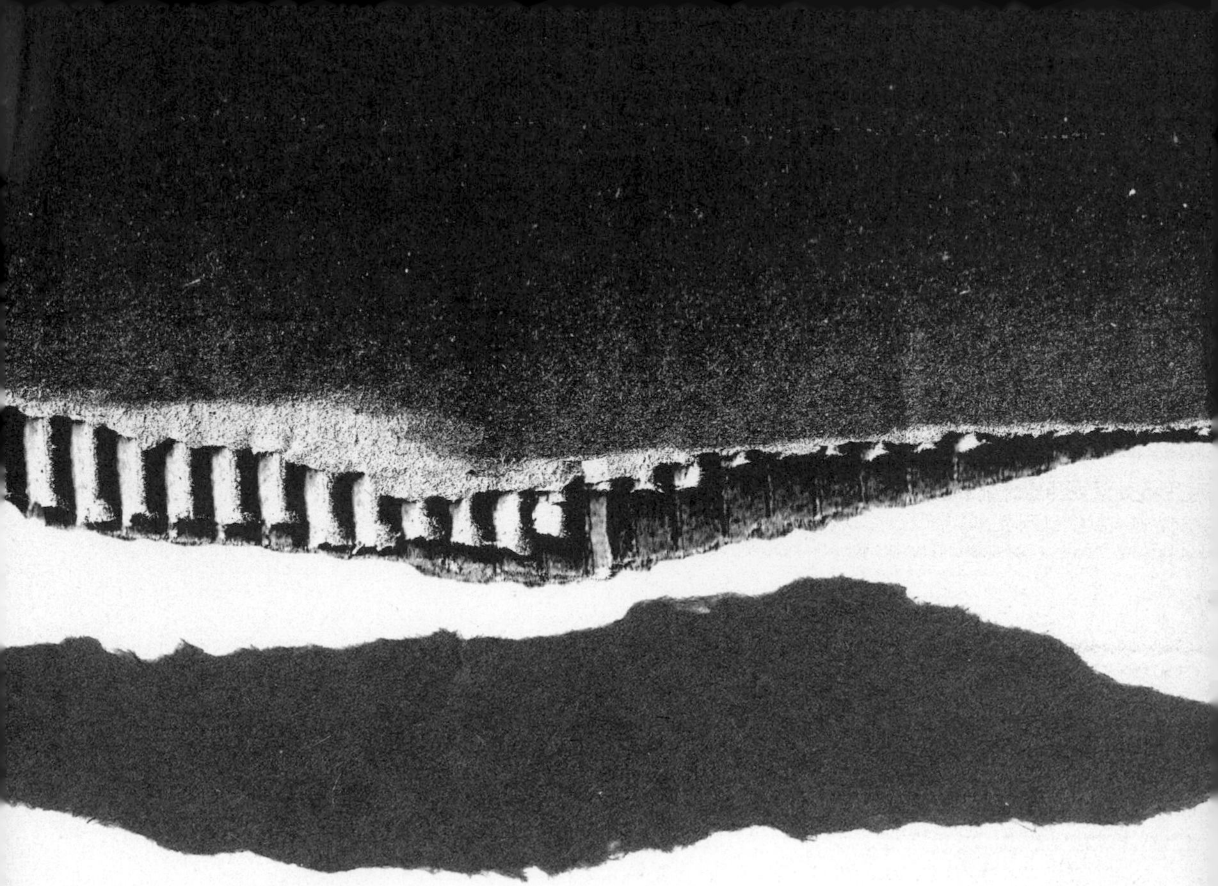

ANDY KHOURI, JAMIE S. RICH Editors – Original Series
MAGGIE HOWELL Assistant Editor – Original Series
JEB WOODARD Group Editor – Collected Editions
ERIKA ROTHBERG Editor – Collected Edition
STEVE COOK Design Director – Books
MEGEN BELLERSEN Publication Design
TOM VALENTE Publication Production

BOB HARRAS Senior VP – Editor-in-Chief, DC Comics
MARK DOYLE Executive Editor, DC Black Label

DAN DiDIO Publisher
JIM LEE Publisher & Chief Creative Officer
BOBBIE CHASE VP – New Publishing Initiatives
DON FALLETTI VP – Manufacturing Operations & Workflow Management
LAWRENCE GANEM VP – Talent Services
ALISON GILL Senior VP – Manufacturing & Operations
HANK KANALZ Senior VP – Publishing Strategy & Support Services
DAN MIRON VP – Publishing Operations
NICK J. NAPOLITANO VP – Manufacturing Administration & Design
NANCY SPEARS VP – Sales
JONAH WEILAND VP – Marketing & Creative Services
MICHELE R. WELLS VP & Executive Editor, Young Reader

COLLAPSER

DC Comics, 2900 West Alameda Ave., Burbank, CA 91505
Printed by LSC Communications, Owensville, MO, USA.
6/26/20. First Printing.
ISBN: 978-1-4012-9581-3

Library of Congress Cataloging-in-Publication Data is available.

PEFC Certified

This product is from
sustainably managed
forests and controlled
sources

PEFC/29-31-337   www.pefc.org

COLLAPSER

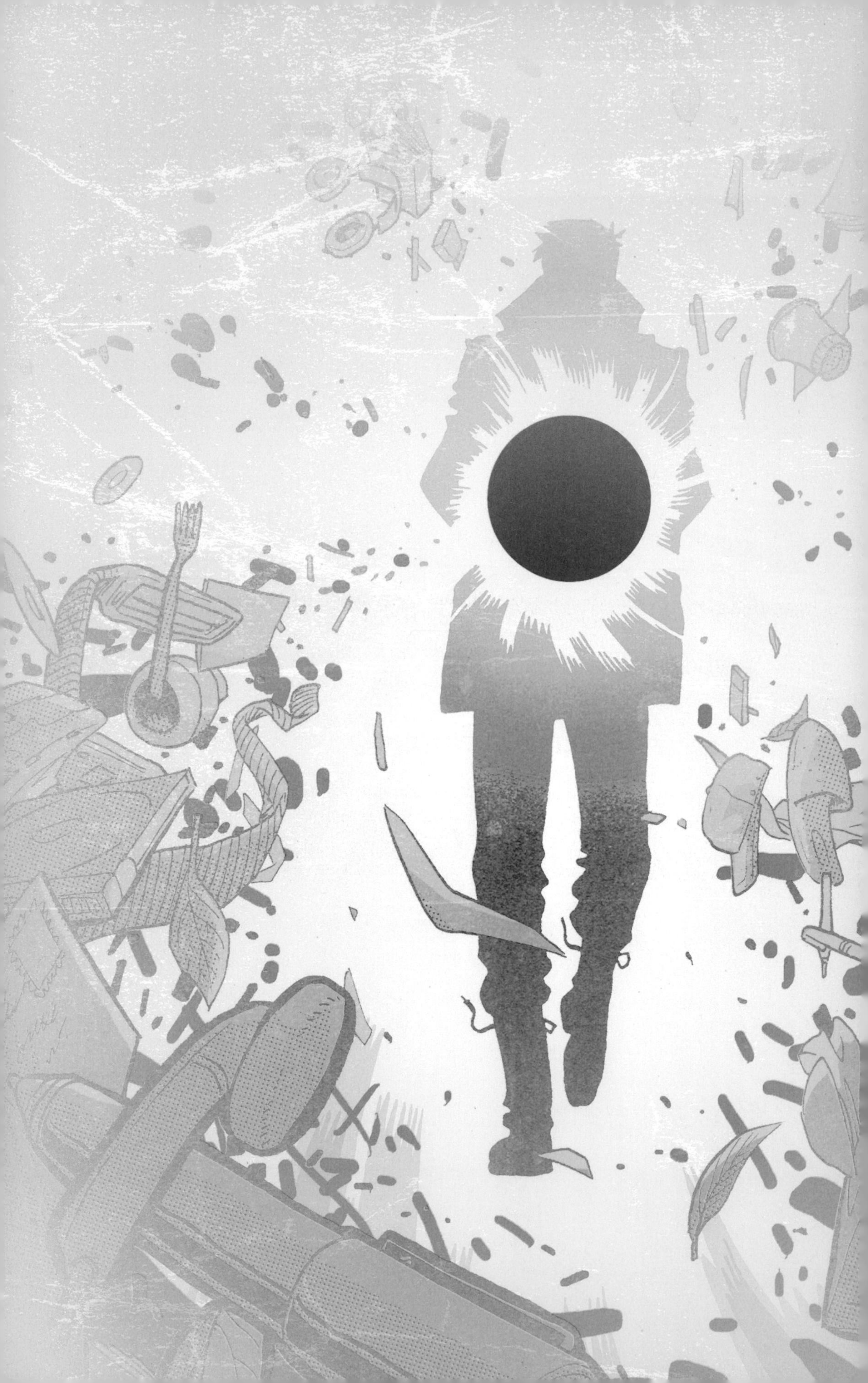

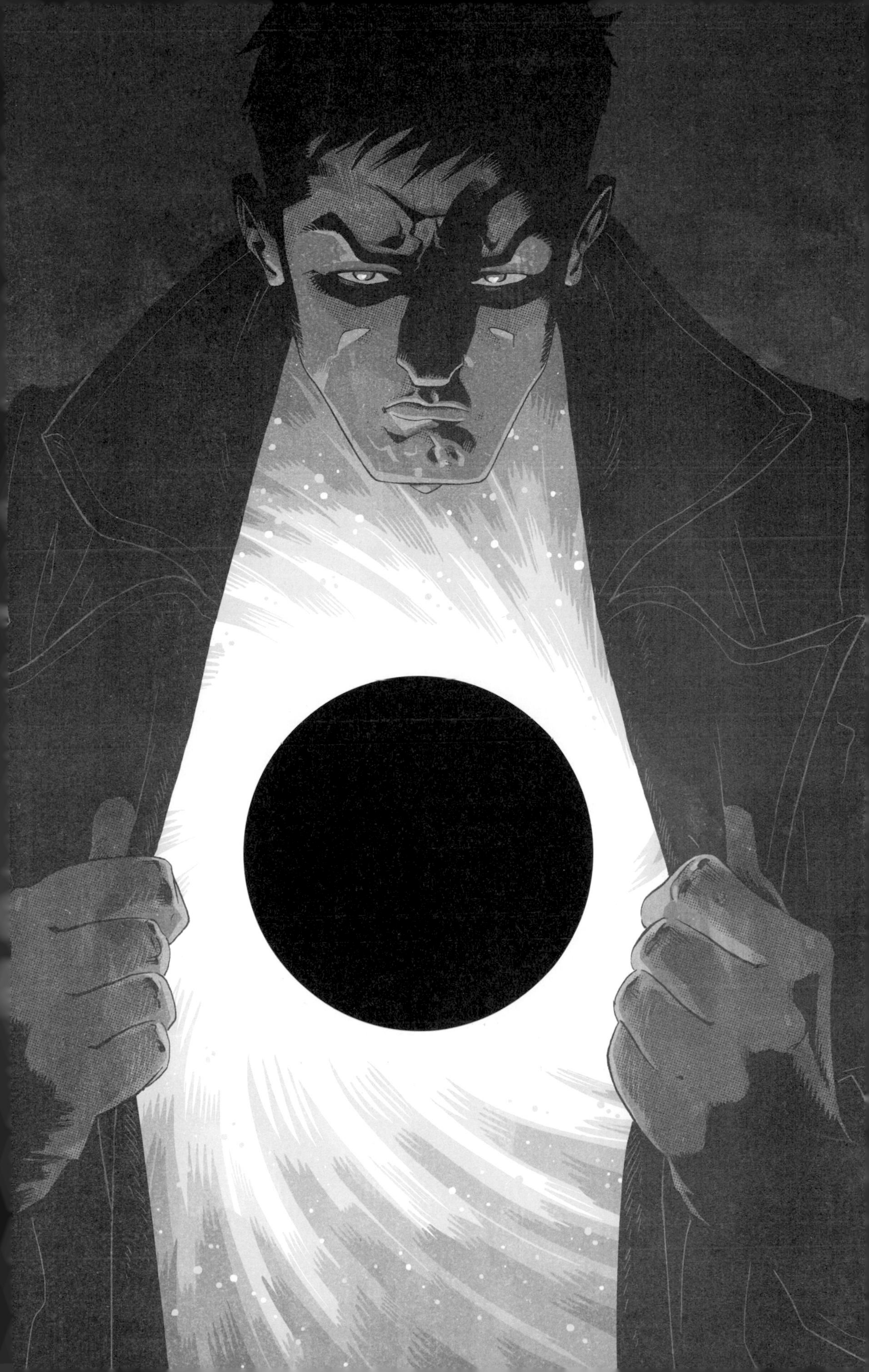

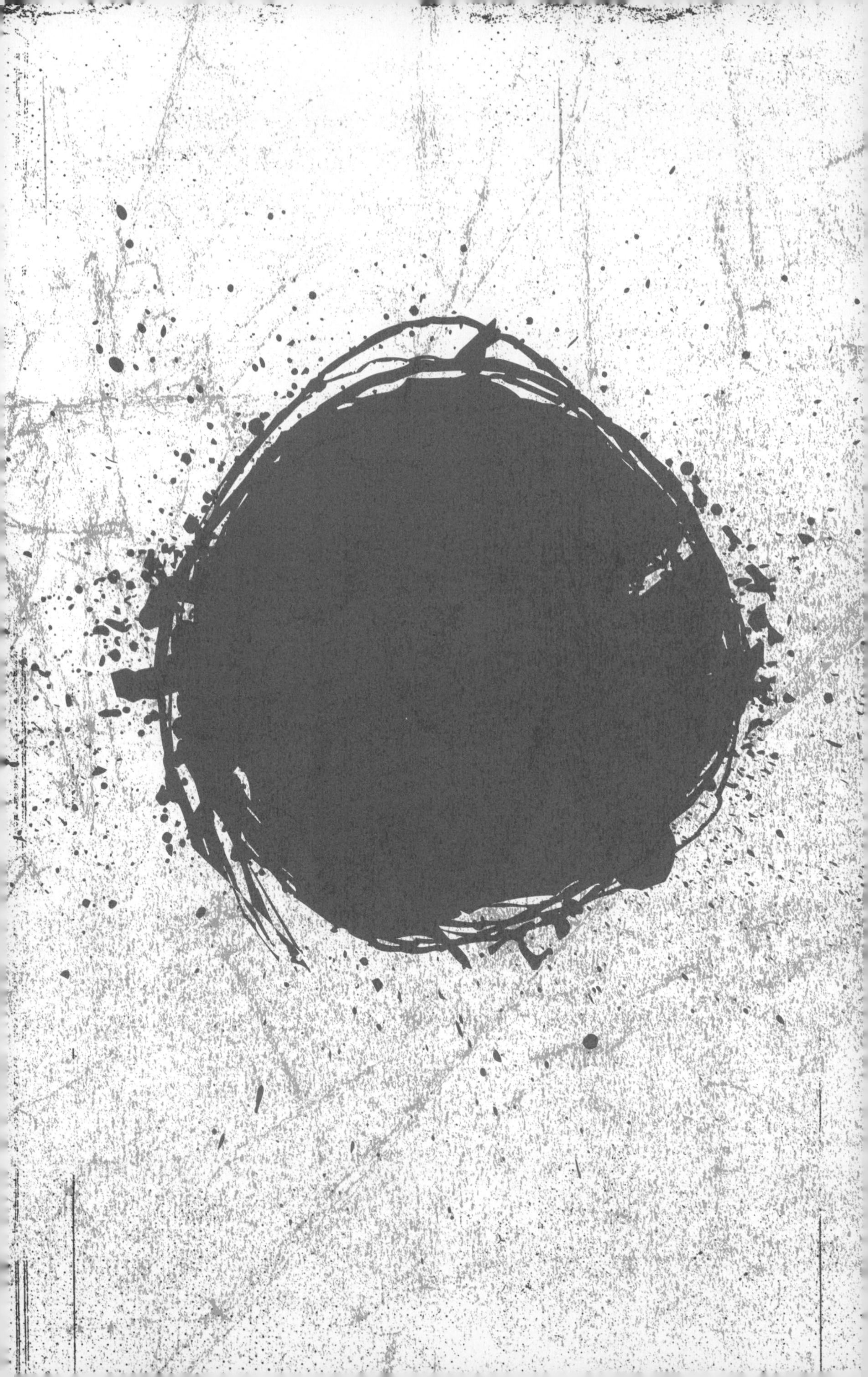

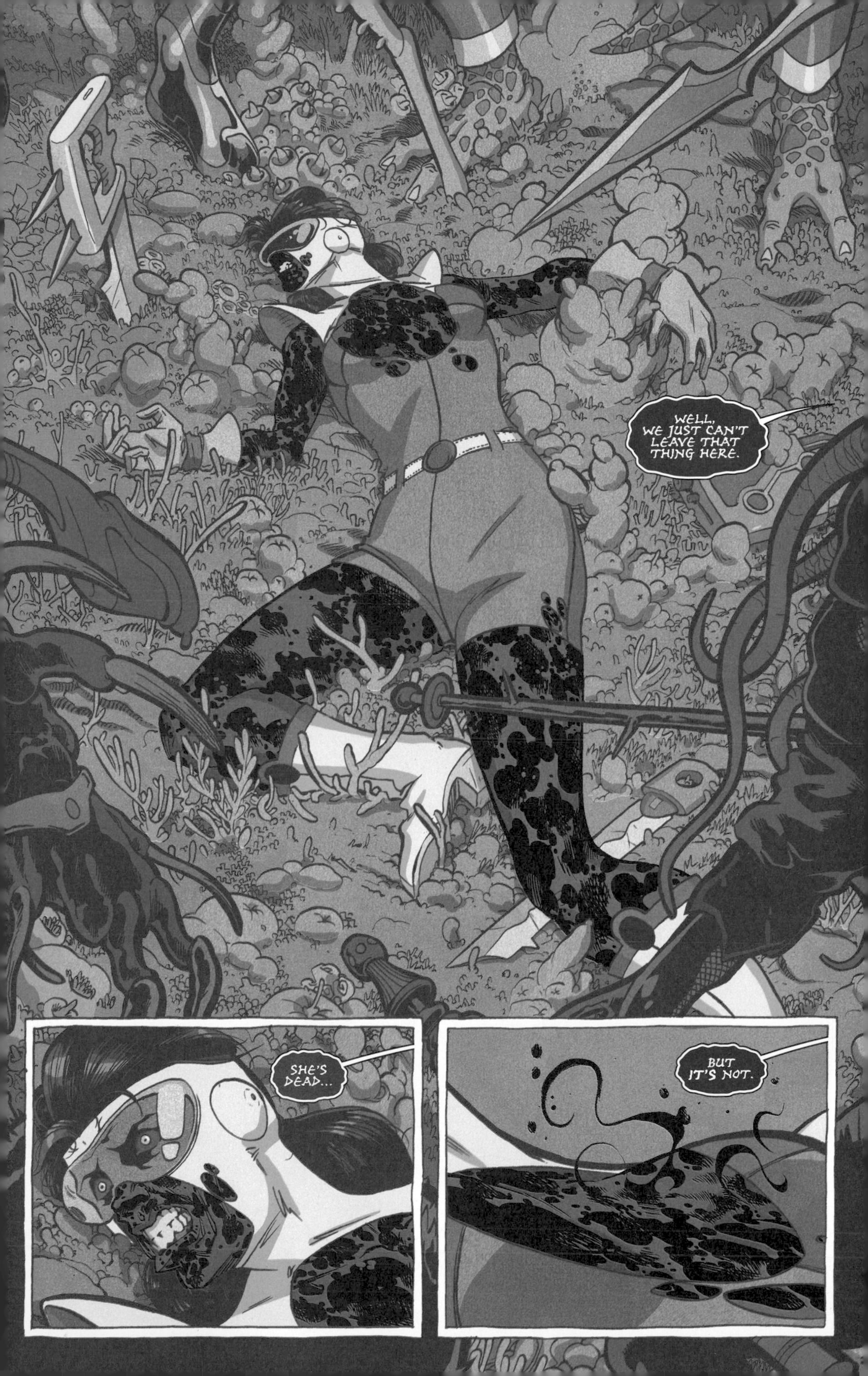
WELL, WE JUST CAN'T LEAVE THAT THING HERE.
SHE'S DEAD...
BUT IT'S NOT.

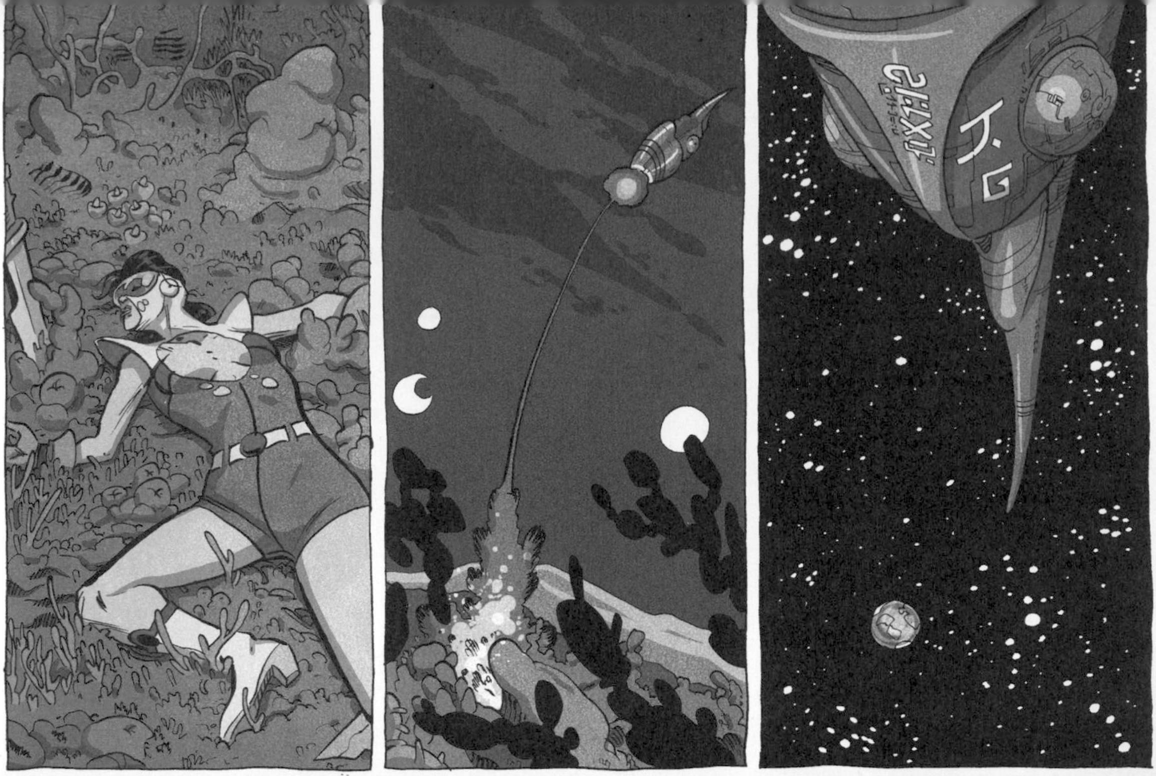

CONSTELLATION PRIZE

story MIKEY WAY and SHAUN SIMON
art ILIAS KYRIAZIS
colors CRIS PETER letters SIMON BOWLAND cover ILIAS KYRIAZIS
editors JAMIE S. RICH & ANDY KHOURI assistant editor MAGGIE HOWELL
created by MIKEY WAY, SHAUN SIMON and ILIAS KYRIAZIS
DC YOUNG ANIMAL curated by GERARD WAY
In memory of DEMETRES KYRIAZIS

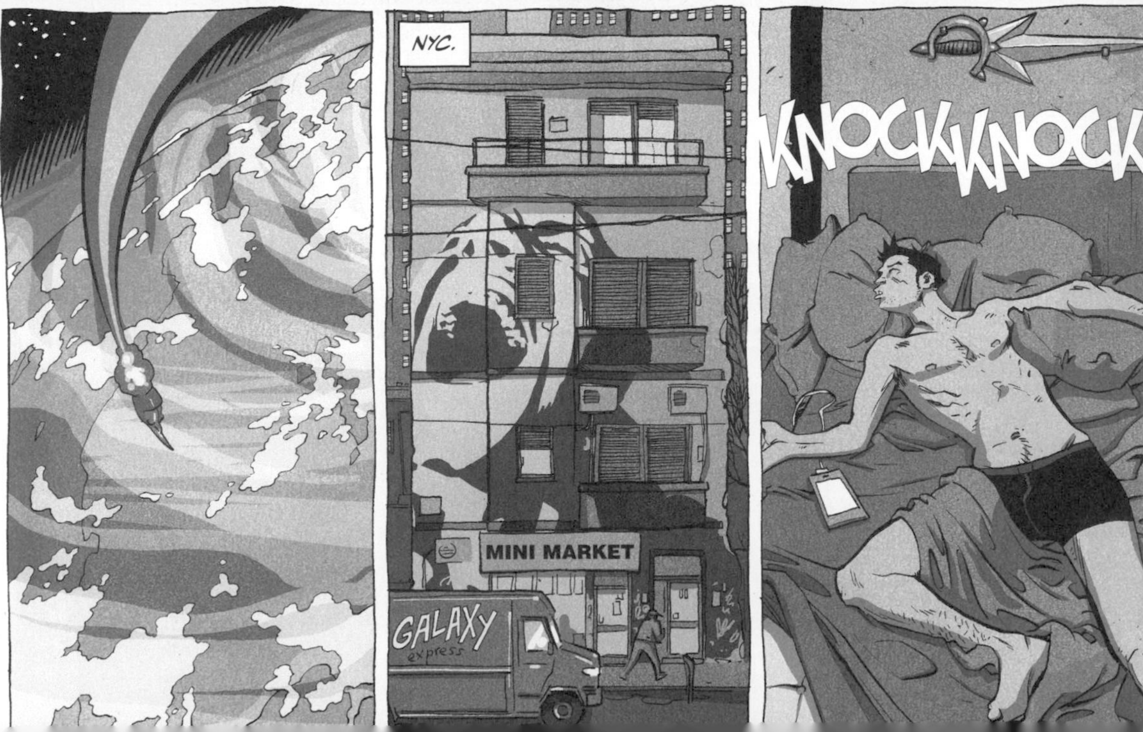
NYC.
MINI MARKET
GALAXY
express
KNOCKKNOCK

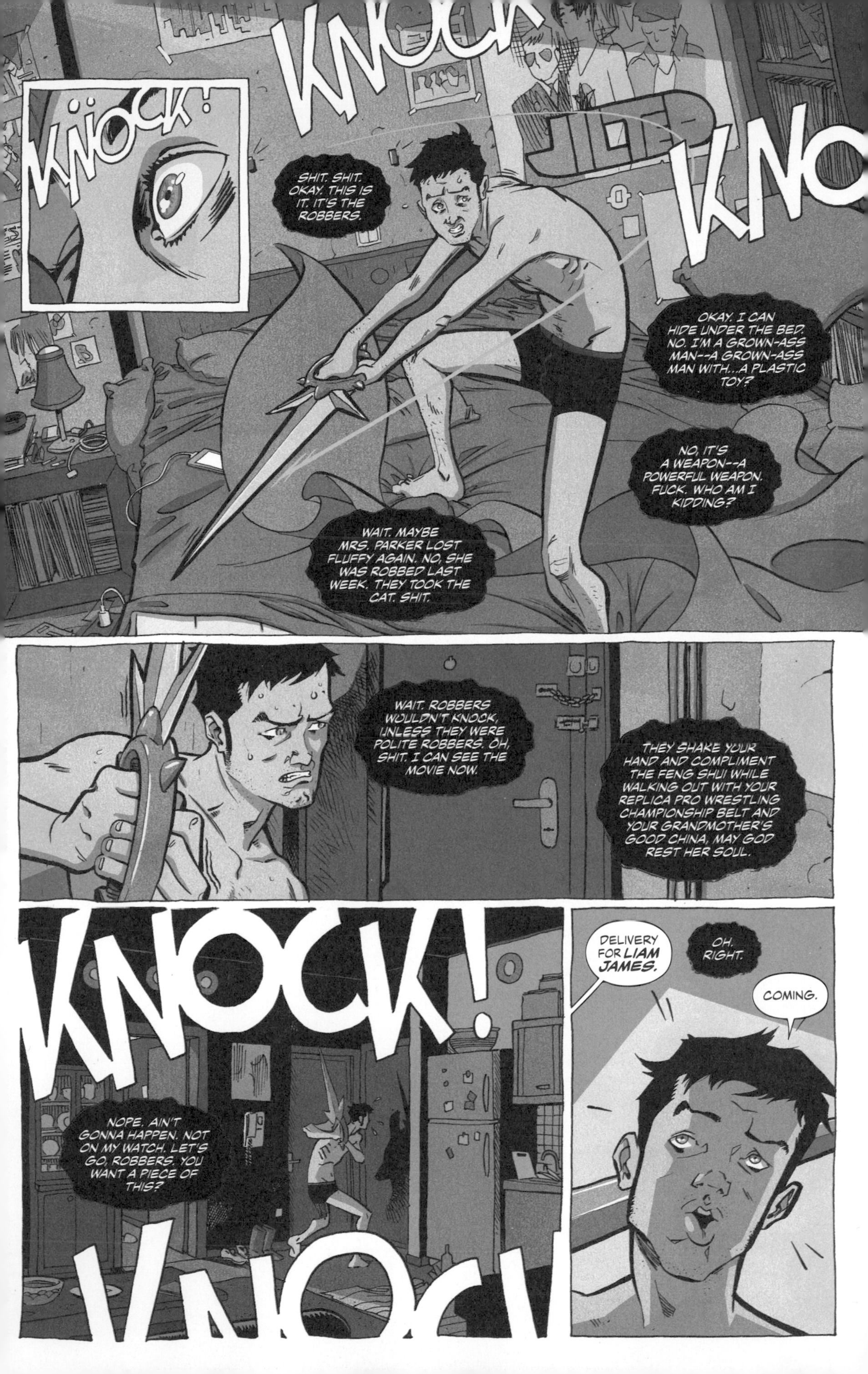
KNOCK
KNÖCK!
KNO
SHIT. SHIT. OKAY. THIS IS IT. IT'S THE ROBBERS.
OKAY. I CAN HIDE UNDER THE BED. NO. I'M A GROWN-ASS MAN--A GROWN-ASS MAN WITH...A PLASTIC TOY?
NO, IT'S A WEAPON--A POWERFUL WEAPON. FUCK. WHO AM I KIDDING?
WAIT. MAYBE MRS. PARKER LOST FLUFFY AGAIN. NO, SHE WAS ROBBED LAST WEEK. THEY TOOK THE CAT. SHIT.
WAIT. ROBBERS WOULDN'T KNOCK, UNLESS THEY WERE POLITE ROBBERS. OH, SHIT. I CAN SEE THE MOVIE NOW.
THEY SHAKE YOUR HAND AND COMPLIMENT THE FENG SHUI WHILE WALKING OUT WITH YOUR REPLICA PRO WRESTLING CHAMPIONSHIP BELT AND YOUR GRANDMOTHER'S GOOD CHINA, MAY GOD REST HER SOUL.
KNOCK!
NOPE. AIN'T GONNA HAPPEN. NOT ON MY WATCH. LET'S GO, ROBBERS. YOU WANT A PIECE OF THIS?
DELIVERY FOR **LIAM JAMES.**
OH. RIGHT.
COMING.

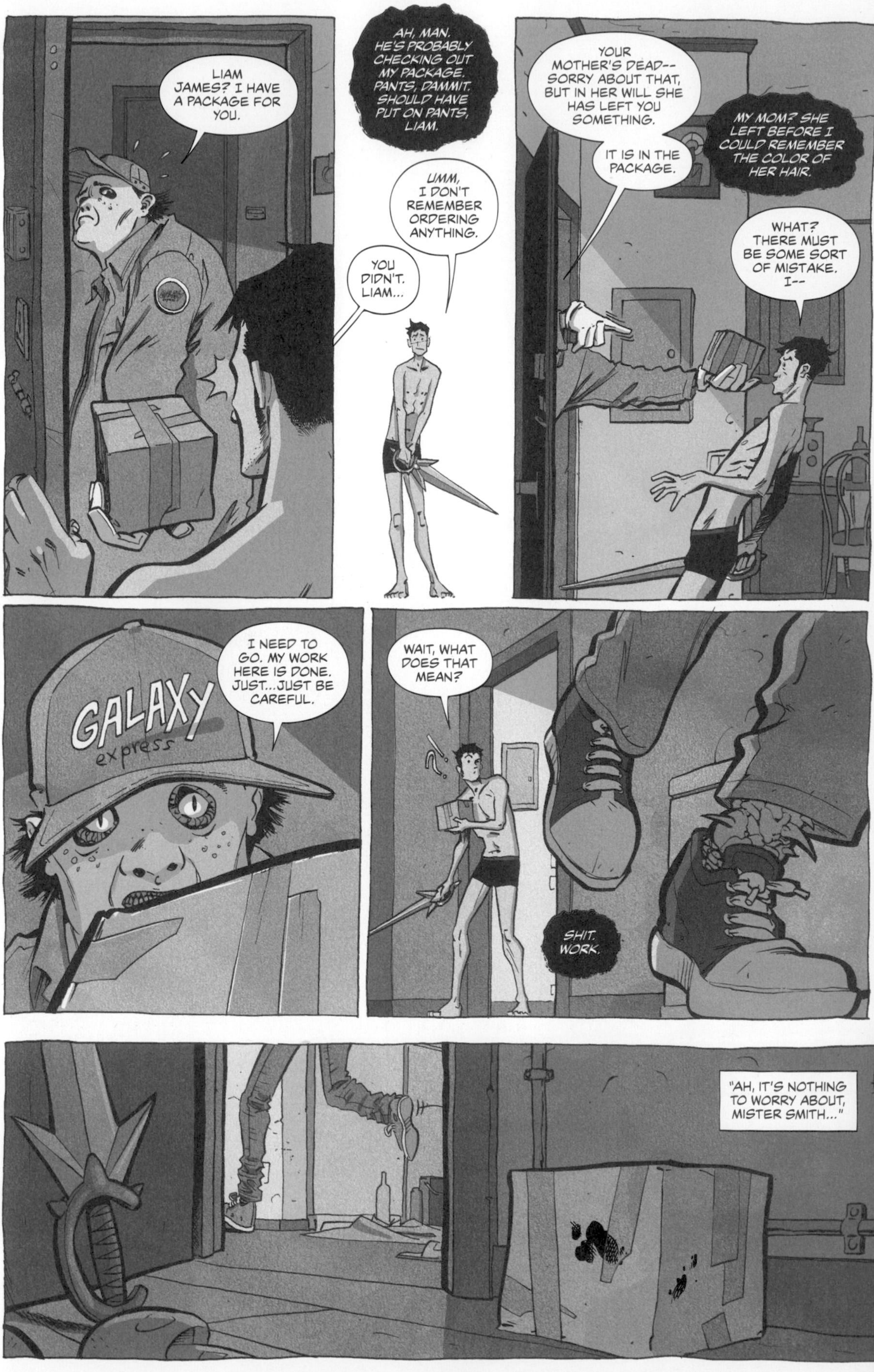
LIAM JAMES? I HAVE A PACKAGE FOR YOU.
AH, MAN. HE'S PROBABLY CHECKING OUT MY PACKAGE. PANTS, DAMMIT. SHOULD HAVE PUT ON PANTS, LIAM.
UMM, I DON'T REMEMBER ORDERING ANYTHING.
YOU DIDN'T. LIAM...
YOUR MOTHER'S DEAD-- SORRY ABOUT THAT, BUT IN HER WILL SHE HAS LEFT YOU SOMETHING.
IT IS IN THE PACKAGE.
MY MOM? SHE LEFT BEFORE I COULD REMEMBER THE COLOR OF HER HAIR.
WHAT? THERE MUST BE SOME SORT OF MISTAKE. I--
GALAXY express
I NEED TO GO. MY WORK HERE IS DONE. JUST...JUST BE CAREFUL.
WAIT, WHAT DOES THAT MEAN?
SHIT. WORK.
"AH, IT'S NOTHING TO WORRY ABOUT, MISTER SMITH..."

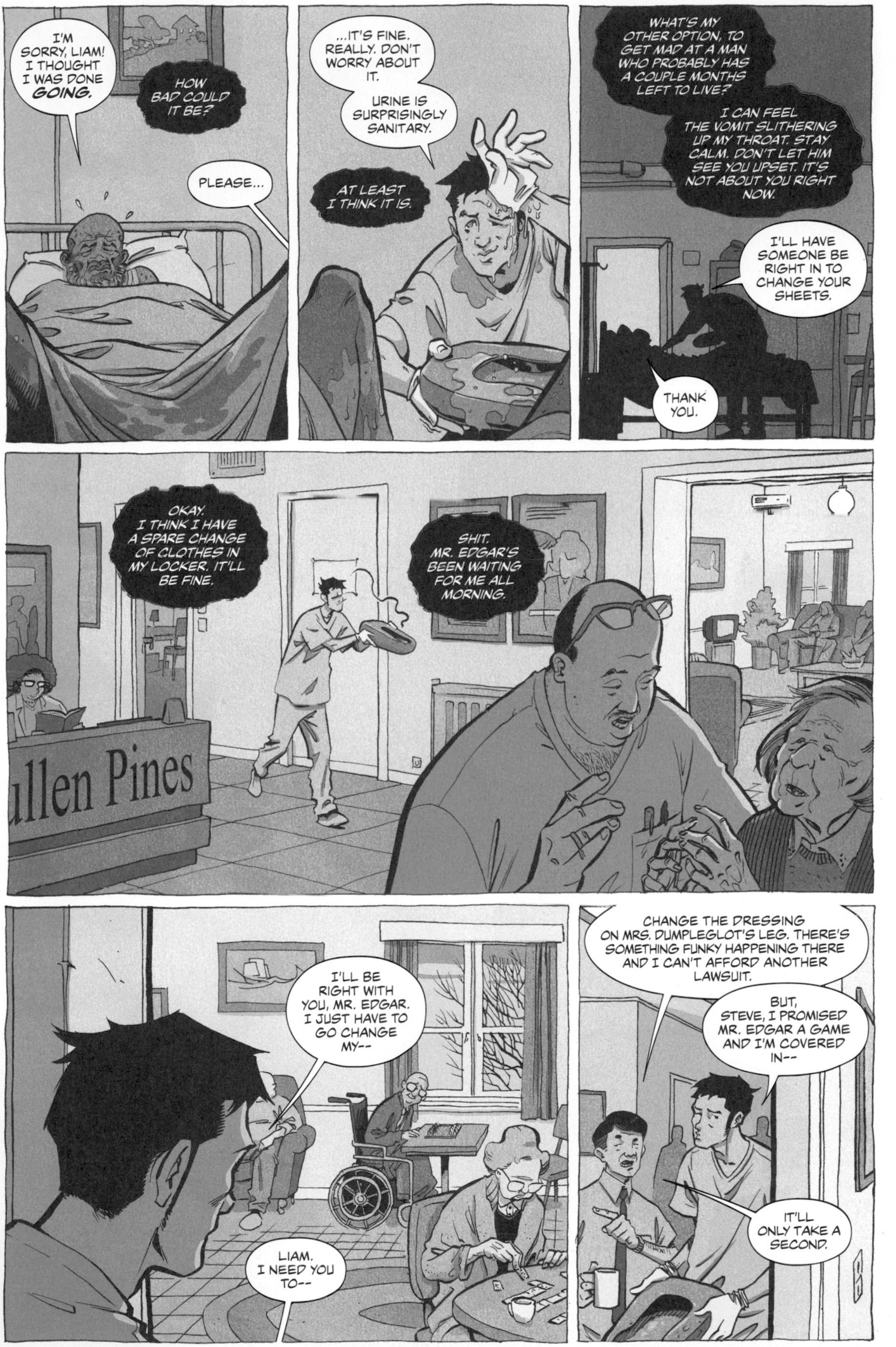
I'M SORRY, LIAM! I THOUGHT I WAS DONE GOING.
HOW BAD COULD IT BE?
PLEASE...
...IT'S FINE. REALLY. DON'T WORRY ABOUT IT.
URINE IS SURPRISINGLY SANITARY.
AT LEAST I THINK IT IS.
WHAT'S MY OTHER OPTION, TO GET MAD AT A MAN WHO PROBABLY HAS A COUPLE MONTHS LEFT TO LIVE?
I CAN FEEL THE VOMIT SLITHERING UP MY THROAT. STAY CALM. DON'T LET HIM SEE YOU UPSET. IT'S NOT ABOUT YOU RIGHT NOW.
I'LL HAVE SOMEONE BE RIGHT IN TO CHANGE YOUR SHEETS.
THANK YOU.
OKAY. I THINK I HAVE A SPARE CHANGE OF CLOTHES IN MY LOCKER. IT'LL BE FINE.
SHIT. MR. EDGAR'S BEEN WAITING FOR ME ALL MORNING.
ullen Pines
I'LL BE RIGHT WITH YOU, MR. EDGAR. I JUST HAVE TO GO CHANGE MY--
LIAM. I NEED YOU TO--
CHANGE THE DRESSING ON MRS. DUMPLEGLOT'S LEG. THERE'S SOMETHING FUNKY HAPPENING THERE AND I CAN'T AFFORD ANOTHER LAWSUIT.
BUT, STEVE, I PROMISED MR. EDGAR A GAME AND I'M COVERED IN--
IT'LL ONLY TAKE A SECOND.

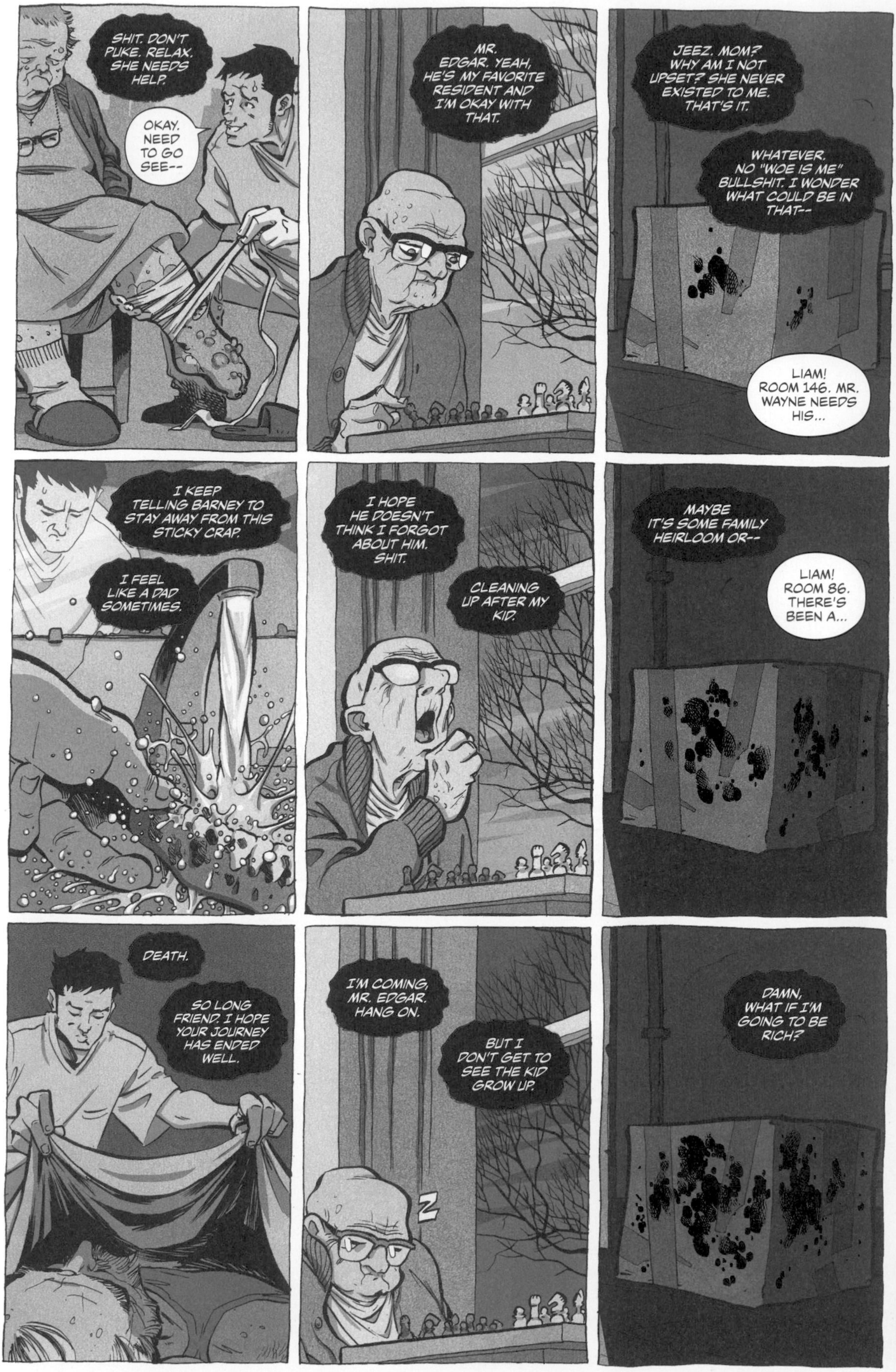

SHIT. DON'T PUKE. RELAX. SHE NEEDS HELP.
OKAY. NEED TO GO SEE--
MR. EDGAR. YEAH, HE'S MY FAVORITE RESIDENT AND I'M OKAY WITH THAT.
JEEZ. MOM? WHY AM I NOT UPSET? SHE NEVER EXISTED TO ME. THAT'S IT.
WHATEVER. NO "WOE IS ME" BULLSHIT. I WONDER WHAT COULD BE IN THAT--
LIAM! ROOM 146. MR. WAYNE NEEDS HIS...
I KEEP TELLING BARNEY TO STAY AWAY FROM THIS STICKY CRAP.
I FEEL LIKE A DAD SOMETIMES.
I HOPE HE DOESN'T THINK I FORGOT ABOUT HIM. SHIT.
CLEANING UP AFTER MY KID.
MAYBE IT'S SOME FAMILY HEIRLOOM OR--
LIAM! ROOM 86. THERE'S BEEN A...
DEATH.
SO LONG FRIEND. I HOPE YOUR JOURNEY HAS ENDED WELL.
I'M COMING, MR. EDGAR. HANG ON.
BUT I DON'T GET TO SEE THE KID GROW UP.
Z
DAMN, WHAT IF I'M GOING TO BE RICH?

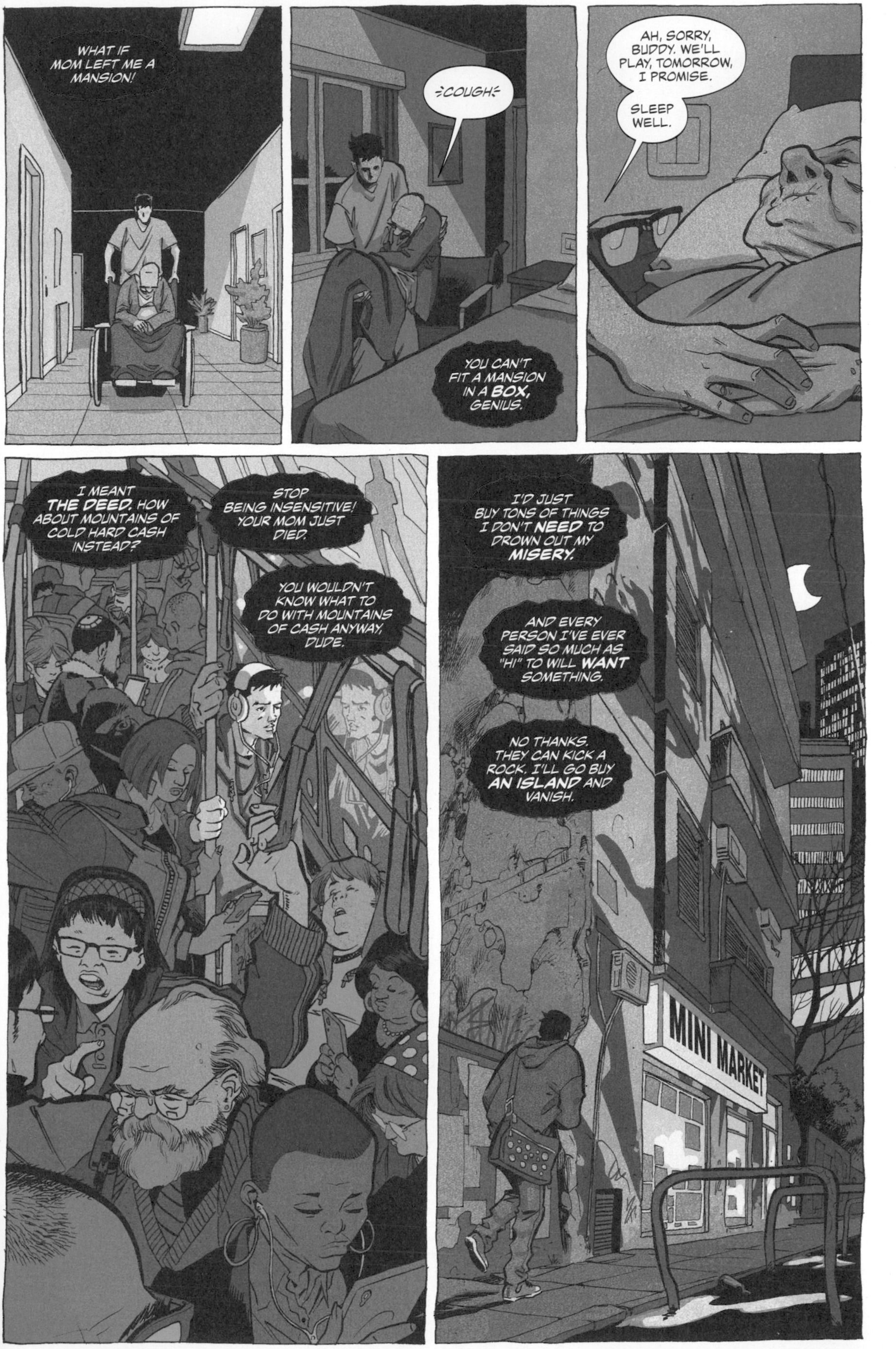
WHAT IF MOM LEFT ME A MANSION!
COUGH
YOU CAN'T FIT A MANSION IN A BOX, GENIUS.
AH, SORRY, BUDDY. WE'LL PLAY, TOMORROW, I PROMISE.
SLEEP WELL.
I MEANT THE DEED. HOW ABOUT MOUNTAINS OF COLD HARD CASH INSTEAD?
STOP BEING INSENSITIVE! YOUR MOM JUST DIED.
YOU WOULDN'T KNOW WHAT TO DO WITH MOUNTAINS OF CASH ANYWAY, DUDE.
I'D JUST BUY TONS OF THINGS I DON'T NEED TO DROWN OUT MY MISERY.
AND EVERY PERSON I'VE EVER SAID SO MUCH AS "HI" TO WILL WANT SOMETHING.
NO THANKS. THEY CAN KICK A ROCK. I'LL GO BUY AN ISLAND AND VANISH.
MINI MARKET

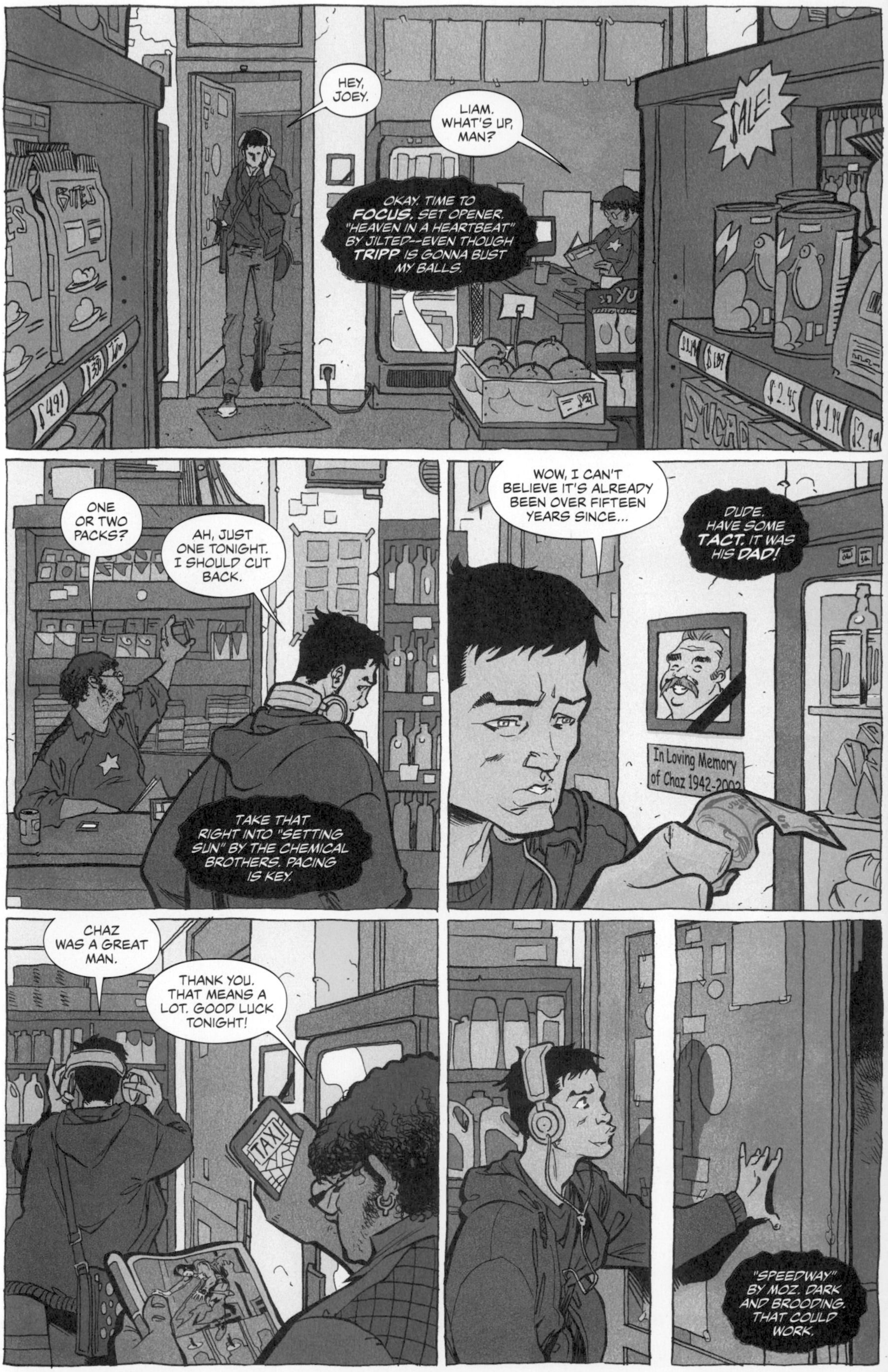
HEY, JOEY.
LIAM. WHAT'S UP, MAN?
OKAY. TIME TO FOCUS. SET OPENER. "HEAVEN IN A HEARTBEAT" BY JILTED--EVEN THOUGH TRIPP IS GONNA BUST MY BALLS.
SALE!
ONE OR TWO PACKS?
AH, JUST ONE TONIGHT. I SHOULD CUT BACK.
TAKE THAT RIGHT INTO "SETTING SUN" BY THE CHEMICAL BROTHERS. PACING IS KEY.
WOW, I CAN'T BELIEVE IT'S ALREADY BEEN OVER FIFTEEN YEARS SINCE...
DUDE. HAVE SOME TACT. IT WAS HIS DAD!
In Loving Memory of Chaz 1942-2002
CHAZ WAS A GREAT MAN.
THANK YOU. THAT MEANS A LOT. GOOD LUCK TONIGHT!
TAXI
"SPEEDWAY" BY MOZ. DARK AND BROODING. THAT COULD WORK.

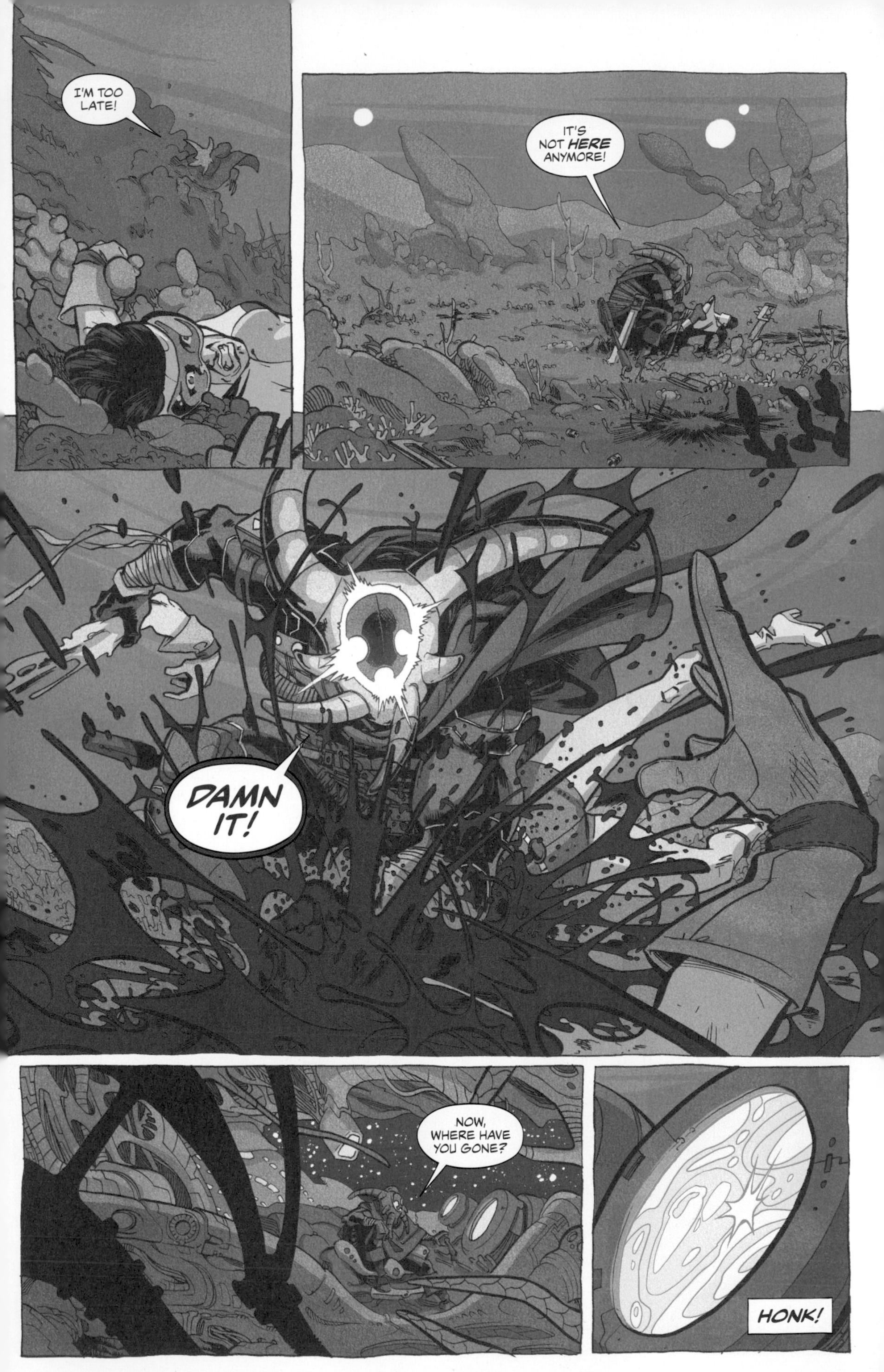
I'M TOO LATE!
IT'S NOT *HERE* ANYMORE!
DAMN IT!
NOW, WHERE HAVE YOU GONE?
HONK!

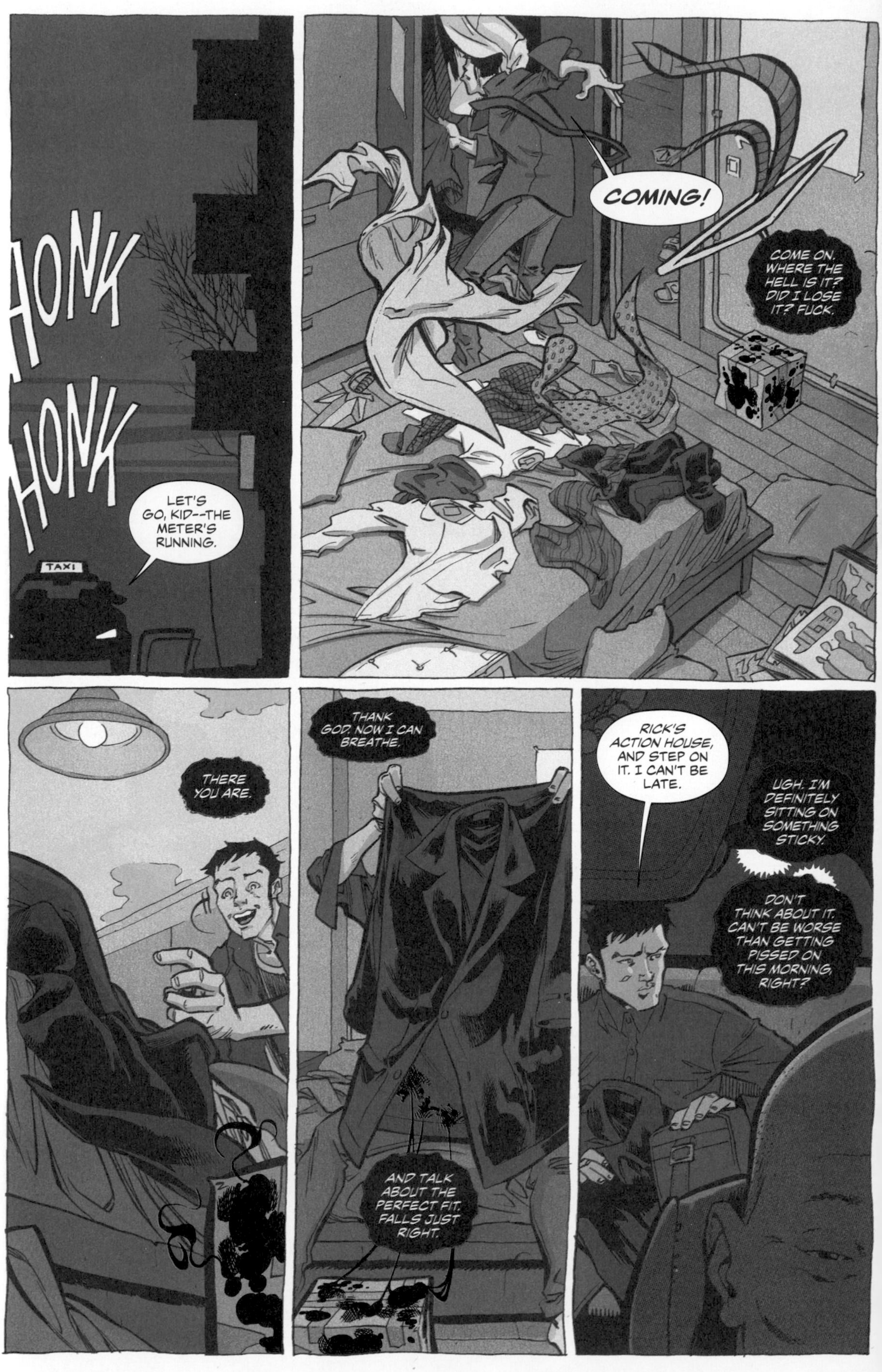
HONK
HONK
LET'S GO, KID--THE METER'S RUNNING.
TAXI
COMING!
COME ON. WHERE THE HELL IS IT? DID I LOSE IT? FUCK.
THERE YOU ARE.
THANK GOD. NOW I CAN BREATHE.
AND TALK ABOUT THE PERFECT FIT. FALLS JUST RIGHT.
RICK'S ACTION HOUSE, AND STEP ON IT. I CAN'T BE LATE.
UGH. I'M DEFINITELY SITTING ON SOMETHING STICKY.
DON'T THINK ABOUT IT. CAN'T BE WORSE THAN GETTING PISSED ON THIS MORNING, RIGHT?

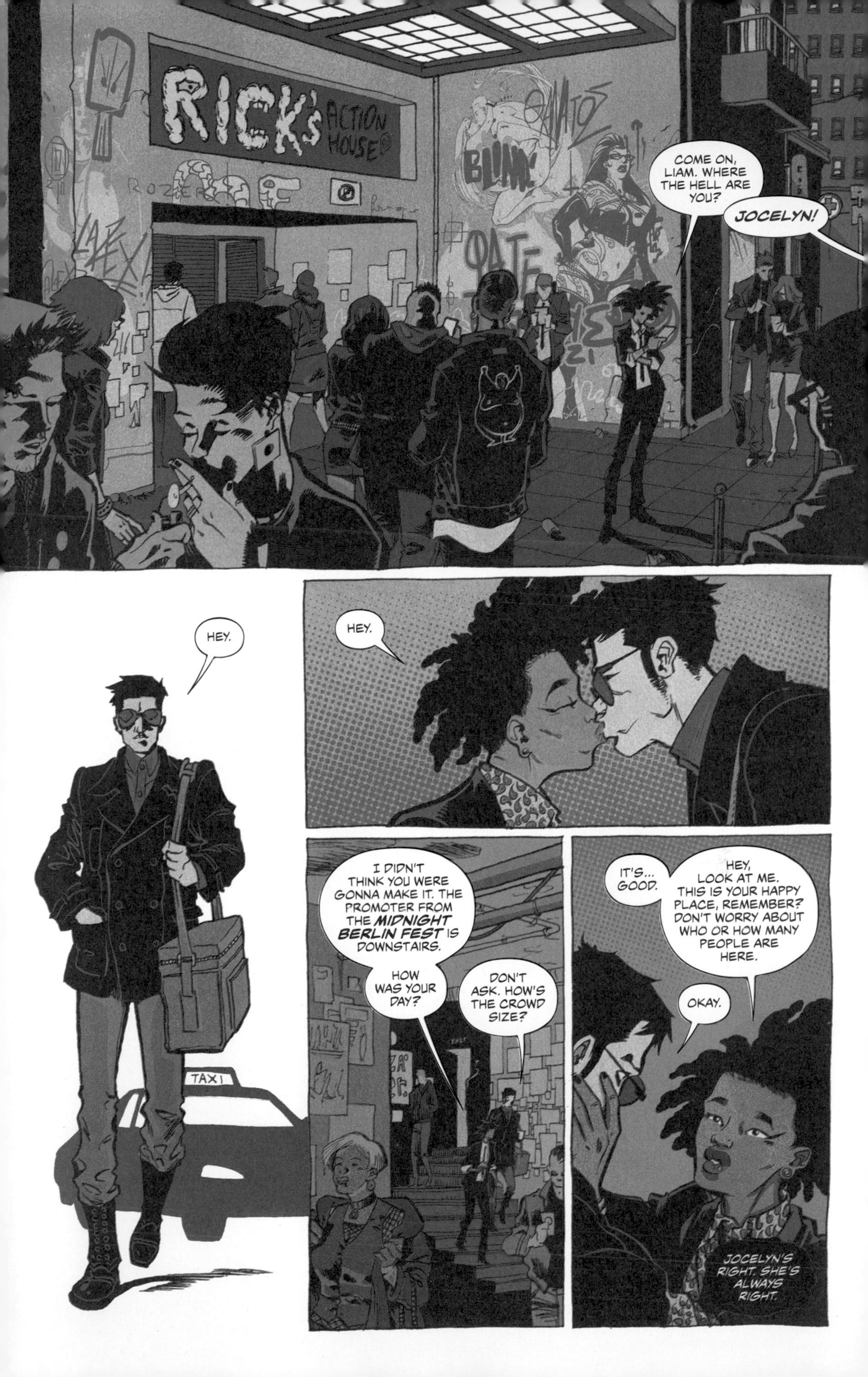
RICK'S ACTION HOUSE
COME ON, LIAM. WHERE THE HELL ARE YOU?
JOCELYN!
HEY.
HEY.
I DIDN'T THINK YOU WERE GONNA MAKE IT. THE PROMOTER FROM THE MIDNIGHT BERLIN FEST IS DOWNSTAIRS.
HOW WAS YOUR DAY?
DON'T ASK. HOW'S THE CROWD SIZE?
IT'S... GOOD.
HEY, LOOK AT ME. THIS IS YOUR HAPPY PLACE, REMEMBER? DON'T WORRY ABOUT WHO OR HOW MANY PEOPLE ARE HERE.
OKAY.
JOCELYN'S RIGHT. SHE'S ALWAYS RIGHT.
TAXI

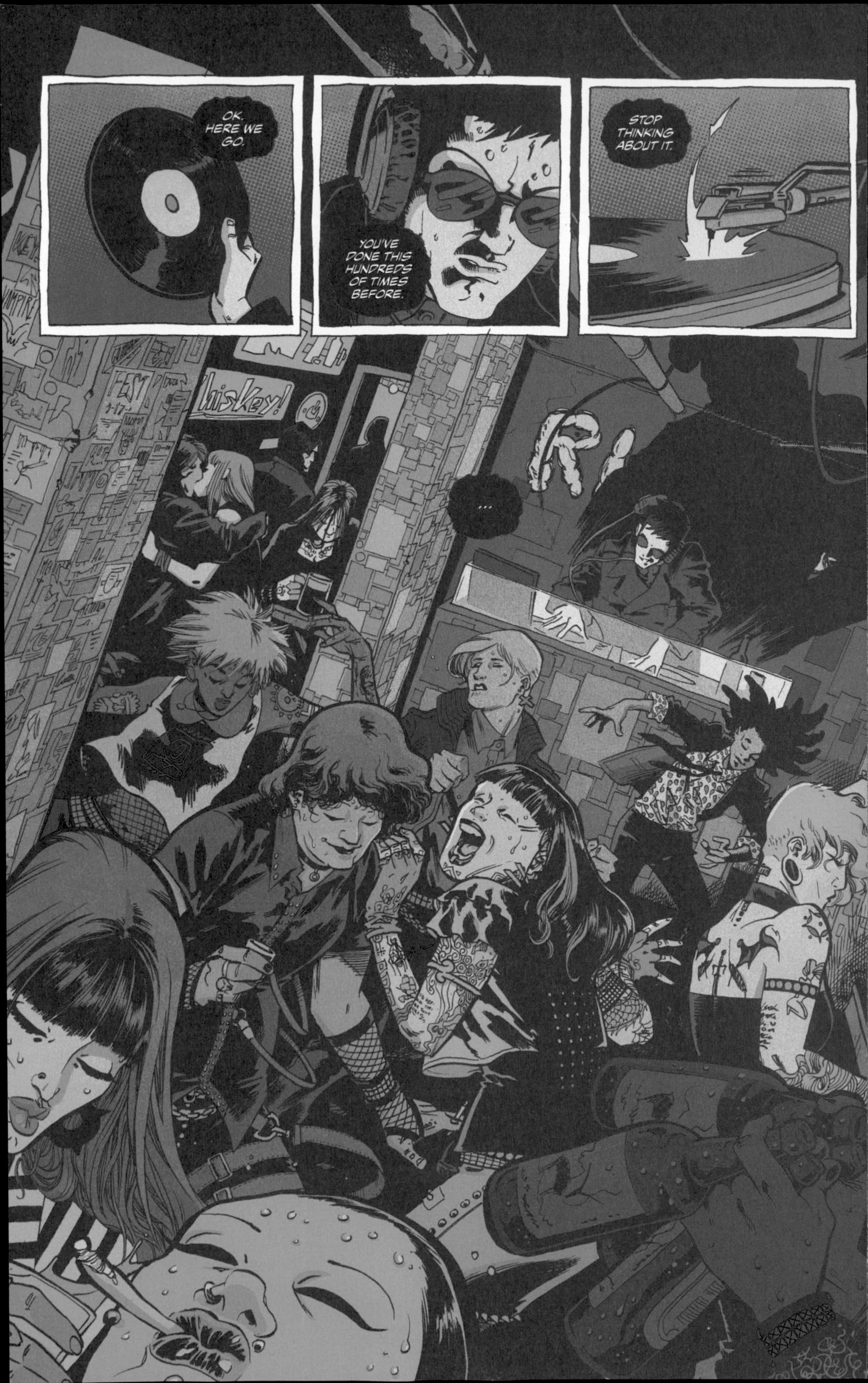
OK. HERE WE GO.
YOU'VE DONE THIS HUNDREDS OF TIMES BEFORE.
STOP THINKING ABOUT IT.
...
Whiskey!
FEST
VAMPIRE

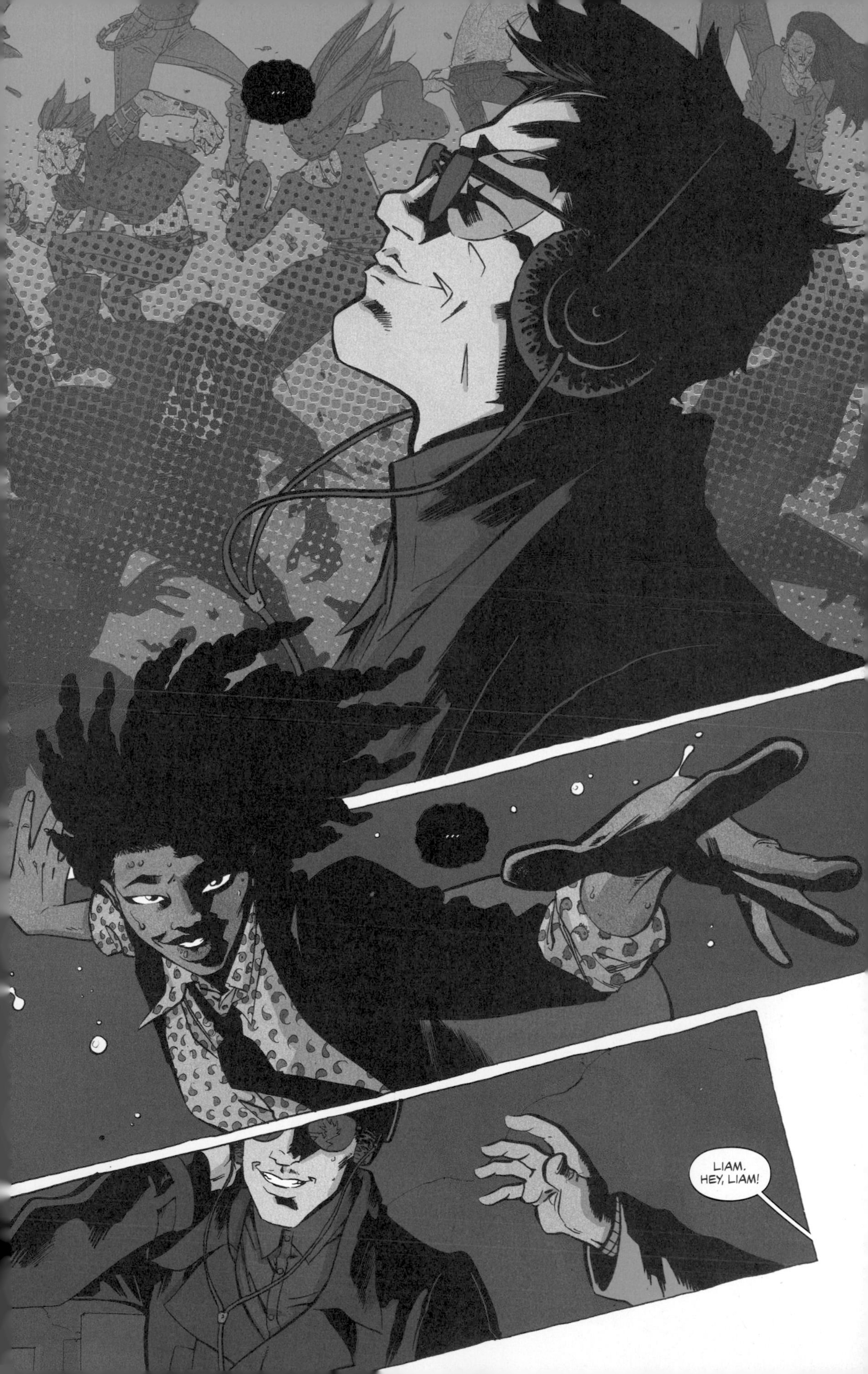
LIAM.
HEY, LIAM!

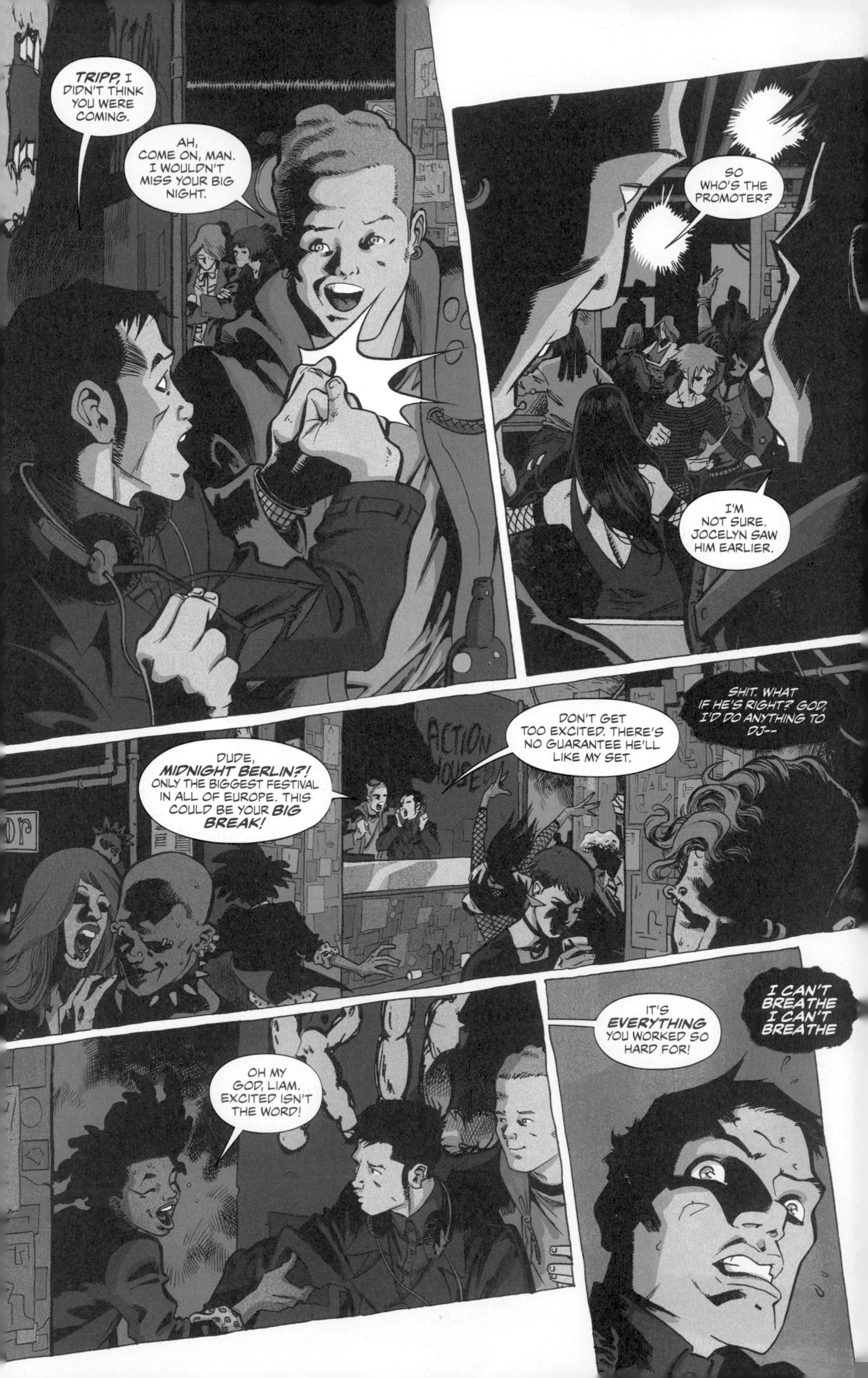
TRIPP, I DIDN'T THINK YOU WERE COMING.
AH, COME ON, MAN. I WOULDN'T MISS YOUR BIG NIGHT.
SO WHO'S THE PROMOTER?
I'M NOT SURE. JOCELYN SAW HIM EARLIER.
DUDE, MIDNIGHT BERLIN?! ONLY THE BIGGEST FESTIVAL IN ALL OF EUROPE. THIS COULD BE YOUR BIG BREAK!
ACTION HOUSE
DON'T GET TOO EXCITED. THERE'S NO GUARANTEE HE'LL LIKE MY SET.
SHIT. WHAT IF HE'S RIGHT? GOD, I'D DO ANYTHING TO DJ--
OH MY GOD, LIAM. EXCITED ISN'T THE WORD!
IT'S EVERYTHING YOU WORKED SO HARD FOR!
I CAN'T BREATHE I CAN'T BREATHE

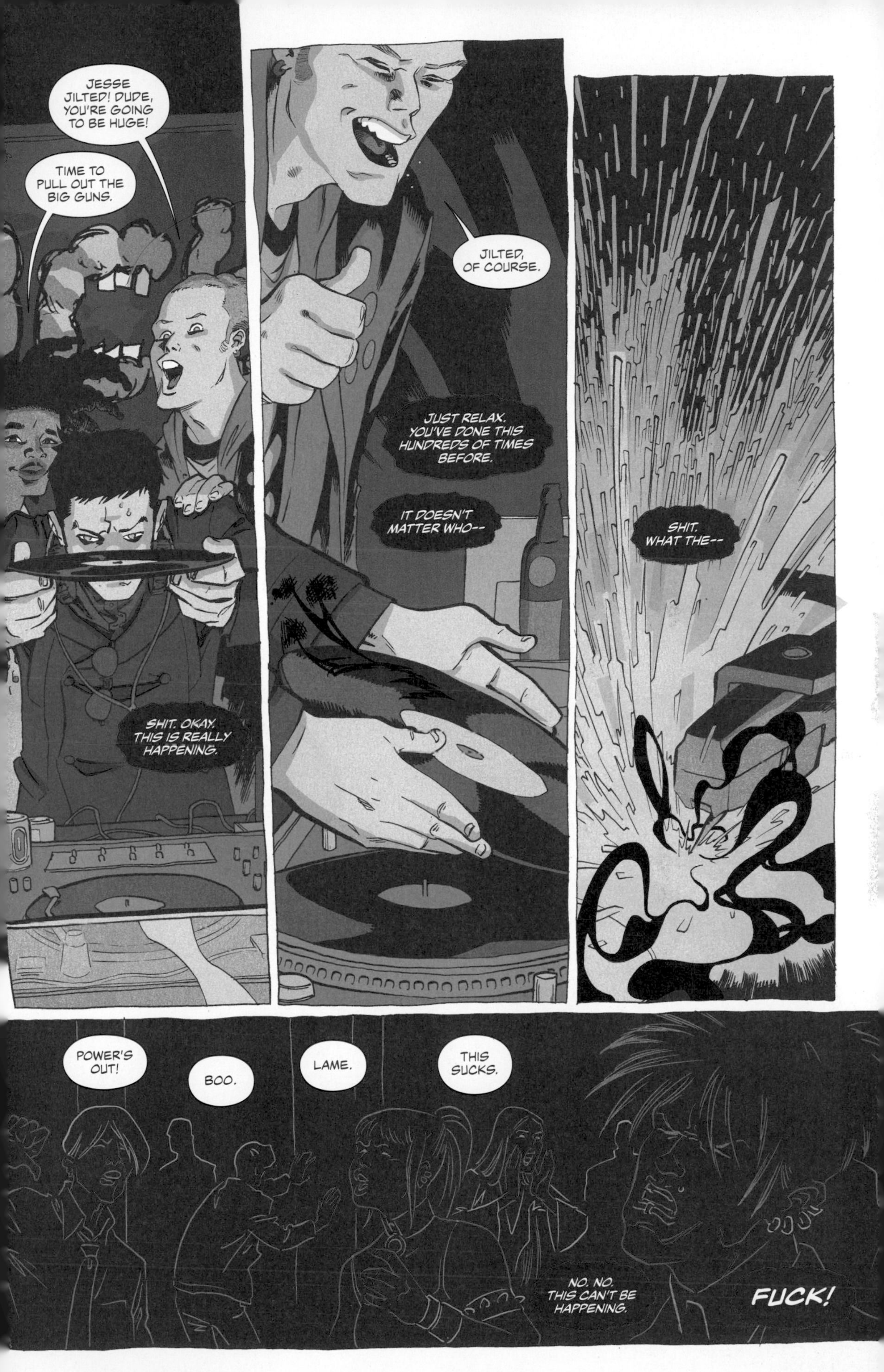
JESSE JILTED! DUDE, YOU'RE GOING TO BE HUGE!
TIME TO PULL OUT THE BIG GUNS.
SHIT. OKAY. THIS IS REALLY HAPPENING.
JILTED, OF COURSE.
JUST RELAX. YOU'VE DONE THIS HUNDREDS OF TIMES BEFORE.
IT DOESN'T MATTER WHO--
SHIT. WHAT THE--
POWER'S OUT!
BOO.
LAME.
THIS SUCKS.
NO. NO. THIS CAN'T BE HAPPENING.
FUCK!

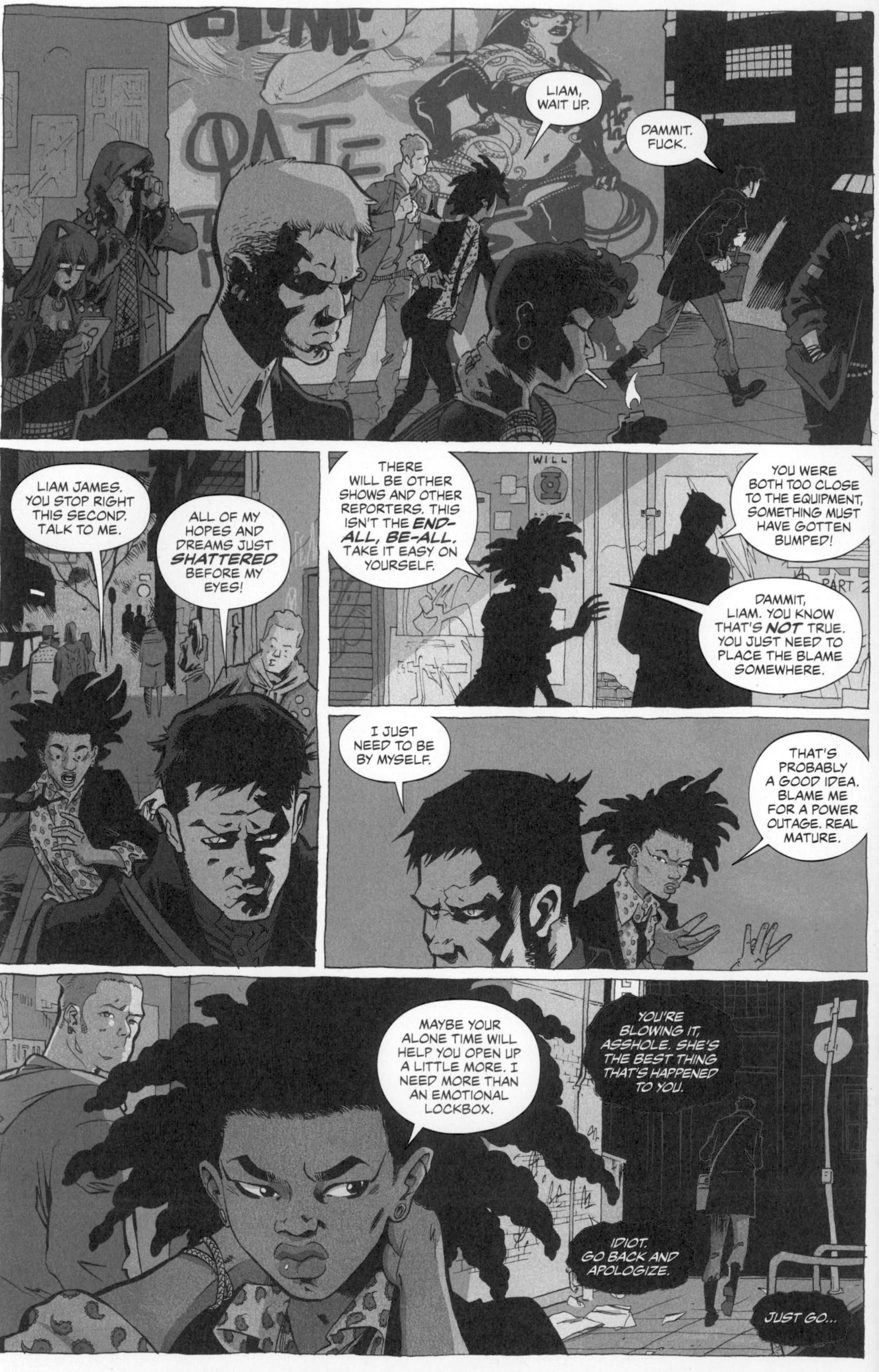
LIAM, WAIT UP.
DAMMIT. FUCK.
LIAM JAMES. YOU STOP RIGHT THIS SECOND. TALK TO ME.
ALL OF MY HOPES AND DREAMS JUST *SHATTERED* BEFORE MY EYES!
THERE WILL BE OTHER SHOWS AND OTHER REPORTERS. THIS ISN'T THE *END-ALL, BE-ALL.* TAKE IT EASY ON YOURSELF.
YOU WERE BOTH TOO CLOSE TO THE EQUIPMENT, SOMETHING MUST HAVE GOTTEN BUMPED!
DAMMIT, LIAM. YOU KNOW THAT'S *NOT* TRUE. YOU JUST NEED TO PLACE THE BLAME SOMEWHERE.
I JUST NEED TO BE BY MYSELF.
THAT'S PROBABLY A GOOD IDEA. BLAME ME FOR A POWER OUTAGE. REAL MATURE.
MAYBE YOUR ALONE TIME WILL HELP YOU OPEN UP A LITTLE MORE. I NEED MORE THAN AN EMOTIONAL LOCKBOX.
YOU'RE BLOWING IT, ASSHOLE. SHE'S THE BEST THING THAT'S HAPPENED TO YOU.
IDIOT. GO BACK AND APOLOGIZE.
JUST GO...

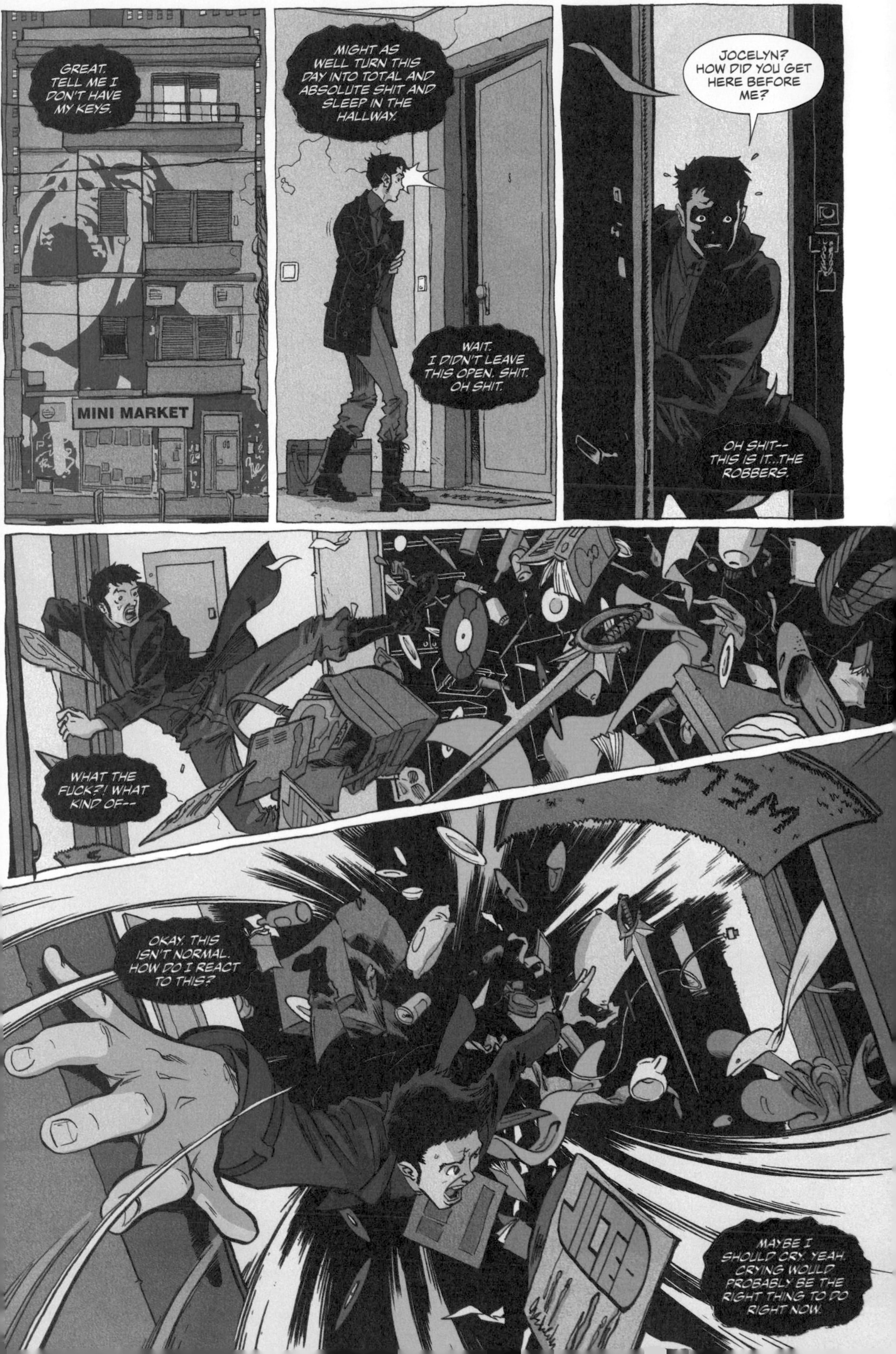
GREAT. TELL ME I DON'T HAVE MY KEYS.
MINI MARKET
MIGHT AS WELL TURN THIS DAY INTO TOTAL AND ABSOLUTE SHIT AND SLEEP IN THE HALLWAY.
WAIT. I DIDN'T LEAVE THIS OPEN. SHIT. OH SHIT.
JOCELYN? HOW DID YOU GET HERE BEFORE ME?
OH SHIT-- THIS IS IT...THE ROBBERS.
WHAT THE FUCK?! WHAT KIND OF--
OKAY. THIS ISN'T NORMAL. HOW DO I REACT TO THIS?
MAYBE I SHOULD CRY. YEAH. CRYING WOULD PROBABLY BE THE RIGHT THING TO DO RIGHT NOW.

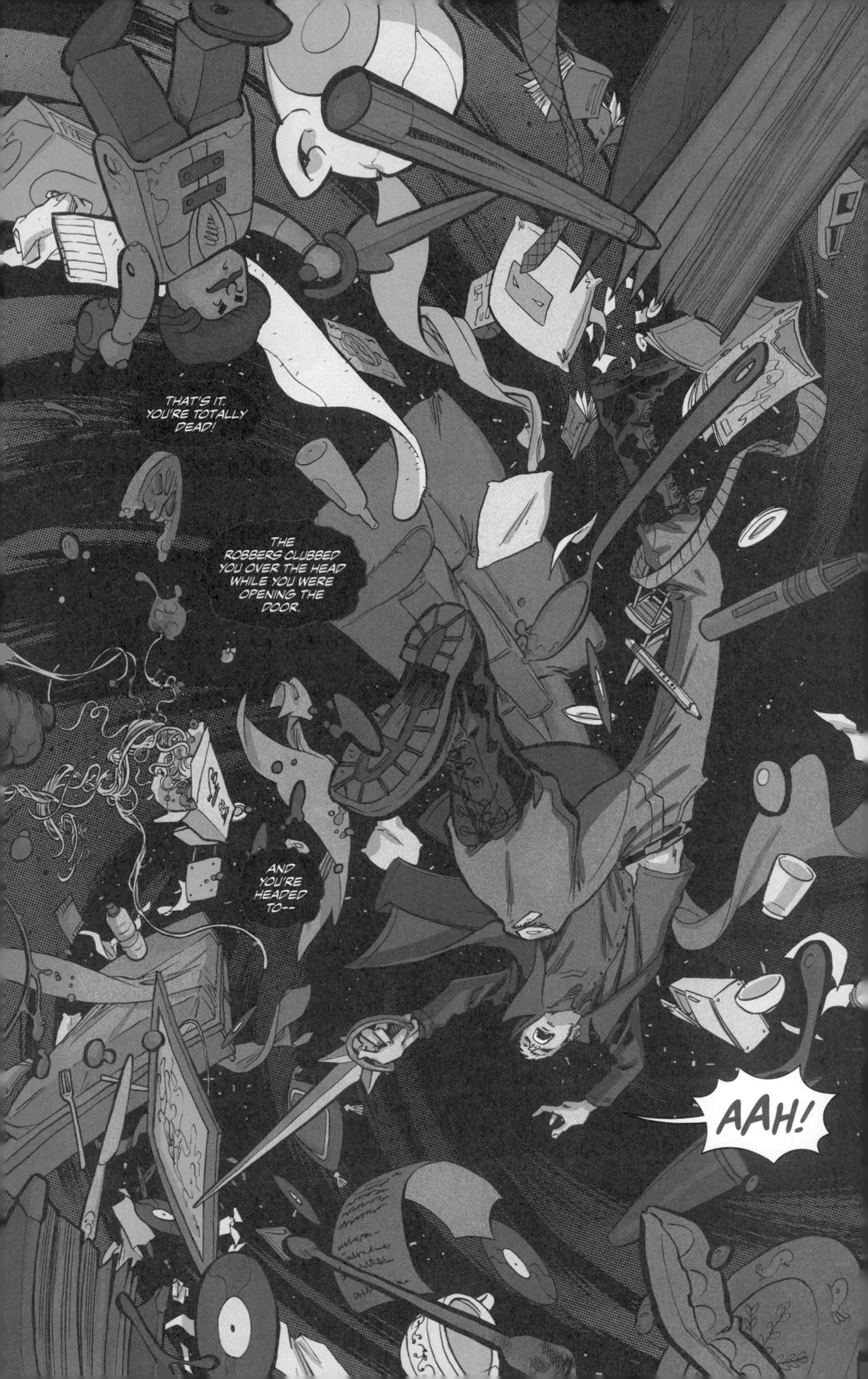
THAT'S IT. YOU'RE TOTALLY DEAD!
THE ROBBERS CLUBBED YOU OVER THE HEAD WHILE YOU WERE OPENING THE DOOR.
AND YOU'RE HEADED TO--
AAH!

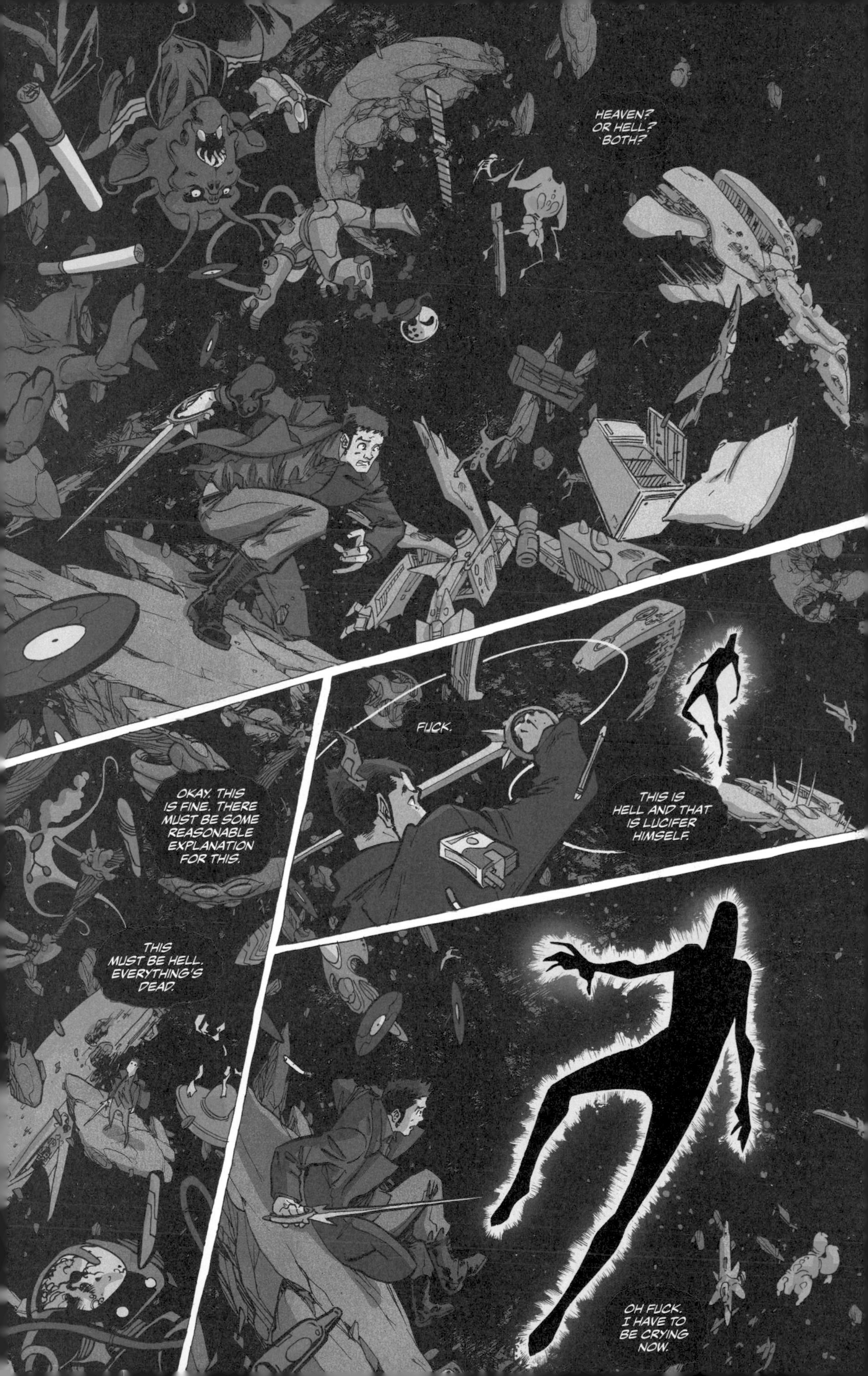
HEAVEN? OR HELL? BOTH?
OKAY. THIS IS FINE. THERE MUST BE SOME REASONABLE EXPLANATION FOR THIS.
THIS MUST BE HELL. EVERYTHING'S DEAD.
FUCK.
THIS IS HELL AND THAT IS LUCIFER HIMSELF.
OH FUCK. I HAVE TO BE CRYING NOW.

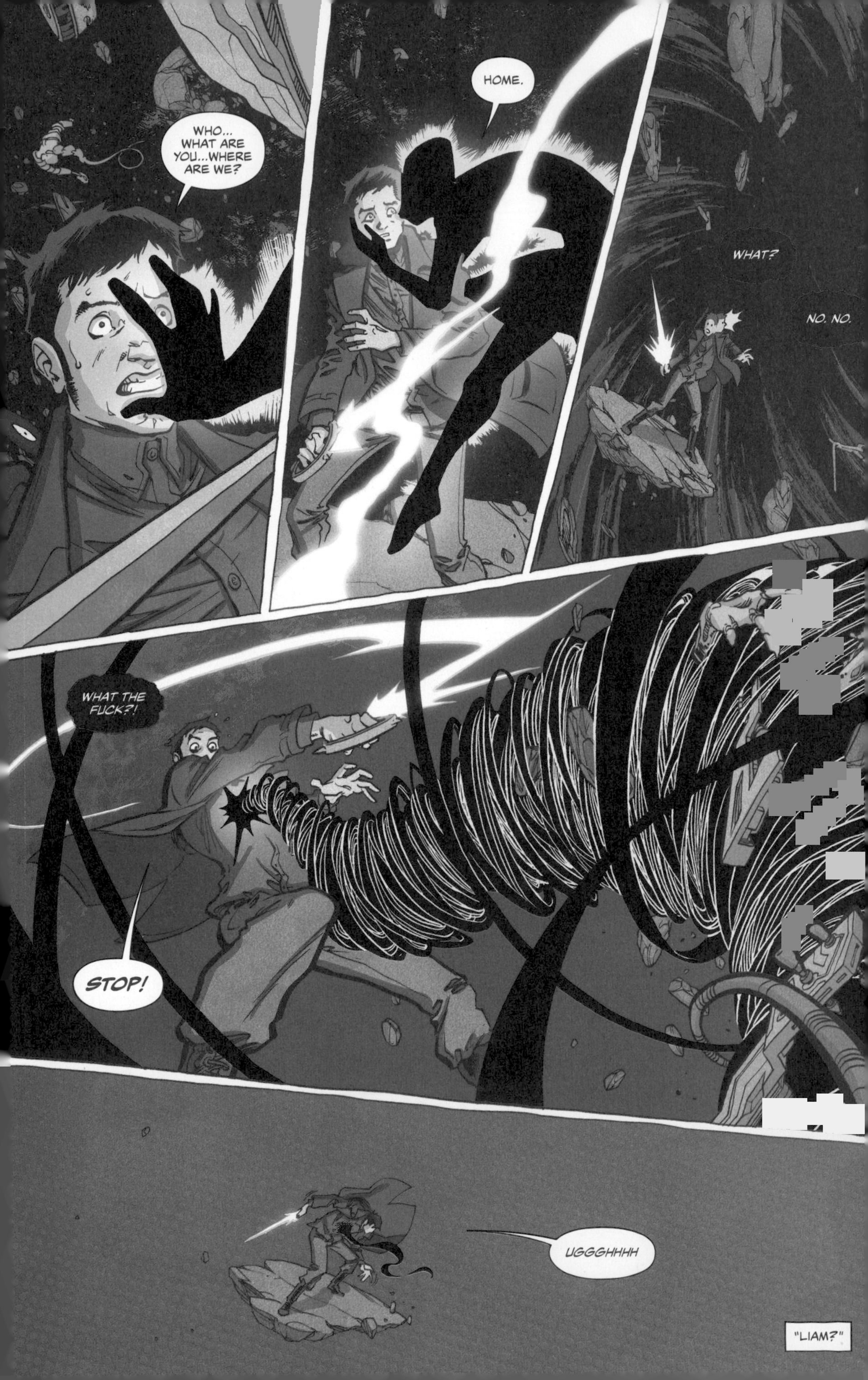

WHO... WHAT ARE YOU...WHERE ARE WE?
HOME.
WHAT?
NO. NO.
WHAT THE FUCK?!
STOP!
UGGGHHHH
"LIAM?"

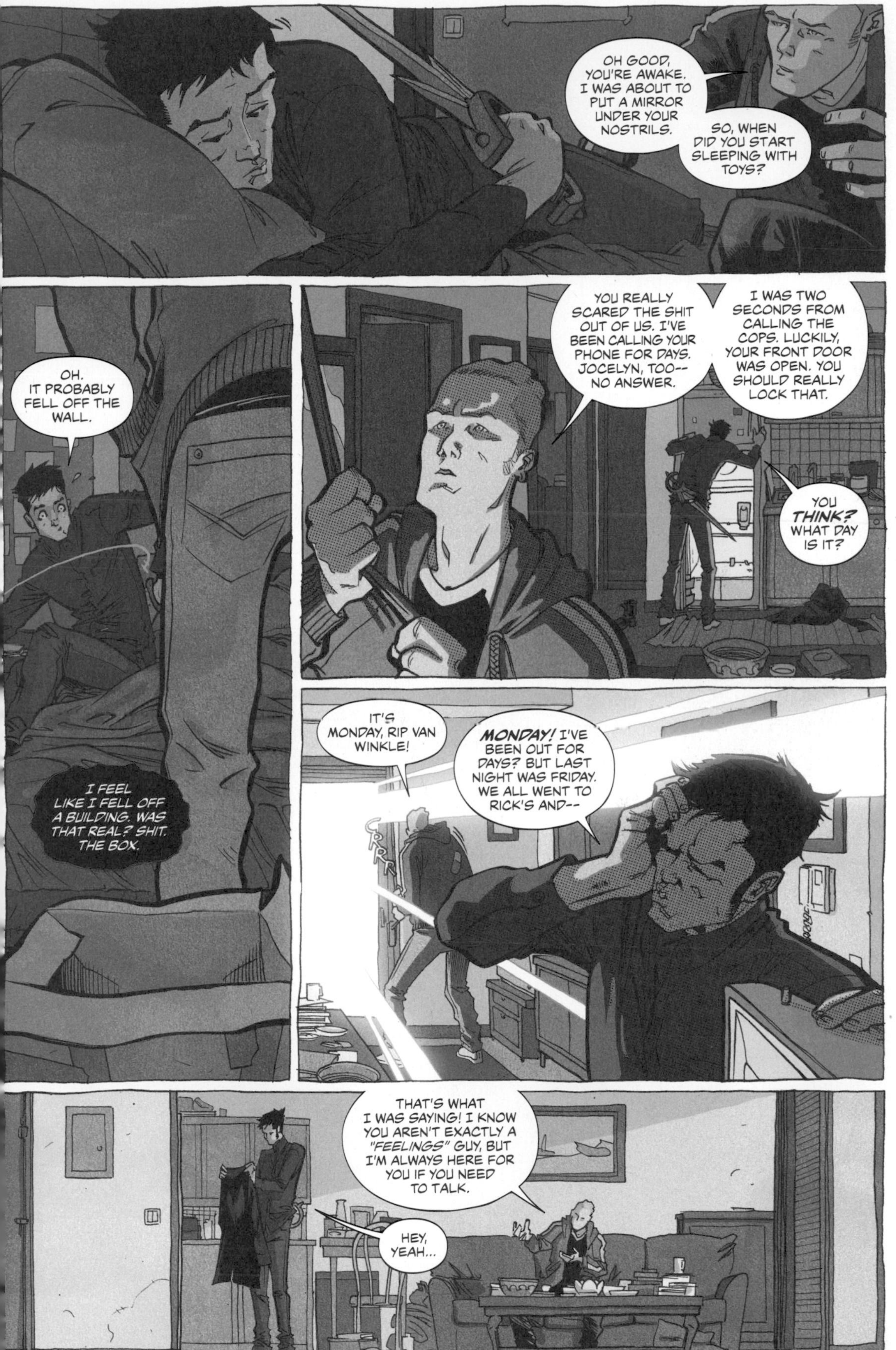
OH GOOD, YOU'RE AWAKE. I WAS ABOUT TO PUT A MIRROR UNDER YOUR NOSTRILS.
SO, WHEN DID YOU START SLEEPING WITH TOYS?
OH. IT PROBABLY FELL OFF THE WALL.
YOU REALLY SCARED THE SHIT OUT OF US. I'VE BEEN CALLING YOUR PHONE FOR DAYS. JOCELYN, TOO-- NO ANSWER.
I WAS TWO SECONDS FROM CALLING THE COPS. LUCKILY, YOUR FRONT DOOR WAS OPEN. YOU SHOULD REALLY LOCK THAT.
YOU *THINK?* WHAT DAY IS IT?
I FEEL LIKE I FELL OFF A BUILDING. WAS THAT REAL? SHIT. THE BOX.
IT'S MONDAY, RIP VAN WINKLE!
MONDAY! I'VE BEEN OUT FOR DAYS? BUT LAST NIGHT WAS FRIDAY. WE ALL WENT TO RICK'S AND--
CRRRR
THAT'S WHAT I WAS SAYING! I KNOW YOU AREN'T EXACTLY A "FEELINGS" GUY, BUT I'M ALWAYS HERE FOR YOU IF YOU NEED TO TALK.
HEY, YEAH...

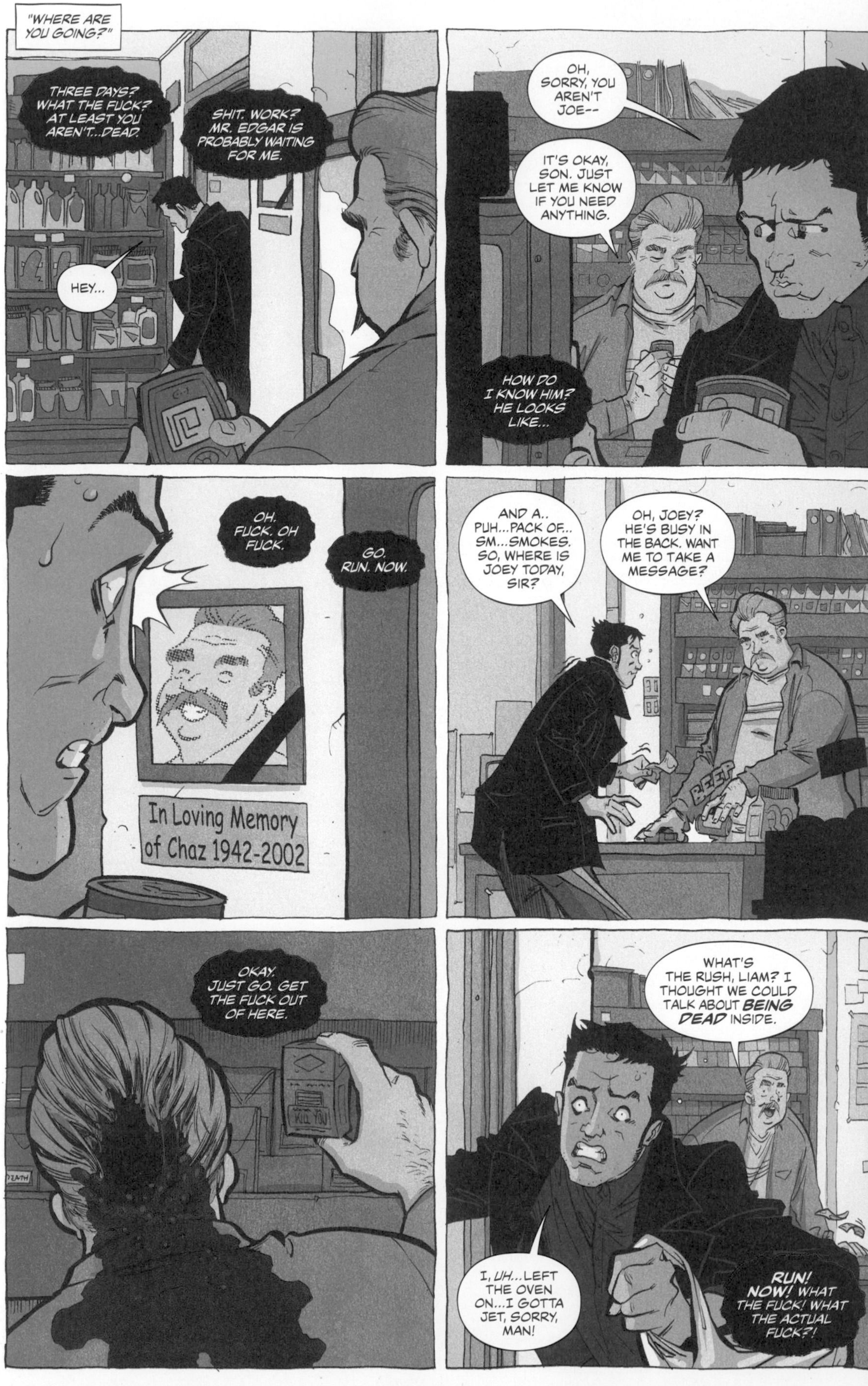
"WHERE ARE YOU GOING?"
THREE DAYS? WHAT THE FUCK? AT LEAST YOU AREN'T...DEAD.
SHIT. WORK? MR. EDGAR IS PROBABLY WAITING FOR ME.
HEY...
OH, SORRY, YOU AREN'T JOE--
IT'S OKAY, SON. JUST LET ME KNOW IF YOU NEED ANYTHING.
HOW DO I KNOW HIM? HE LOOKS LIKE...
OH. FUCK. OH FUCK.
GO. RUN. NOW.
In Loving Memory of Chaz 1942-2002
AND A.. PUH...PACK OF... SM...SMOKES. SO, WHERE IS JOEY TODAY, SIR?
OH, JOEY? HE'S BUSY IN THE BACK. WANT ME TO TAKE A MESSAGE?
BEEP
OKAY. JUST GO. GET THE FUCK OUT OF HERE.
KILL YOU
WHAT'S THE RUSH, LIAM? I THOUGHT WE COULD TALK ABOUT BEING DEAD INSIDE.
I, UH...LEFT THE OVEN ON...I GOTTA JET, SORRY, MAN!
RUN! NOW! WHAT THE FUCK! WHAT THE ACTUAL FUCK?!

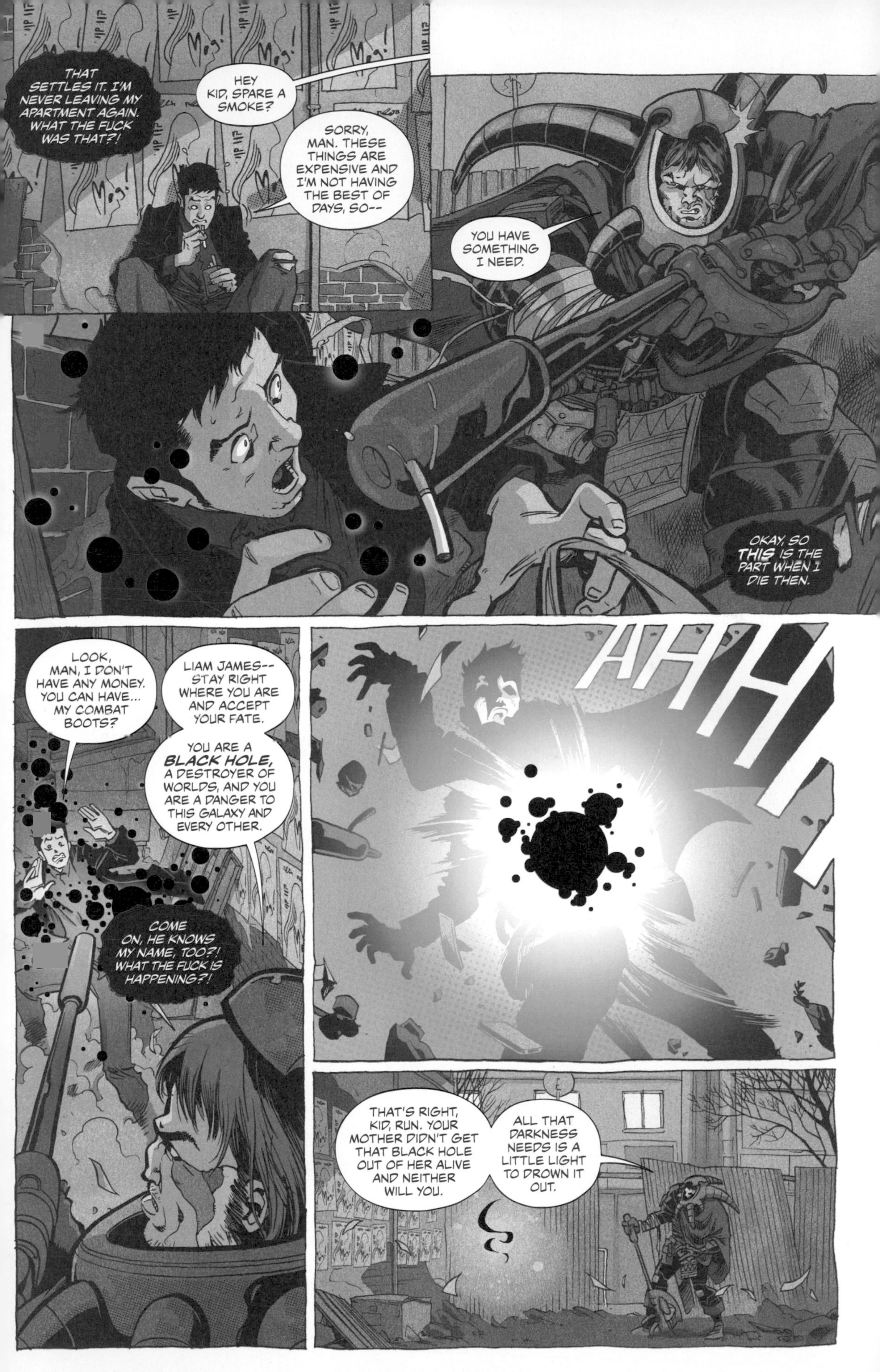

THAT SETTLES IT. I'M NEVER LEAVING MY APARTMENT AGAIN. WHAT THE FUCK WAS THAT?!
HEY KID, SPARE A SMOKE?
SORRY, MAN. THESE THINGS ARE EXPENSIVE AND I'M NOT HAVING THE BEST OF DAYS, SO--
YOU HAVE SOMETHING I NEED.
OKAY, SO THIS IS THE PART WHEN I DIE THEN.
LOOK, MAN, I DON'T HAVE ANY MONEY. YOU CAN HAVE... MY COMBAT BOOTS?
LIAM JAMES--STAY RIGHT WHERE YOU ARE AND ACCEPT YOUR FATE.
YOU ARE A BLACK HOLE, A DESTROYER OF WORLDS, AND YOU ARE A DANGER TO THIS GALAXY AND EVERY OTHER.
COME ON, HE KNOWS MY NAME, TOO?! WHAT THE FUCK IS HAPPENING?!
AHH!
THAT'S RIGHT, KID, RUN. YOUR MOTHER DIDN'T GET THAT BLACK HOLE OUT OF HER ALIVE AND NEITHER WILL YOU.
ALL THAT DARKNESS NEEDS IS A LITTLE LIGHT TO DROWN IT OUT.

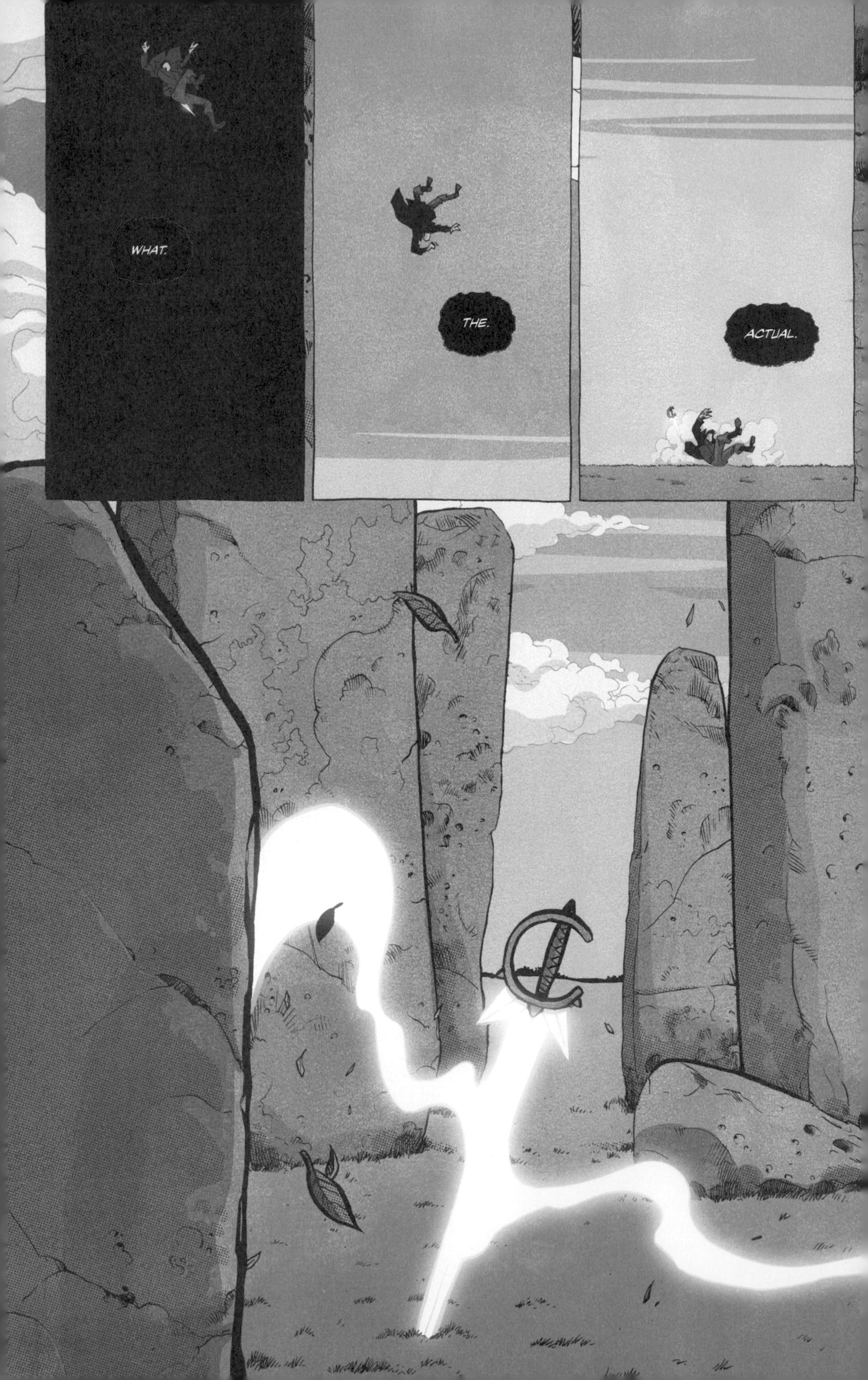
WHAT.
THE.
ACTUAL.

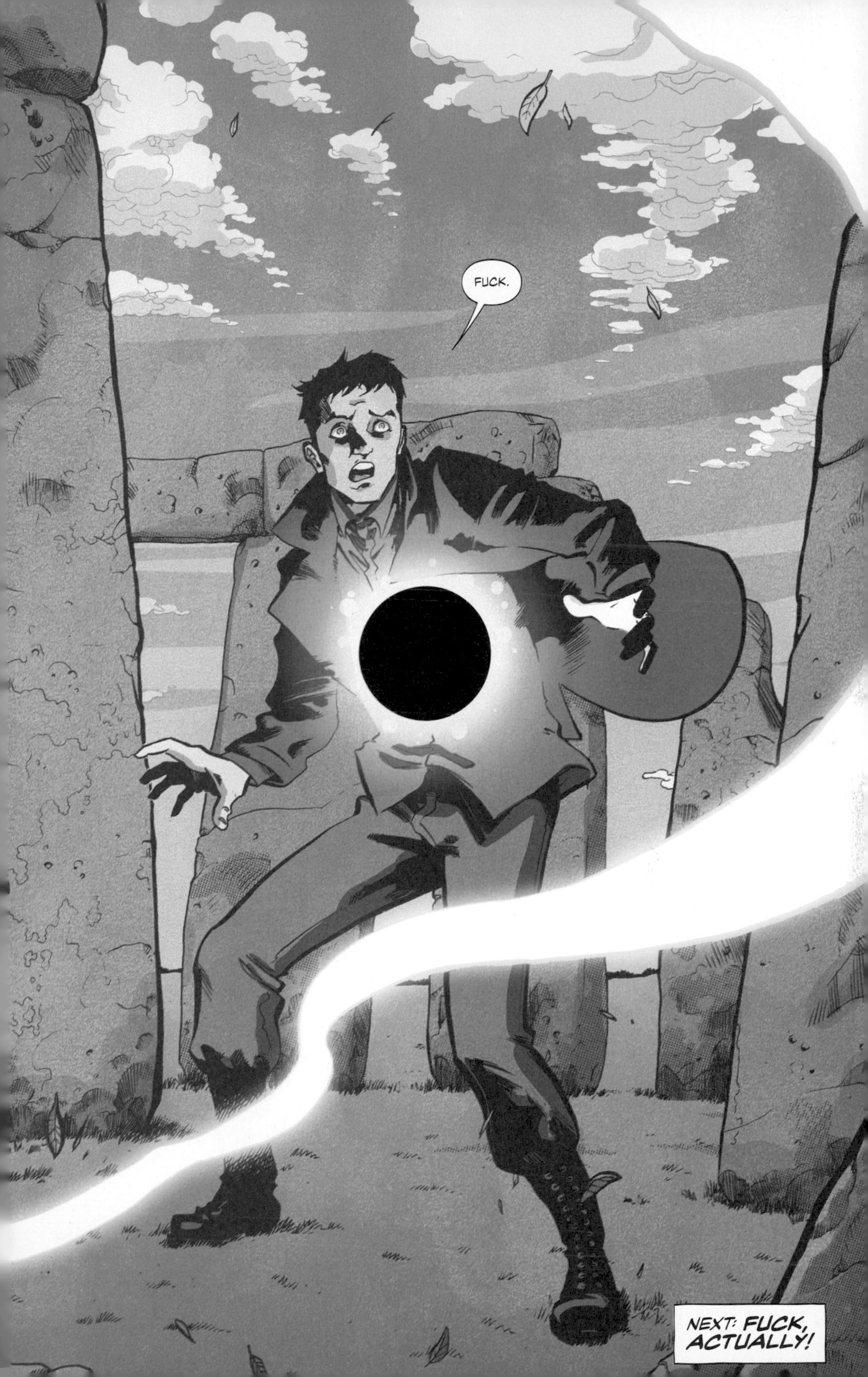
FUCK.
NEXT: FUCK, ACTUALLY!

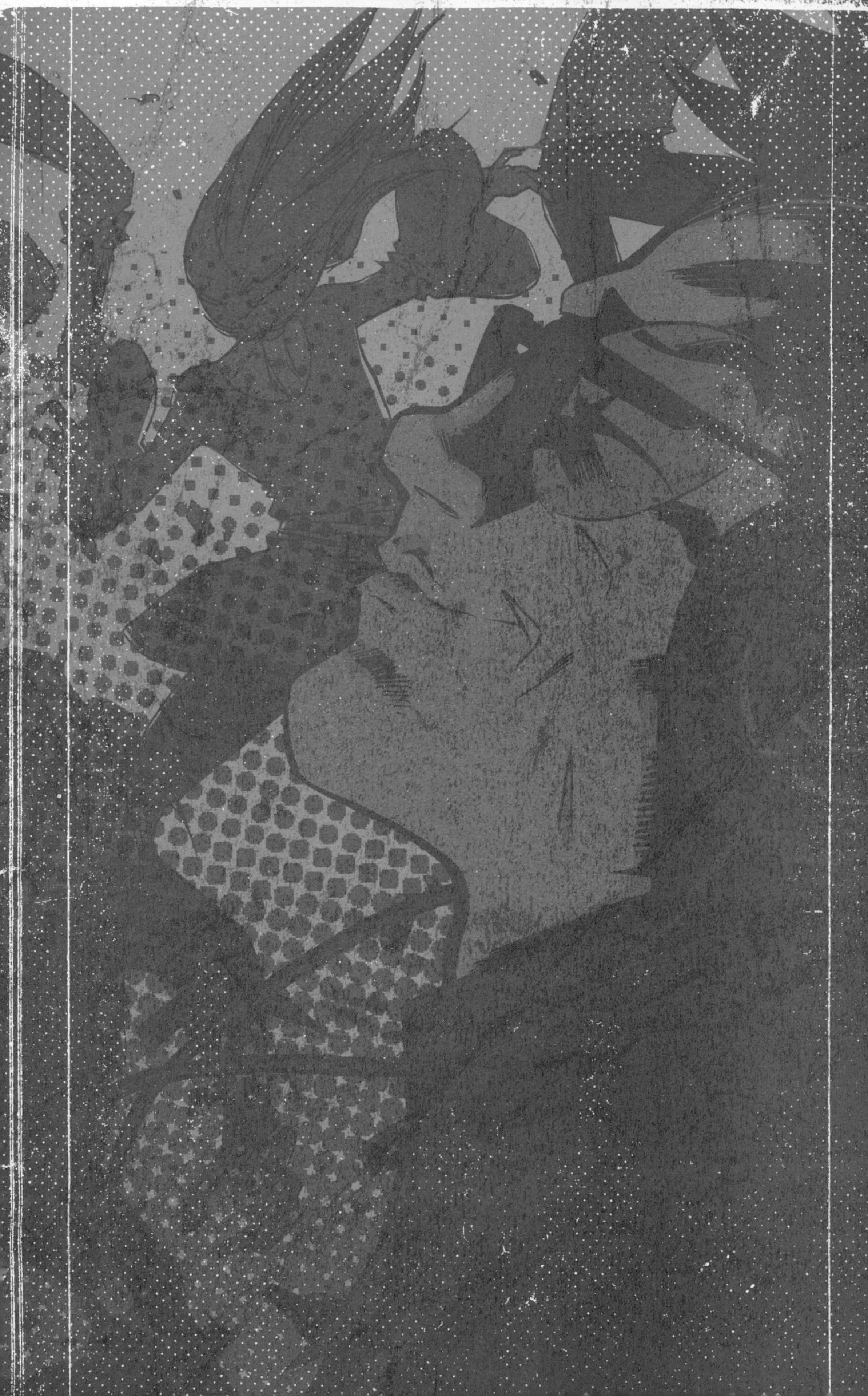

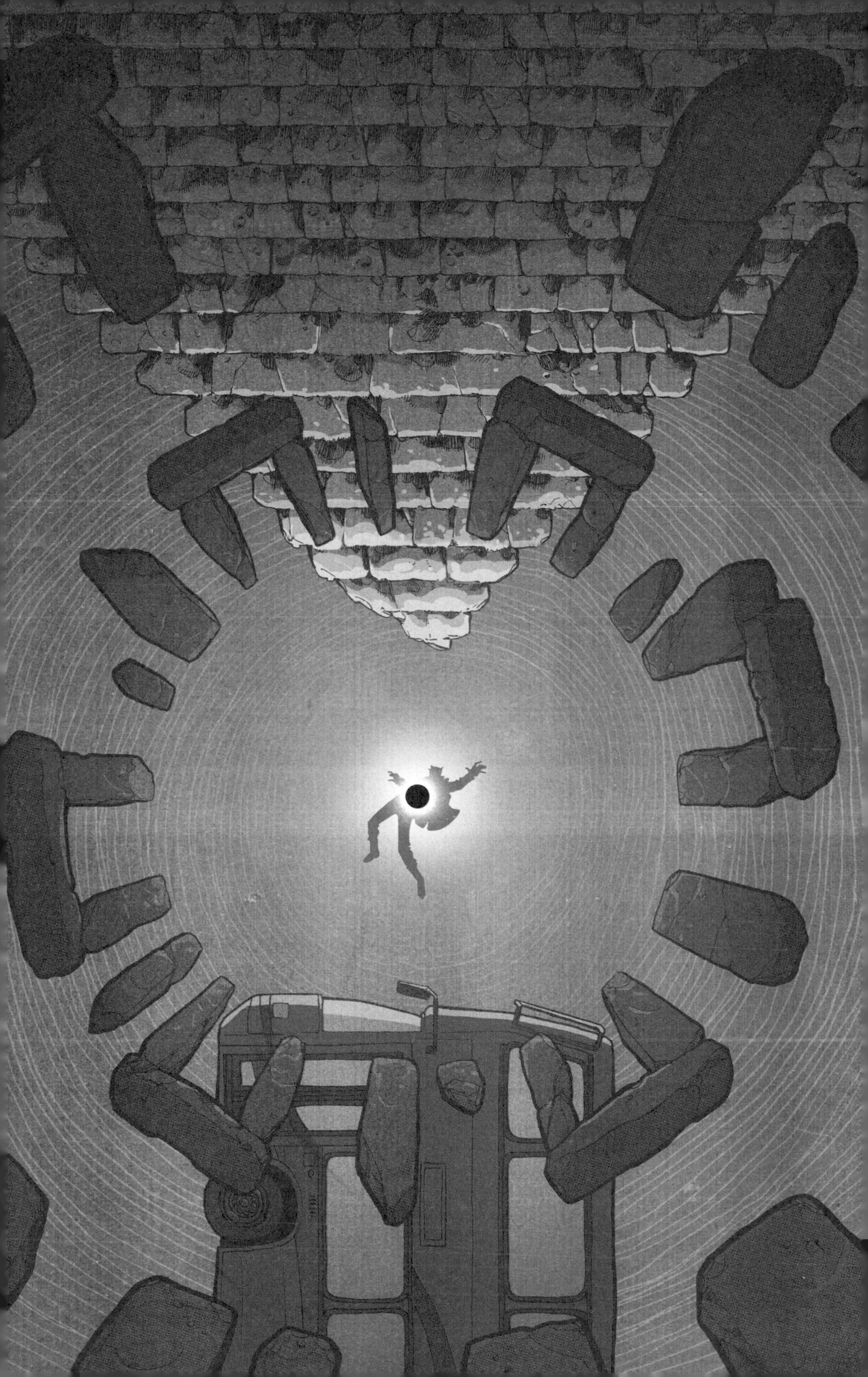

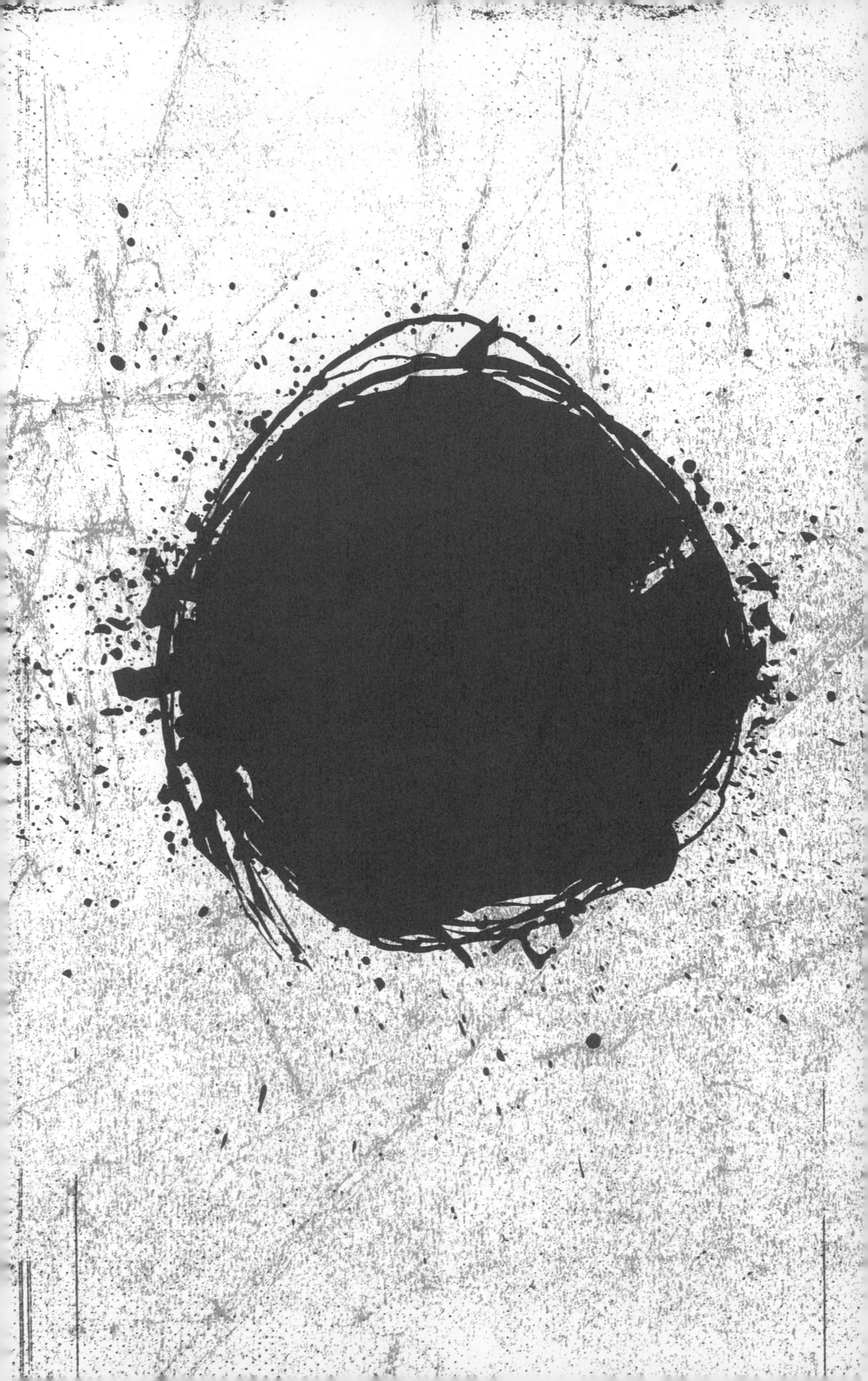

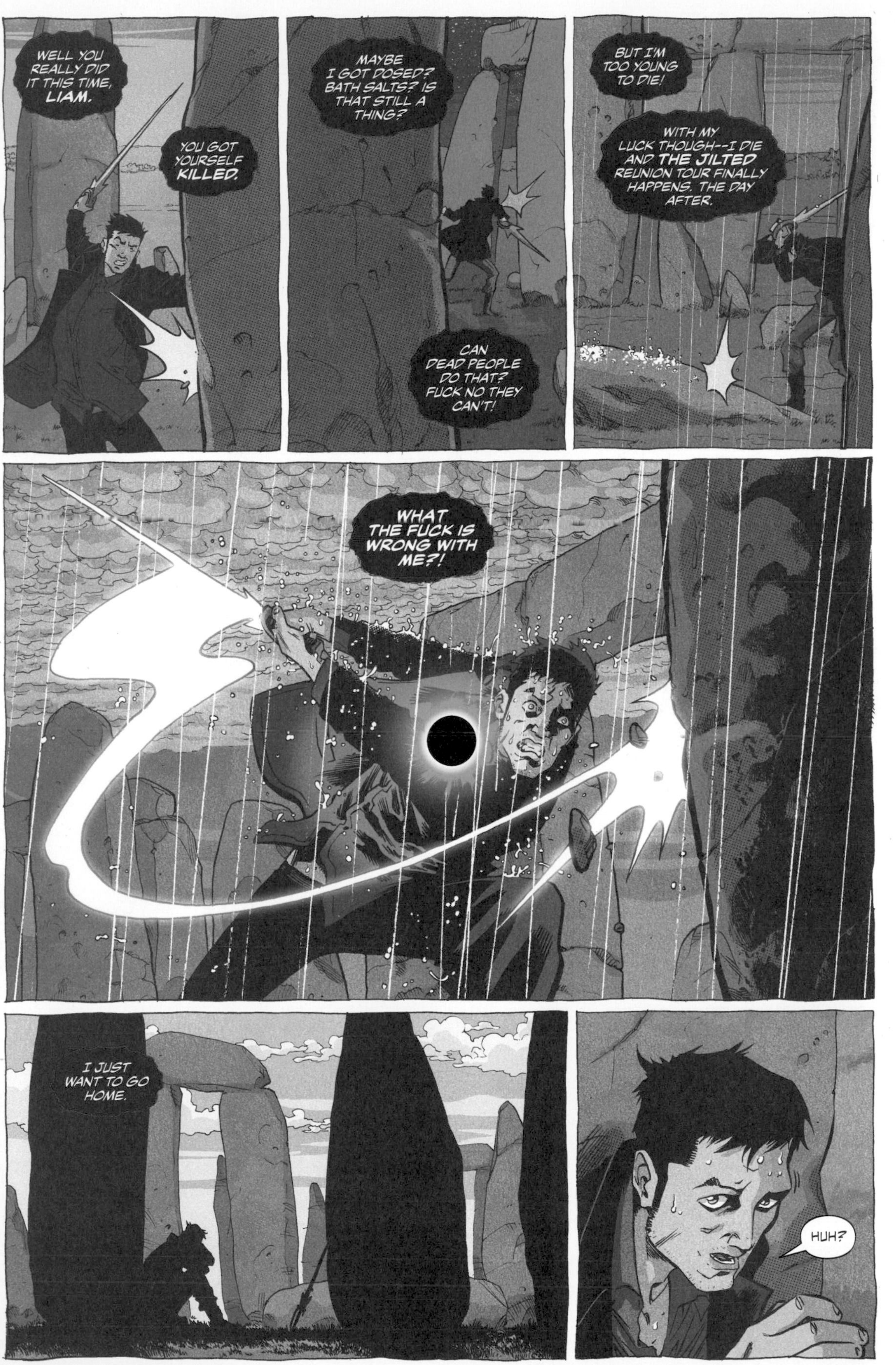
WELL YOU REALLY DID IT THIS TIME, LIAM.
YOU GOT YOURSELF KILLED.
MAYBE I GOT DOSED? BATH SALTS? IS THAT STILL A THING?
CAN DEAD PEOPLE DO THAT? FUCK NO THEY CAN'T!
BUT I'M TOO YOUNG TO DIE!
WITH MY LUCK THOUGH--I DIE AND THE JILTED REUNION TOUR FINALLY HAPPENS. THE DAY AFTER.
WHAT THE FUCK IS WRONG WITH ME?!
I JUST WANT TO GO HOME.
HUH?

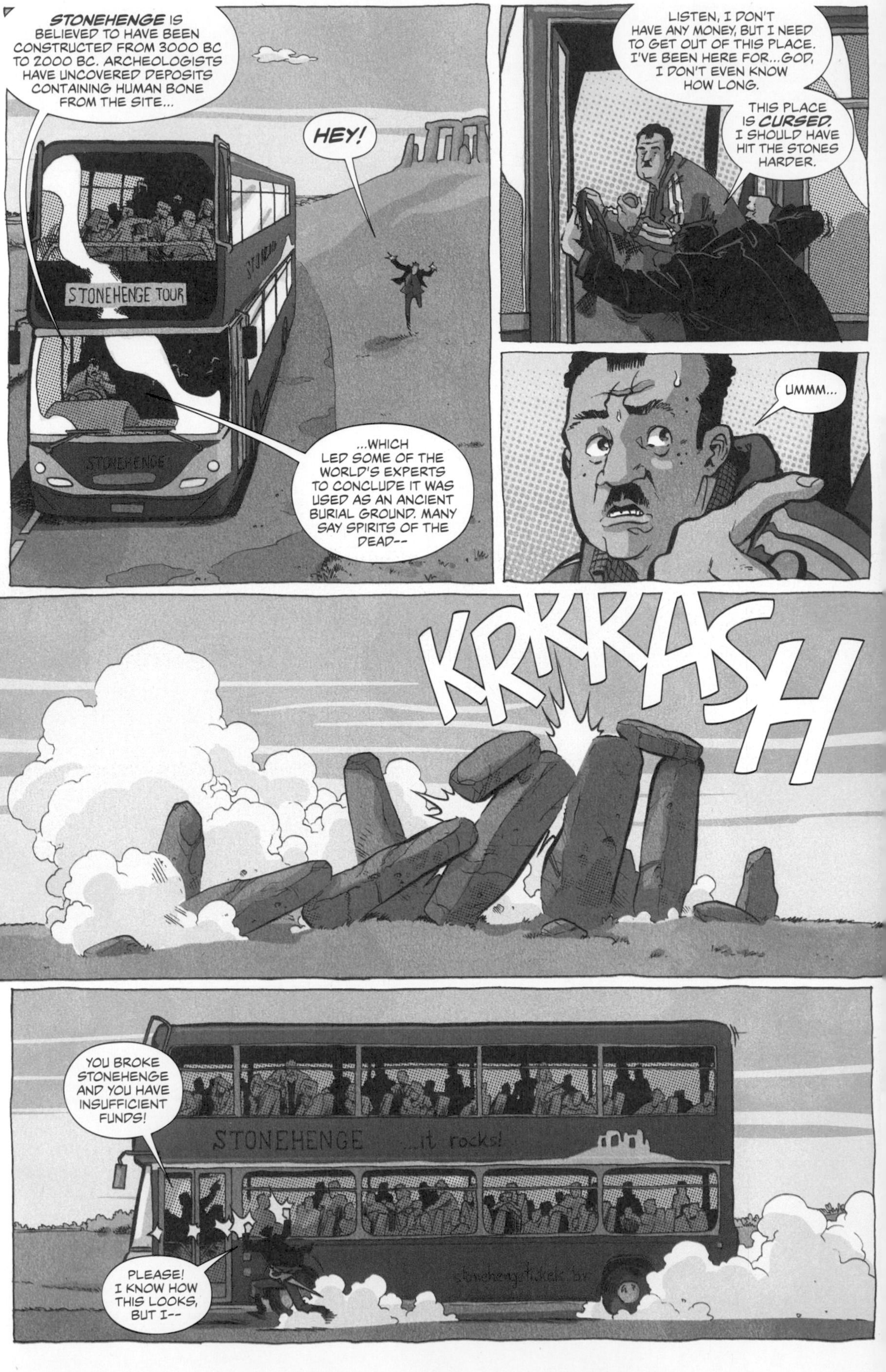
STONEHENGE IS BELIEVED TO HAVE BEEN CONSTRUCTED FROM 3000 BC TO 2000 BC. ARCHEOLOGISTS HAVE UNCOVERED DEPOSITS CONTAINING HUMAN BONE FROM THE SITE...
HEY!
STONEHENGE TOUR
STONEHENGE
...WHICH LED SOME OF THE WORLD'S EXPERTS TO CONCLUDE IT WAS USED AS AN ANCIENT BURIAL GROUND. MANY SAY SPIRITS OF THE DEAD--
LISTEN, I DON'T HAVE ANY MONEY, BUT I NEED TO GET OUT OF THIS PLACE. I'VE BEEN HERE FOR...GOD, I DON'T EVEN KNOW HOW LONG.
THIS PLACE IS CURSED. I SHOULD HAVE HIT THE STONES HARDER.
UMMM...
KRKKASH
YOU BROKE STONEHENGE AND YOU HAVE INSUFFICIENT FUNDS!
STONEHENGE ...it rocks!
PLEASE! I KNOW HOW THIS LOOKS, BUT I--

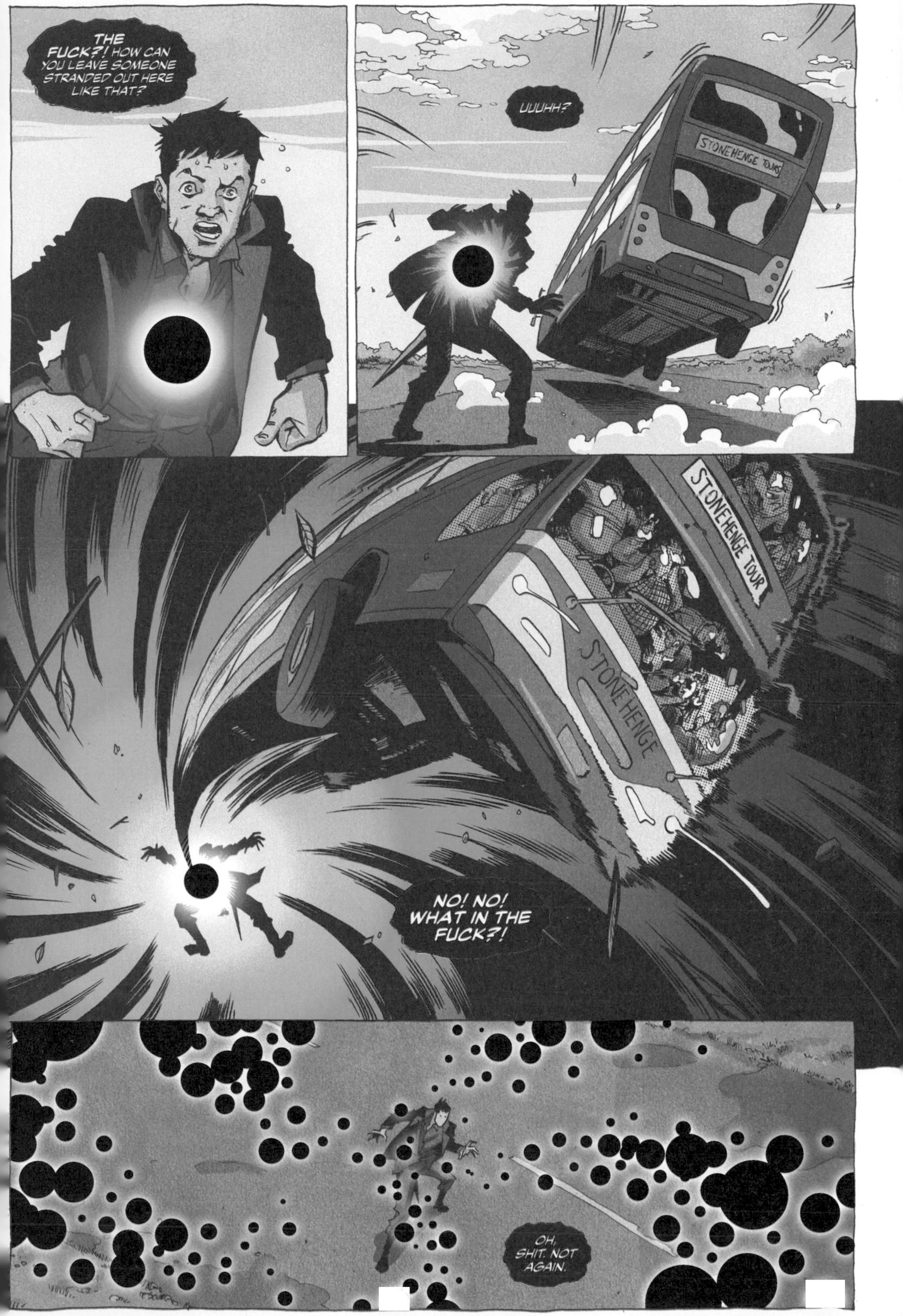
THE FUCK?! HOW CAN YOU LEAVE SOMEONE STRANDED OUT HERE LIKE THAT?
UUUHH?
STONEHENGE TOURS
STONEHENGE TOUR
STONEHENGE
NO! NO! WHAT IN THE FUCK?!
OH, SHIT. NOT AGAIN.

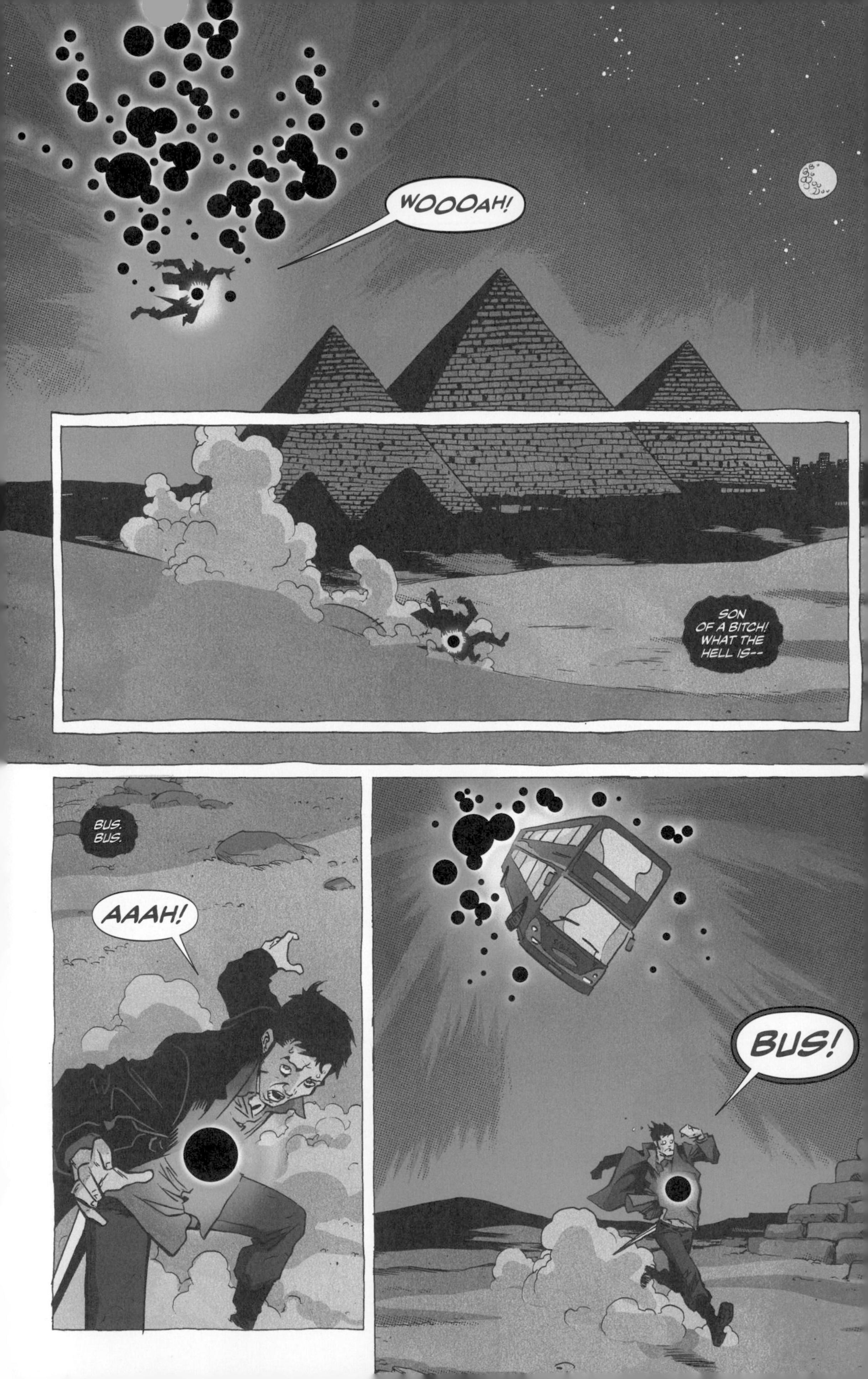
WOOOAH!
SON OF A BITCH! WHAT THE HELL IS--
BUS. BUS.
AAAH!
BUS!

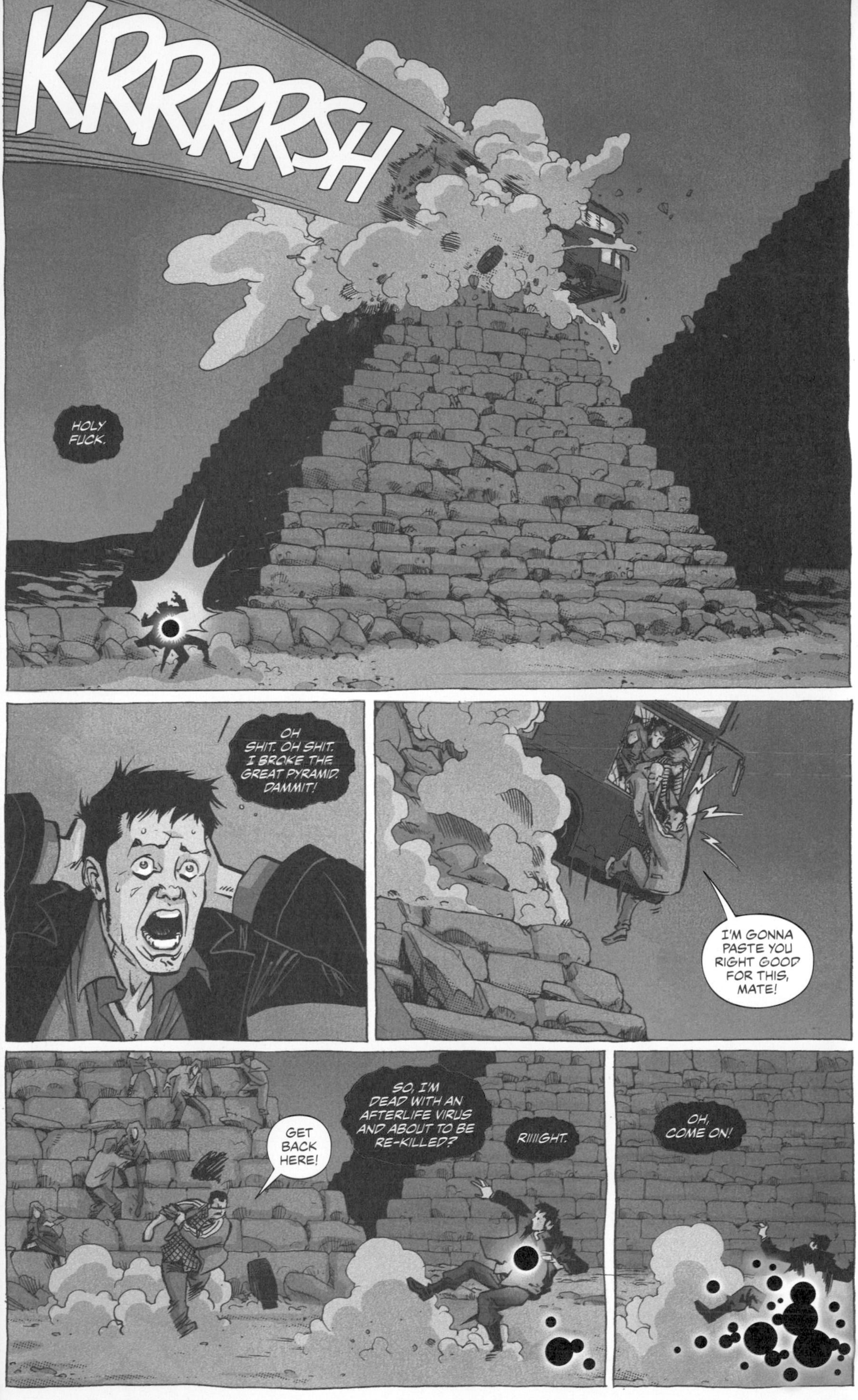
KRRRRSH
HOLY FUCK.
OH SHIT. OH SHIT. I BROKE THE GREAT PYRAMID. DAMMIT!
I'M GONNA PASTE YOU RIGHT GOOD FOR THIS, MATE!
GET BACK HERE!
SO, I'M DEAD WITH AN AFTERLIFE VIRUS AND ABOUT TO BE RE-KILLED?
RIIIGHT.
OH, COME ON!

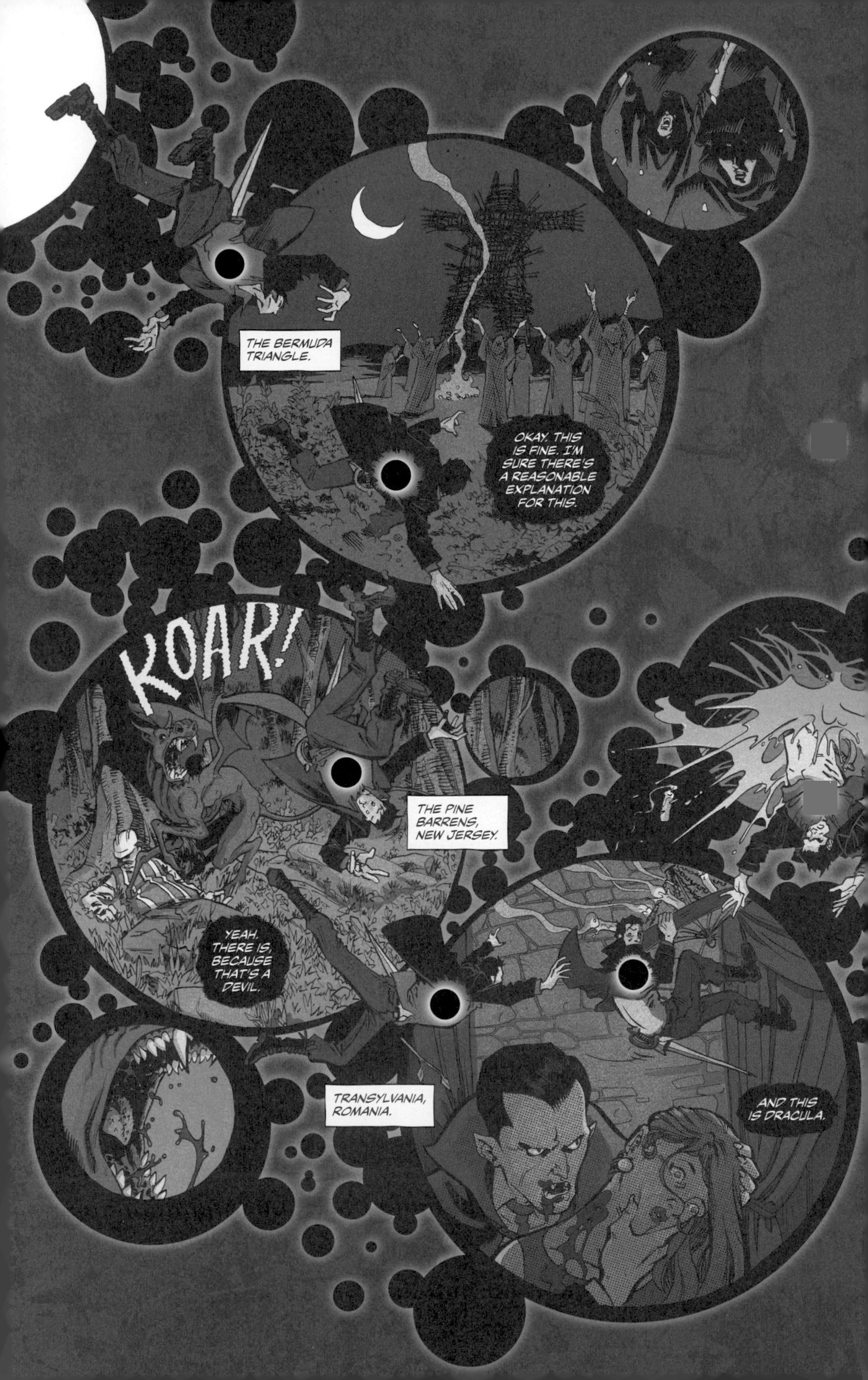
THE BERMUDA TRIANGLE.
OKAY. THIS IS FINE. I'M SURE THERE'S A REASONABLE EXPLANATION FOR THIS.
KOAR!
THE PINE BARRENS, NEW JERSEY.
YEAH. THERE IS, BECAUSE THAT'S A DEVIL.
TRANSYLVANIA, ROMANIA.
AND THIS IS DRACULA.

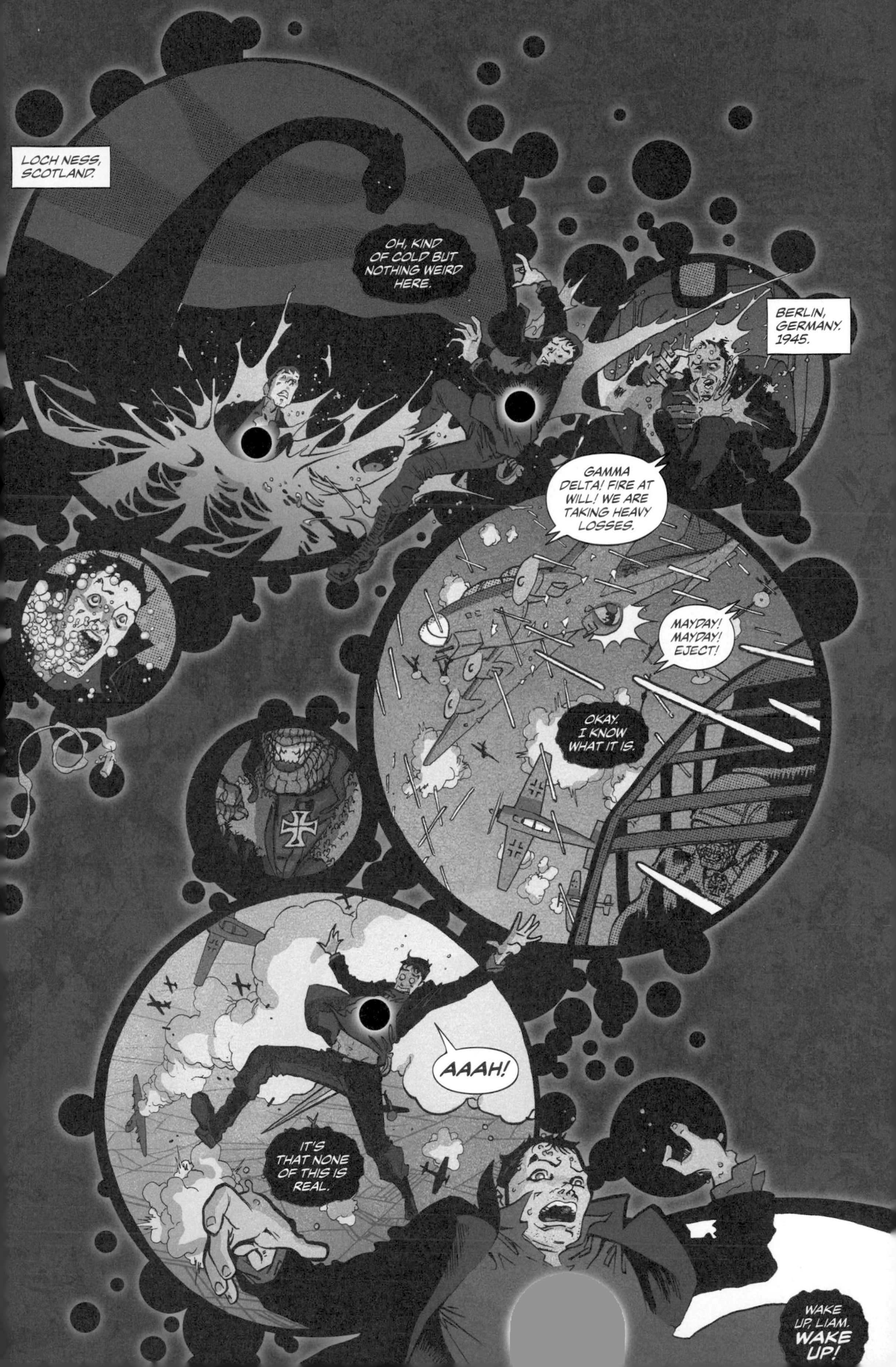
LOCH NESS, SCOTLAND.
OH, KIND OF COLD BUT NOTHING WEIRD HERE.
BERLIN, GERMANY. 1945.
GAMMA DELTA! FIRE AT WILL! WE ARE TAKING HEAVY LOSSES.
MAYDAY! MAYDAY! EJECT!
OKAY. I KNOW WHAT IT IS.
AAAH!
IT'S THAT NONE OF THIS IS REAL.
WAKE UP, LIAM. WAKE UP!

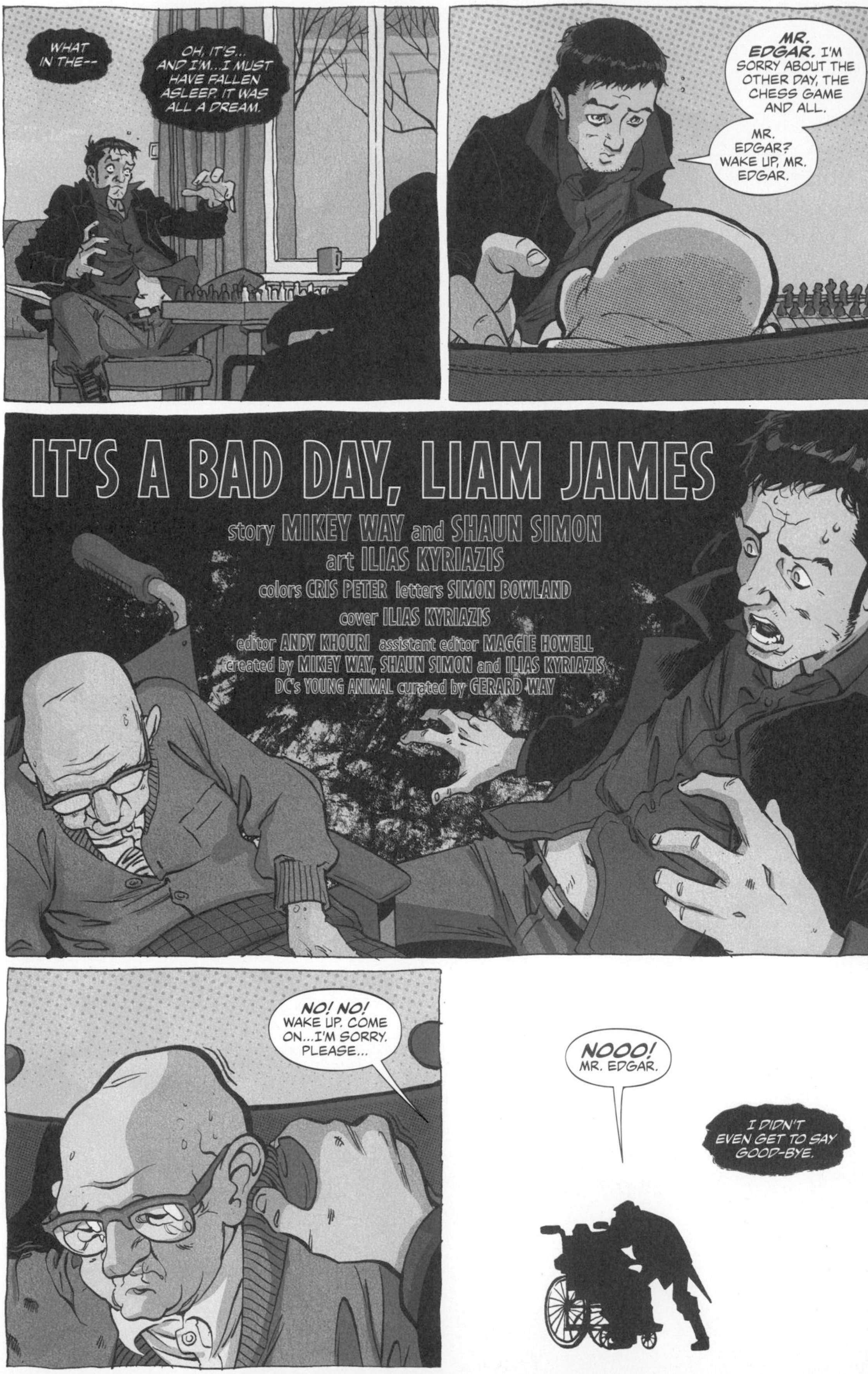
WHAT IN THE--
OH, IT'S... AND I'M...I MUST HAVE FALLEN ASLEEP. IT WAS ALL A DREAM.
MR. EDGAR. I'M SORRY ABOUT THE OTHER DAY, THE CHESS GAME AND ALL.
MR. EDGAR? WAKE UP, MR. EDGAR.
IT'S A BAD DAY, LIAM JAMES
story MIKEY WAY and SHAUN SIMON
art ILIAS KYRIAZIS
colors CRIS PETER letters SIMON BOWLAND
cover ILIAS KYRIAZIS
editor ANDY KHOURI assistant editor MAGGIE HOWELL
created by MIKEY WAY, SHAUN SIMON and ILIAS KYRIAZIS
DC's YOUNG ANIMAL curated by GERARD WAY
NO! NO! WAKE UP. COME ON...I'M SORRY. PLEASE...
NOOO! MR. EDGAR.
I DIDN'T EVEN GET TO SAY GOOD-BYE.

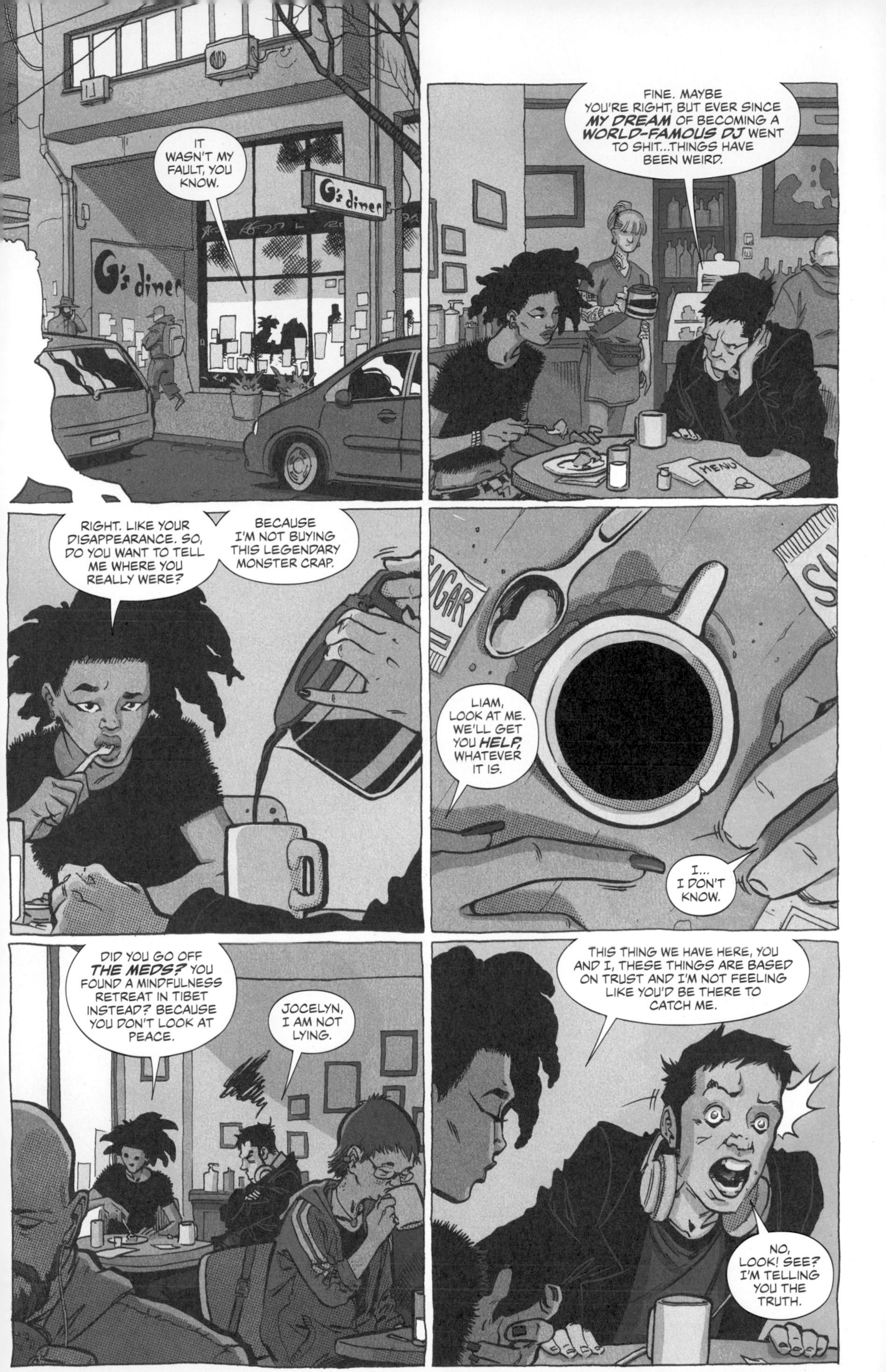
G's diner
IT WASN'T MY FAULT, YOU KNOW.
G's diner
FINE. MAYBE YOU'RE RIGHT, BUT EVER SINCE MY DREAM OF BECOMING A WORLD-FAMOUS DJ WENT TO SHIT...THINGS HAVE BEEN WEIRD.
MENU
RIGHT. LIKE YOUR DISAPPEARANCE. SO, DO YOU WANT TO TELL ME WHERE YOU REALLY WERE?
BECAUSE I'M NOT BUYING THIS LEGENDARY MONSTER CRAP.
SUGAR
LIAM, LOOK AT ME. WE'LL GET YOU HELP, WHATEVER IT IS.
I... I DON'T KNOW.
DID YOU GO OFF THE MEDS? YOU FOUND A MINDFULNESS RETREAT IN TIBET INSTEAD? BECAUSE YOU DON'T LOOK AT PEACE.
JOCELYN, I AM NOT LYING.
THIS THING WE HAVE HERE, YOU AND I, THESE THINGS ARE BASED ON TRUST AND I'M NOT FEELING LIKE YOU'D BE THERE TO CATCH ME.
NO, LOOK! SEE? I'M TELLING YOU THE TRUTH.

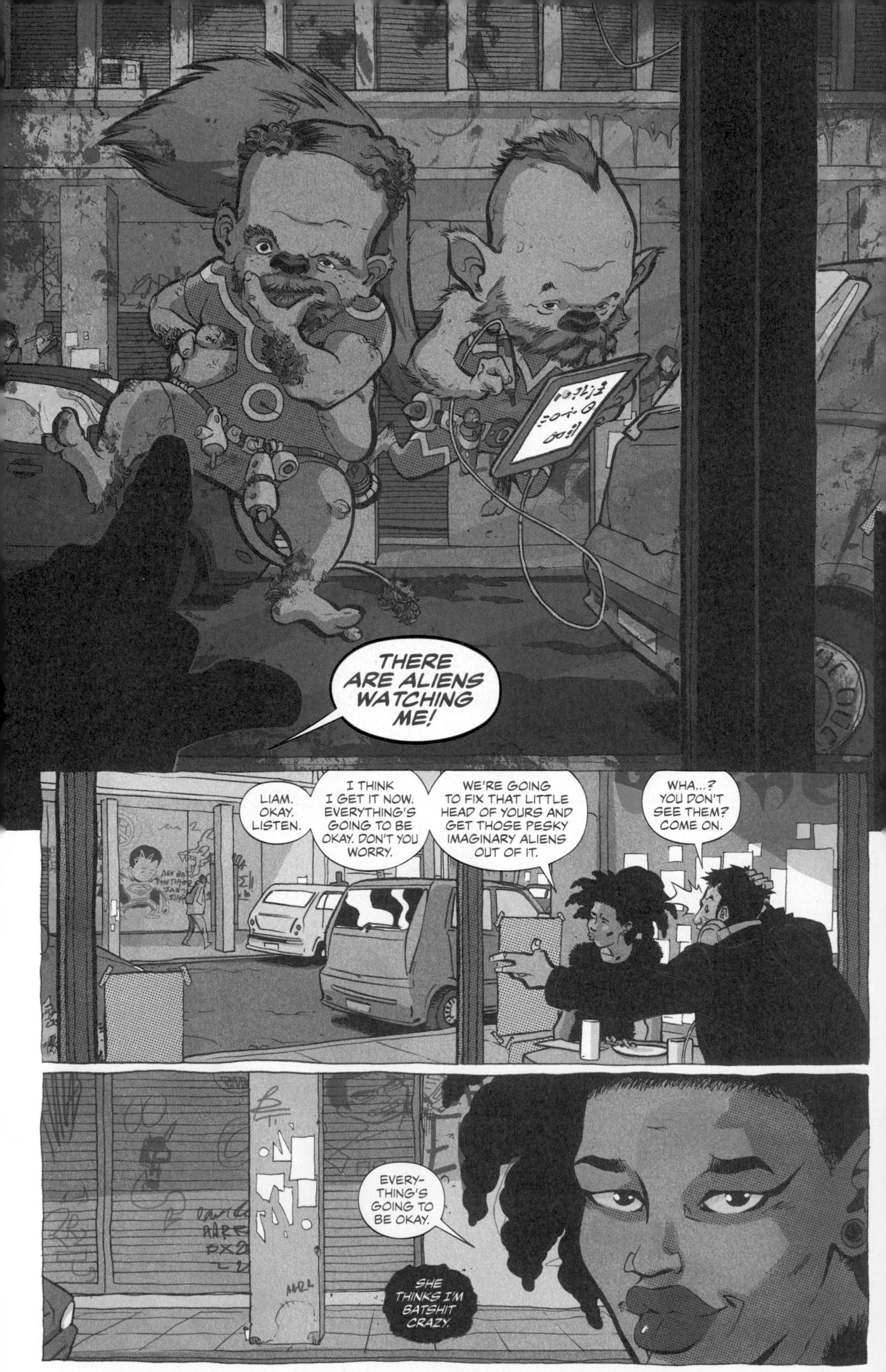
THERE ARE ALIENS WATCHING ME!
LIAM. OKAY. LISTEN.
I THINK I GET IT NOW. EVERYTHING'S GOING TO BE OKAY. DON'T YOU WORRY.
WE'RE GOING TO FIX THAT LITTLE HEAD OF YOURS AND GET THOSE PESKY IMAGINARY ALIENS OUT OF IT.
WHA...? YOU DON'T SEE THEM? COME ON.
EVERY-THING'S GOING TO BE OKAY.
SHE THINKS I'M BATSHIT CRAZY.

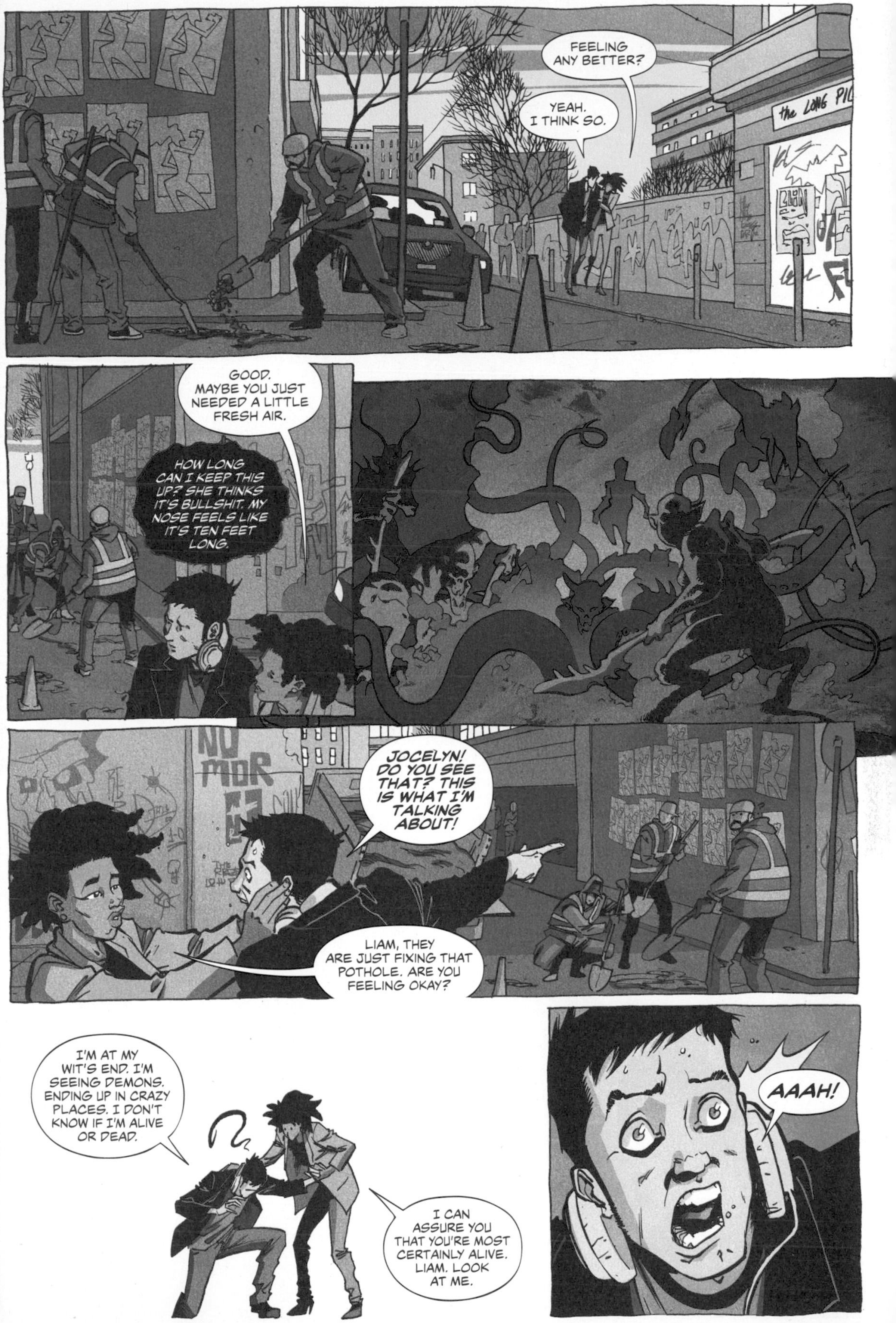
FEELING ANY BETTER?
YEAH. I THINK SO.
the LONG PI
GOOD. MAYBE YOU JUST NEEDED A LITTLE FRESH AIR.
HOW LONG CAN I KEEP THIS UP? SHE THINKS IT'S BULLSHIT. MY NOSE FEELS LIKE IT'S TEN FEET LONG.
NO MOR
JOCELYN! DO YOU SEE THAT? THIS IS WHAT I'M TALKING ABOUT!
LIAM, THEY ARE JUST FIXING THAT POTHOLE. ARE YOU FEELING OKAY?
I'M AT MY WIT'S END. I'M SEEING DEMONS. ENDING UP IN CRAZY PLACES. I DON'T KNOW IF I'M ALIVE OR DEAD.
I CAN ASSURE YOU THAT YOU'RE MOST CERTAINLY ALIVE. LIAM. LOOK AT ME.
AAAH!

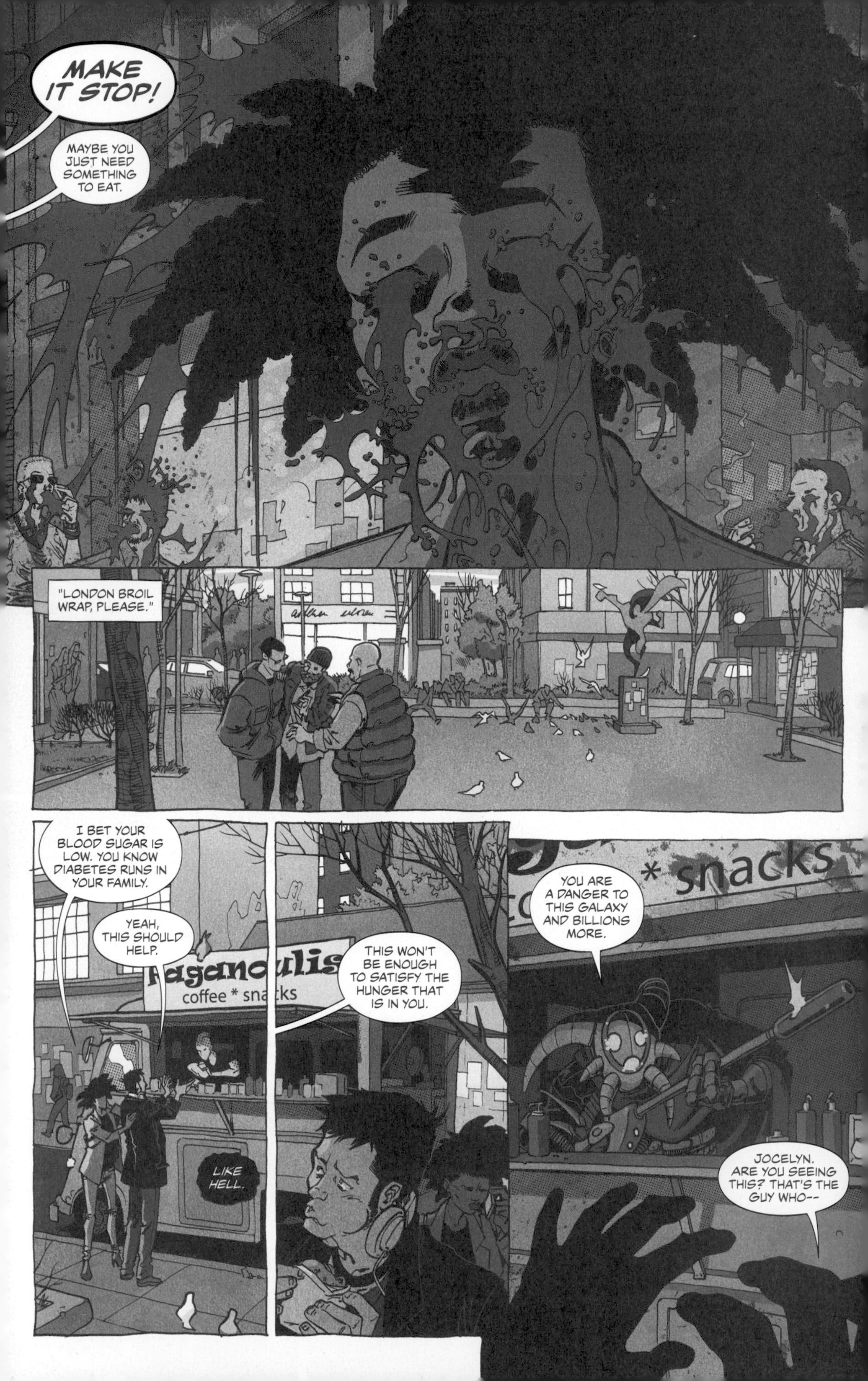
MAKE IT STOP!
MAYBE YOU JUST NEED SOMETHING TO EAT.
"LONDON BROIL WRAP, PLEASE."
I BET YOUR BLOOD SUGAR IS LOW. YOU KNOW DIABETES RUNS IN YOUR FAMILY.
YEAH, THIS SHOULD HELP.
coffee * snacks
LIKE HELL.
THIS WON'T BE ENOUGH TO SATISFY THE HUNGER THAT IS IN YOU.
* snacks
YOU ARE A DANGER TO THIS GALAXY AND BILLIONS MORE.
JOCELYN. ARE YOU SEEING THIS? THAT'S THE GUY WHO--

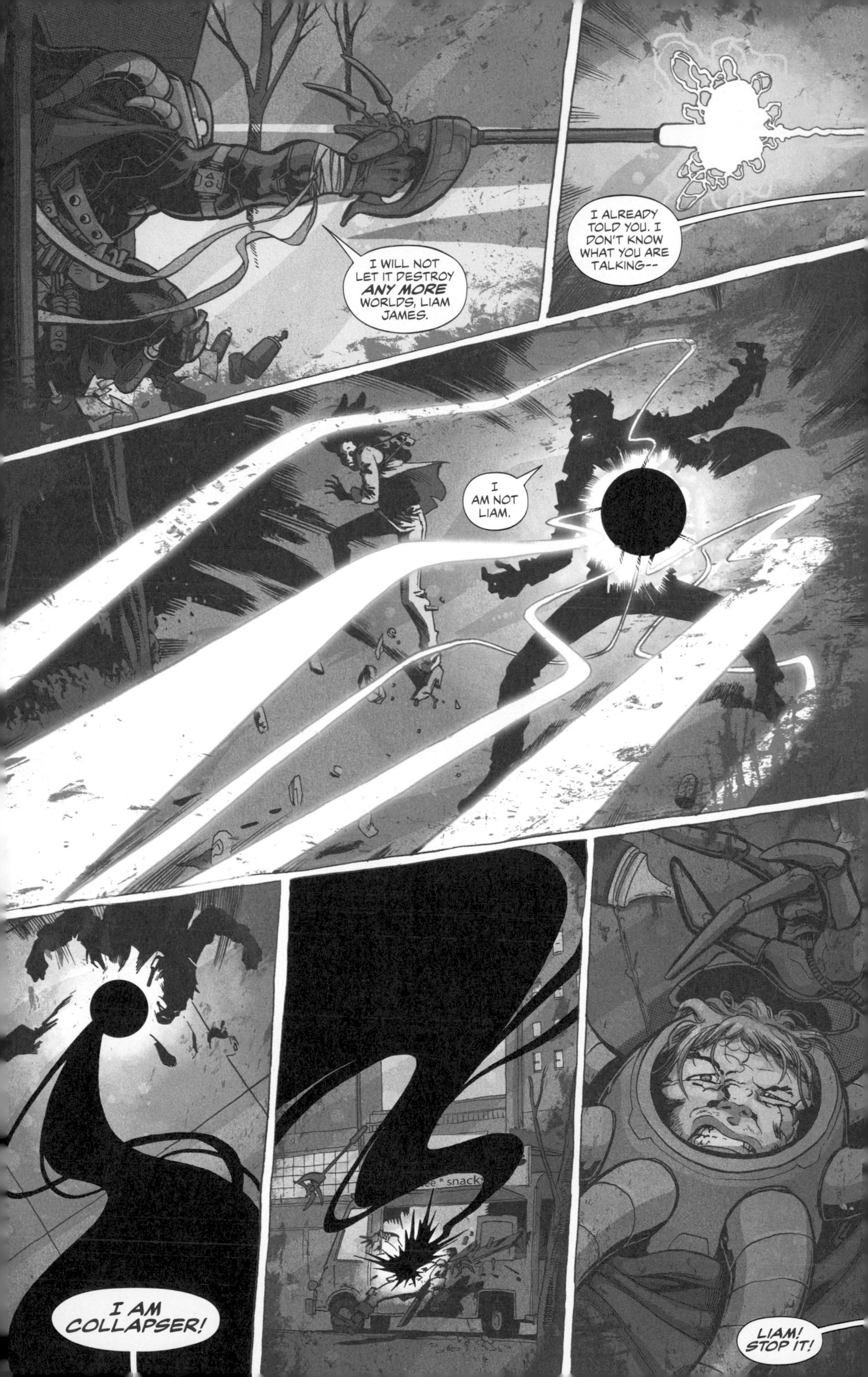
I WILL NOT LET IT DESTROY ***ANY MORE*** WORLDS, LIAM JAMES.
I ALREADY TOLD YOU. I DON'T KNOW WHAT YOU ARE TALKING--
I AM NOT LIAM.
I AM COLLAPSER!
LIAM! STOP IT!

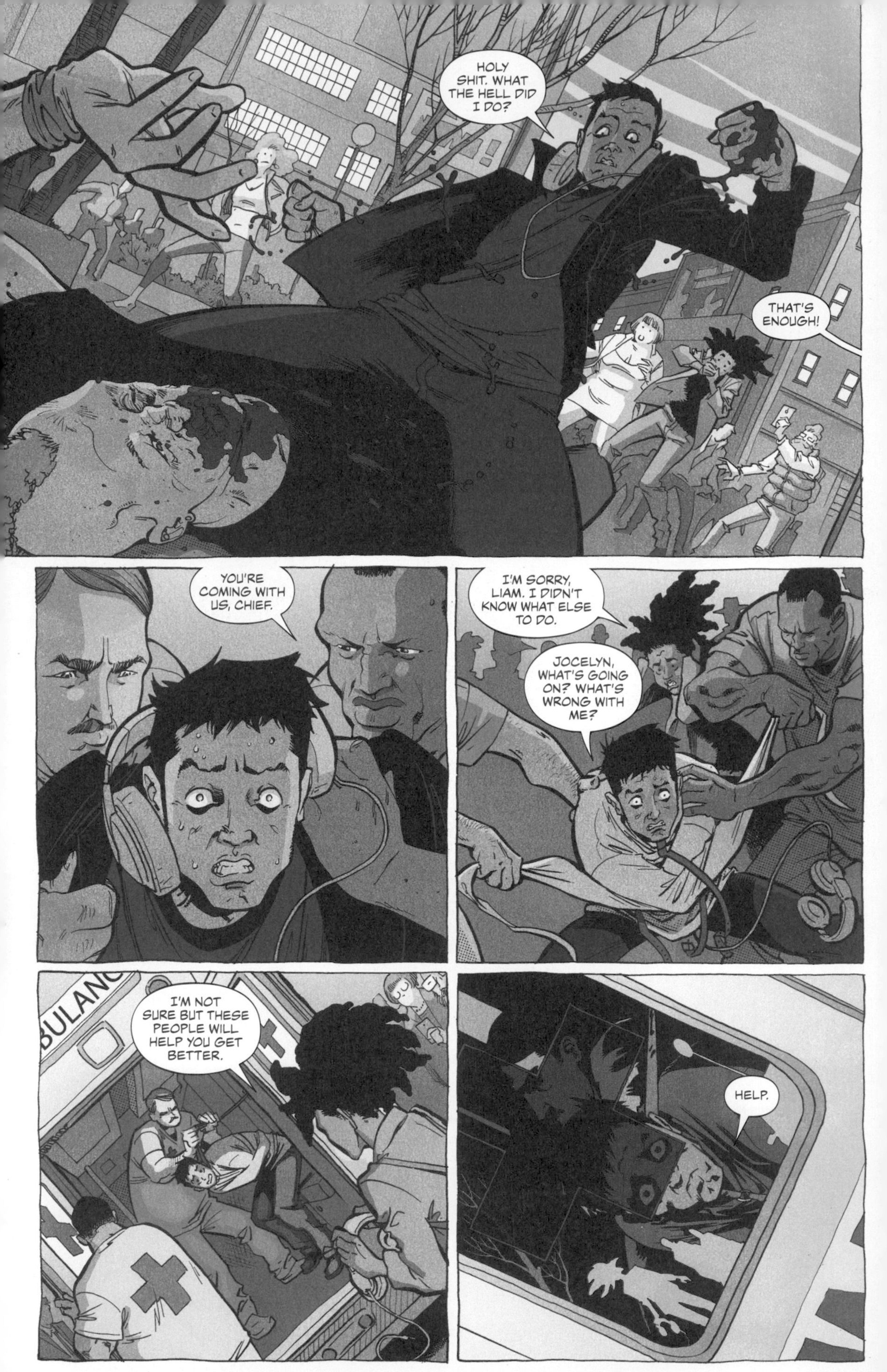
HOLY SHIT. WHAT THE HELL DID I DO?
THAT'S ENOUGH!
YOU'RE COMING WITH US, CHIEF.
I'M SORRY, LIAM. I DIDN'T KNOW WHAT ELSE TO DO.
JOCELYN, WHAT'S GOING ON? WHAT'S WRONG WITH ME?
I'M NOT SURE BUT THESE PEOPLE WILL HELP YOU GET BETTER.
BULANC
HELP.

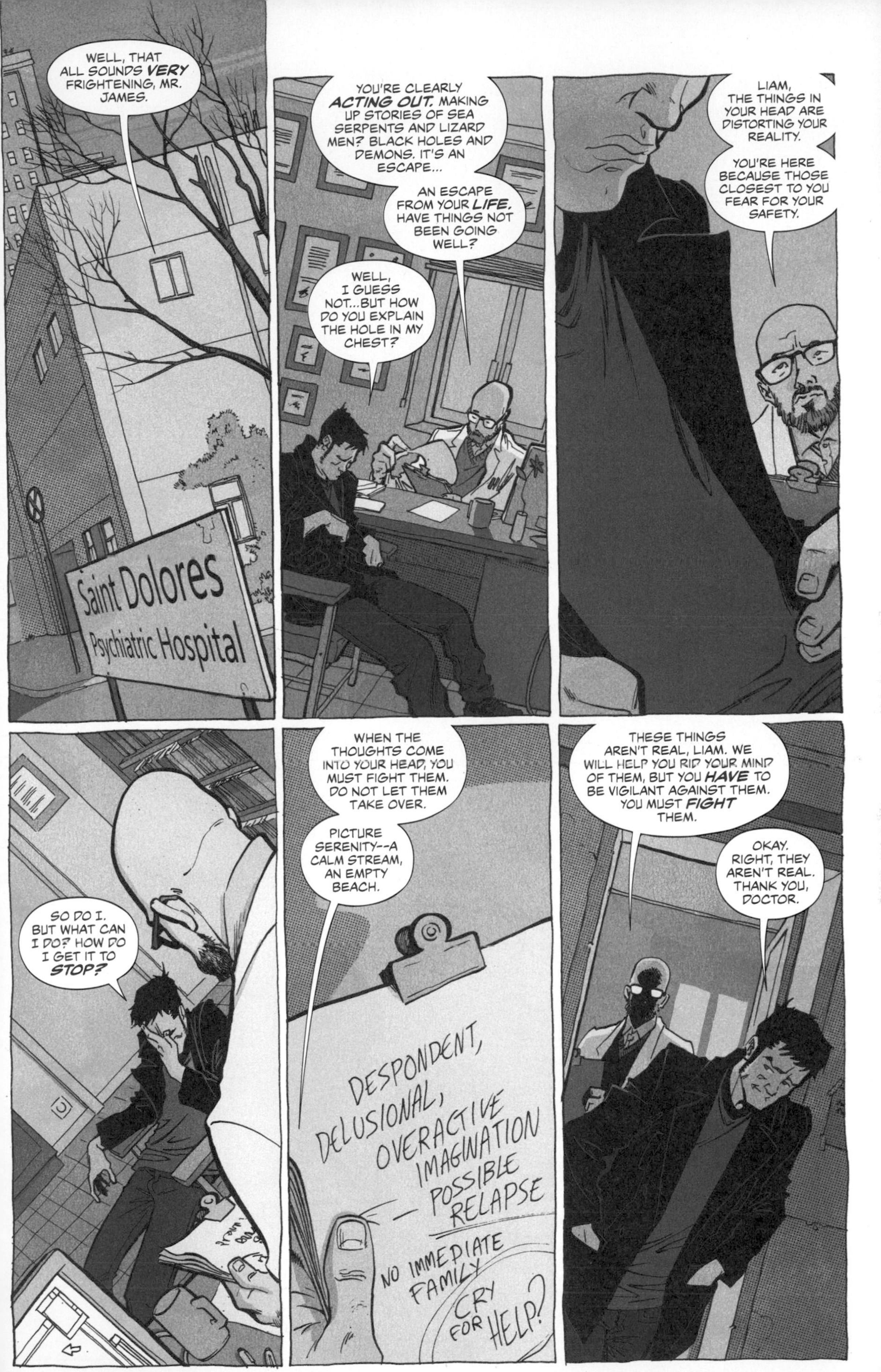
WELL, THAT ALL SOUNDS VERY FRIGHTENING, MR. JAMES.
Saint Dolores Psychiatric Hospital
YOU'RE CLEARLY ACTING OUT. MAKING UP STORIES OF SEA SERPENTS AND LIZARD MEN? BLACK HOLES AND DEMONS. IT'S AN ESCAPE...
AN ESCAPE FROM YOUR LIFE. HAVE THINGS NOT BEEN GOING WELL?
WELL, I GUESS NOT...BUT HOW DO YOU EXPLAIN THE HOLE IN MY CHEST?
LIAM, THE THINGS IN YOUR HEAD ARE DISTORTING YOUR REALITY.
YOU'RE HERE BECAUSE THOSE CLOSEST TO YOU FEAR FOR YOUR SAFETY.
SO DO I. BUT WHAT CAN I DO? HOW DO I GET IT TO STOP?
WHEN THE THOUGHTS COME INTO YOUR HEAD, YOU MUST FIGHT THEM. DO NOT LET THEM TAKE OVER.
PICTURE SERENITY--A CALM STREAM, AN EMPTY BEACH.
DESPONDENT, DELUSIONAL, OVERACTIVE IMAGINATION
— POSSIBLE RELAPSE
NO IMMEDIATE FAMILY
CRY FOR HELP?
THESE THINGS AREN'T REAL, LIAM. WE WILL HELP YOU RID YOUR MIND OF THEM, BUT YOU HAVE TO BE VIGILANT AGAINST THEM. YOU MUST FIGHT THEM.
OKAY. RIGHT, THEY AREN'T REAL. THANK YOU, DOCTOR.

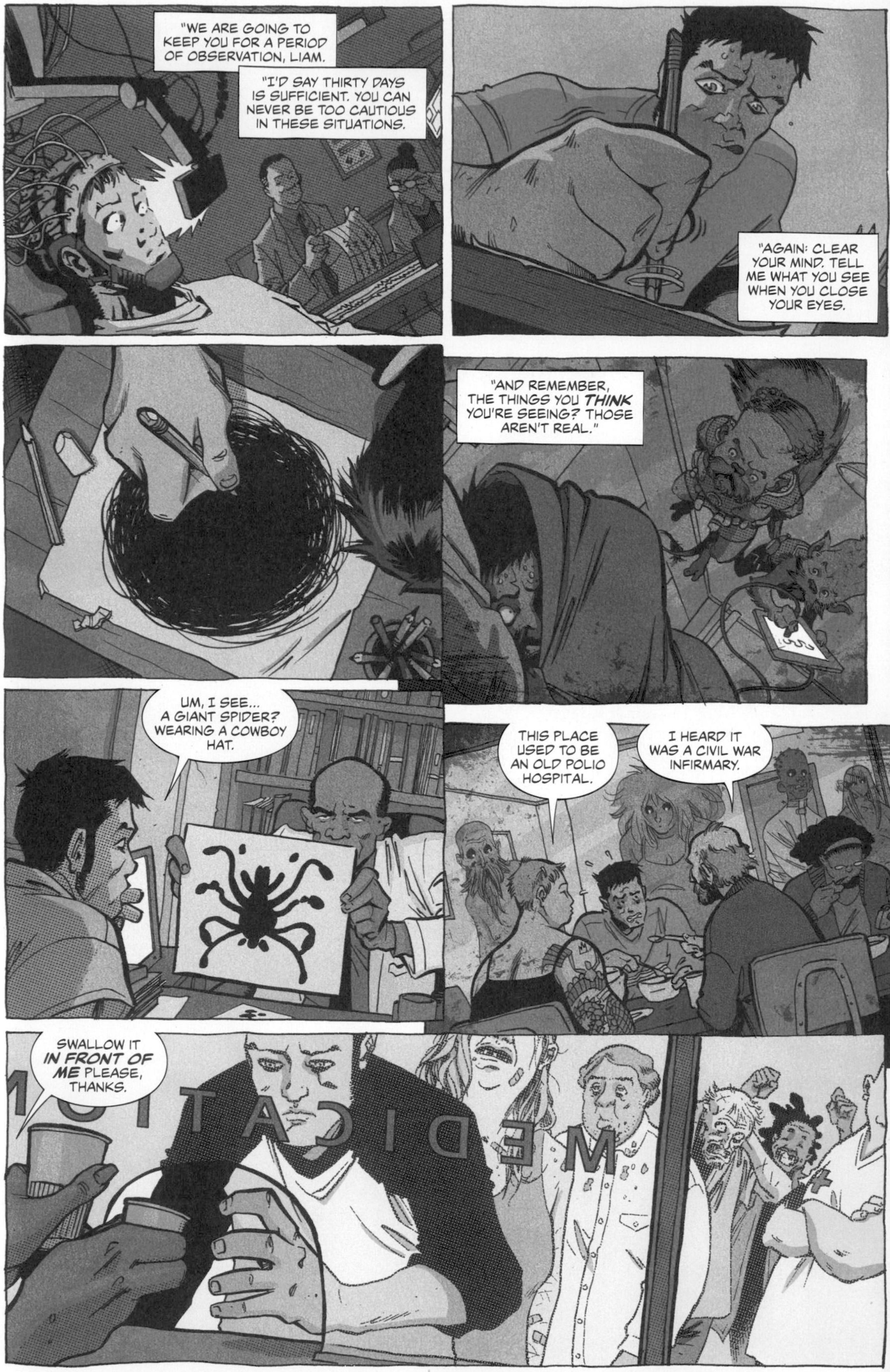
"WE ARE GOING TO KEEP YOU FOR A PERIOD OF OBSERVATION, LIAM.
"I'D SAY THIRTY DAYS IS SUFFICIENT. YOU CAN NEVER BE TOO CAUTIOUS IN THESE SITUATIONS.
"AGAIN: CLEAR YOUR MIND. TELL ME WHAT YOU SEE WHEN YOU CLOSE YOUR EYES.
"AND REMEMBER, THE THINGS YOU *THINK* YOU'RE SEEING? THOSE AREN'T REAL."
UM, I SEE... A GIANT SPIDER? WEARING A COWBOY HAT.
THIS PLACE USED TO BE AN OLD POLIO HOSPITAL.
I HEARD IT WAS A CIVIL WAR INFIRMARY.
SWALLOW IT ***IN FRONT OF ME*** PLEASE, THANKS.
MEDICATION

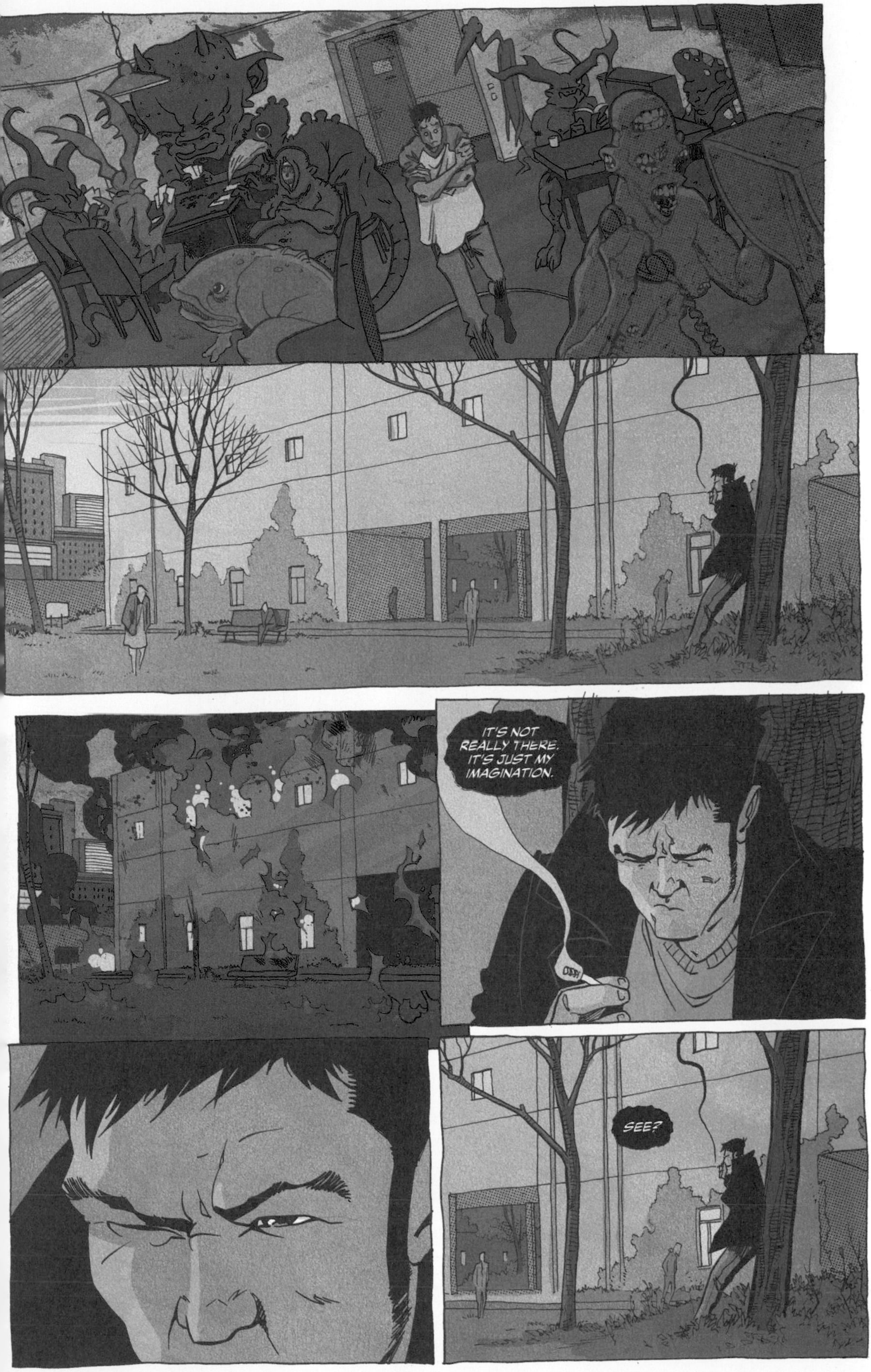
IT'S NOT REALLY THERE. IT'S JUST MY IMAGINATION.
SEE?

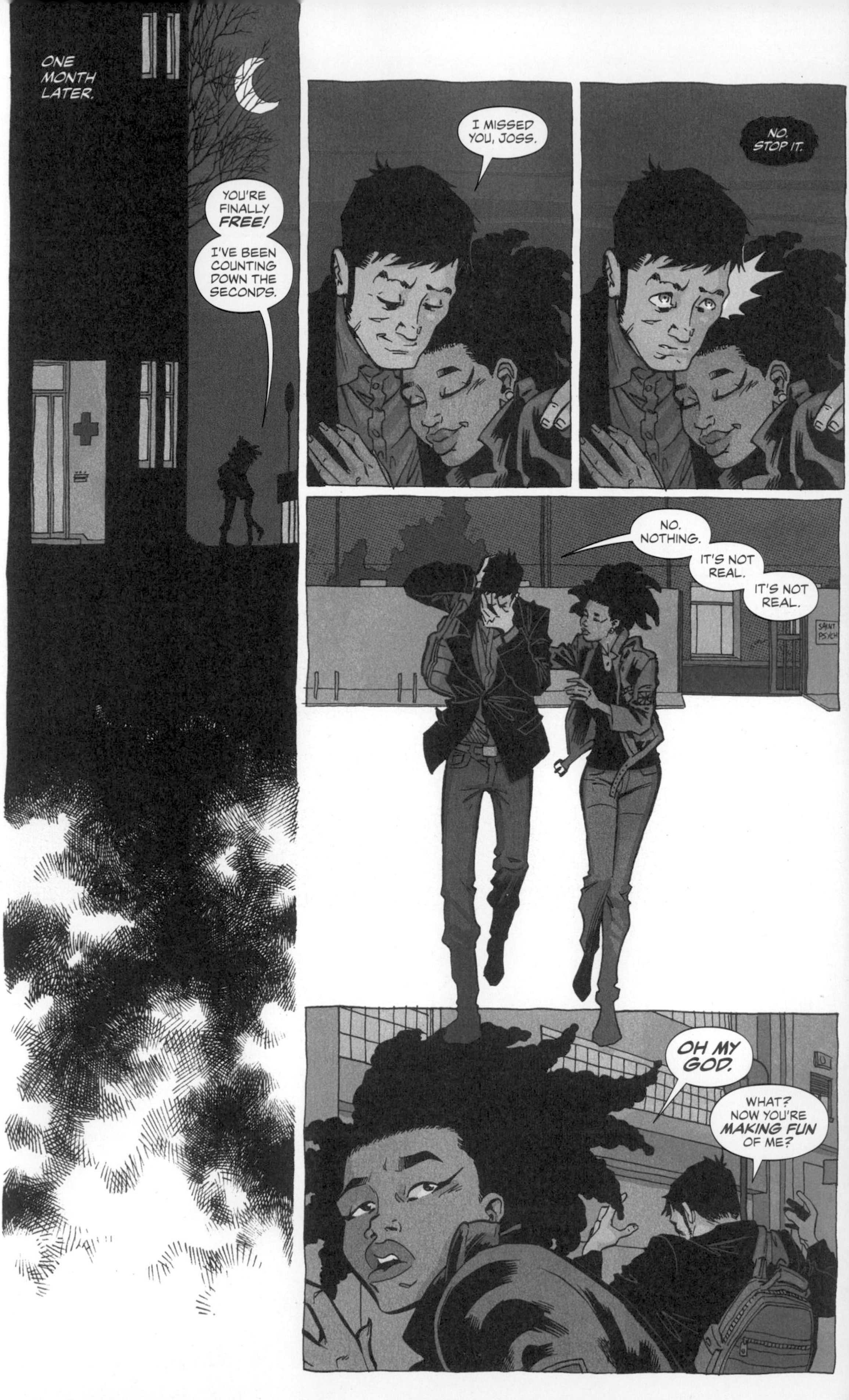
ONE MONTH LATER.
YOU'RE FINALLY FREE!
I'VE BEEN COUNTING DOWN THE SECONDS.
I MISSED YOU, JOSS.
NO. STOP IT.
NO. NOTHING.
IT'S NOT REAL.
IT'S NOT REAL.
SAINT PSYCH
OH MY GOD.
WHAT? NOW YOU'RE MAKING FUN OF ME?

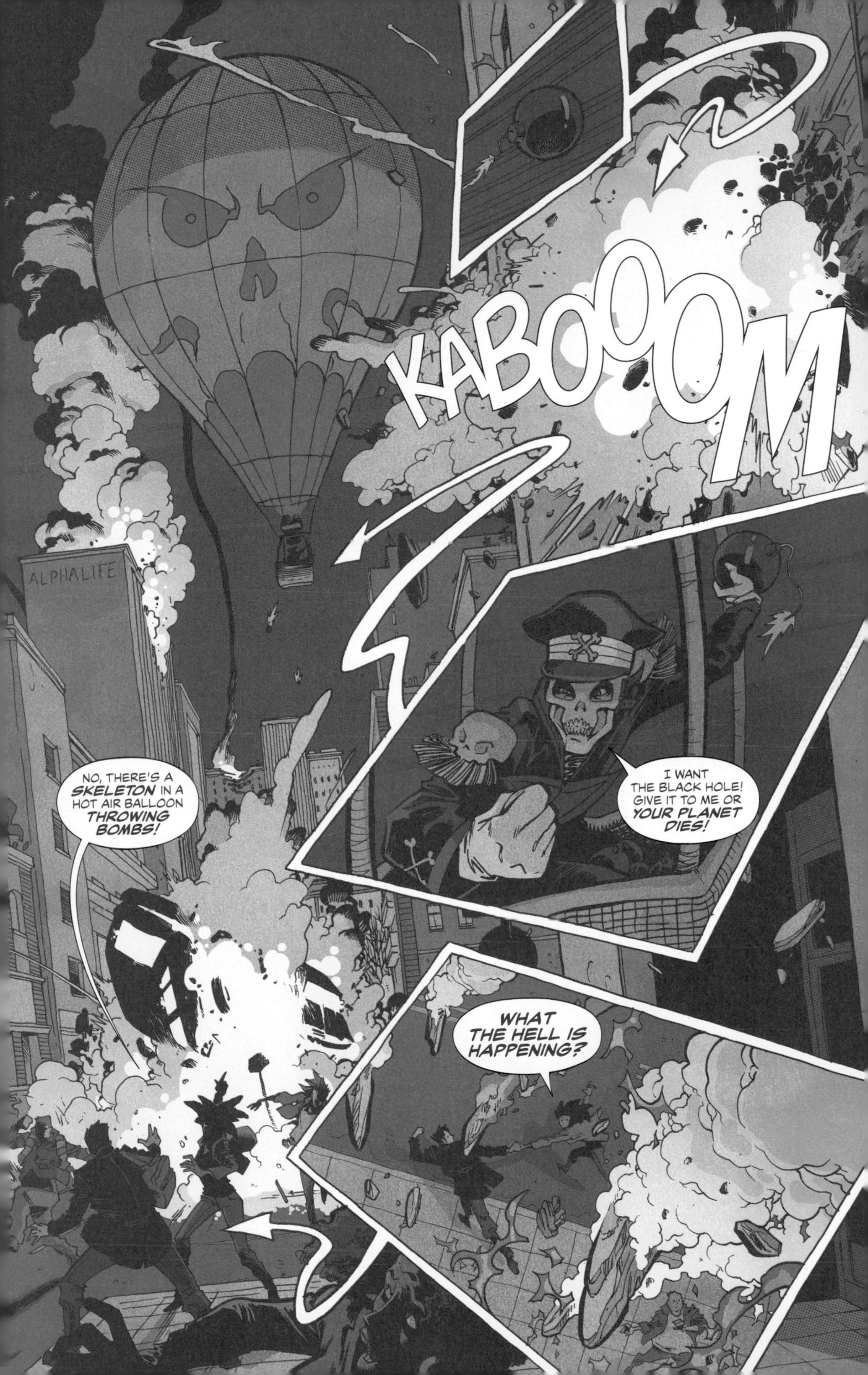
KABOOOOM
ALPHALIFE
I WANT THE BLACK HOLE! GIVE IT TO ME OR YOUR PLANET DIES!
NO, THERE'S A SKELETON IN A HOT AIR BALLOON THROWING BOMBS!
WHAT THE HELL IS HAPPENING?

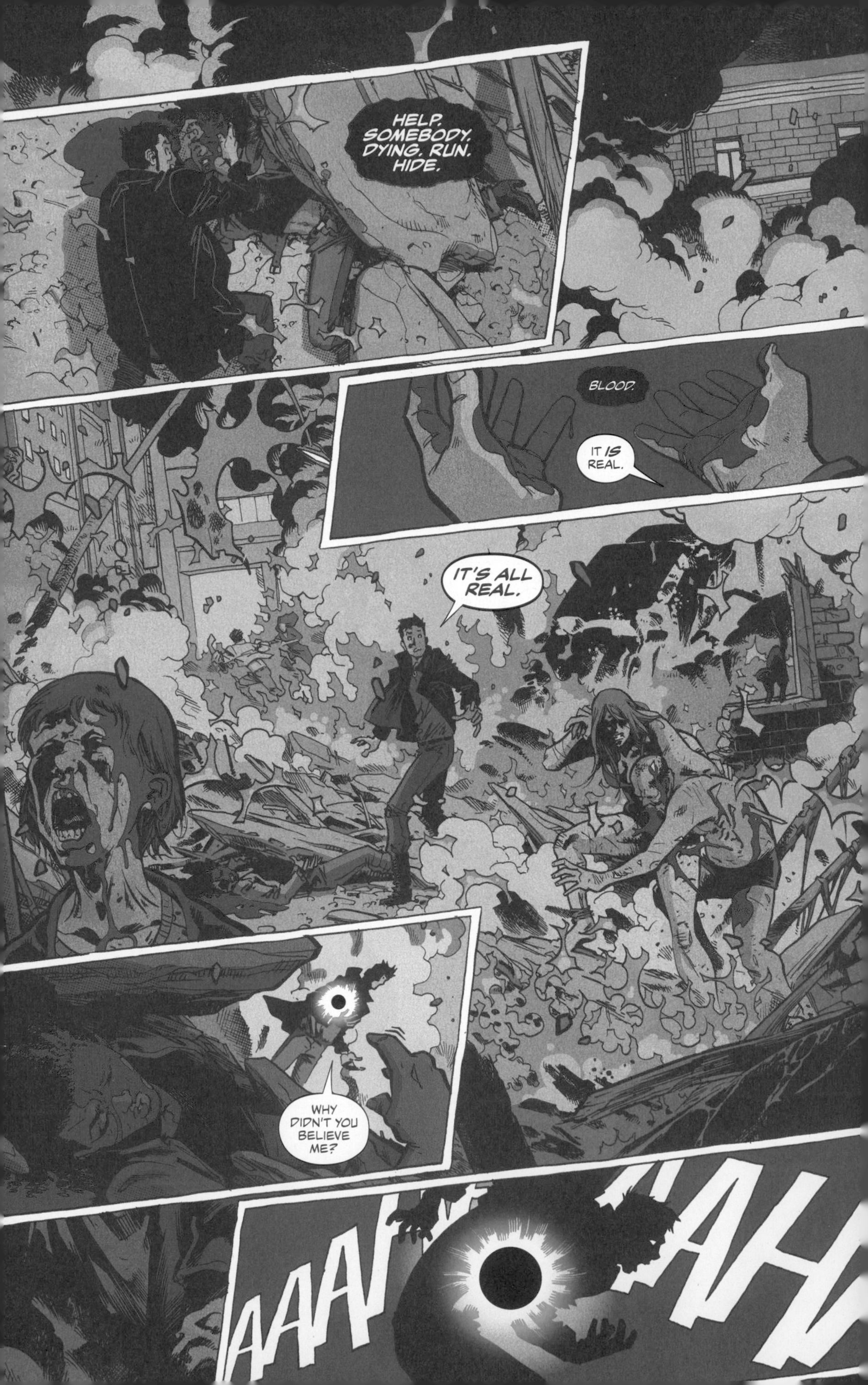
HELP. SOMEBODY. DYING. RUN. HIDE.
BLOOD.
IT IS REAL.
IT'S ALL REAL.
WHY DIDN'T YOU BELIEVE ME?
AAAHHH

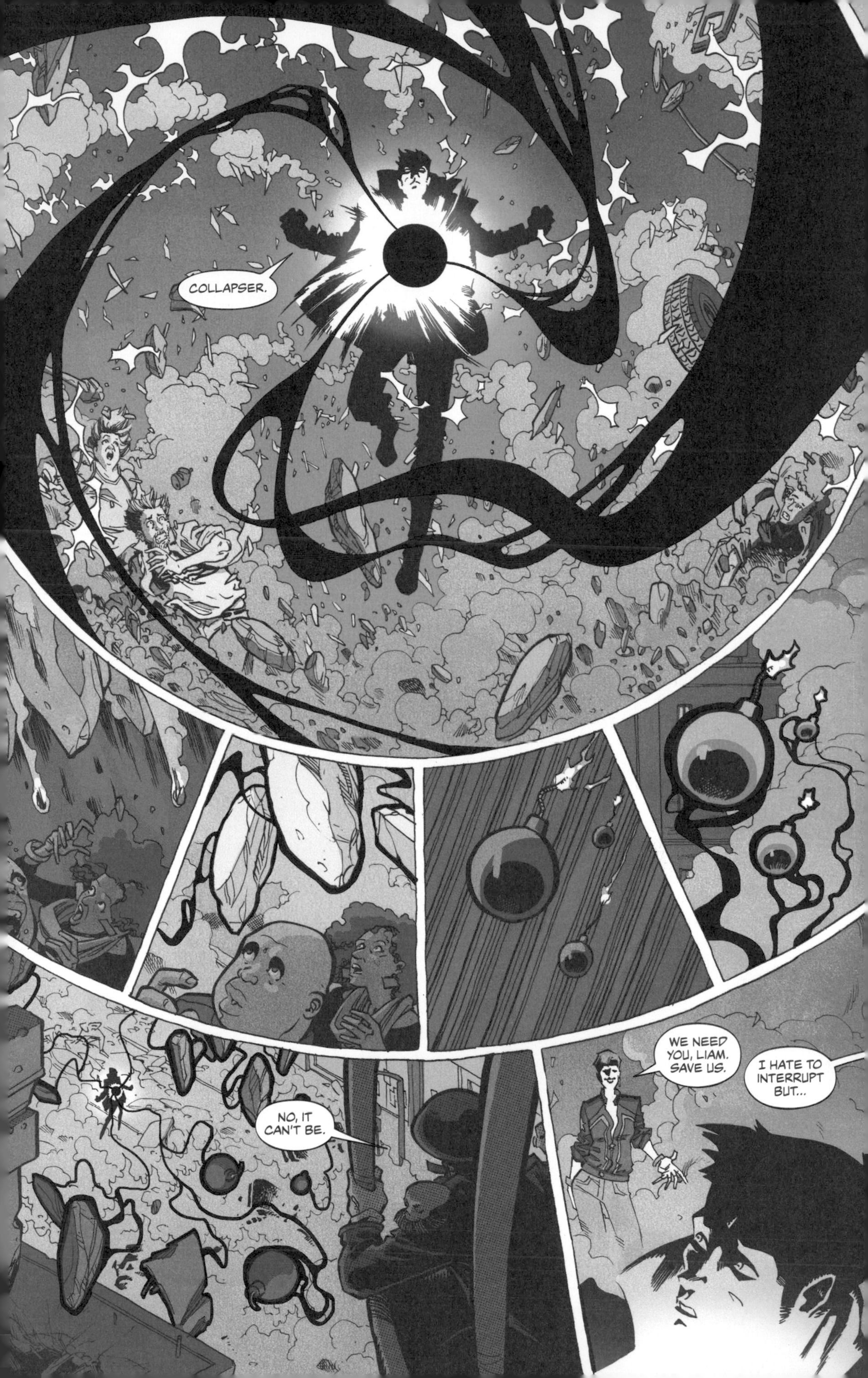
COLLAPSER.
NO, IT CAN'T BE.
WE NEED YOU, LIAM. SAVE US.
I HATE TO INTERRUPT BUT...

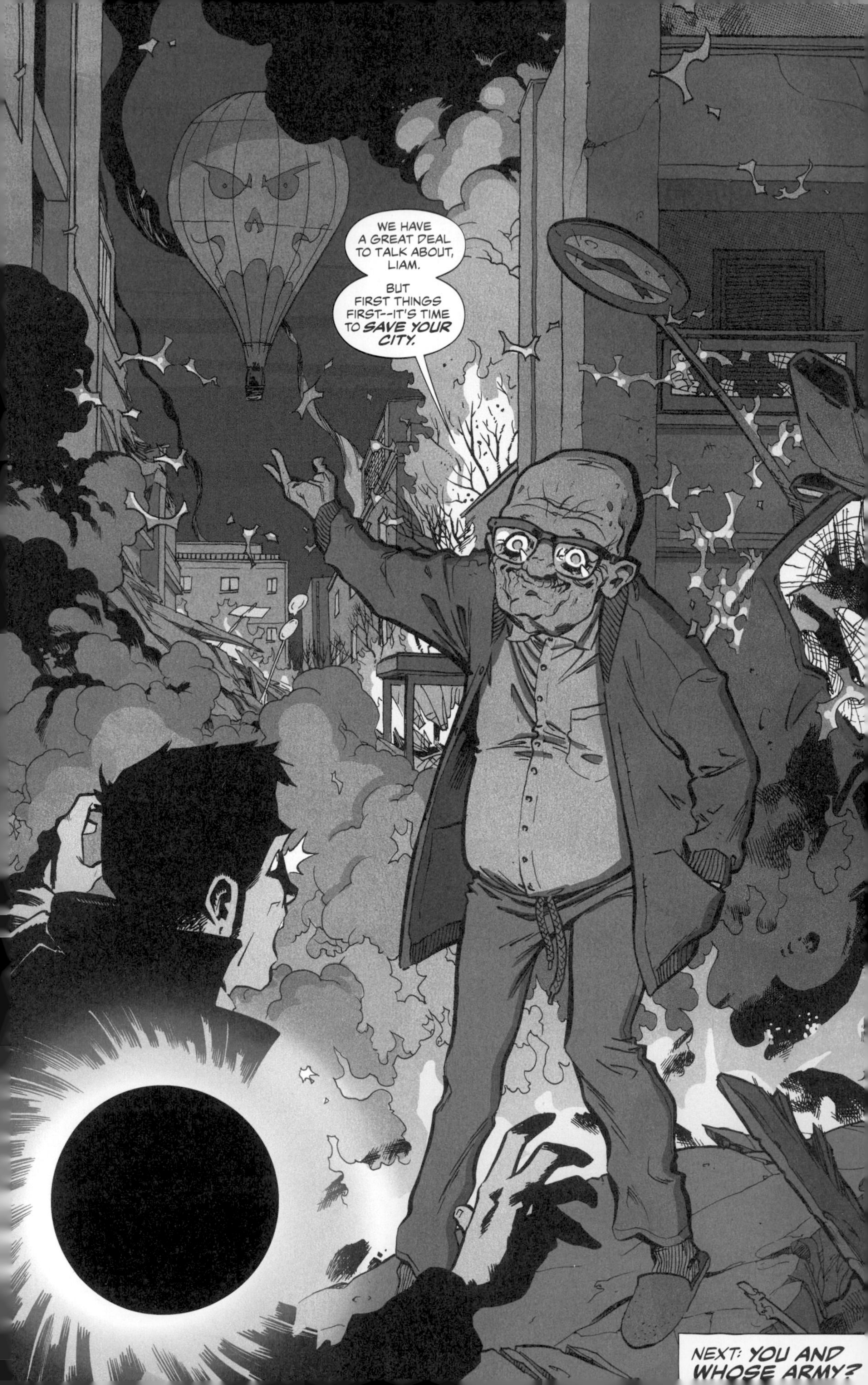
WE HAVE A GREAT DEAL TO TALK ABOUT, LIAM.
BUT FIRST THINGS FIRST--IT'S TIME TO SAVE YOUR CITY.
NEXT: YOU AND WHOSE ARMY?

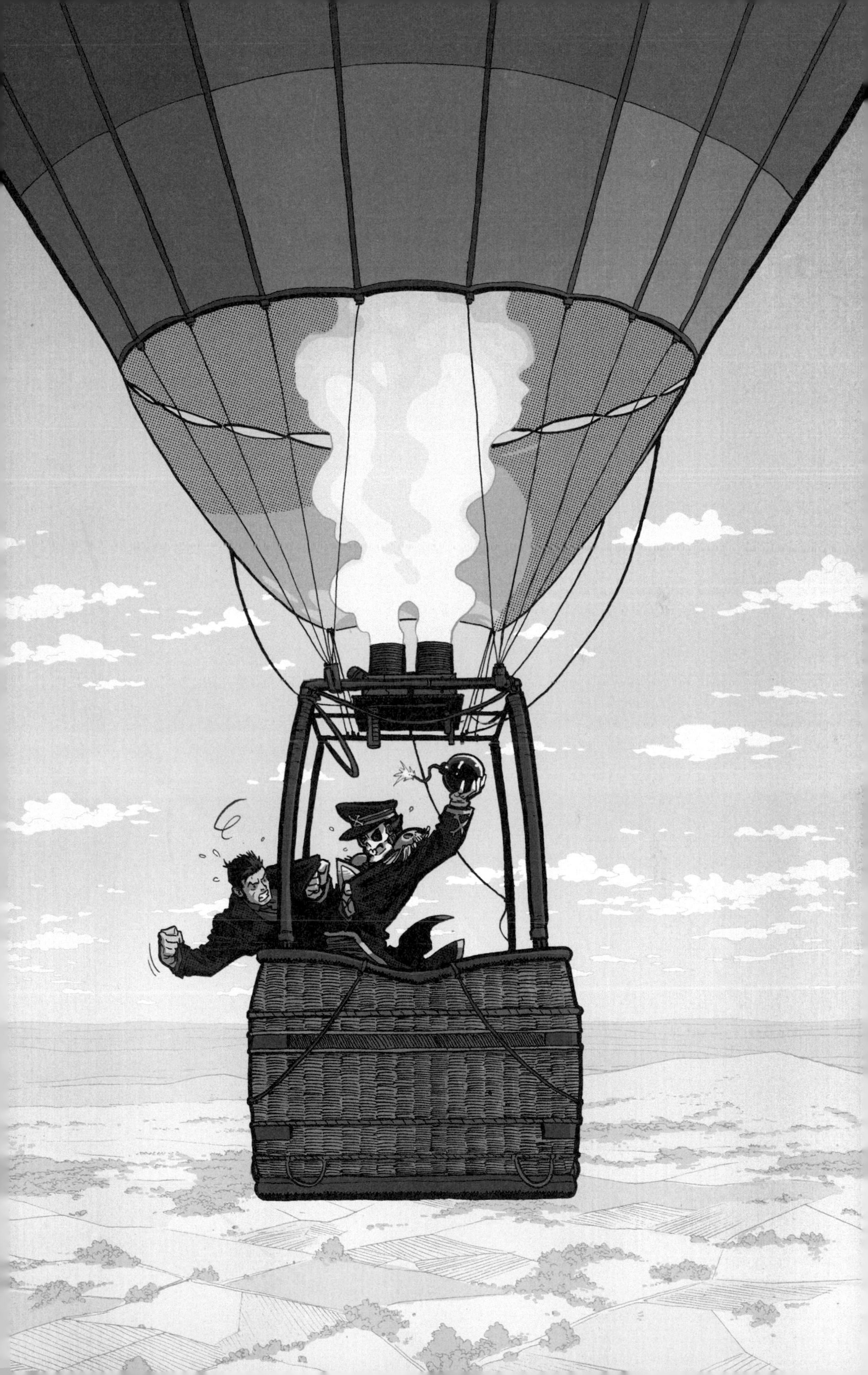

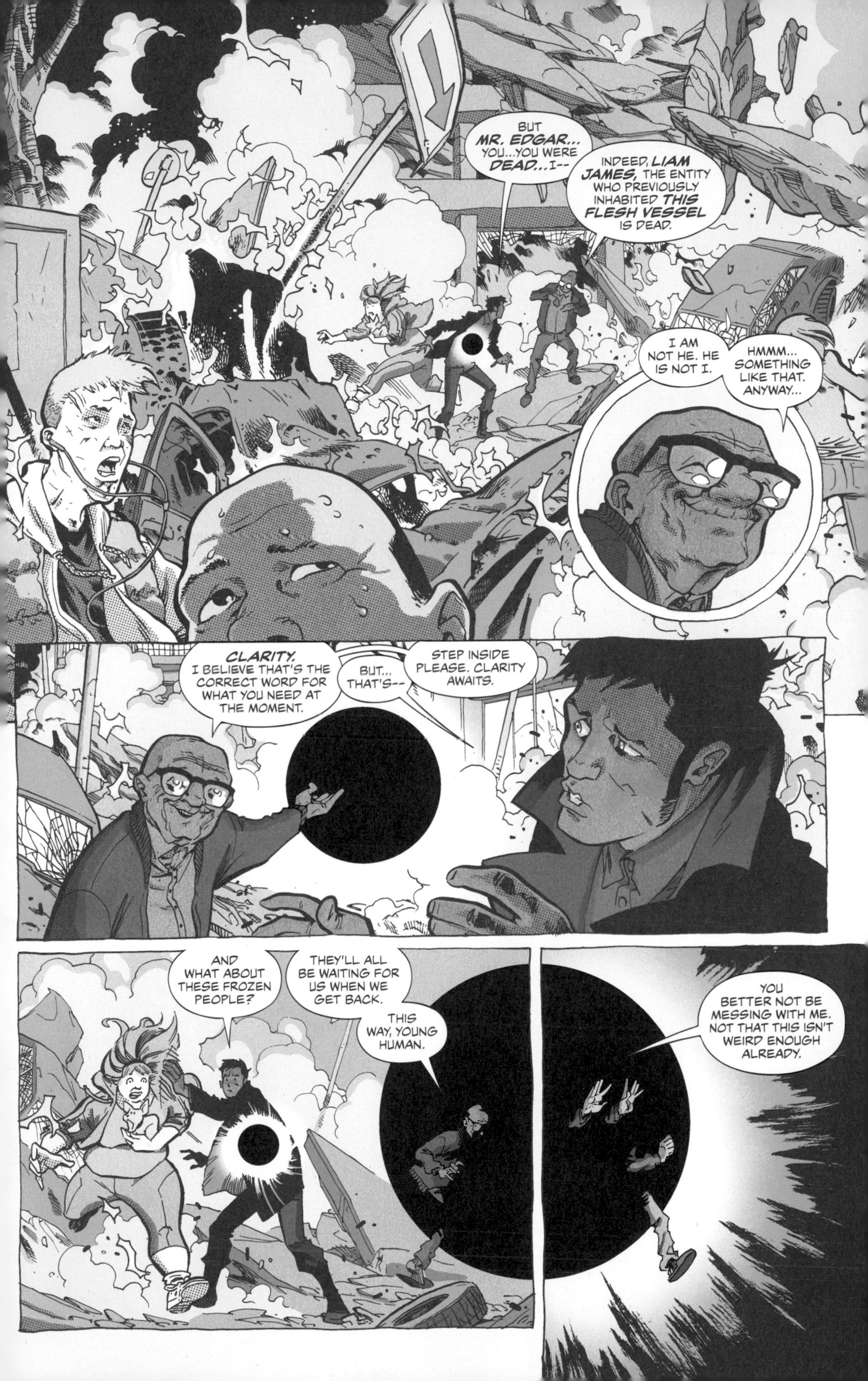
BUT MR. EDGAR... YOU...YOU WERE DEAD...I--
INDEED, LIAM JAMES, THE ENTITY WHO PREVIOUSLY INHABITED THIS FLESH VESSEL IS DEAD.
I AM NOT HE. HE IS NOT I.
HMMM... SOMETHING LIKE THAT. ANYWAY...
CLARITY. I BELIEVE THAT'S THE CORRECT WORD FOR WHAT YOU NEED AT THE MOMENT.
BUT... THAT'S--
STEP INSIDE PLEASE. CLARITY AWAITS.
AND WHAT ABOUT THESE FROZEN PEOPLE?
THEY'LL ALL BE WAITING FOR US WHEN WE GET BACK.
THIS WAY, YOUNG HUMAN.
YOU BETTER NOT BE MESSING WITH ME. NOT THAT THIS ISN'T WEIRD ENOUGH ALREADY.

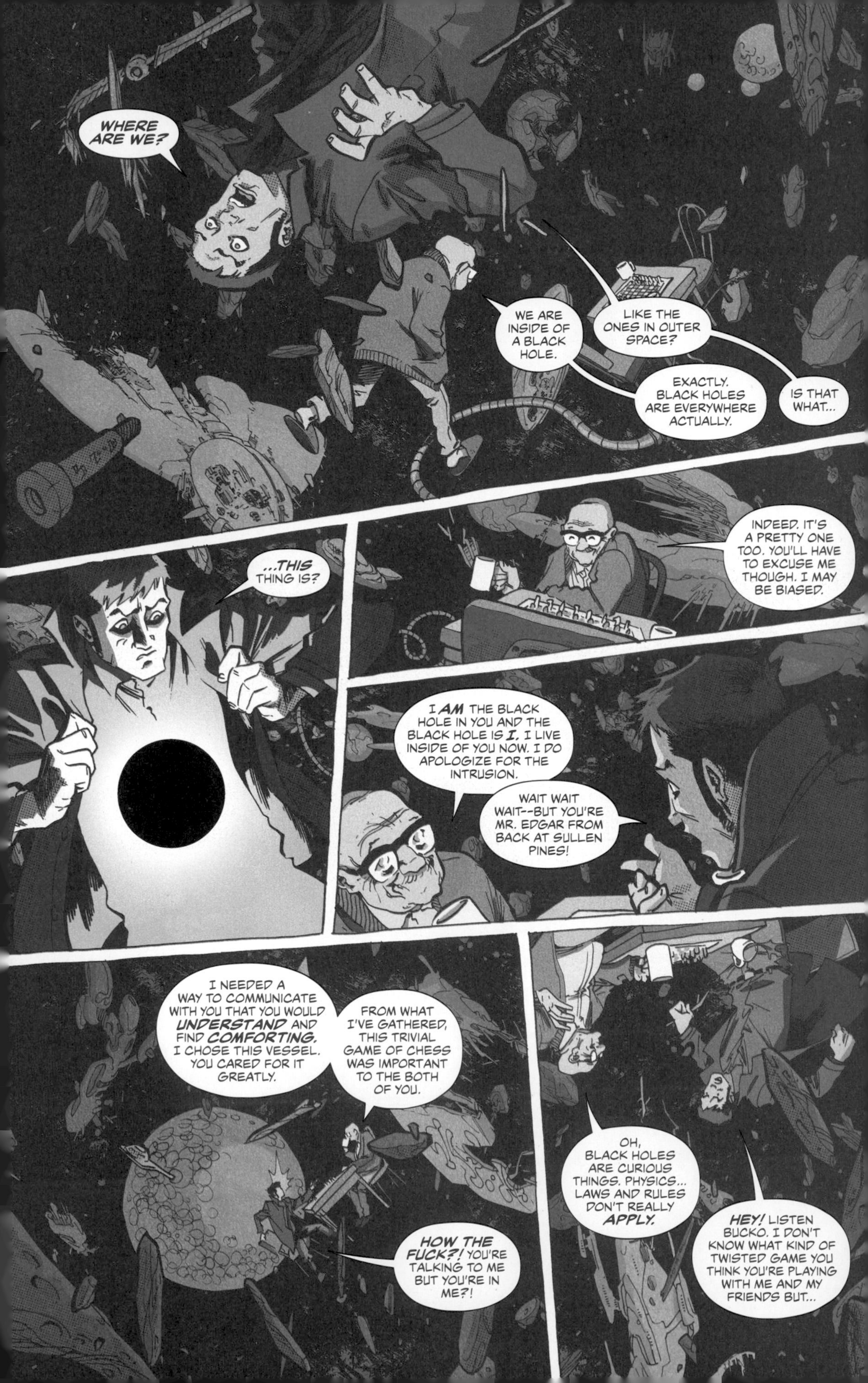
WHERE ARE WE?
WE ARE INSIDE OF A BLACK HOLE.
LIKE THE ONES IN OUTER SPACE?
EXACTLY. BLACK HOLES ARE EVERYWHERE ACTUALLY.
IS THAT WHAT...
...THIS THING IS?
INDEED. IT'S A PRETTY ONE TOO. YOU'LL HAVE TO EXCUSE ME THOUGH. I MAY BE BIASED.
I AM THE BLACK HOLE IN YOU AND THE BLACK HOLE IS I. I LIVE INSIDE OF YOU NOW. I DO APOLOGIZE FOR THE INTRUSION.
WAIT WAIT WAIT--BUT YOU'RE MR. EDGAR FROM BACK AT SULLEN PINES!
I NEEDED A WAY TO COMMUNICATE WITH YOU THAT YOU WOULD UNDERSTAND AND FIND COMFORTING. I CHOSE THIS VESSEL. YOU CARED FOR IT GREATLY.
FROM WHAT I'VE GATHERED, THIS TRIVIAL GAME OF CHESS WAS IMPORTANT TO THE BOTH OF YOU.
HOW THE FUCK?! YOU'RE TALKING TO ME BUT YOU'RE IN ME?!
OH, BLACK HOLES ARE CURIOUS THINGS. PHYSICS... LAWS AND RULES DON'T REALLY APPLY.
HEY! LISTEN BUCKO. I DON'T KNOW WHAT KIND OF TWISTED GAME YOU THINK YOU'RE PLAYING WITH ME AND MY FRIENDS BUT...

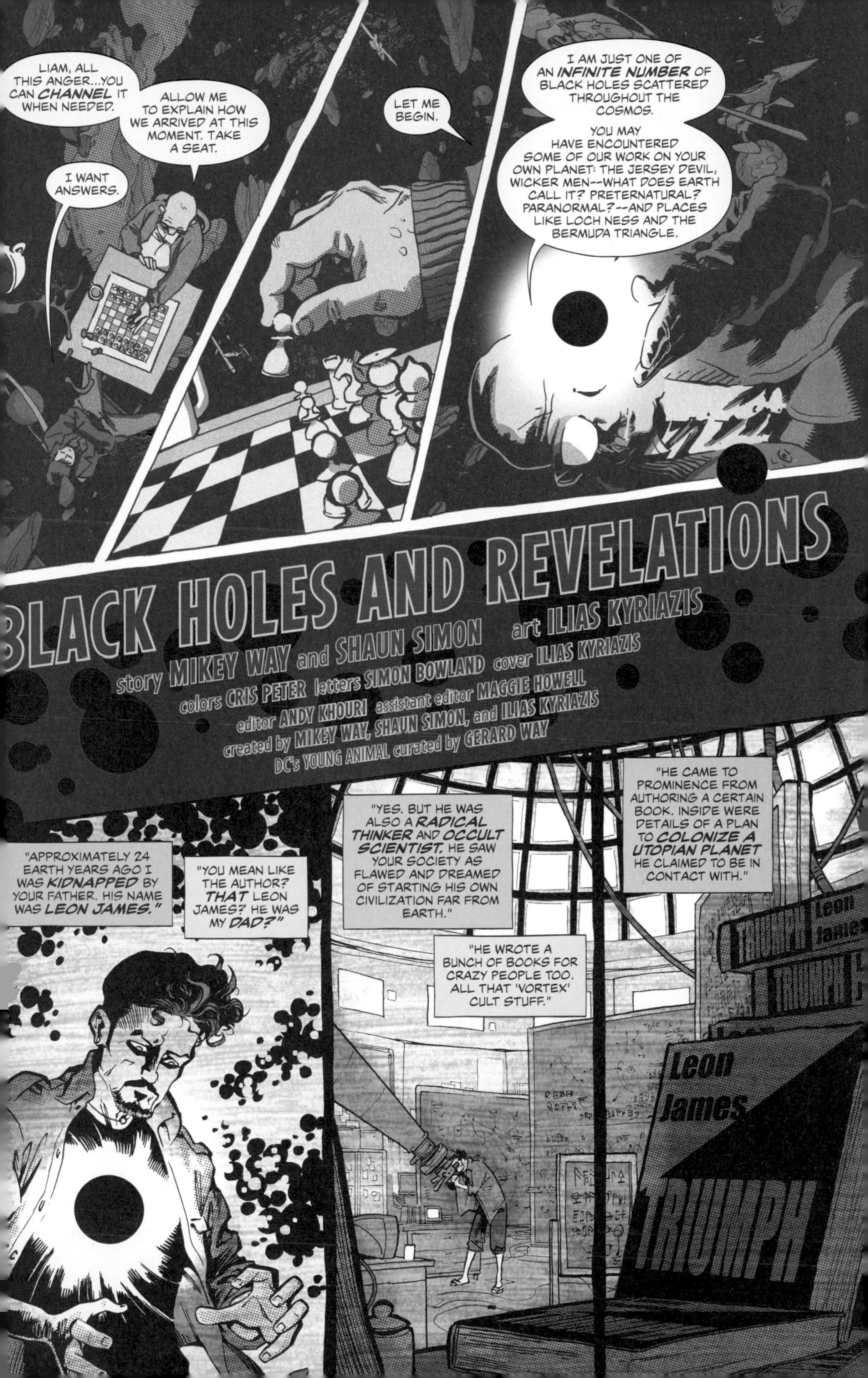
LIAM, ALL THIS ANGER...YOU CAN CHANNEL IT WHEN NEEDED.
I WANT ANSWERS.
ALLOW ME TO EXPLAIN HOW WE ARRIVED AT THIS MOMENT. TAKE A SEAT.
LET ME BEGIN.
I AM JUST ONE OF AN INFINITE NUMBER OF BLACK HOLES SCATTERED THROUGHOUT THE COSMOS.
YOU MAY HAVE ENCOUNTERED SOME OF OUR WORK ON YOUR OWN PLANET: THE JERSEY DEVIL, WICKER MEN--WHAT DOES EARTH CALL IT? PRETERNATURAL? PARANORMAL?--AND PLACES LIKE LOCH NESS AND THE BERMUDA TRIANGLE.
BLACK HOLES AND REVELATIONS
story MIKEY WAY and SHAUN SIMON art ILIAS KYRIAZIS
colors CRIS PETER letters SIMON BOWLAND cover ILIAS KYRIAZIS
editor ANDY KHOURI assistant editor MAGGIE HOWELL
created by MIKEY WAY, SHAUN SIMON, and ILIAS KYRIAZIS
DC's YOUNG ANIMAL curated by GERARD WAY
"APPROXIMATELY 24 EARTH YEARS AGO I WAS KIDNAPPED BY YOUR FATHER. HIS NAME WAS LEON JAMES."
"YOU MEAN LIKE THE AUTHOR? THAT LEON JAMES? HE WAS MY DAD?"
"YES. BUT HE WAS ALSO A RADICAL THINKER AND OCCULT SCIENTIST. HE SAW YOUR SOCIETY AS FLAWED AND DREAMED OF STARTING HIS OWN CIVILIZATION FAR FROM EARTH."
"HE WROTE A BUNCH OF BOOKS FOR CRAZY PEOPLE TOO. ALL THAT 'VORTEX' CULT STUFF."
"HE CAME TO PROMINENCE FROM AUTHORING A CERTAIN BOOK. INSIDE WERE DETAILS OF A PLAN TO COLONIZE A UTOPIAN PLANET HE CLAIMED TO BE IN CONTACT WITH."
TRIUMPH
Leon James
Leon James
TRIUMPH

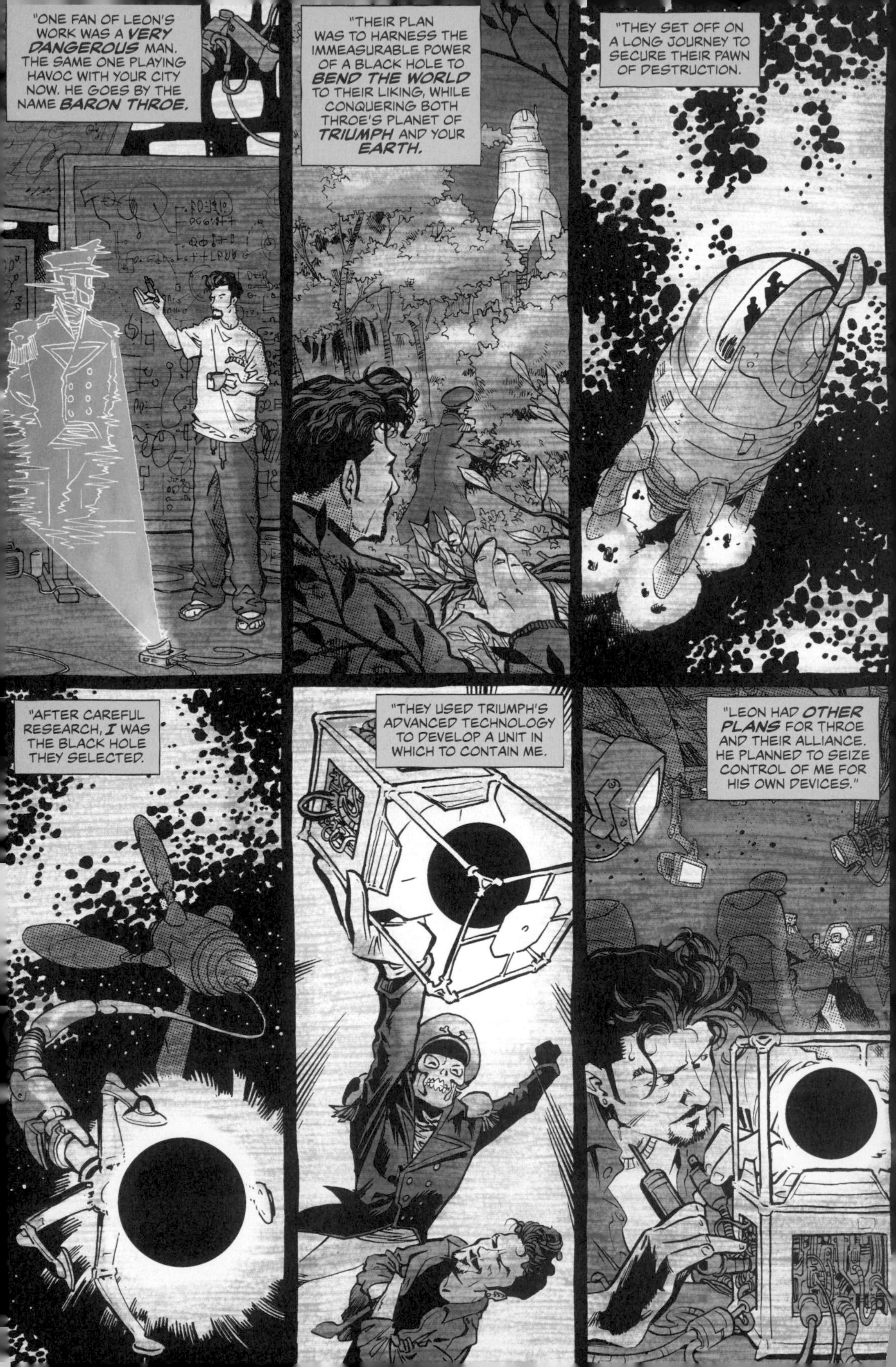
"ONE FAN OF LEON'S WORK WAS A VERY DANGEROUS MAN. THE SAME ONE PLAYING HAVOC WITH YOUR CITY NOW. HE GOES BY THE NAME BARON THROE.
"THEIR PLAN WAS TO HARNESS THE IMMEASURABLE POWER OF A BLACK HOLE TO BEND THE WORLD TO THEIR LIKING, WHILE CONQUERING BOTH THROE'S PLANET OF TRIUMPH AND YOUR EARTH.
"THEY SET OFF ON A LONG JOURNEY TO SECURE THEIR PAWN OF DESTRUCTION.
"AFTER CAREFUL RESEARCH, I WAS THE BLACK HOLE THEY SELECTED.
"THEY USED TRIUMPH'S ADVANCED TECHNOLOGY TO DEVELOP A UNIT IN WHICH TO CONTAIN ME.
"LEON HAD OTHER PLANS FOR THROE AND THEIR ALLIANCE. HE PLANNED TO SEIZE CONTROL OF ME FOR HIS OWN DEVICES."

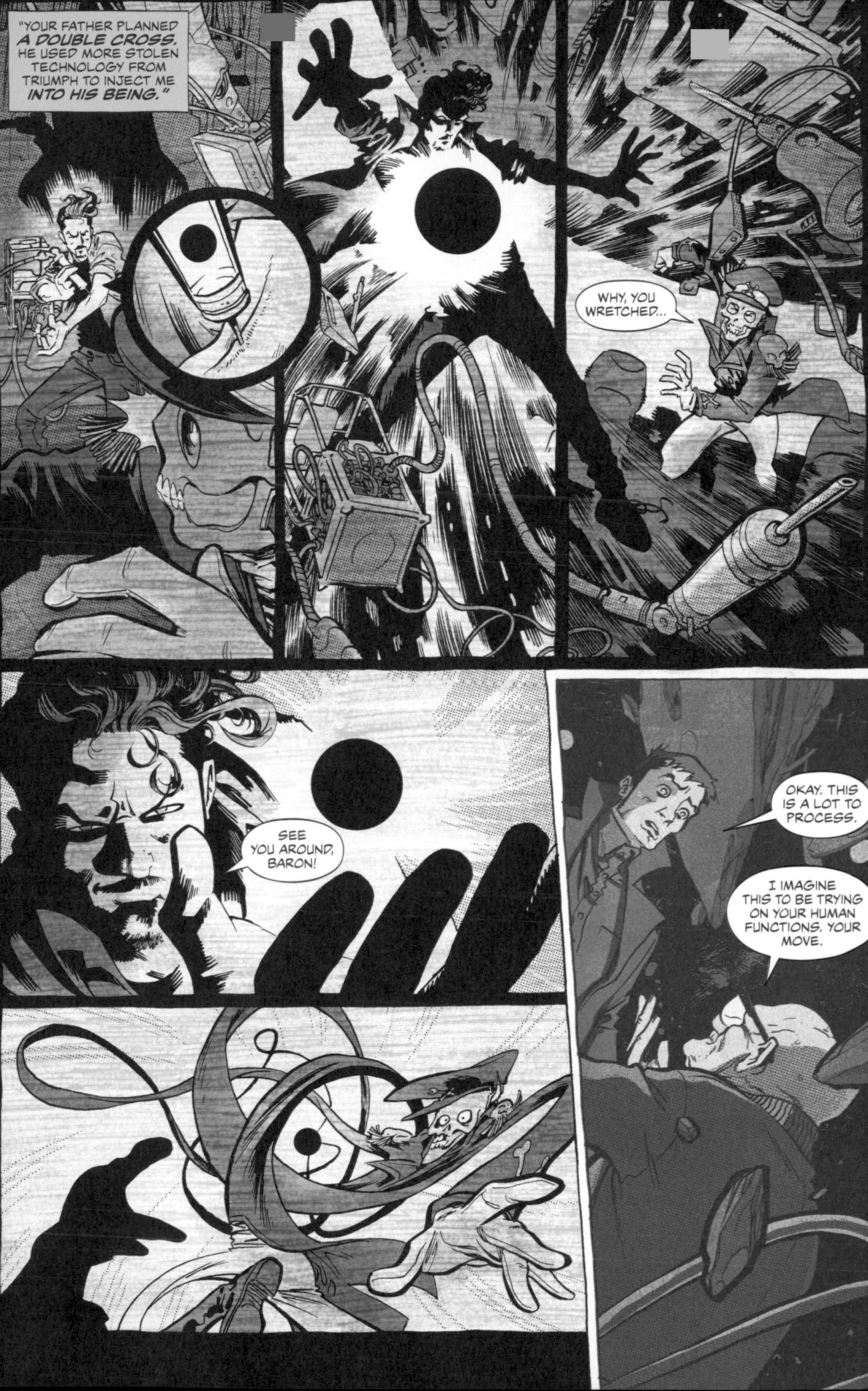
"YOUR FATHER PLANNED A DOUBLE CROSS. HE USED MORE STOLEN TECHNOLOGY FROM TRIUMPH TO INJECT ME INTO HIS BEING."
WHY, YOU WRETCHED...
SEE YOU AROUND, BARON!
OKAY. THIS IS A LOT TO PROCESS.
I IMAGINE THIS TO BE TRYING ON YOUR HUMAN FUNCTIONS. YOUR MOVE.

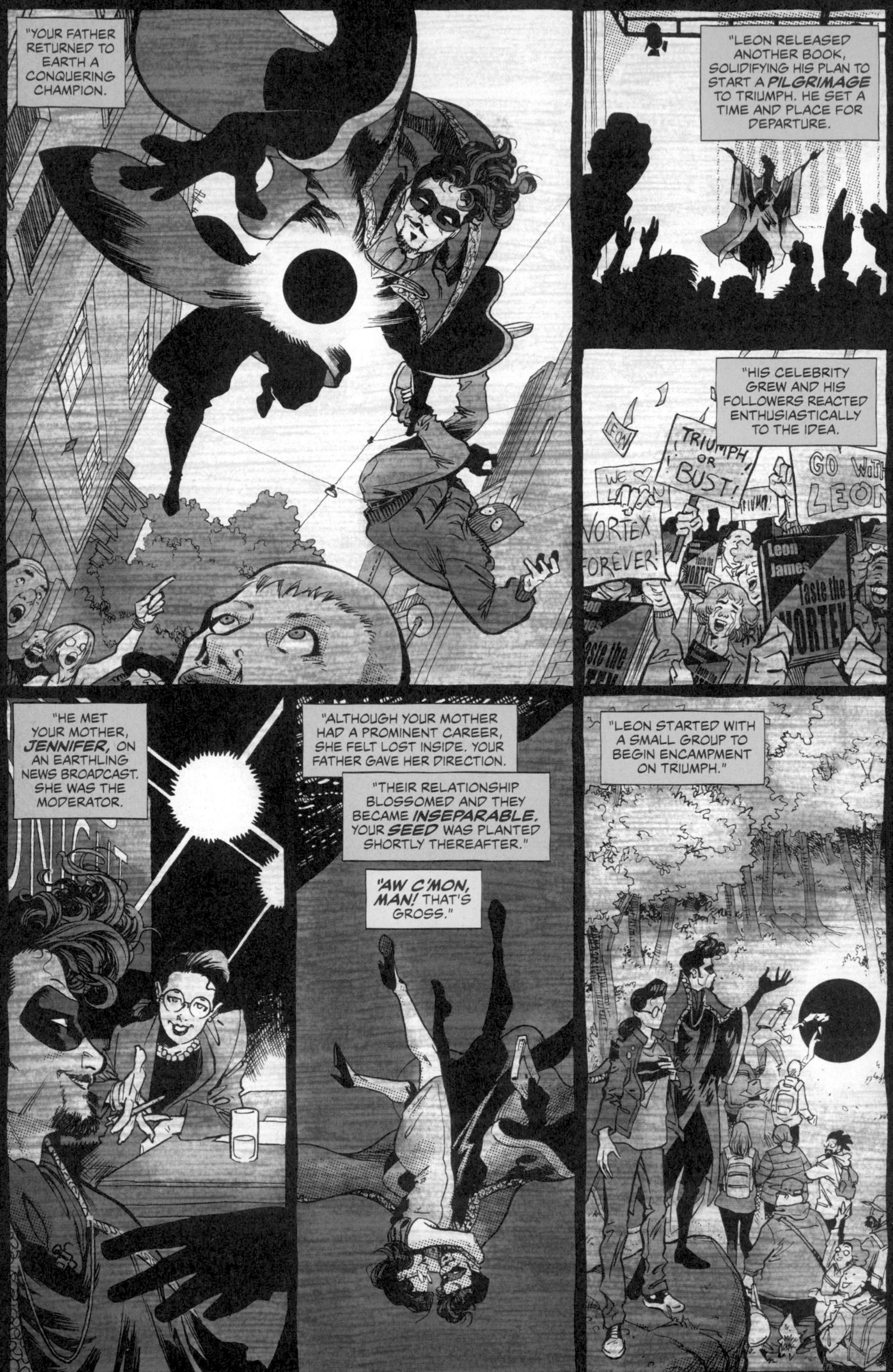
"YOUR FATHER RETURNED TO EARTH A CONQUERING CHAMPION.
"LEON RELEASED ANOTHER BOOK, SOLIDIFYING HIS PLAN TO START A PILGRIMAGE TO TRIUMPH. HE SET A TIME AND PLACE FOR DEPARTURE.
"HIS CELEBRITY GREW AND HIS FOLLOWERS REACTED ENTHUSIASTICALLY TO THE IDEA.
LEON
TRIUMPH OR BUST!
GO WITH LEON
VORTEX FOREVER!
Leon James Taste the VORTEX
"HE MET YOUR MOTHER, JENNIFER, ON AN EARTHLING NEWS BROADCAST. SHE WAS THE MODERATOR.
"ALTHOUGH YOUR MOTHER HAD A PROMINENT CAREER, SHE FELT LOST INSIDE. YOUR FATHER GAVE HER DIRECTION.
"THEIR RELATIONSHIP BLOSSOMED AND THEY BECAME INSEPARABLE. YOUR SEED WAS PLANTED SHORTLY THEREAFTER."
"AW C'MON, MAN! THAT'S GROSS."
"LEON STARTED WITH A SMALL GROUP TO BEGIN ENCAMPMENT ON TRIUMPH."

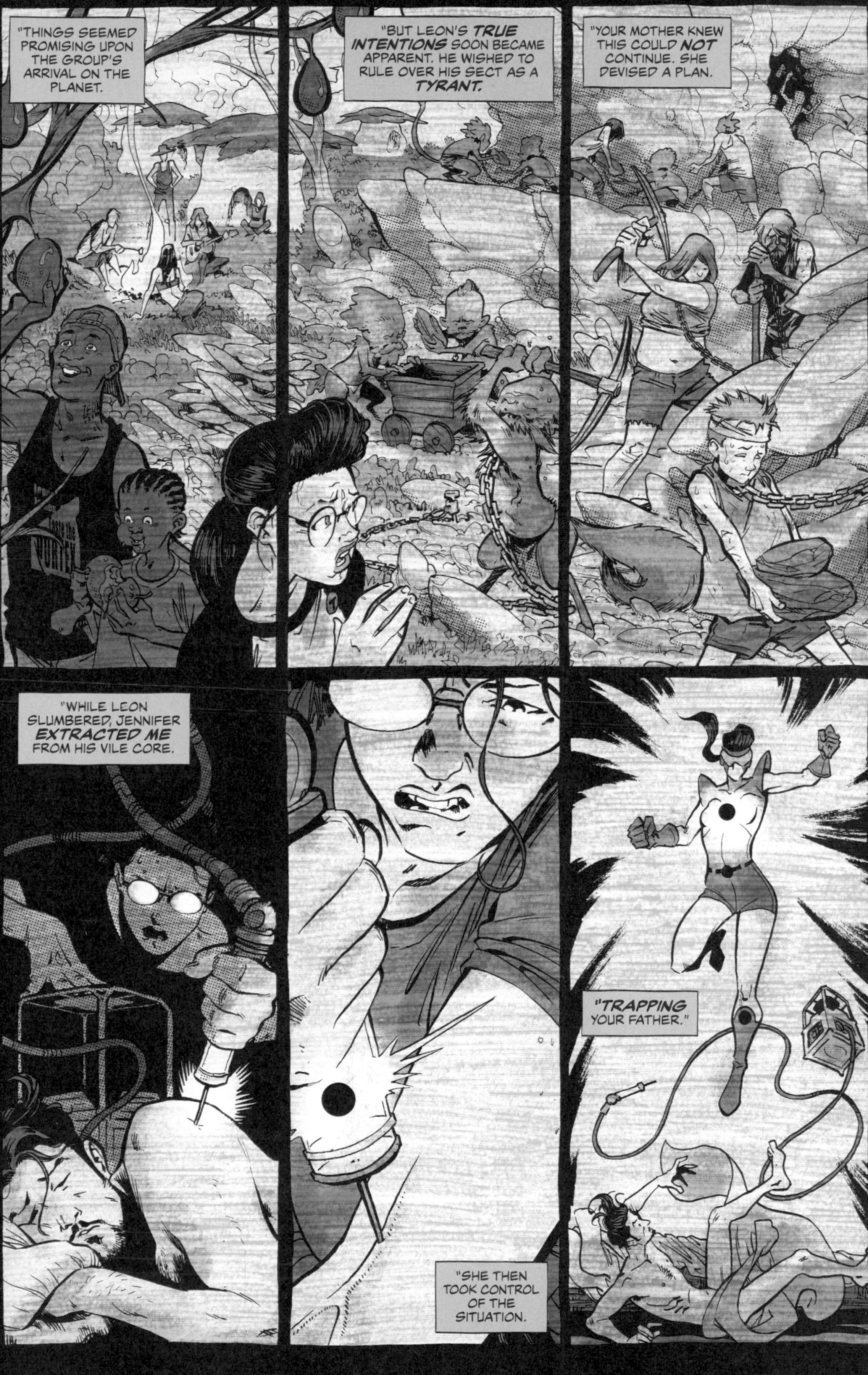
"THINGS SEEMED PROMISING UPON THE GROUP'S ARRIVAL ON THE PLANET.
TASTE THE VORTEX
"BUT LEON'S TRUE INTENTIONS SOON BECAME APPARENT. HE WISHED TO RULE OVER HIS SECT AS A TYRANT.
"YOUR MOTHER KNEW THIS COULD NOT CONTINUE. SHE DEVISED A PLAN.
"WHILE LEON SLUMBERED, JENNIFER EXTRACTED ME FROM HIS VILE CORE.
"SHE THEN TOOK CONTROL OF THE SITUATION.
"TRAPPING YOUR FATHER."

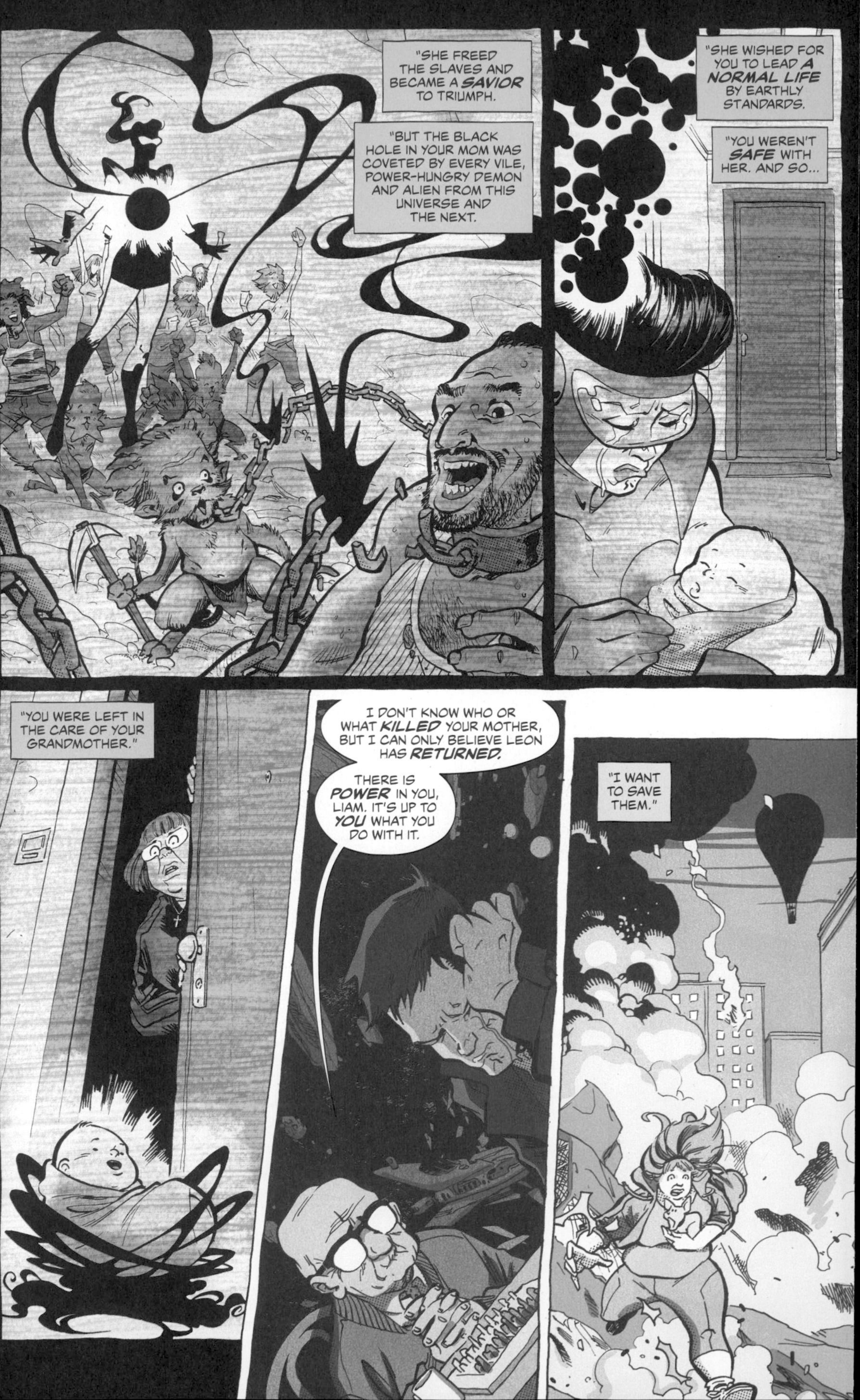
"SHE FREED THE SLAVES AND BECAME A SAVIOR TO TRIUMPH.
"BUT THE BLACK HOLE IN YOUR MOM WAS COVETED BY EVERY VILE, POWER-HUNGRY DEMON AND ALIEN FROM THIS UNIVERSE AND THE NEXT.
"SHE WISHED FOR YOU TO LEAD A NORMAL LIFE BY EARTHLY STANDARDS.
"YOU WEREN'T SAFE WITH HER. AND SO...
"YOU WERE LEFT IN THE CARE OF YOUR GRANDMOTHER."
I DON'T KNOW WHO OR WHAT KILLED YOUR MOTHER, BUT I CAN ONLY BELIEVE LEON HAS RETURNED.
THERE IS POWER IN YOU, LIAM. IT'S UP TO YOU WHAT YOU DO WITH IT.
"I WANT TO SAVE THEM."

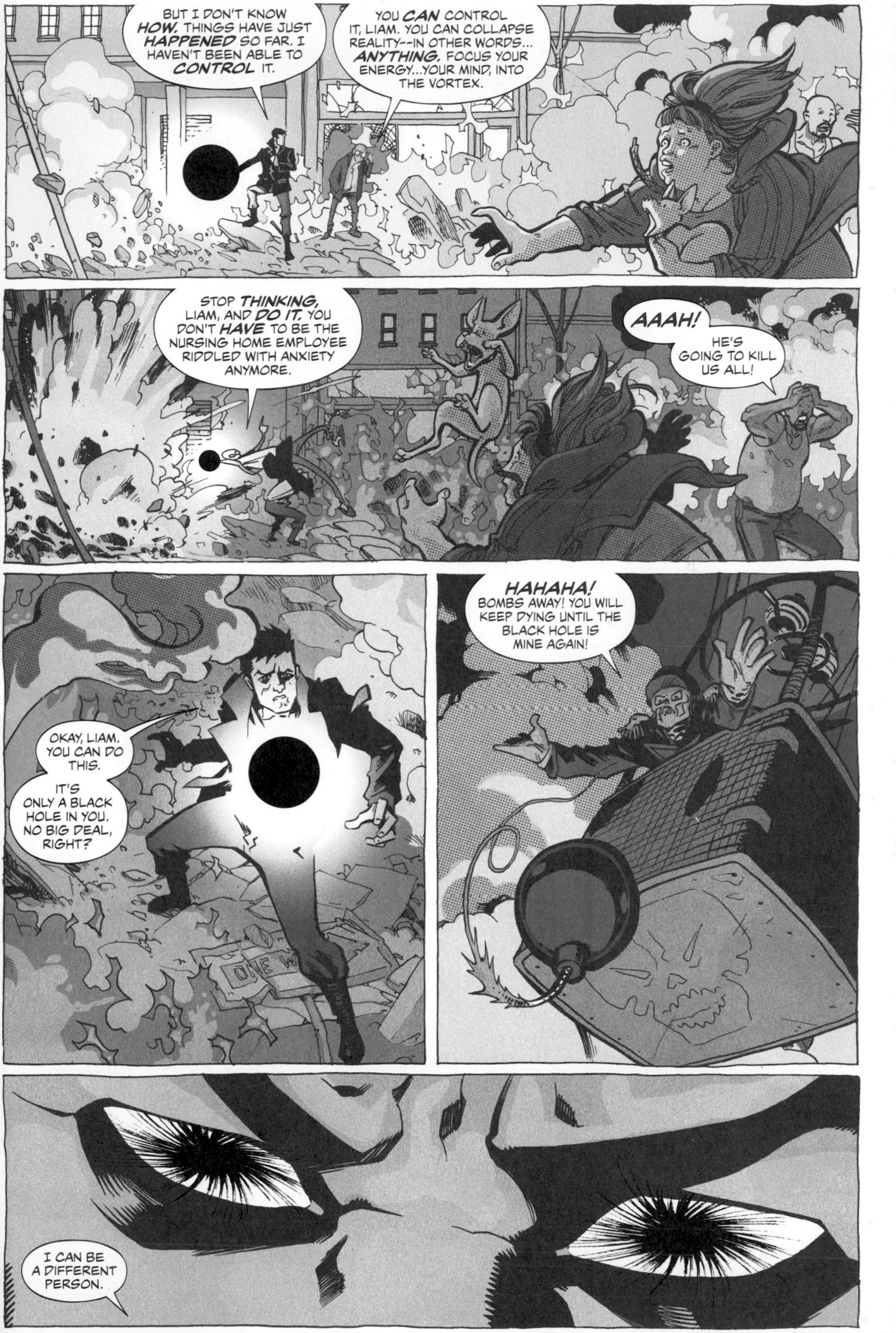
BUT I DON'T KNOW **HOW.** THINGS HAVE JUST **HAPPENED** SO FAR. I HAVEN'T BEEN ABLE TO **CONTROL** IT.
YOU **CAN** CONTROL IT, LIAM. YOU CAN COLLAPSE REALITY--IN OTHER WORDS... **ANYTHING.** FOCUS YOUR ENERGY...YOUR MIND, INTO THE VORTEX.
STOP **THINKING,** LIAM, AND **DO IT.** YOU DON'T **HAVE** TO BE THE NURSING HOME EMPLOYEE RIDDLED WITH ANXIETY ANYMORE.
AAAH!
HE'S GOING TO KILL US ALL!
OKAY, LIAM. YOU CAN DO THIS.
IT'S ONLY A BLACK HOLE IN YOU. NO BIG DEAL, RIGHT?
ONE W
HAHAHA!
BOMBS AWAY! YOU WILL KEEP DYING UNTIL THE BLACK HOLE IS MINE AGAIN!
I CAN BE A DIFFERENT PERSON.

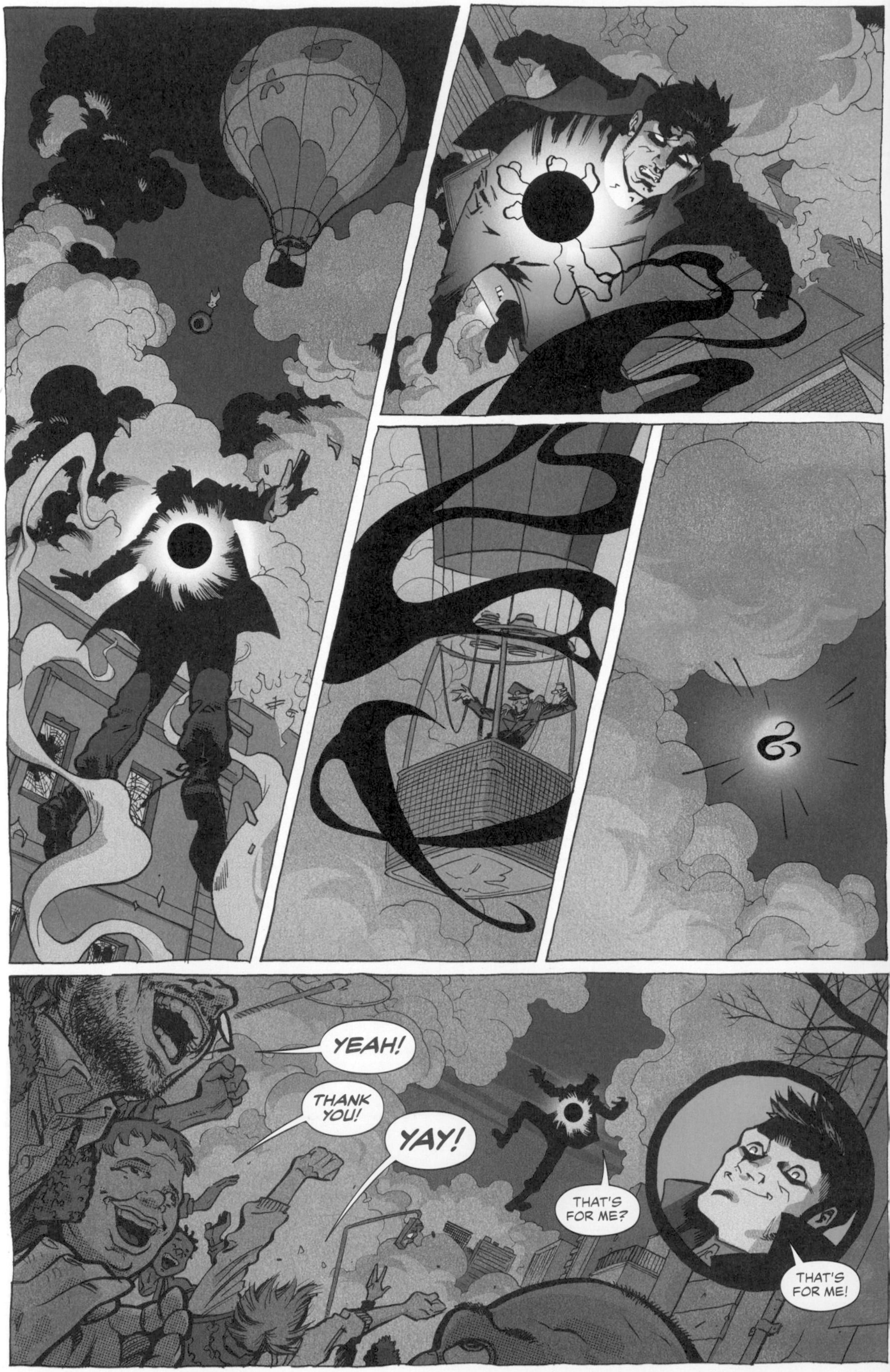
YEAH!
THANK YOU!
YAY!
THAT'S FOR ME?
THAT'S FOR ME!

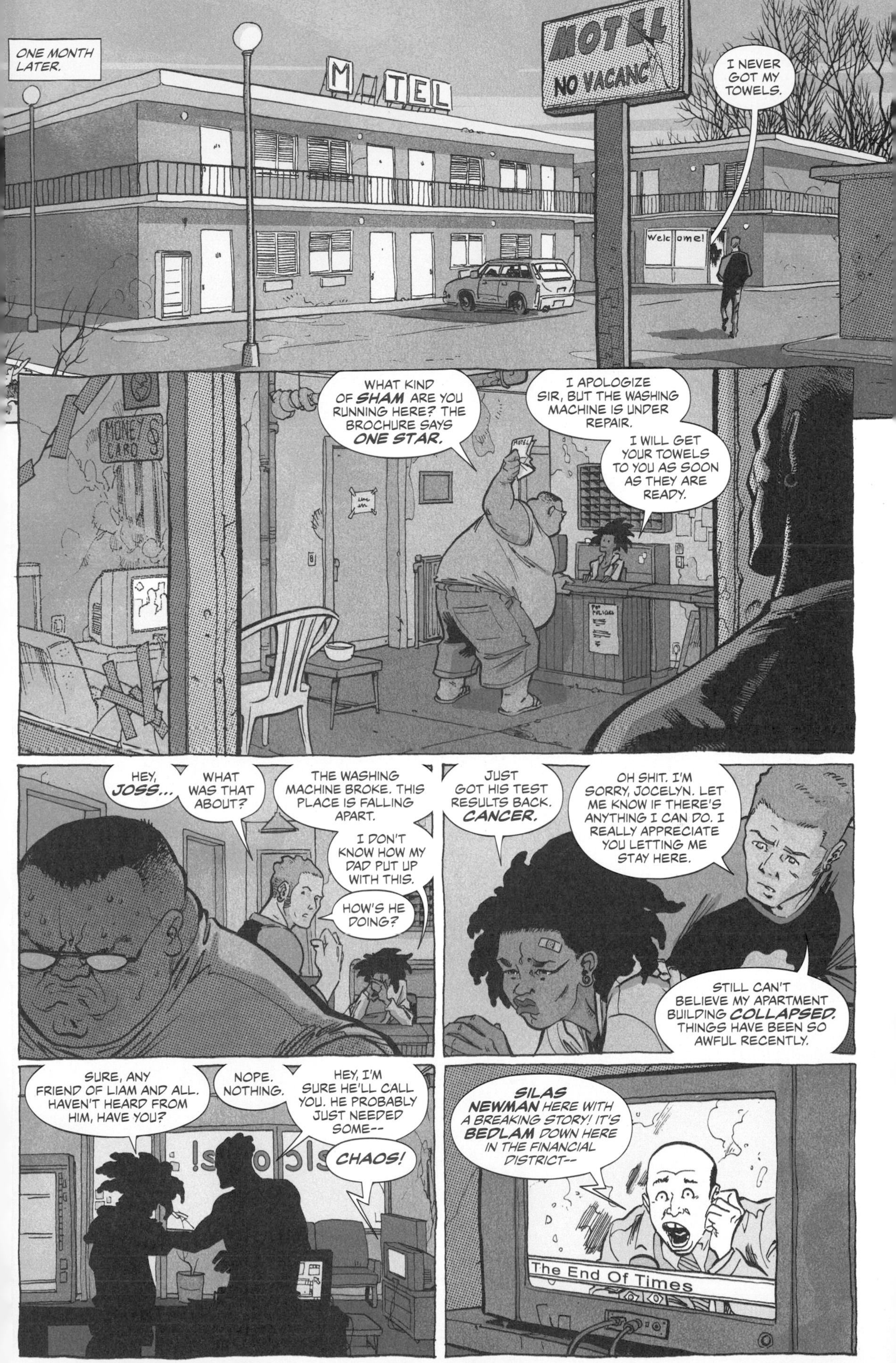
ONE MONTH LATER.
MOTEL
MOTEL NO VACANC
I NEVER GOT MY TOWELS.
Welcome!
WHAT KIND OF SHAM ARE YOU RUNNING HERE? THE BROCHURE SAYS ONE STAR.
I APOLOGIZE SIR, BUT THE WASHING MACHINE IS UNDER REPAIR.
I WILL GET YOUR TOWELS TO YOU AS SOON AS THEY ARE READY.
HEY, JOSS...
WHAT WAS THAT ABOUT?
THE WASHING MACHINE BROKE. THIS PLACE IS FALLING APART.
I DON'T KNOW HOW MY DAD PUT UP WITH THIS.
HOW'S HE DOING?
JUST GOT HIS TEST RESULTS BACK. CANCER.
OH SHIT. I'M SORRY, JOCELYN. LET ME KNOW IF THERE'S ANYTHING I CAN DO. I REALLY APPRECIATE YOU LETTING ME STAY HERE.
STILL CAN'T BELIEVE MY APARTMENT BUILDING COLLAPSED. THINGS HAVE BEEN SO AWFUL RECENTLY.
SURE, ANY FRIEND OF LIAM AND ALL. HAVEN'T HEARD FROM HIM, HAVE YOU?
NOPE. NOTHING.
HEY, I'M SURE HE'LL CALL YOU. HE PROBABLY JUST NEEDED SOME--
CHAOS!
SILAS NEWMAN HERE WITH A BREAKING STORY! IT'S BEDLAM DOWN HERE IN THE FINANCIAL DISTRICT--
The End Of Times

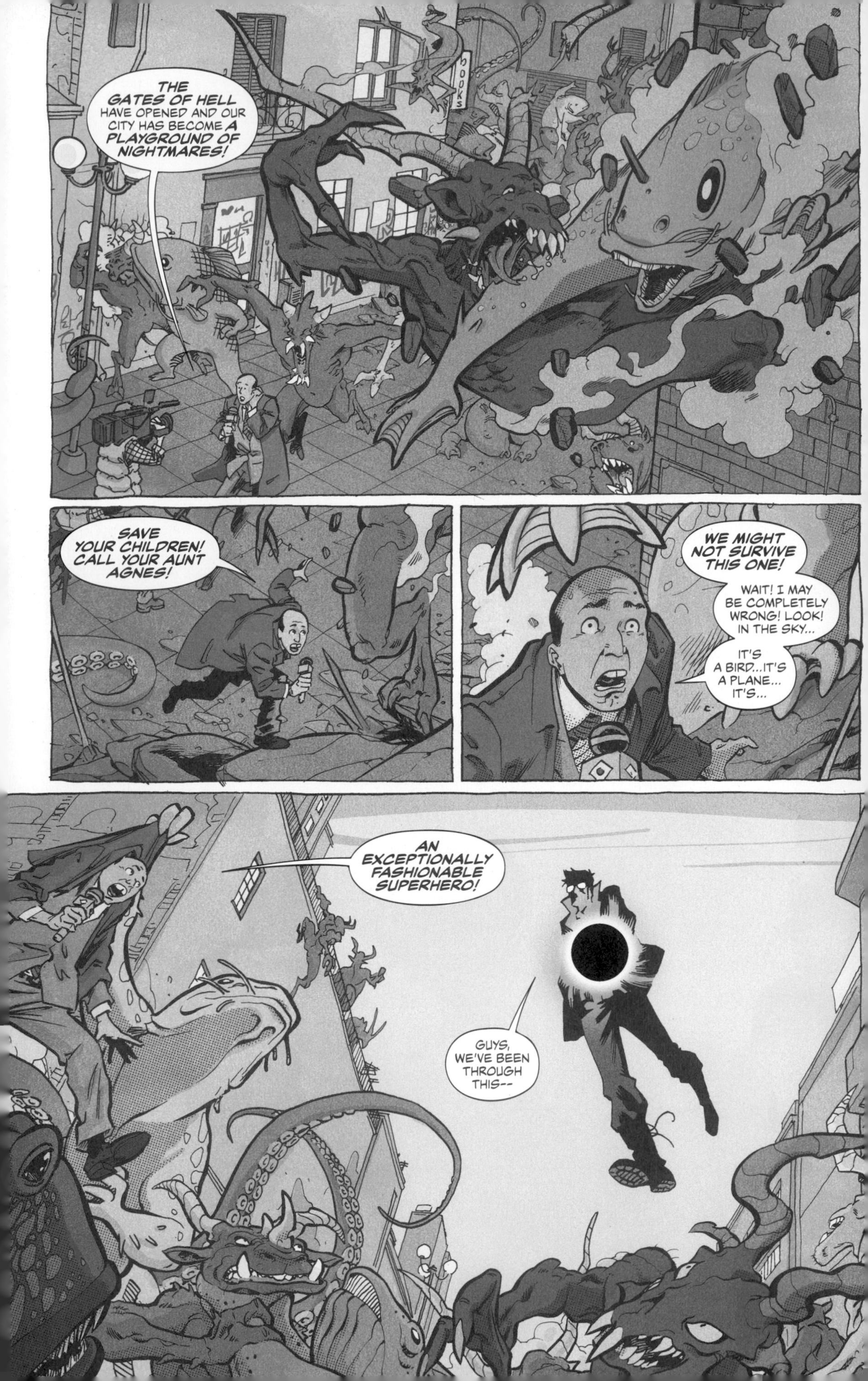
THE GATES OF HELL HAVE OPENED AND OUR CITY HAS BECOME A PLAYGROUND OF NIGHTMARES!
SAVE YOUR CHILDREN! CALL YOUR AUNT AGNES!
WE MIGHT NOT SURVIVE THIS ONE!
WAIT! I MAY BE COMPLETELY WRONG! LOOK! IN THE SKY...
IT'S A BIRD...IT'S A PLANE... IT'S...
AN EXCEPTIONALLY FASHIONABLE SUPERHERO!
GUYS, WE'VE BEEN THROUGH THIS--

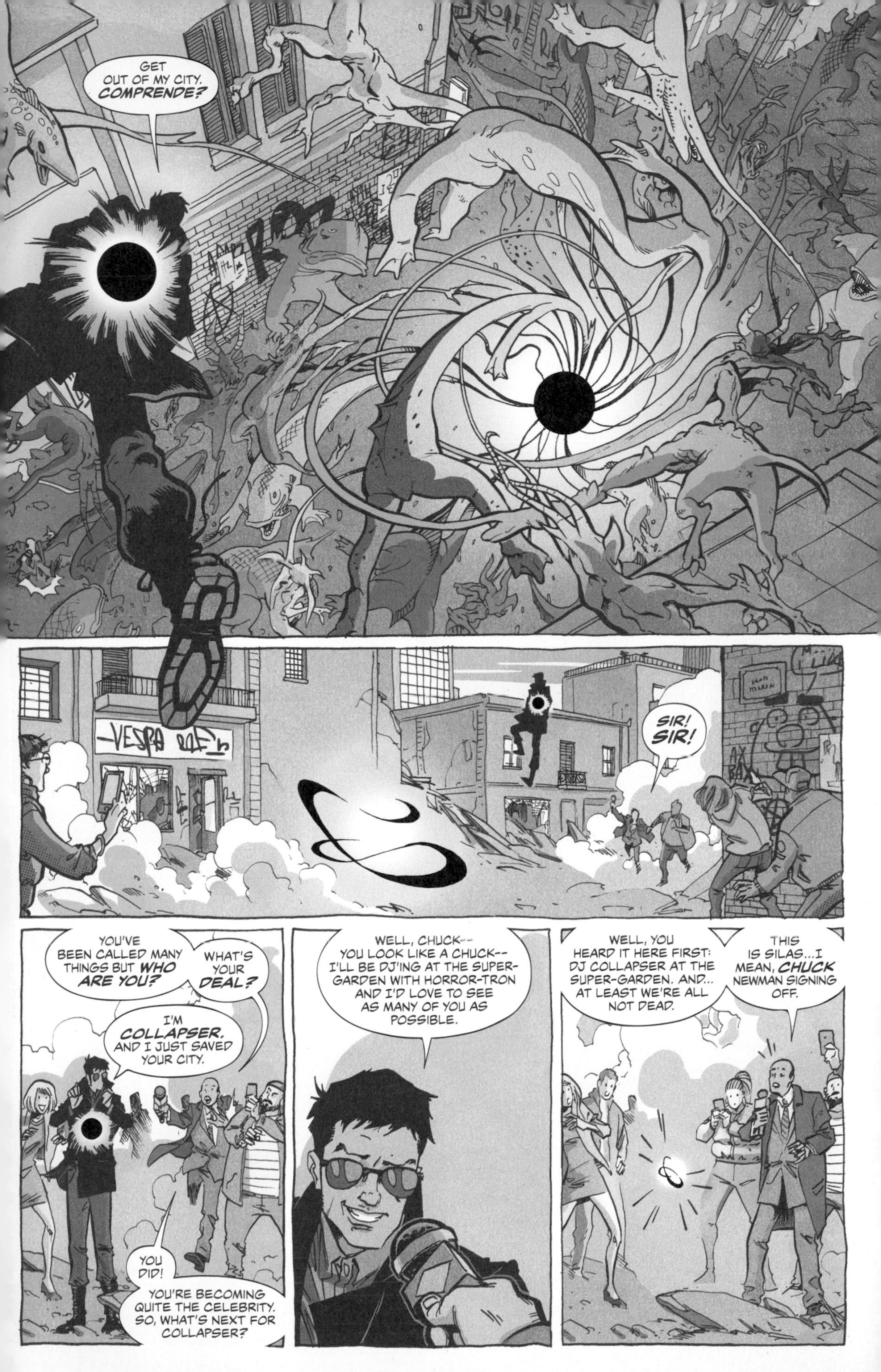
GET OUT OF MY CITY. COMPRENDE?
SIR! SIR!
YOU'VE BEEN CALLED MANY THINGS BUT WHO ARE YOU?
WHAT'S YOUR DEAL?
I'M COLLAPSER. AND I JUST SAVED YOUR CITY.
YOU DID!
YOU'RE BECOMING QUITE THE CELEBRITY. SO, WHAT'S NEXT FOR COLLAPSER?
WELL, CHUCK-- YOU LOOK LIKE A CHUCK-- I'LL BE DJ'ING AT THE SUPER-GARDEN WITH HORROR-TRON AND I'D LOVE TO SEE AS MANY OF YOU AS POSSIBLE.
WELL, YOU HEARD IT HERE FIRST: DJ COLLAPSER AT THE SUPER-GARDEN. AND... AT LEAST WE'RE ALL NOT DEAD.
THIS IS SILAS...I MEAN, CHUCK NEWMAN SIGNING OFF.

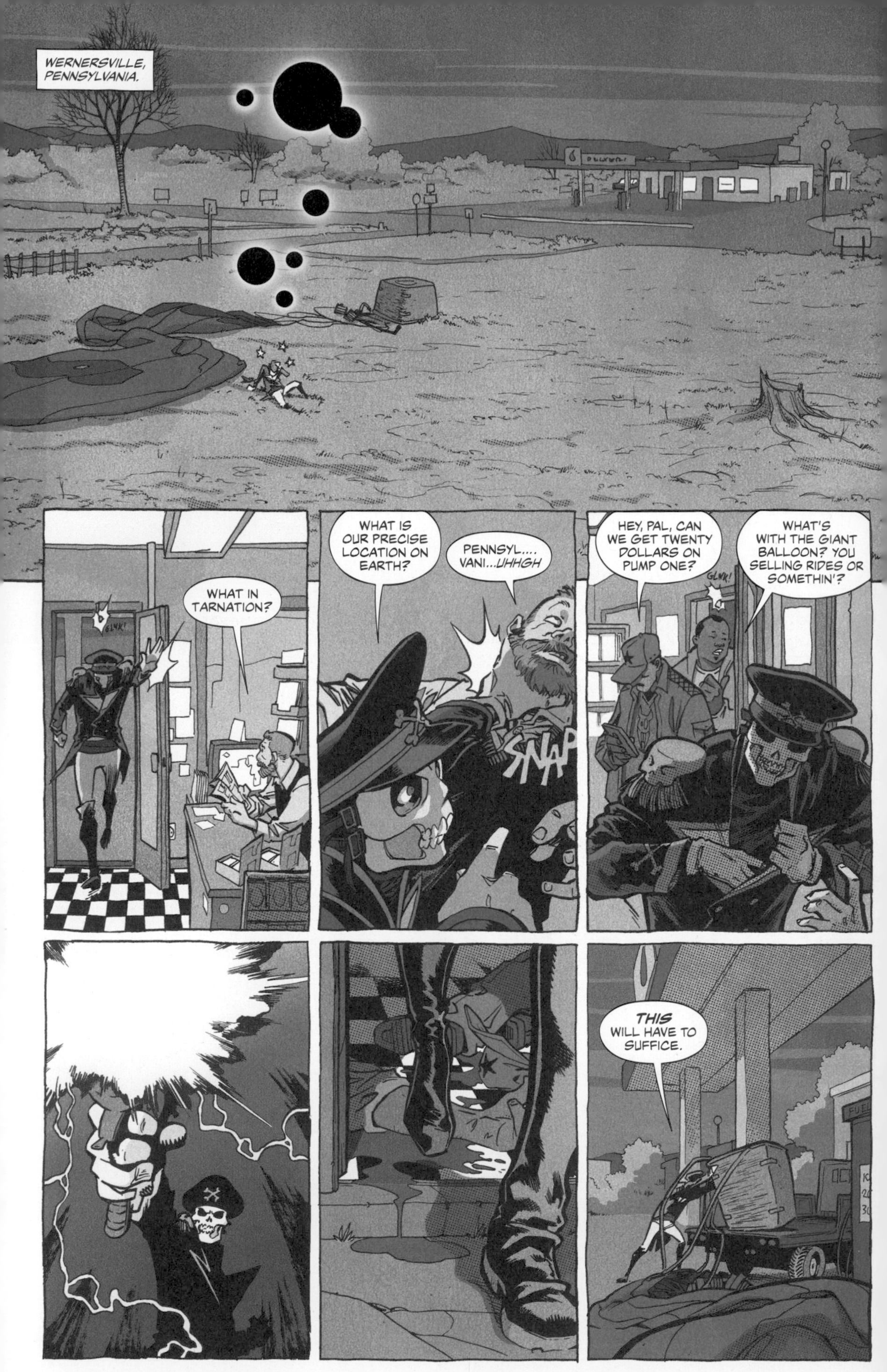
WERNERSVILLE, PENNSYLVANIA.
GLNK!
WHAT IN TARNATION?
WHAT IS OUR PRECISE LOCATION ON EARTH?
PENNSYL.... VANI...UHHGH
SNAP
HEY, PAL, CAN WE GET TWENTY DOLLARS ON PUMP ONE?
GLNK!
WHAT'S WITH THE GIANT BALLOON? YOU SELLING RIDES OR SOMETHIN'?
THIS WILL HAVE TO SUFFICE.

SUPERGARDEN

TONIGHT DJs
HORR TRON COLLAP

TONIGHT: DJs HORR TRON COLLAPSE

I DON'T KNOW HOW I FEEL ABOUT THIS, TRIPP. MAYBE IT'S A MISTAKE.

AREN'T YOU THAT KID FROM THOSE COMMERCIALS?

I AM.

ME AND DR. CREAMY, WE HAD SOME GOOD TIMES BACK THEN. LEFT THE SET COVERED IN MILK MORE THAN ONCE.

EWW. THAT'S GROSS. THAT DR. CREAMY GUY ALWAYS CREEPED ME OUT.

NAH, HE WAS A GREAT--

HERE HE COMES!

OVER HERE!

I'M YOUR BIGGEST FAN!

COLLAPSER!

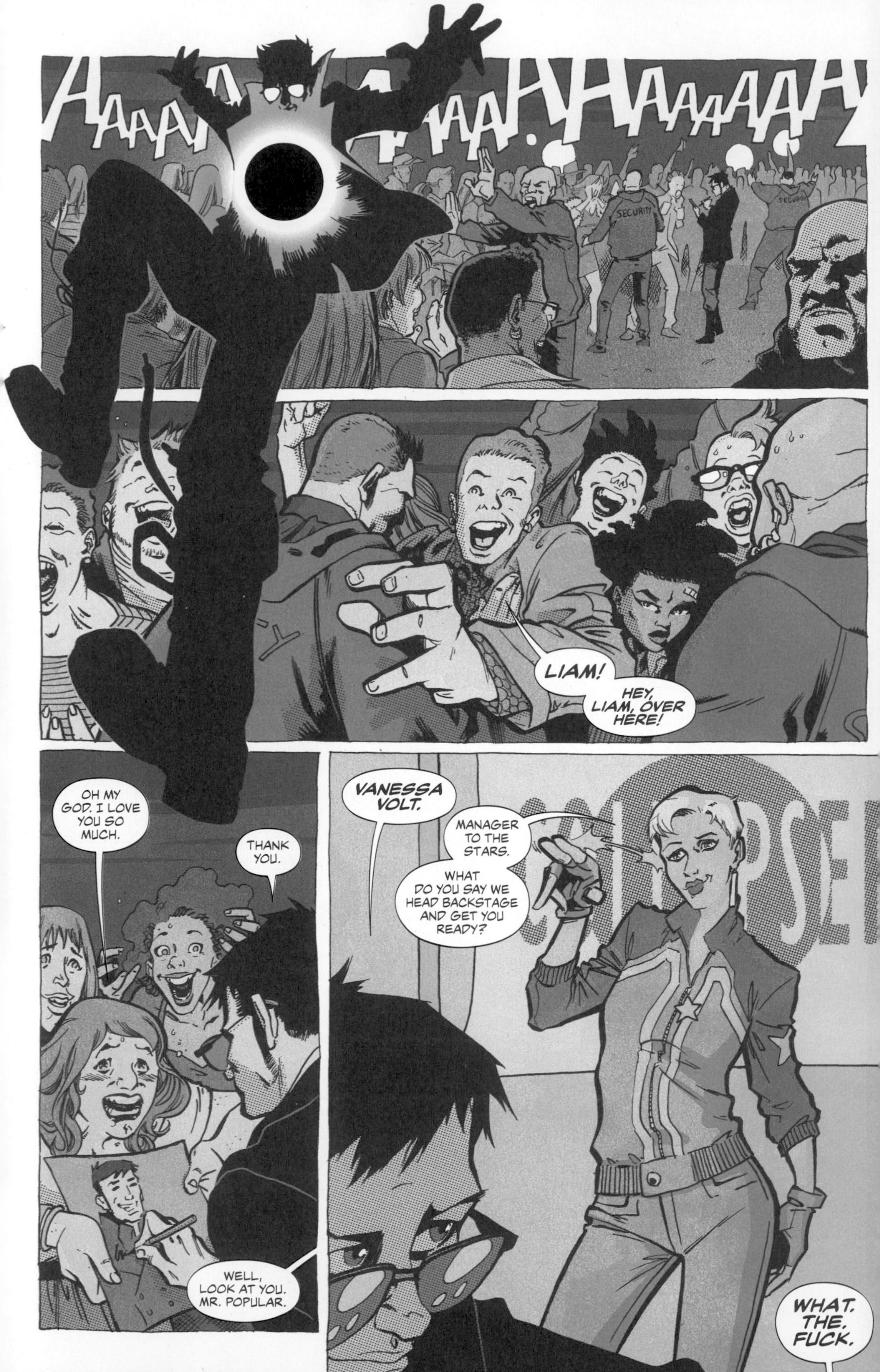

AAAAAAAAAAAHHAAAAAAH
LIAM!
HEY, LIAM, OVER HERE!
OH MY GOD. I LOVE YOU SO MUCH.
THANK YOU.
WELL, LOOK AT YOU. MR. POPULAR.
VANESSA VOLT.
MANAGER TO THE STARS.
WHAT DO YOU SAY WE HEAD BACKSTAGE AND GET YOU READY?
WHAT. THE. FUCK.

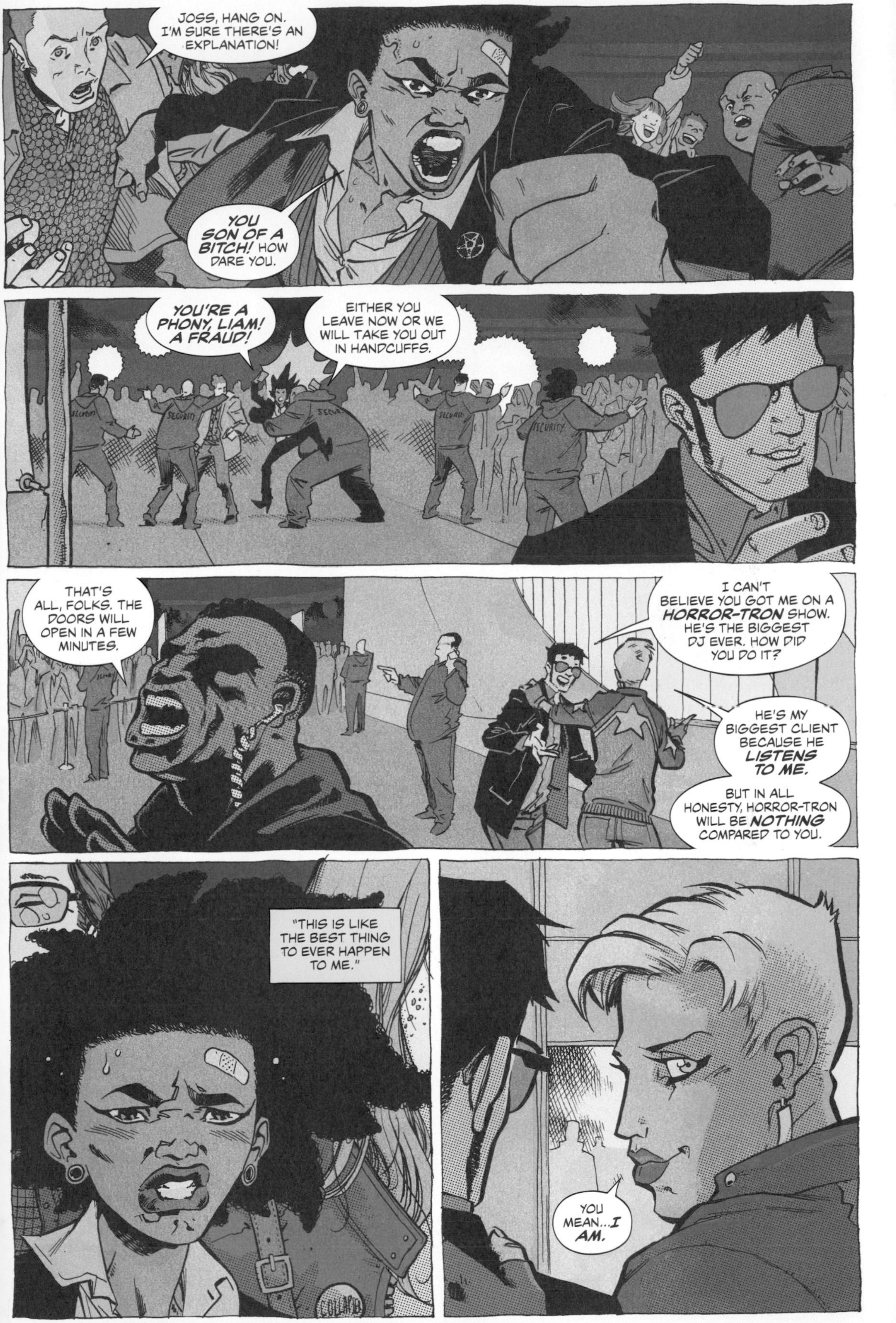
JOSS, HANG ON. I'M SURE THERE'S AN EXPLANATION!
YOU SON OF A BITCH! HOW DARE YOU.
YOU'RE A PHONY, LIAM! A FRAUD!
EITHER YOU LEAVE NOW OR WE WILL TAKE YOU OUT IN HANDCUFFS.
SECURITY
THAT'S ALL, FOLKS. THE DOORS WILL OPEN IN A FEW MINUTES.
I CAN'T BELIEVE YOU GOT ME ON A HORROR-TRON SHOW. HE'S THE BIGGEST DJ EVER. HOW DID YOU DO IT?
HE'S MY BIGGEST CLIENT BECAUSE HE LISTENS TO ME.
BUT IN ALL HONESTY, HORROR-TRON WILL BE NOTHING COMPARED TO YOU.
"THIS IS LIKE THE BEST THING TO EVER HAPPEN TO ME."
YOU MEAN...I AM.

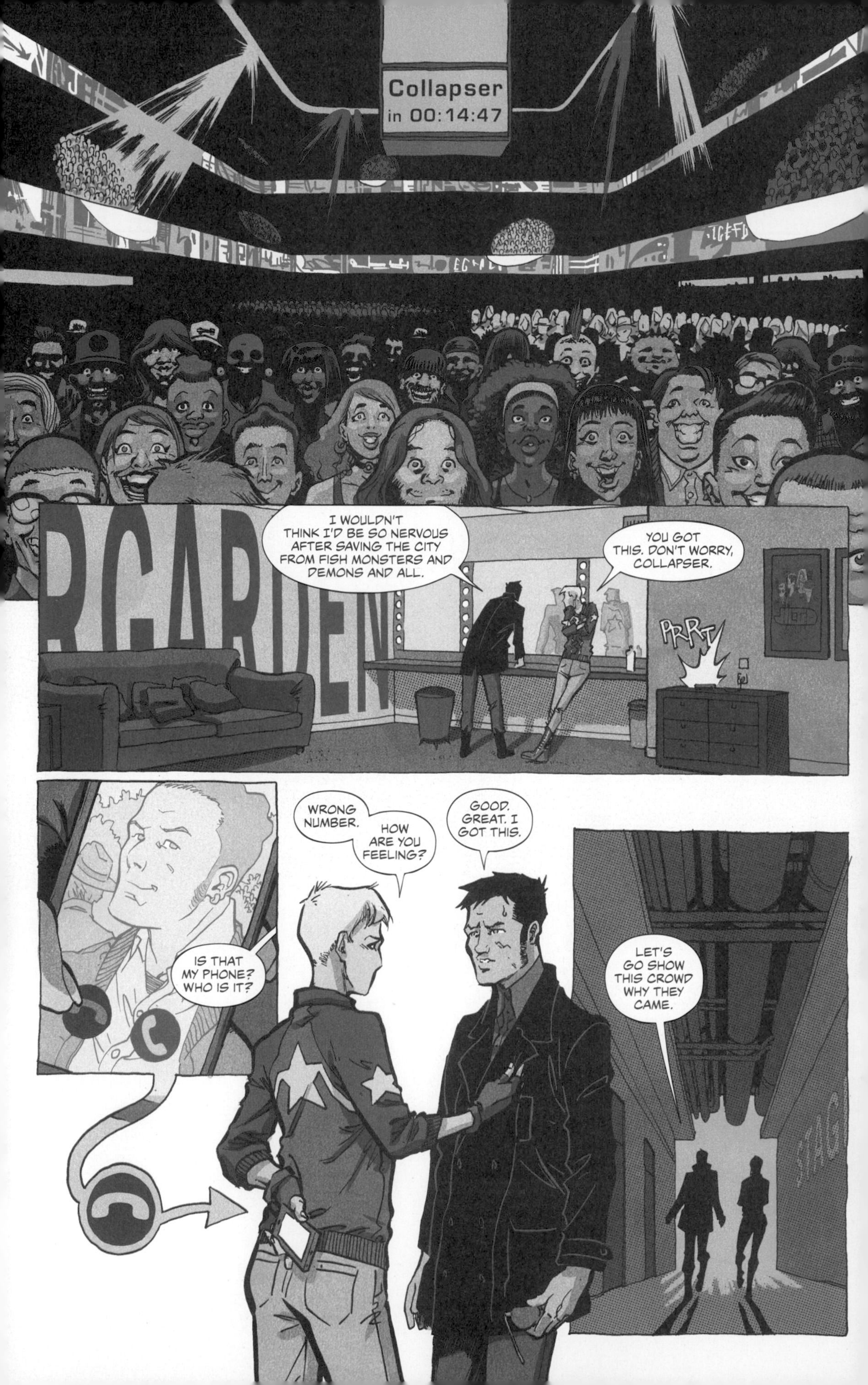
Collapser
in 00:14:47
I WOULDN'T THINK I'D BE SO NERVOUS AFTER SAVING THE CITY FROM FISH MONSTERS AND DEMONS AND ALL.
YOU GOT THIS. DON'T WORRY, COLLAPSER.
PRRRT
IS THAT MY PHONE? WHO IS IT?
WRONG NUMBER.
HOW ARE YOU FEELING?
GOOD. GREAT. I GOT THIS.
LET'S GO SHOW THIS CROWD WHY THEY CAME.

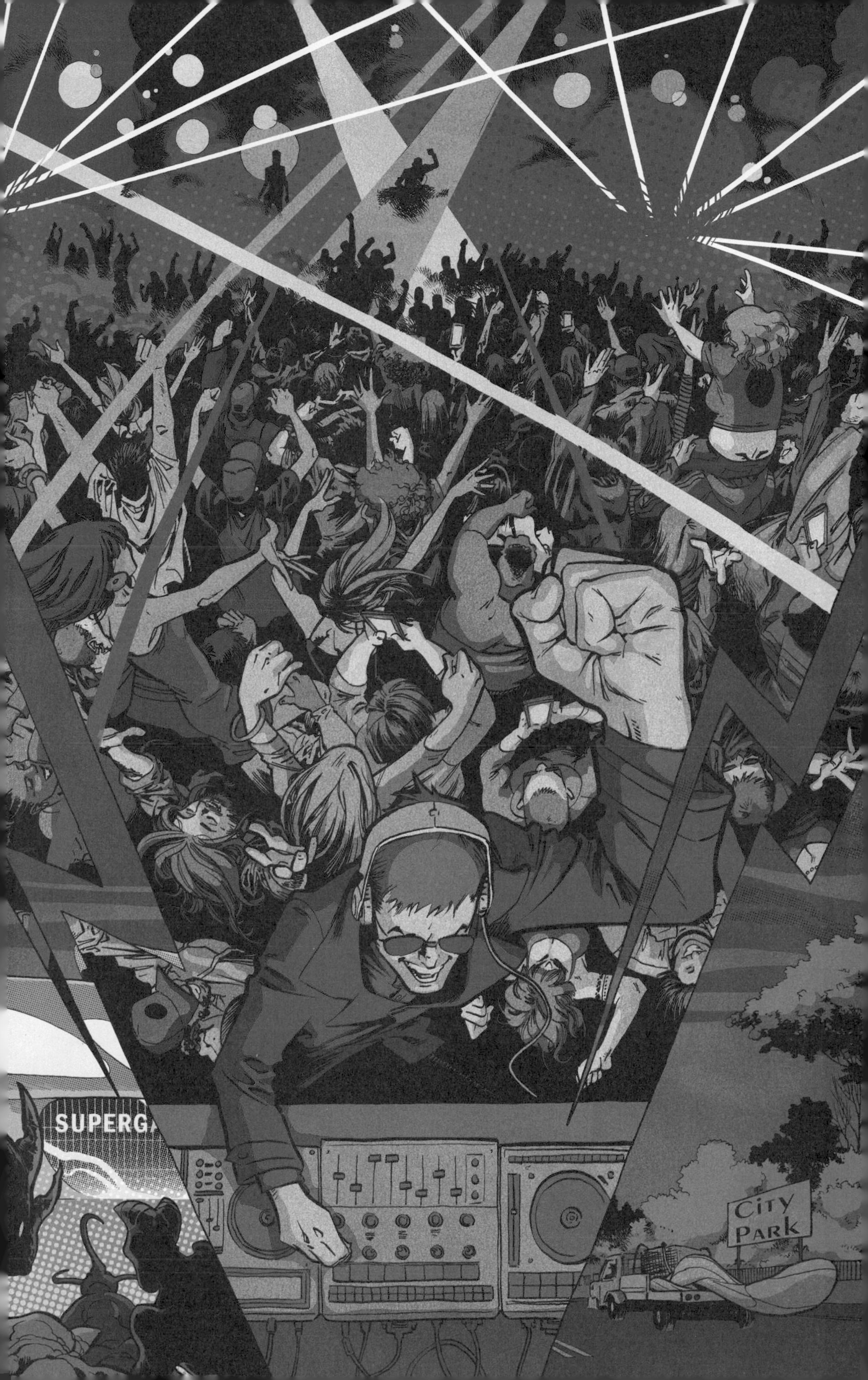
SUPERGA
City
Park

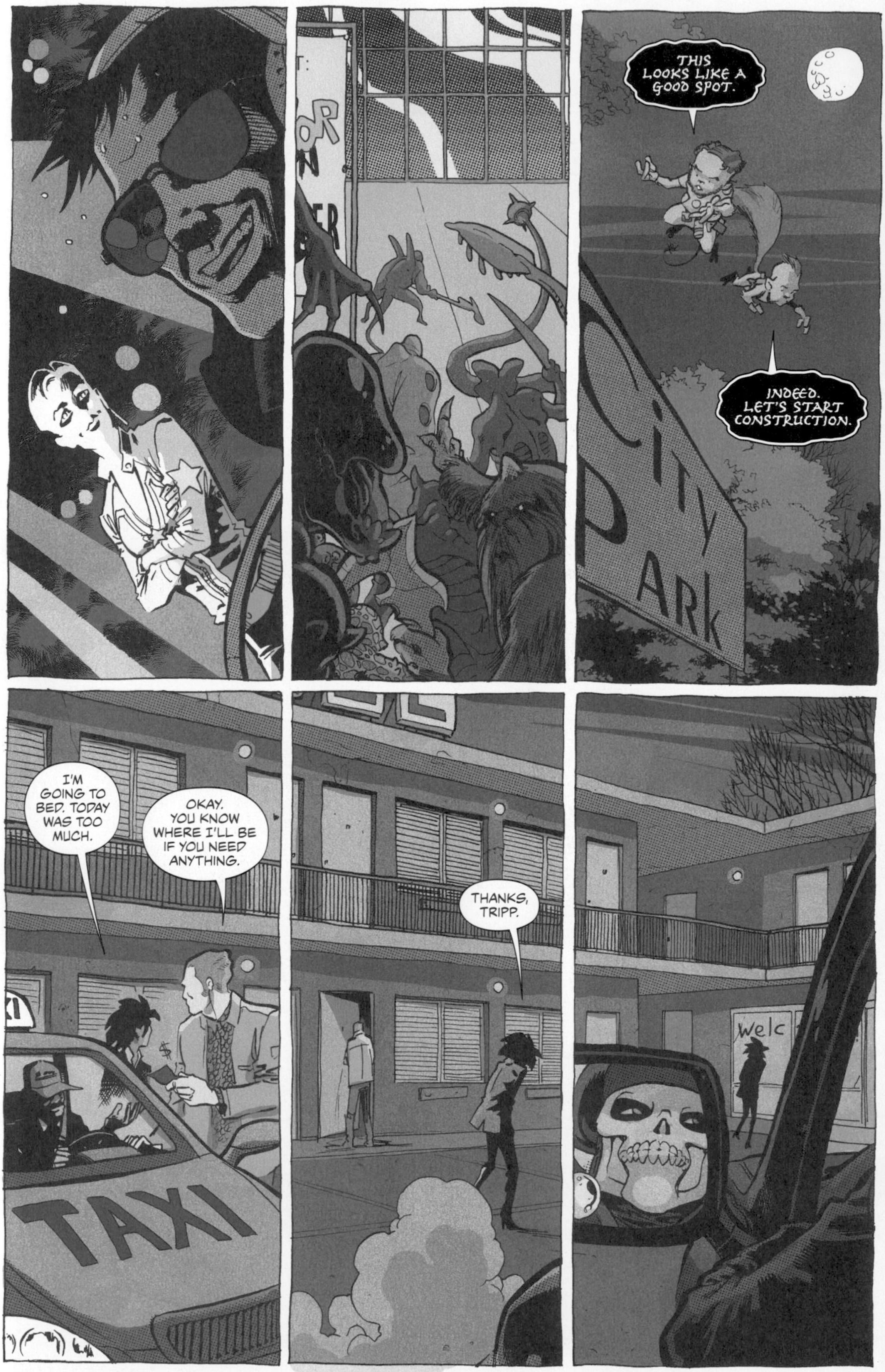
THIS LOOKS LIKE A GOOD SPOT.
INDEED. LET'S START CONSTRUCTION.
I'M GOING TO BED. TODAY WAS TOO MUCH.
OKAY. YOU KNOW WHERE I'LL BE IF YOU NEED ANYTHING.
TAXI
THANKS, TRIPP.

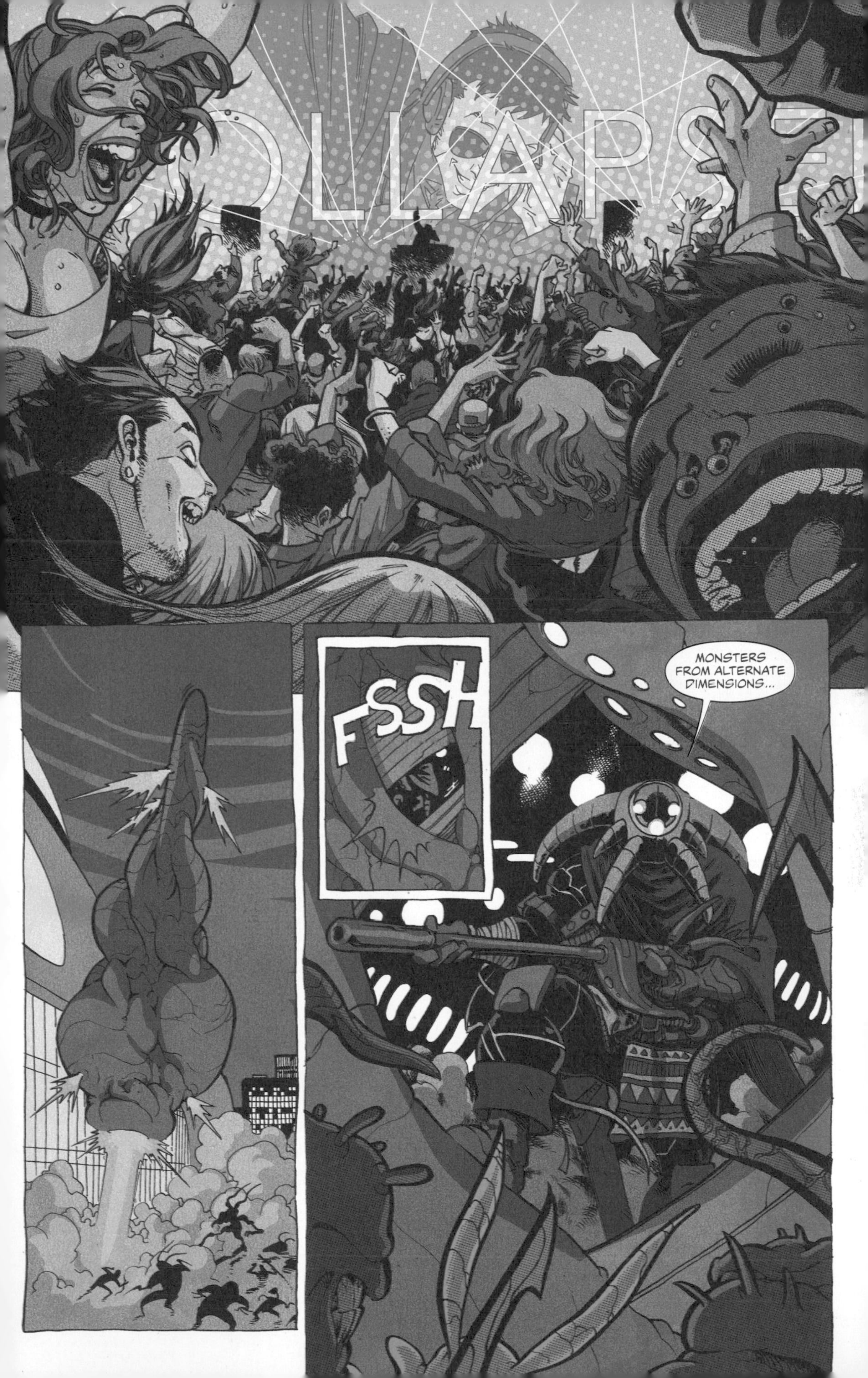
FSSH
MONSTERS FROM ALTERNATE DIMENSIONS...

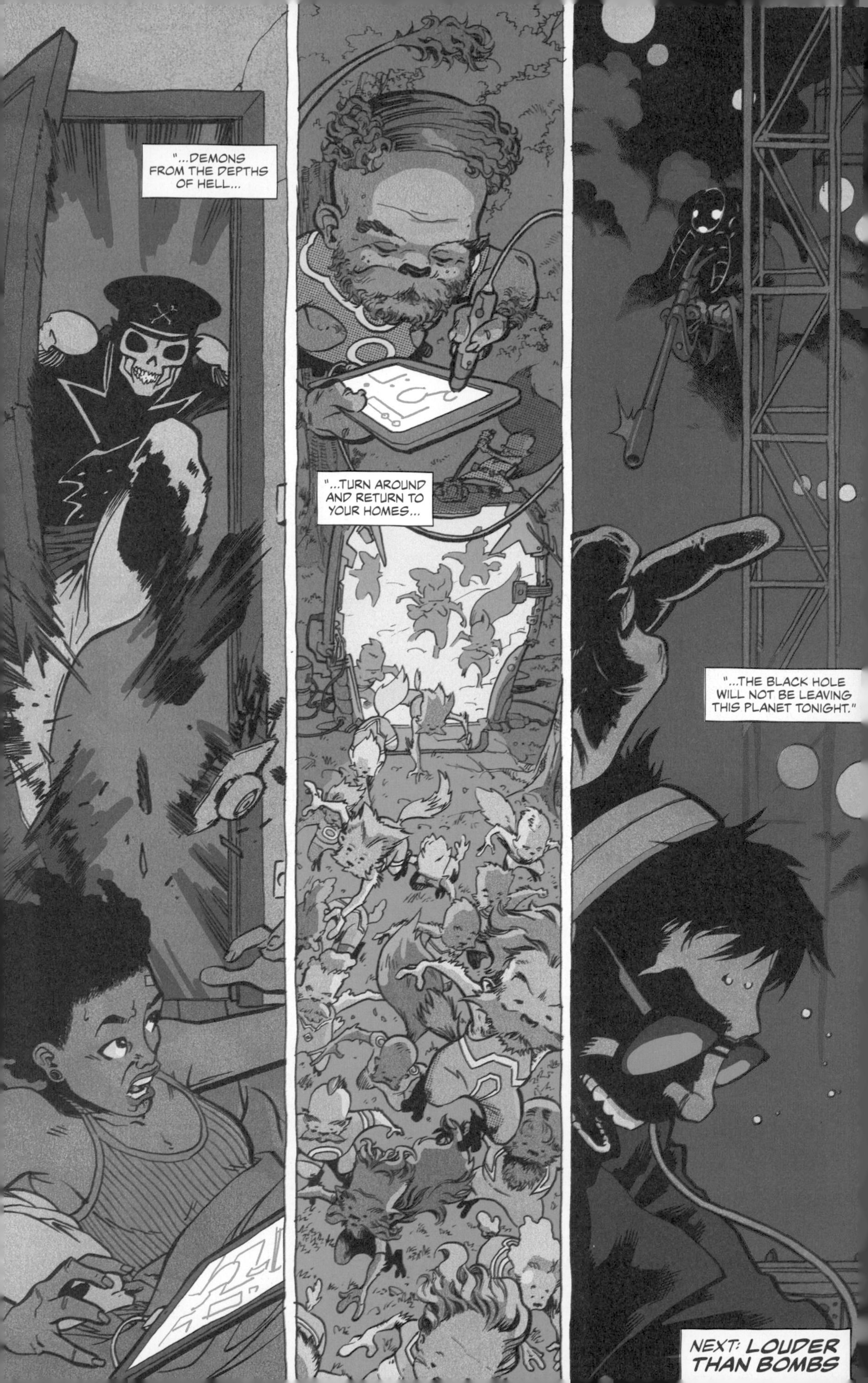
"...DEMONS FROM THE DEPTHS OF HELL...
"...TURN AROUND AND RETURN TO YOUR HOMES...
"...THE BLACK HOLE WILL NOT BE LEAVING THIS PLANET TONIGHT."
NEXT: LOUDER THAN BOMBS

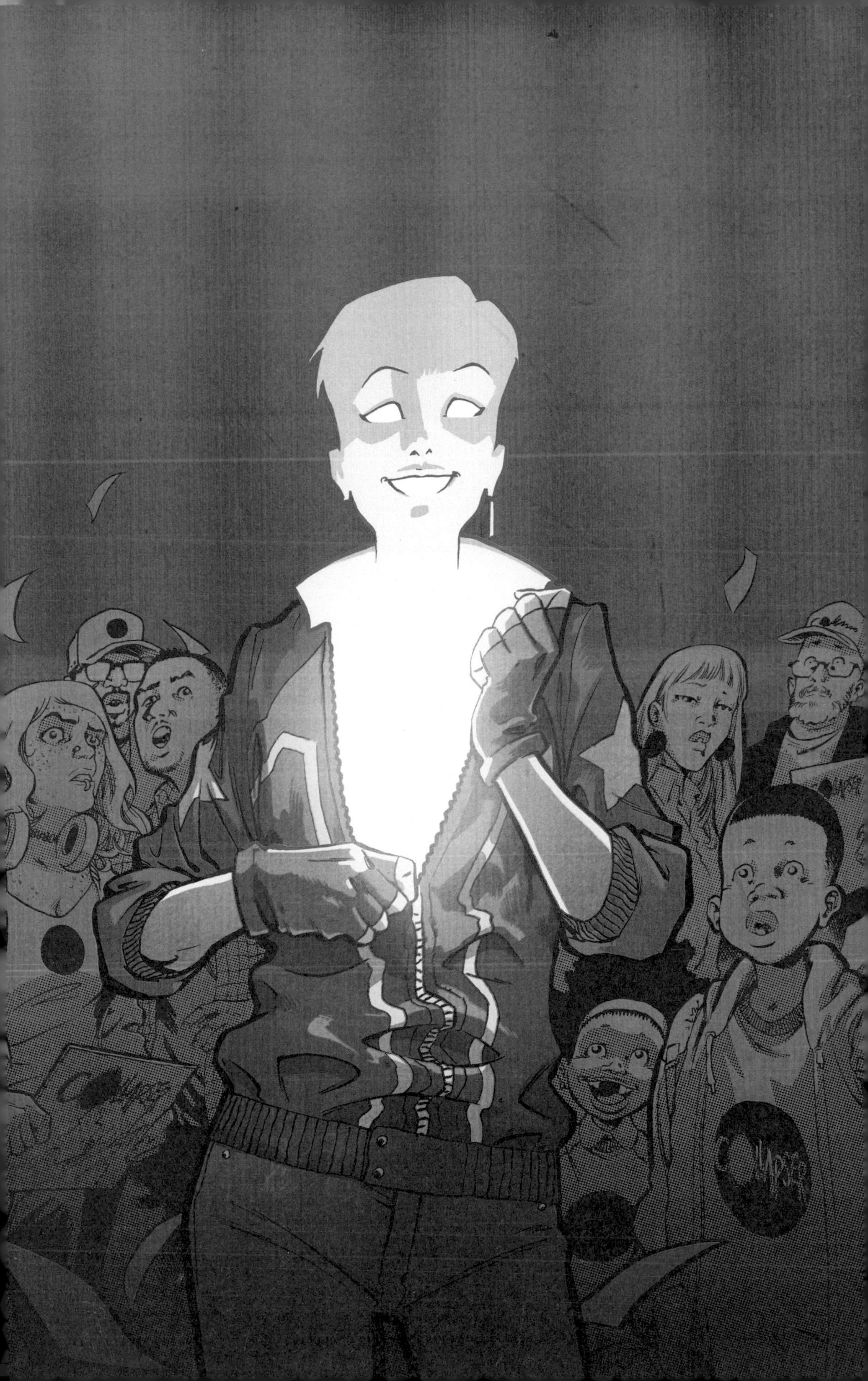

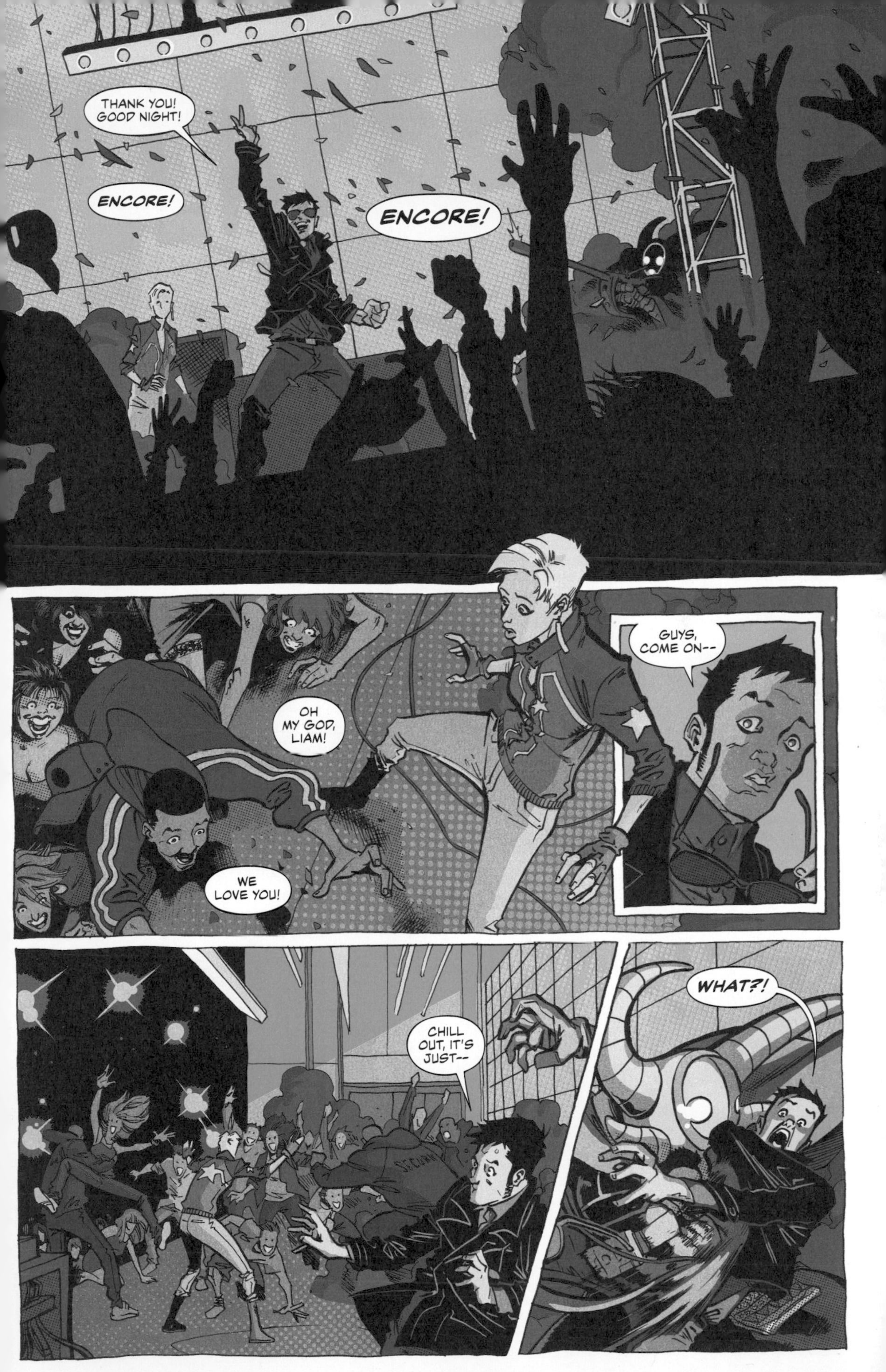
THANK YOU! GOOD NIGHT!
ENCORE!
ENCORE!
OH MY GOD, LIAM!
WE LOVE YOU!
GUYS, COME ON--
CHILL OUT, IT'S JUST--
WHAT?!

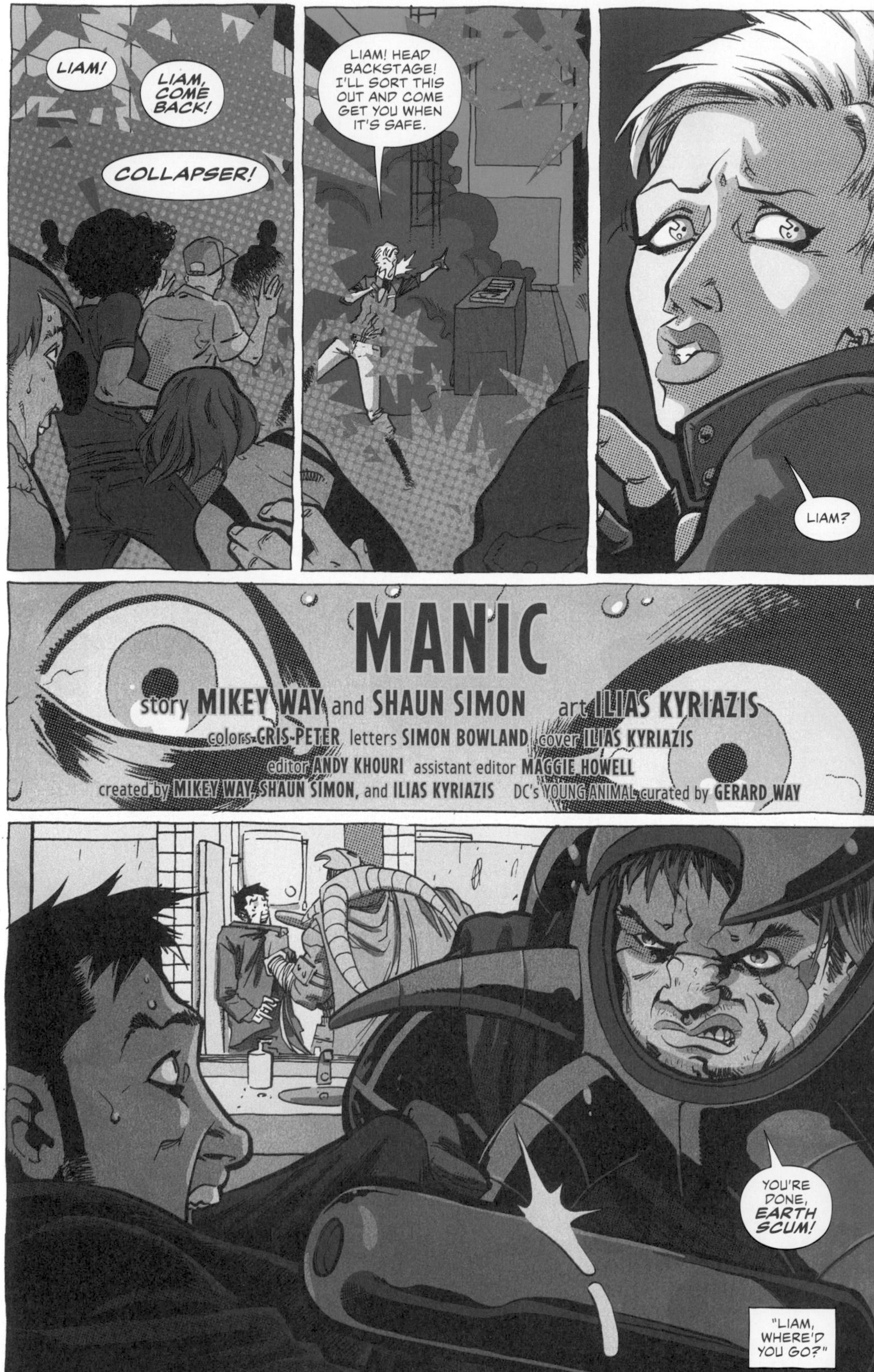
LIAM!
LIAM, COME BACK!
COLLAPSER!
LIAM! HEAD BACKSTAGE! I'LL SORT THIS OUT AND COME GET YOU WHEN IT'S SAFE.
LIAM?
MANIC
story MIKEY WAY and SHAUN SIMON art ILIAS KYRIAZIS
colors CRIS PETER letters SIMON BOWLAND cover ILIAS KYRIAZIS
editor ANDY KHOURI assistant editor MAGGIE HOWELL
created by MIKEY WAY, SHAUN SIMON, and ILIAS KYRIAZIS DC's YOUNG ANIMAL curated by GERARD WAY
YOU'RE DONE, EARTH SCUM!
"LIAM, WHERE'D YOU GO?"

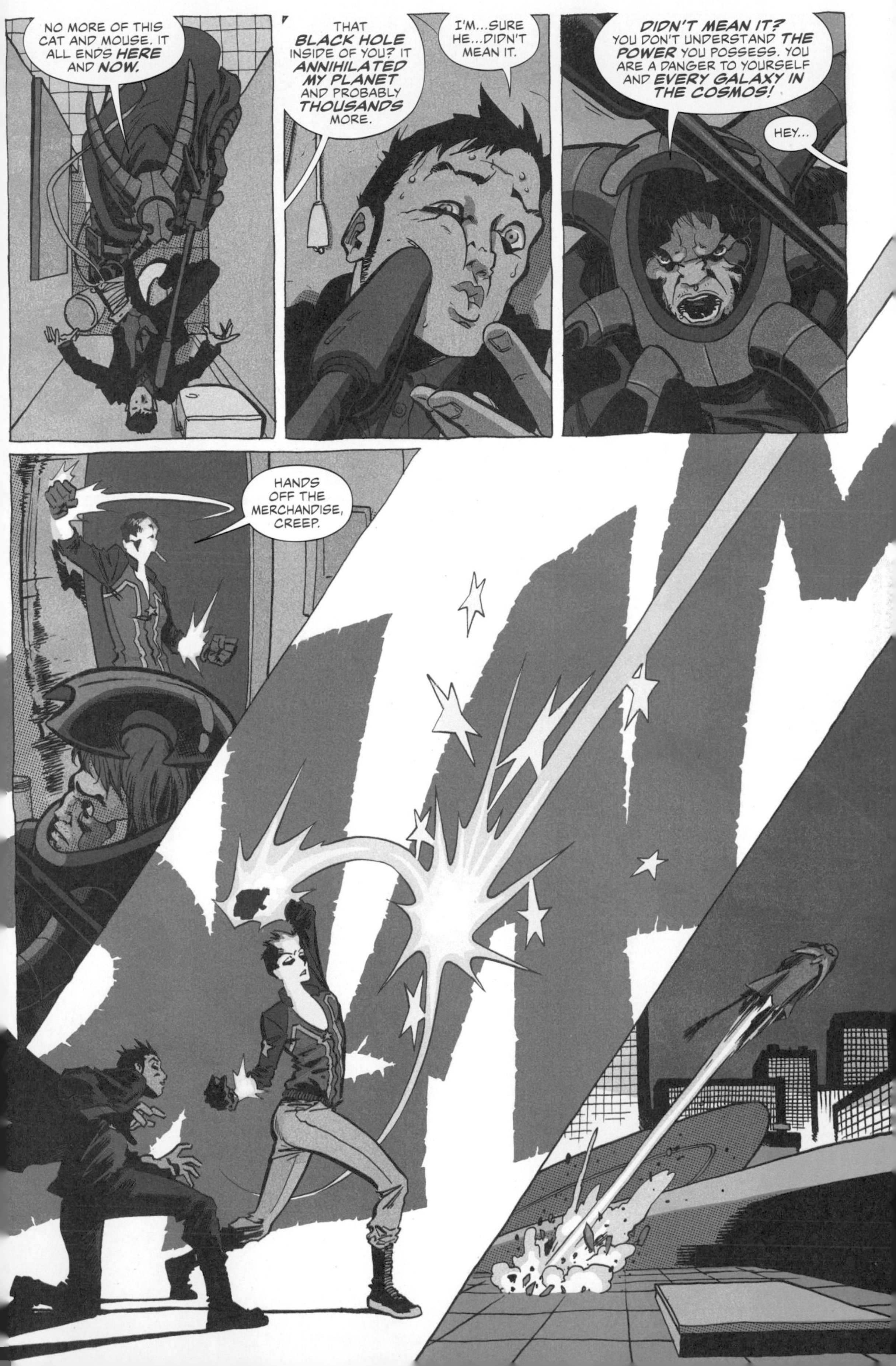
NO MORE OF THIS CAT AND MOUSE. IT ALL ENDS **HERE** AND **NOW.**
THAT **BLACK HOLE** INSIDE OF YOU? IT **ANNIHILATED MY PLANET** AND PROBABLY **THOUSANDS** MORE.
I'M...SURE HE...DIDN'T MEAN IT.
DIDN'T MEAN IT? YOU DON'T UNDERSTAND **THE POWER** YOU POSSESS. YOU ARE A DANGER TO YOURSELF AND **EVERY GALAXY IN THE COSMOS!**
HEY...
HANDS OFF THE MERCHANDISE, CREEP.

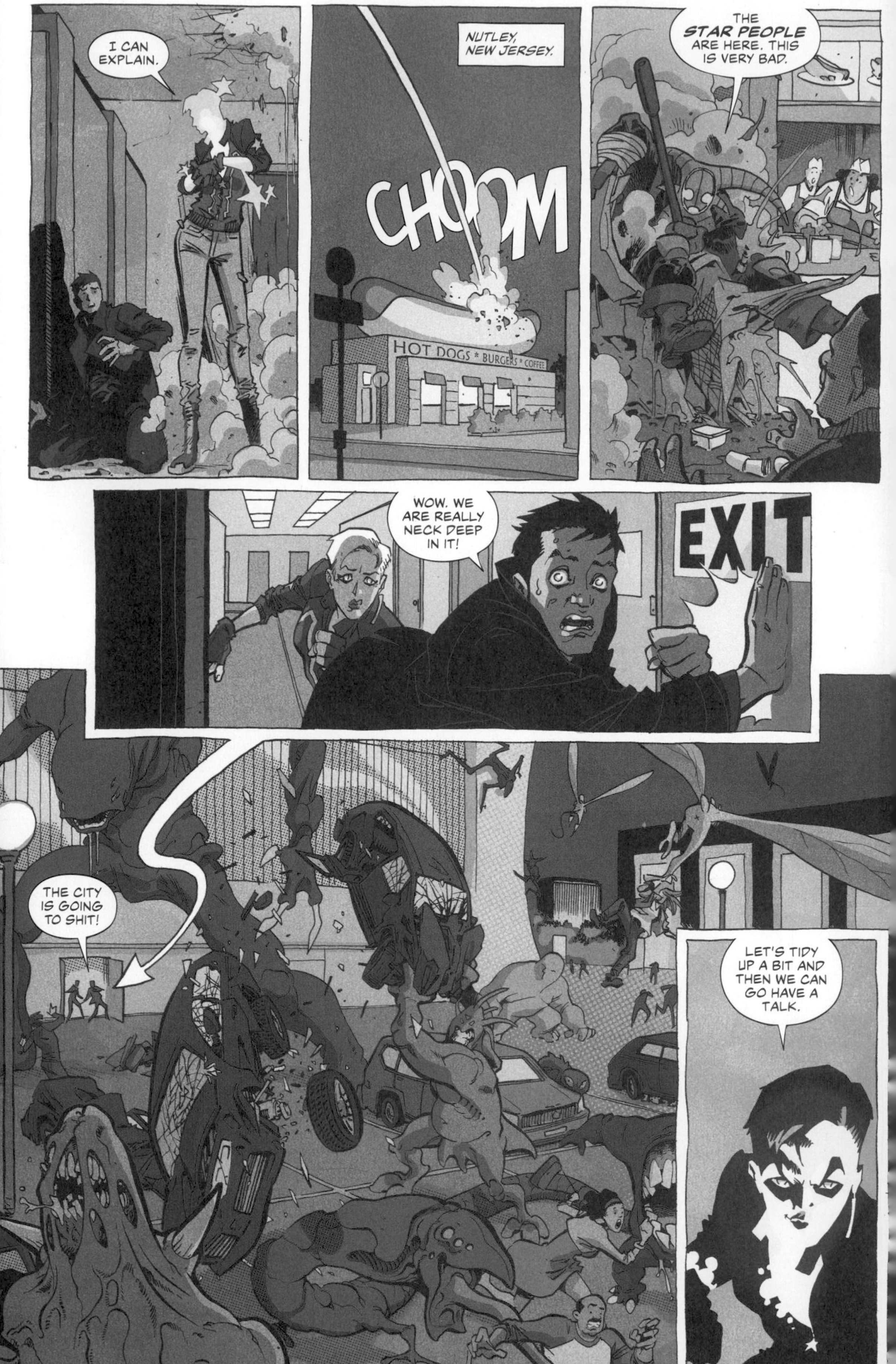
I CAN EXPLAIN.
NUTLEY, NEW JERSEY.
CHOOM
HOT DOGS * BURGERS * COFFEE
THE STAR PEOPLE ARE HERE. THIS IS VERY BAD.
WOW. WE ARE REALLY NECK DEEP IN IT!
EXIT
THE CITY IS GOING TO SHIT!
LET'S TIDY UP A BIT AND THEN WE CAN GO HAVE A TALK.

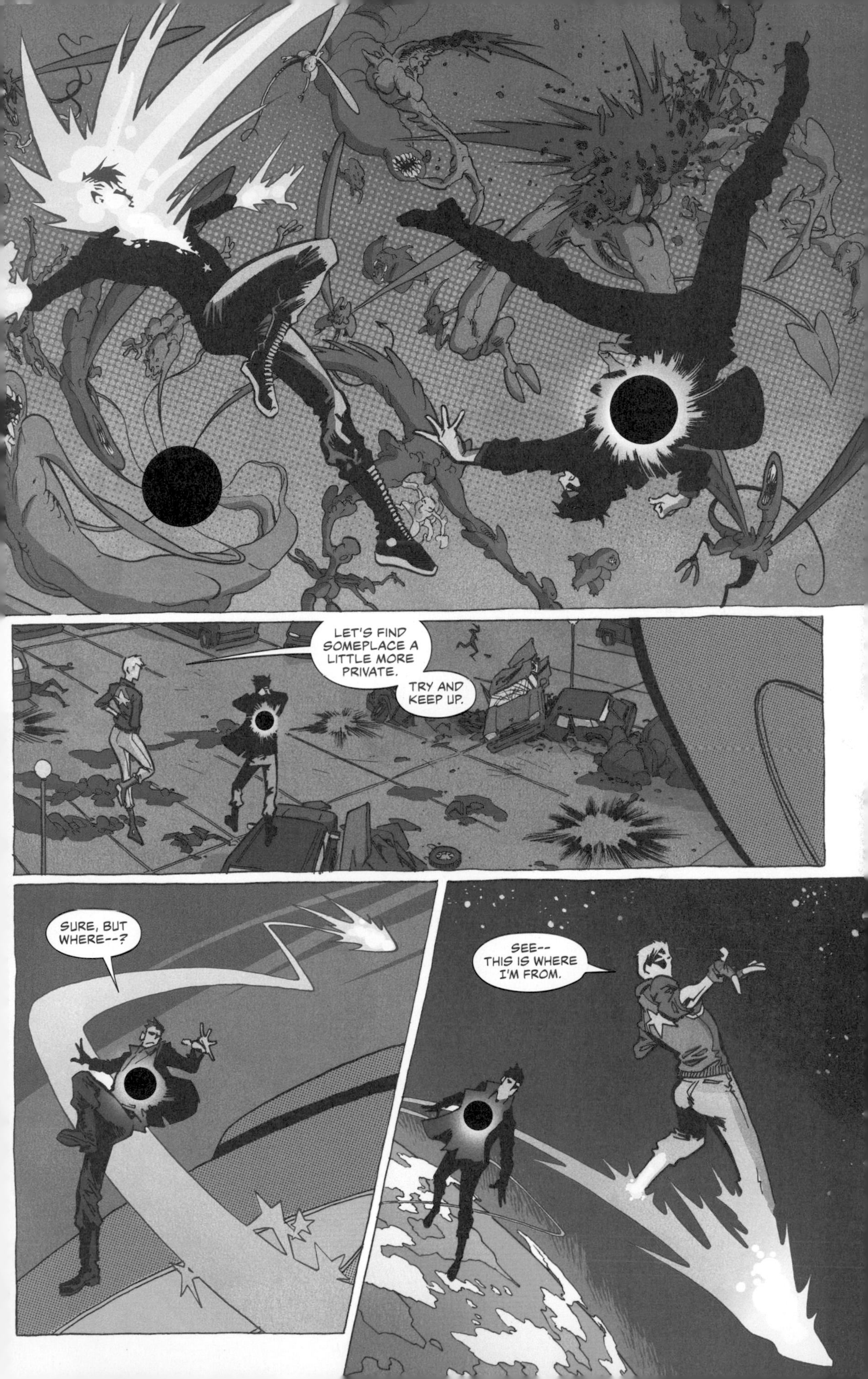
LET'S FIND SOMEPLACE A LITTLE MORE PRIVATE.
TRY AND KEEP UP.
SURE, BUT WHERE--?
SEE-- THIS IS WHERE I'M FROM.

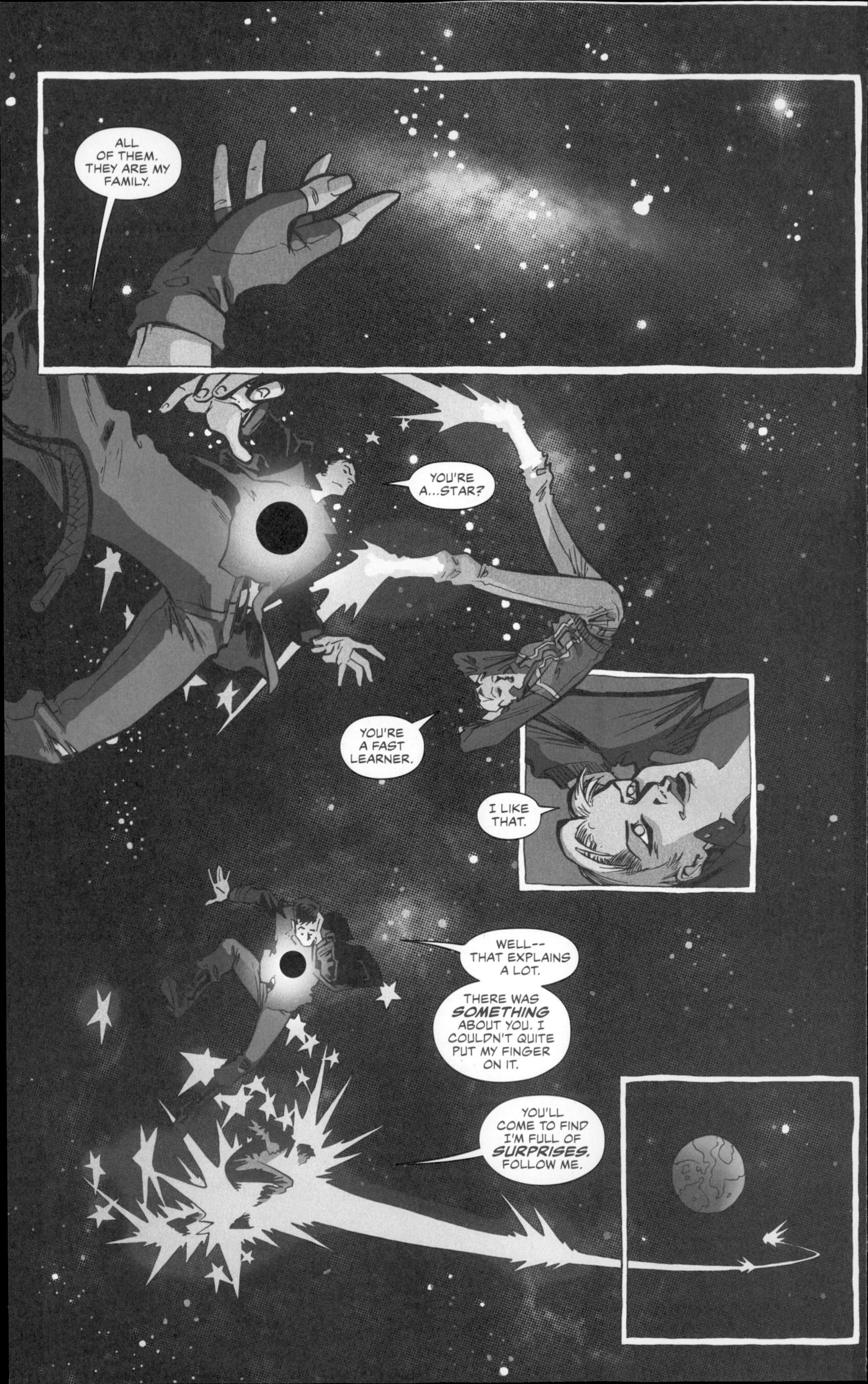

ALL OF THEM. THEY ARE MY FAMILY.
YOU'RE A...STAR?
YOU'RE A FAST LEARNER.
I LIKE THAT.
WELL-- THAT EXPLAINS A LOT.
THERE WAS SOMETHING ABOUT YOU. I COULDN'T QUITE PUT MY FINGER ON IT.
YOU'LL COME TO FIND I'M FULL OF SURPRISES. FOLLOW ME.

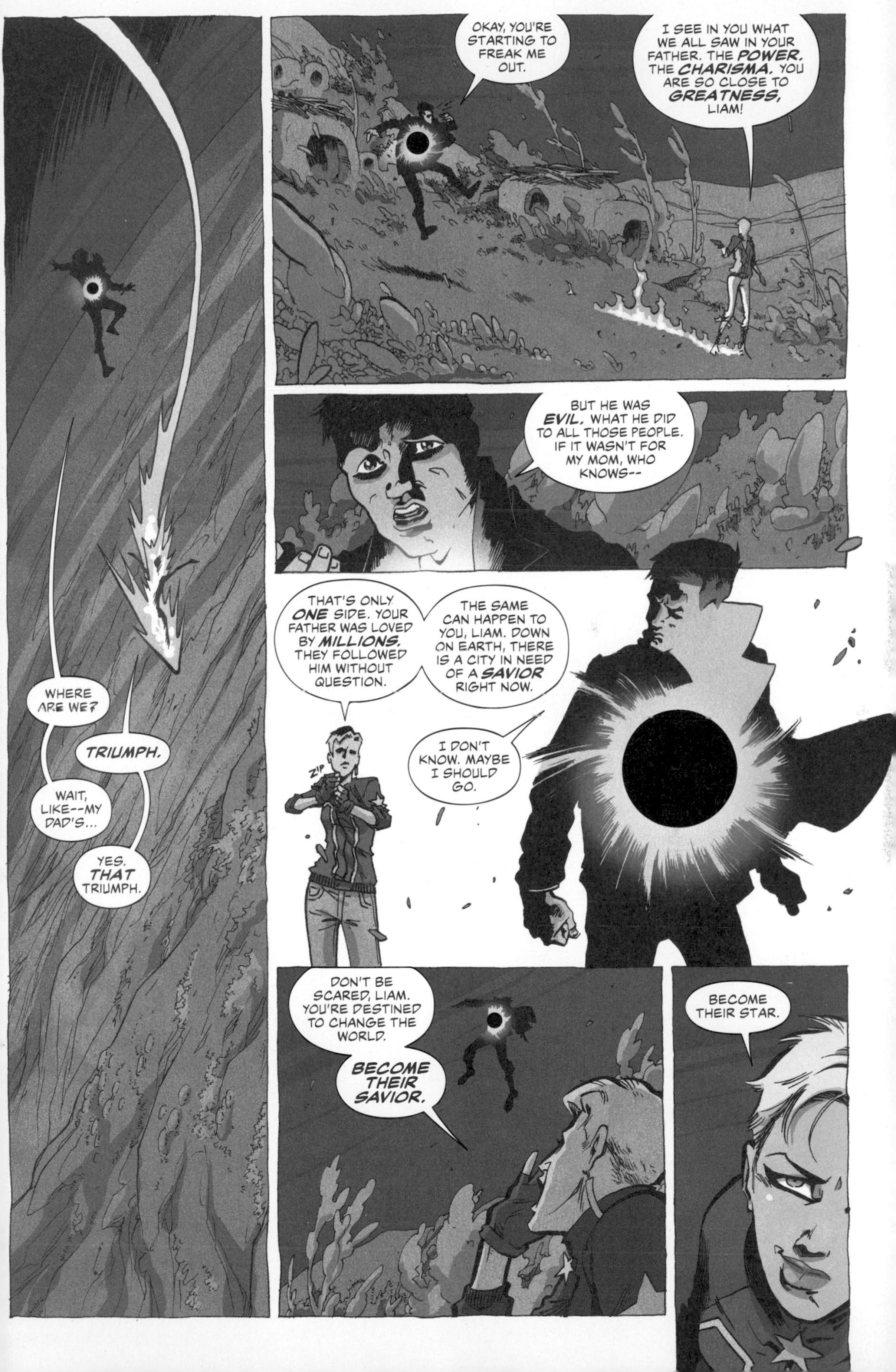
WHERE ARE WE?
TRIUMPH.
WAIT, LIKE--MY DAD'S...
YES. THAT TRIUMPH.
OKAY, YOU'RE STARTING TO FREAK ME OUT.
I SEE IN YOU WHAT WE ALL SAW IN YOUR FATHER. THE POWER. THE CHARISMA. YOU ARE SO CLOSE TO GREATNESS, LIAM!
BUT HE WAS EVIL. WHAT HE DID TO ALL THOSE PEOPLE. IF IT WASN'T FOR MY MOM, WHO KNOWS--
THAT'S ONLY ONE SIDE. YOUR FATHER WAS LOVED BY MILLIONS. THEY FOLLOWED HIM WITHOUT QUESTION.
THE SAME CAN HAPPEN TO YOU, LIAM. DOWN ON EARTH, THERE IS A CITY IN NEED OF A SAVIOR RIGHT NOW.
ZIP
I DON'T KNOW. MAYBE I SHOULD GO.
DON'T BE SCARED, LIAM. YOU'RE DESTINED TO CHANGE THE WORLD.
BECOME THEIR SAVIOR.
BECOME THEIR STAR.

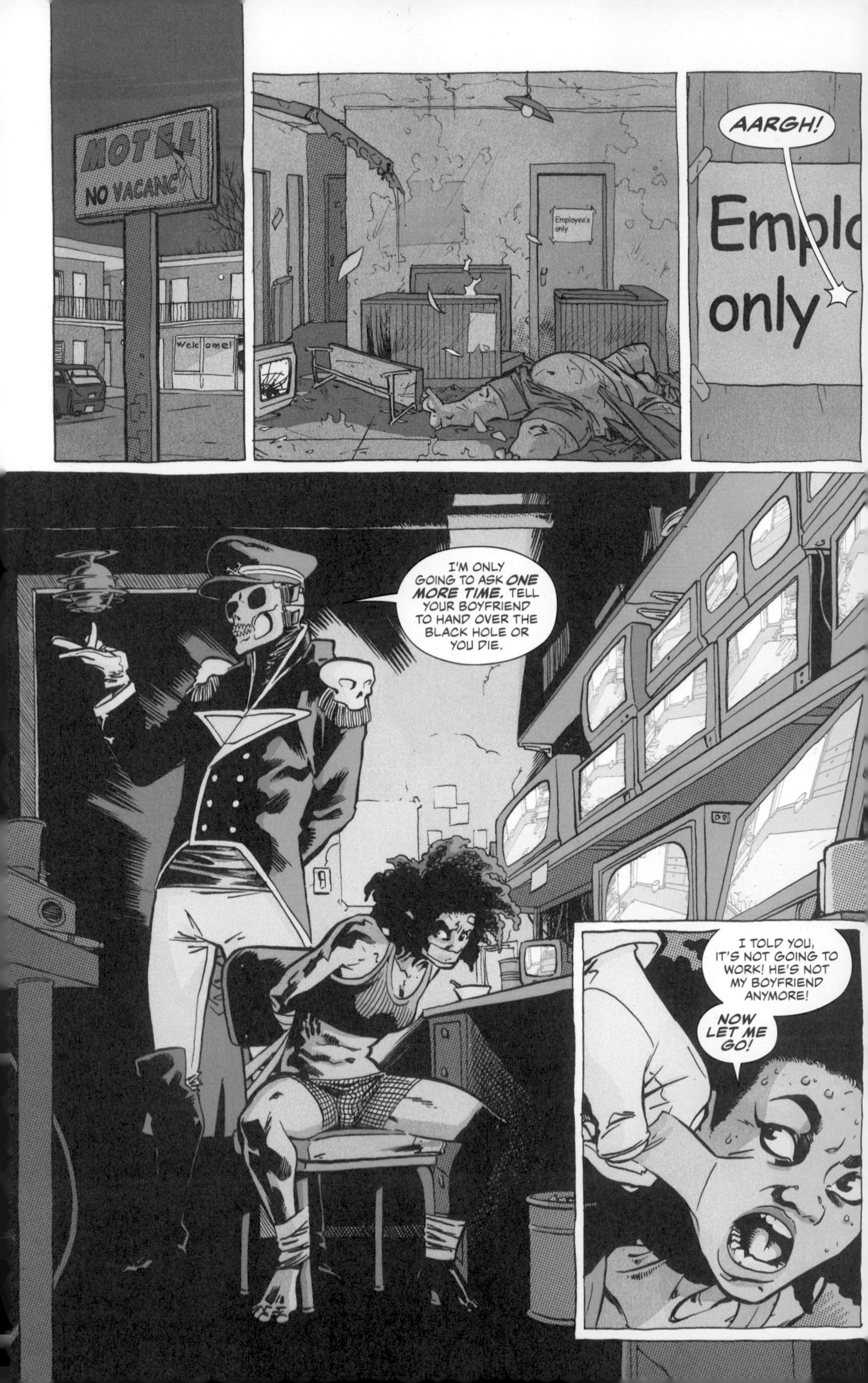
MOTEL
NO VACANC
Welcome!
Employee's only
AARGH!
Emplo only
I'M ONLY GOING TO ASK ONE MORE TIME. TELL YOUR BOYFRIEND TO HAND OVER THE BLACK HOLE OR YOU DIE.
I TOLD YOU, IT'S NOT GOING TO WORK! HE'S NOT MY BOYFRIEND ANYMORE!
NOW LET ME GO!

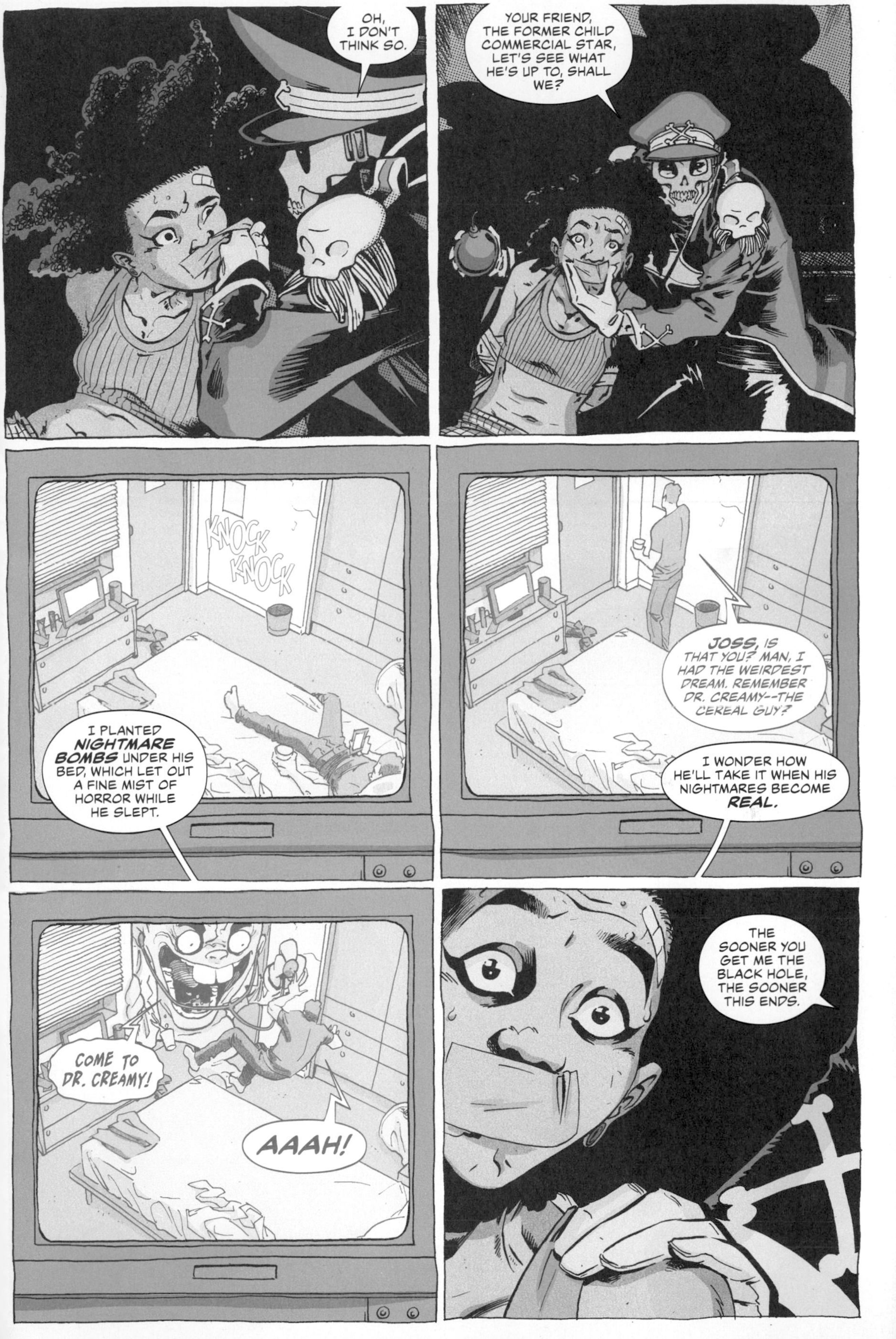
OH, I DON'T THINK SO.
YOUR FRIEND, THE FORMER CHILD COMMERCIAL STAR, LET'S SEE WHAT HE'S UP TO, SHALL WE?
KNOCK KNOCK
I PLANTED NIGHTMARE BOMBS UNDER HIS BED, WHICH LET OUT A FINE MIST OF HORROR WHILE HE SLEPT.
JOSS, IS THAT YOU? MAN, I HAD THE WEIRDEST DREAM. REMEMBER DR. CREAMY--THE CEREAL GUY?
I WONDER HOW HE'LL TAKE IT WHEN HIS NIGHTMARES BECOME REAL.
COME TO DR. CREAMY!
AAAH!
THE SOONER YOU GET ME THE BLACK HOLE, THE SOONER THIS ENDS.

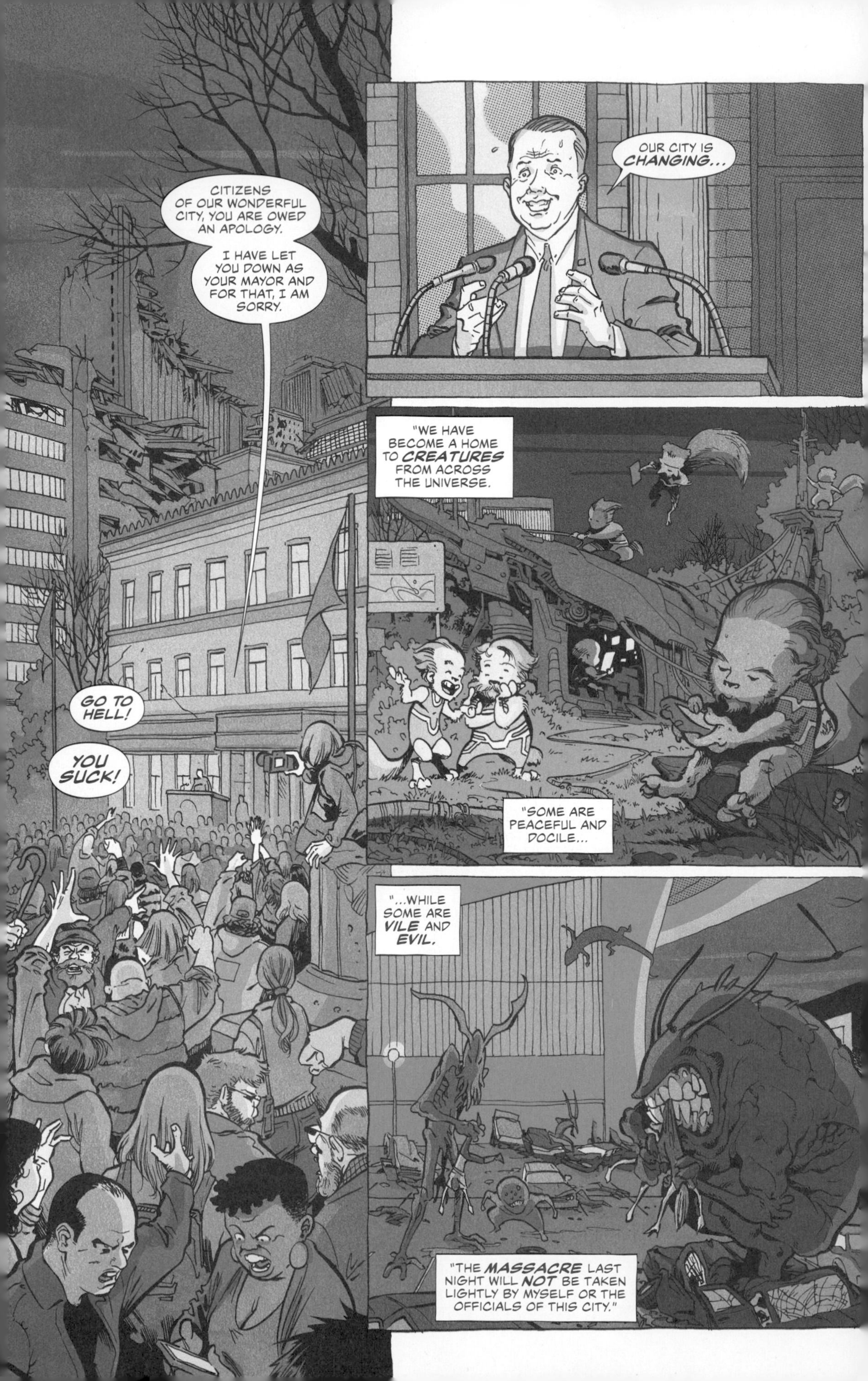
CITIZENS OF OUR WONDERFUL CITY, YOU ARE OWED AN APOLOGY.
I HAVE LET YOU DOWN AS YOUR MAYOR AND FOR THAT, I AM SORRY.
GO TO HELL!
YOU SUCK!
OUR CITY IS CHANGING...
"WE HAVE BECOME A HOME TO CREATURES FROM ACROSS THE UNIVERSE.
"SOME ARE PEACEFUL AND DOCILE...
"...WHILE SOME ARE VILE AND EVIL.
"THE MASSACRE LAST NIGHT WILL NOT BE TAKEN LIGHTLY BY MYSELF OR THE OFFICIALS OF THIS CITY."

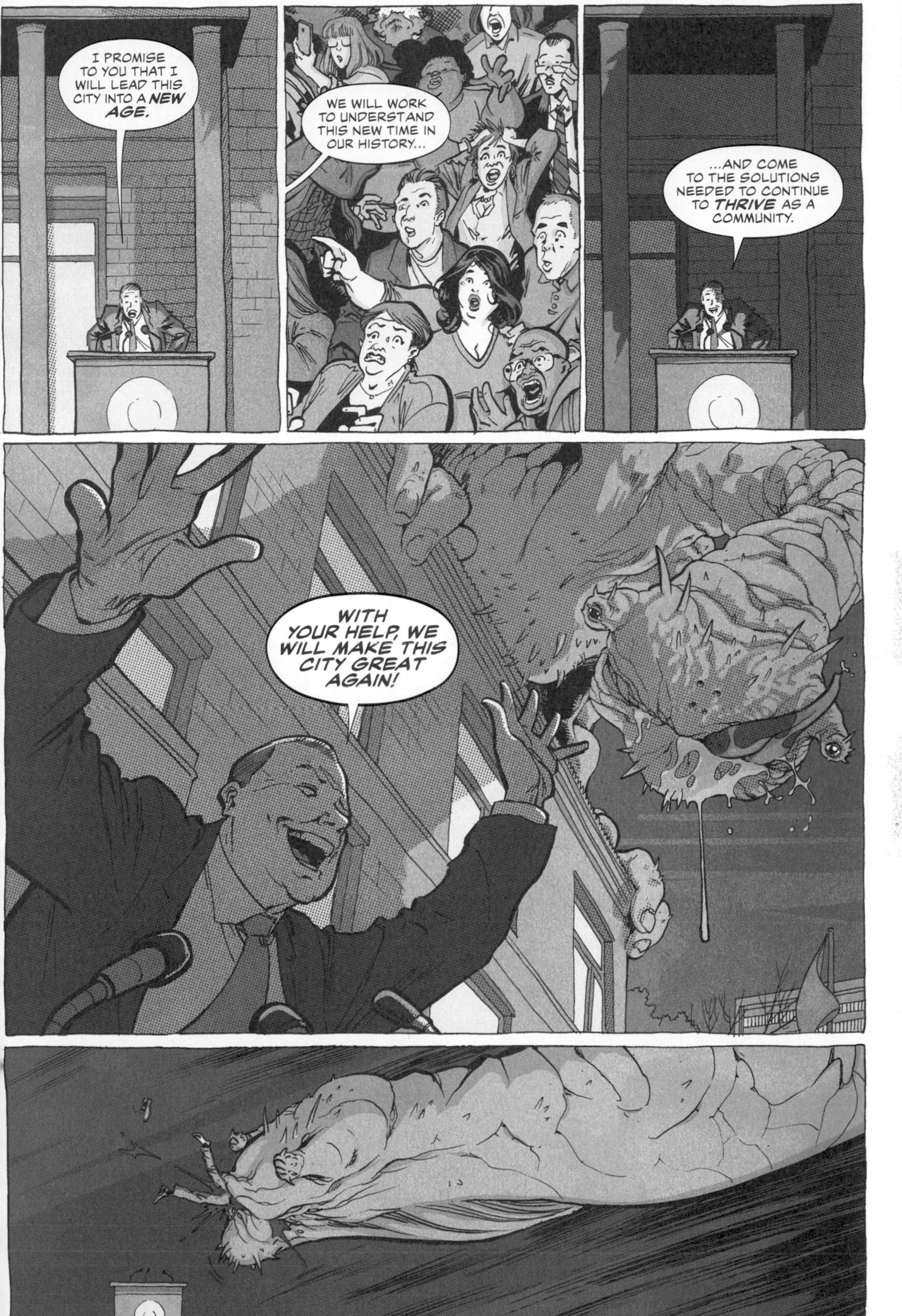
I PROMISE TO YOU THAT I WILL LEAD THIS CITY INTO A NEW AGE.
WE WILL WORK TO UNDERSTAND THIS NEW TIME IN OUR HISTORY...
...AND COME TO THE SOLUTIONS NEEDED TO CONTINUE TO THRIVE AS A COMMUNITY.
WITH YOUR HELP, WE WILL MAKE THIS CITY GREAT AGAIN!

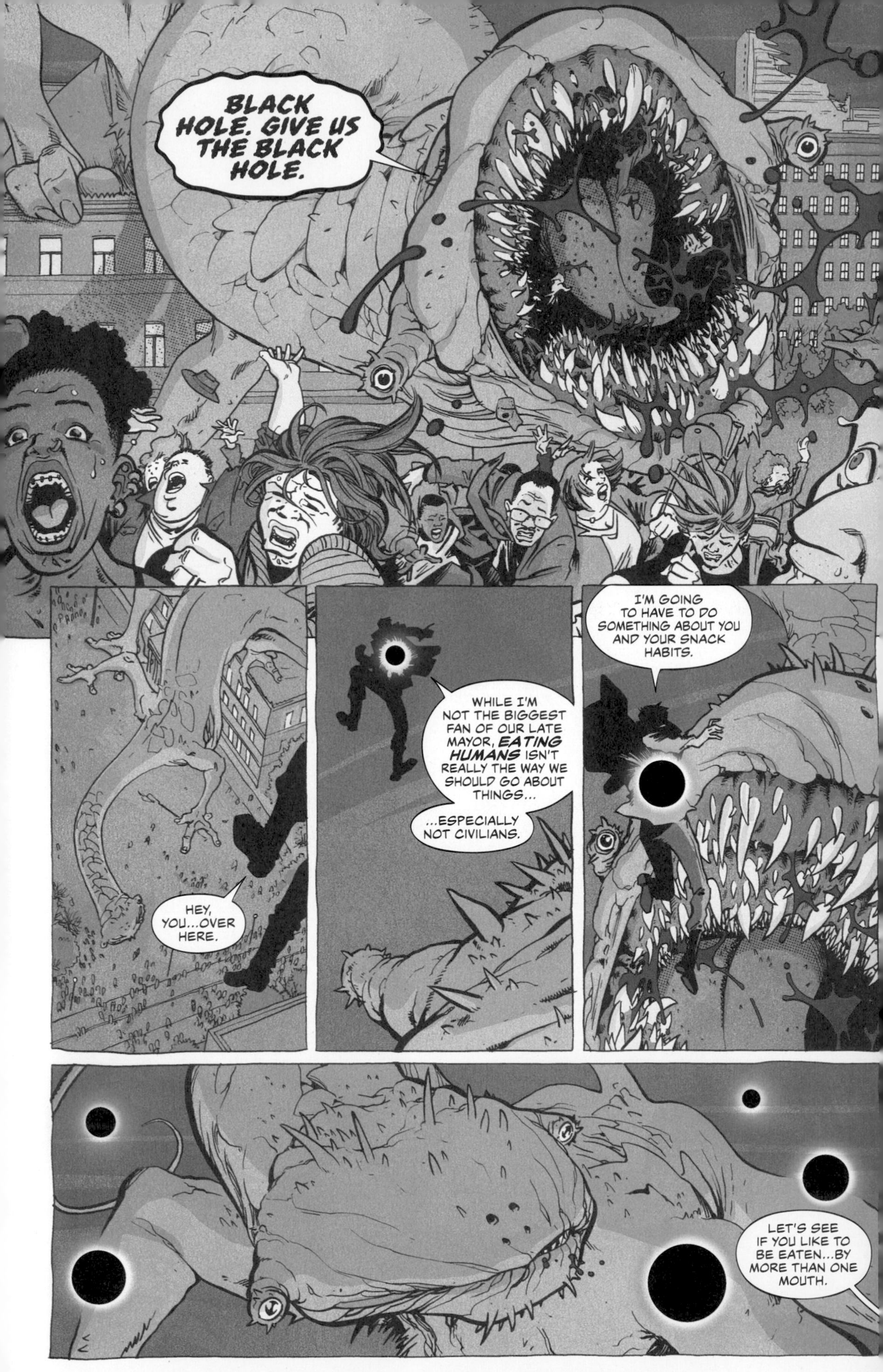
BLACK HOLE. GIVE US THE BLACK HOLE.
HEY, YOU...OVER HERE.
WHILE I'M NOT THE BIGGEST FAN OF OUR LATE MAYOR, EATING HUMANS ISN'T REALLY THE WAY WE SHOULD GO ABOUT THINGS...
...ESPECIALLY NOT CIVILIANS.
I'M GOING TO HAVE TO DO SOMETHING ABOUT YOU AND YOUR SNACK HABITS.
LET'S SEE IF YOU LIKE TO BE EATEN...BY MORE THAN ONE MOUTH.

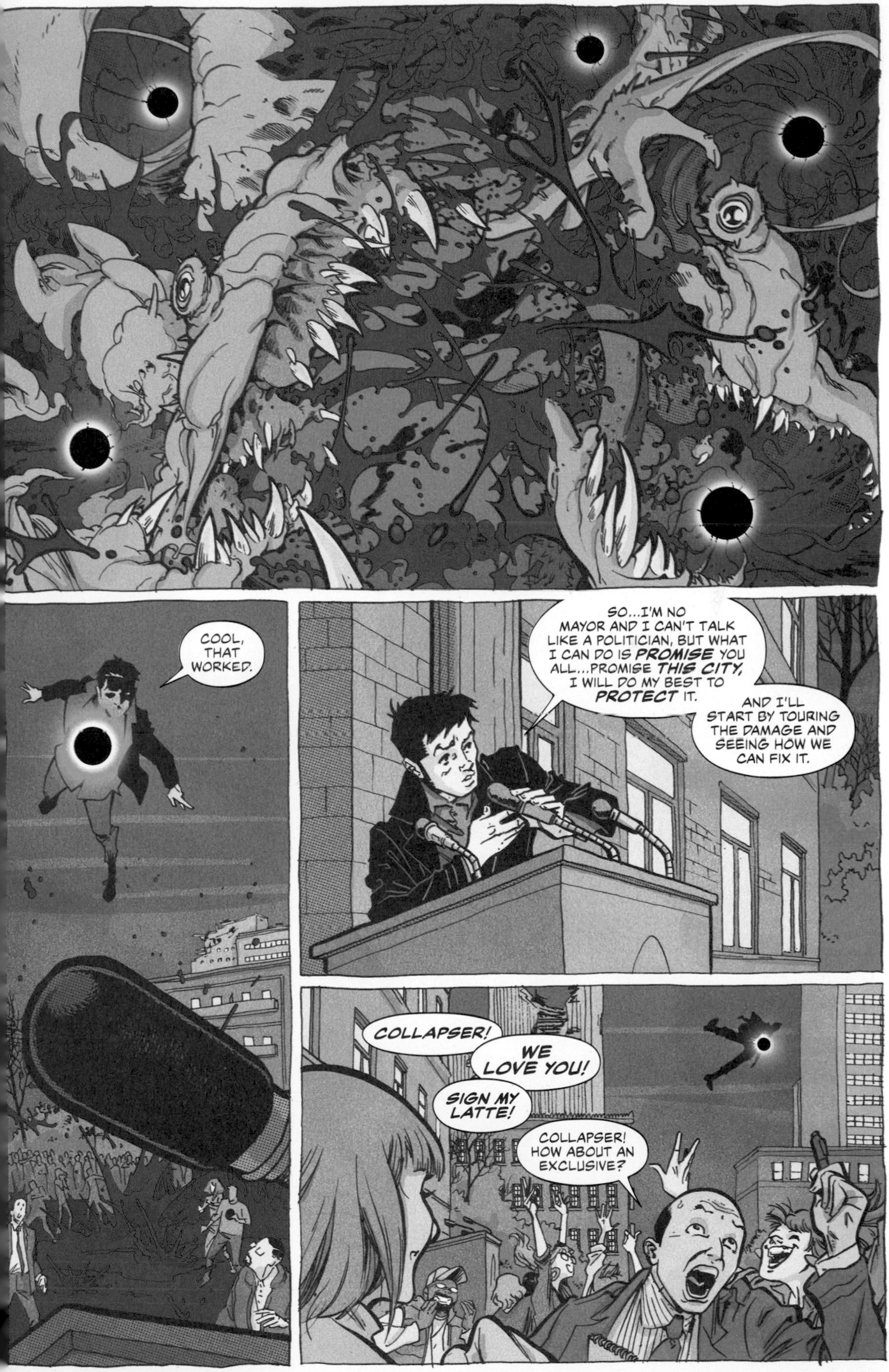
COOL, THAT WORKED.
SO...I'M NO MAYOR AND I CAN'T TALK LIKE A POLITICIAN, BUT WHAT I CAN DO IS PROMISE YOU ALL...PROMISE THIS CITY, I WILL DO MY BEST TO PROTECT IT.
AND I'LL START BY TOURING THE DAMAGE AND SEEING HOW WE CAN FIX IT.
COLLAPSER!
WE LOVE YOU!
SIGN MY LATTE!
COLLAPSER! HOW ABOUT AN EXCLUSIVE?

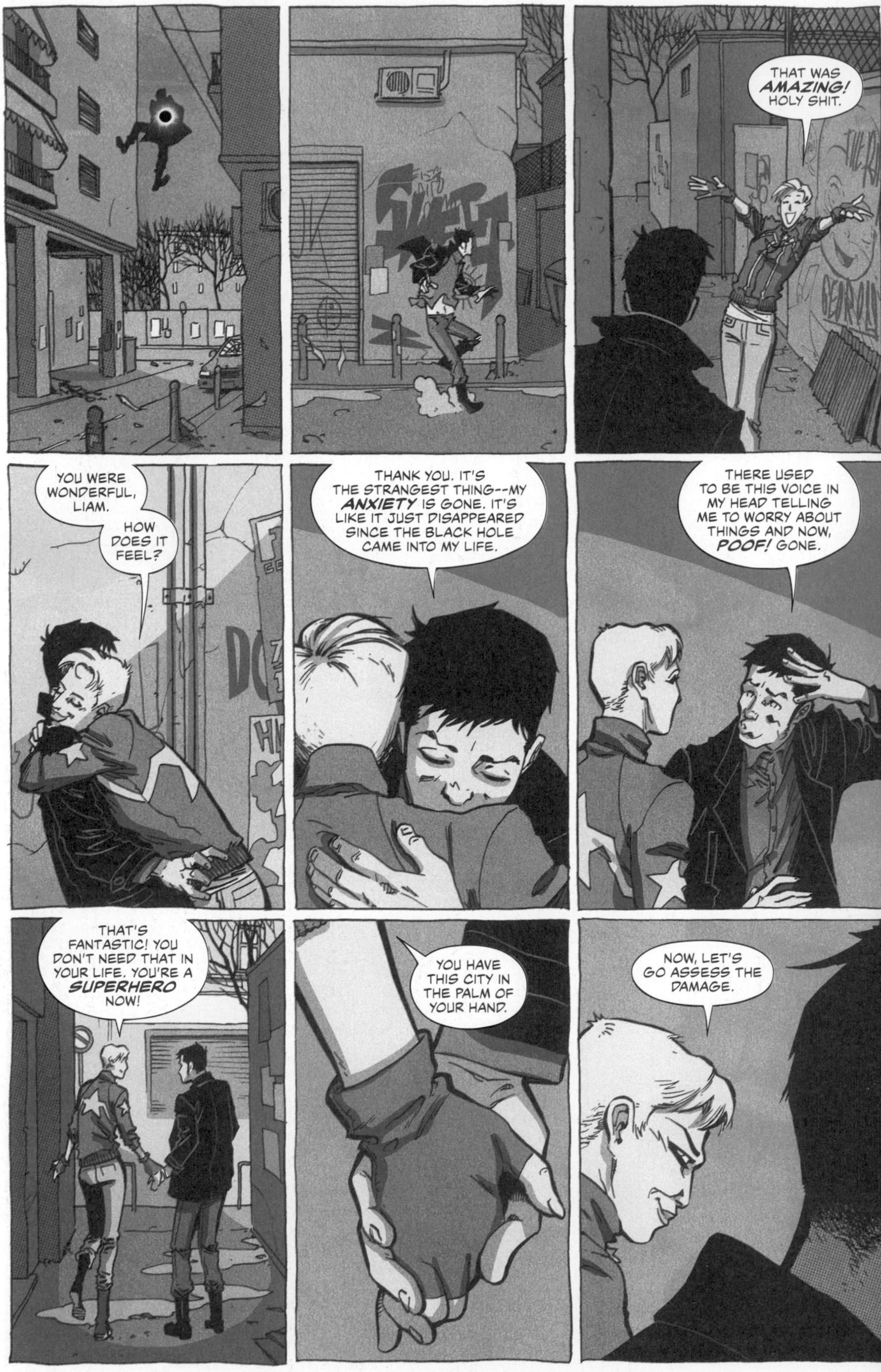

THAT WAS AMAZING! HOLY SHIT.
YOU WERE WONDERFUL, LIAM.
HOW DOES IT FEEL?
THANK YOU. IT'S THE STRANGEST THING--MY ANXIETY IS GONE. IT'S LIKE IT JUST DISAPPEARED SINCE THE BLACK HOLE CAME INTO MY LIFE.
THERE USED TO BE THIS VOICE IN MY HEAD TELLING ME TO WORRY ABOUT THINGS AND NOW, POOF! GONE.
THAT'S FANTASTIC! YOU DON'T NEED THAT IN YOUR LIFE. YOU'RE A SUPERHERO NOW!
YOU HAVE THIS CITY IN THE PALM OF YOUR HAND.
NOW, LET'S GO ASSESS THE DAMAGE.

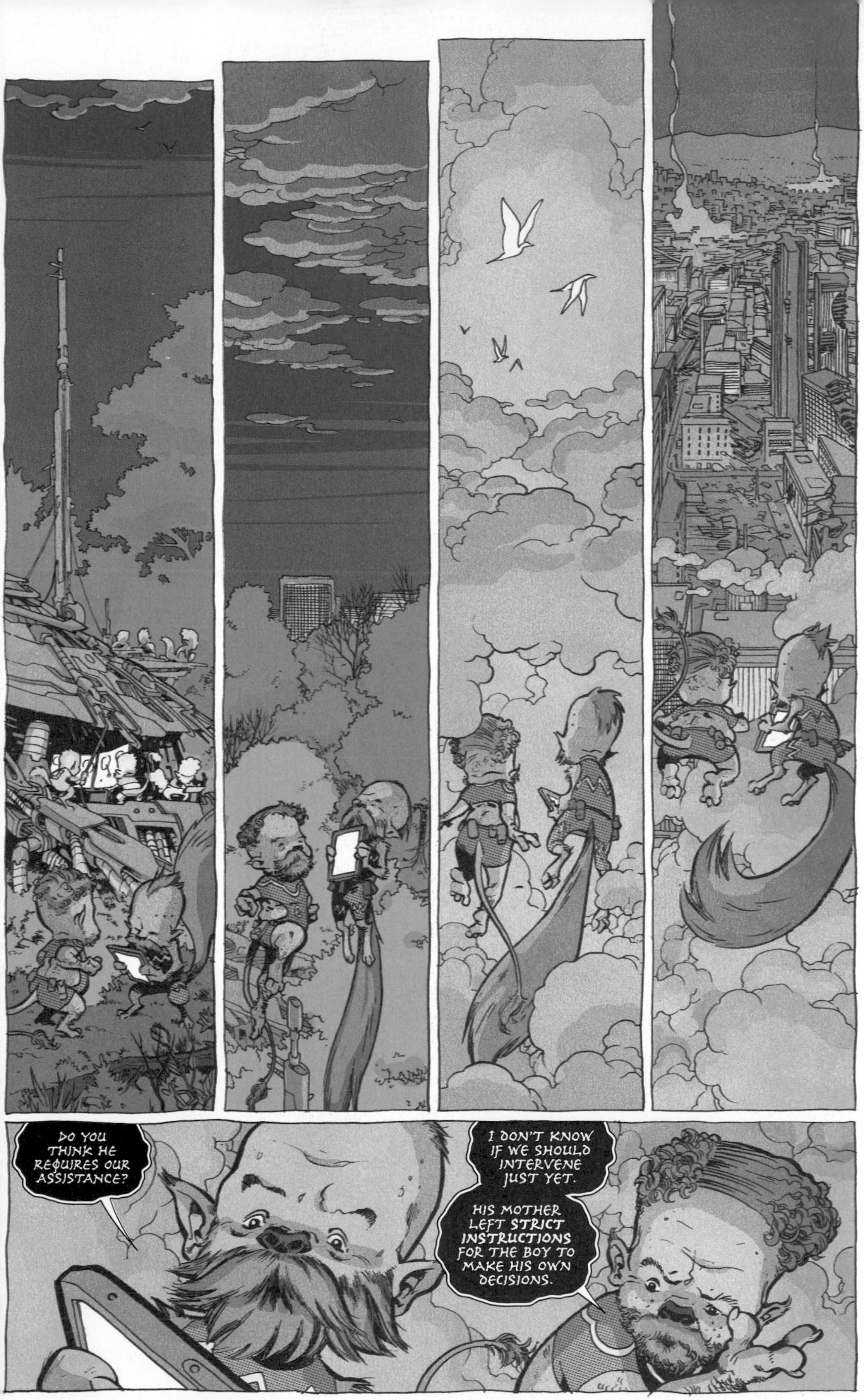

DO YOU THINK HE REQUIRES OUR ASSISTANCE?
I DON'T KNOW IF WE SHOULD INTERVENE JUST YET.
HIS MOTHER LEFT STRICT INSTRUCTIONS FOR THE BOY TO MAKE HIS OWN DECISIONS.

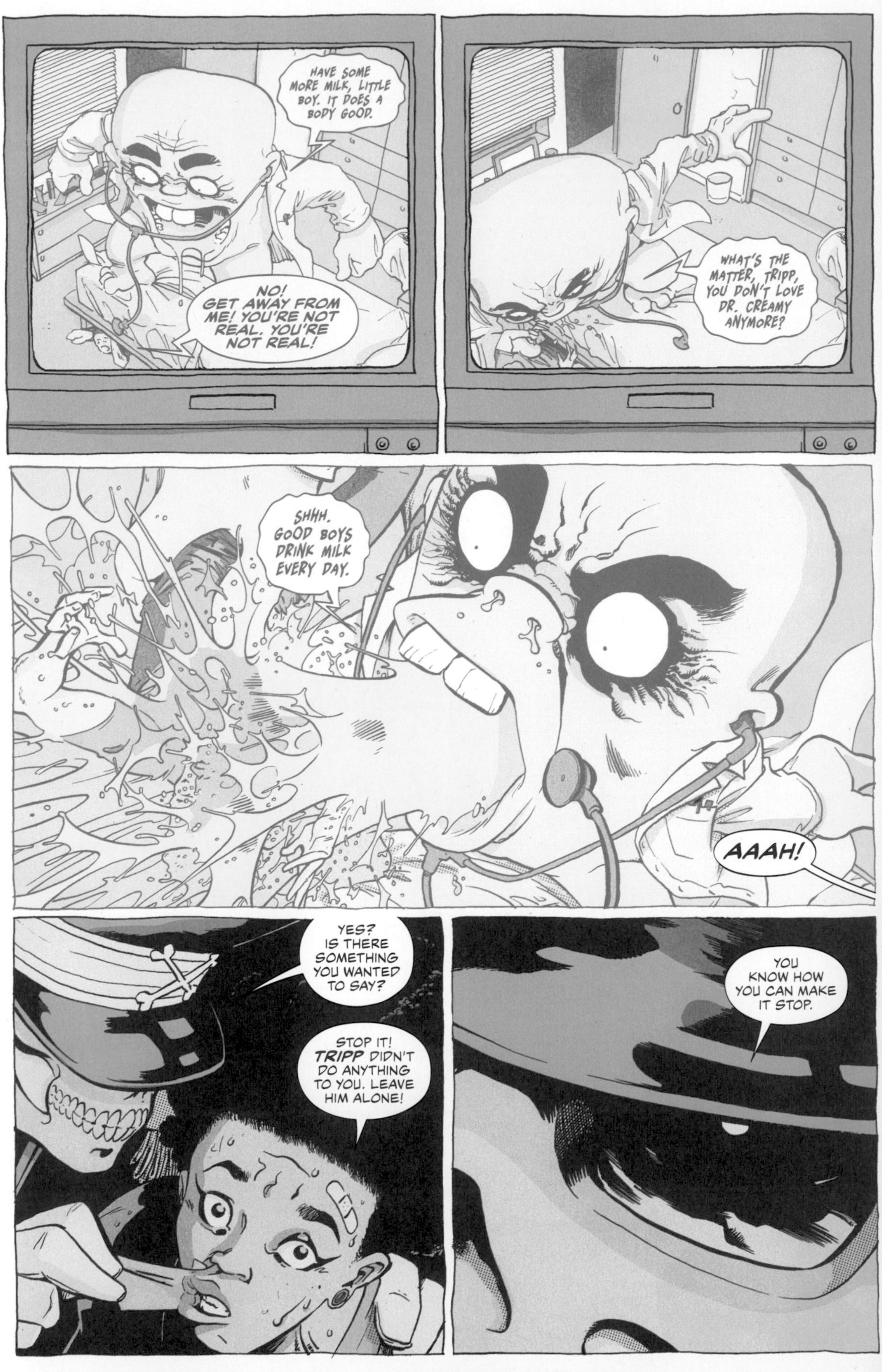
HAVE SOME MORE MILK, LITTLE BOY. IT DOES A BODY GOOD.
NO! GET AWAY FROM ME! YOU'RE NOT REAL. YOU'RE NOT REAL!
WHAT'S THE MATTER, TRIPP, YOU DON'T LOVE DR. CREAMY ANYMORE?
SHHH. GOOD BOYS DRINK MILK EVERY DAY.
AAAH!
YES? IS THERE SOMETHING YOU WANTED TO SAY?
STOP IT! TRIPP DIDN'T DO ANYTHING TO YOU. LEAVE HIM ALONE!
YOU KNOW HOW YOU CAN MAKE IT STOP.

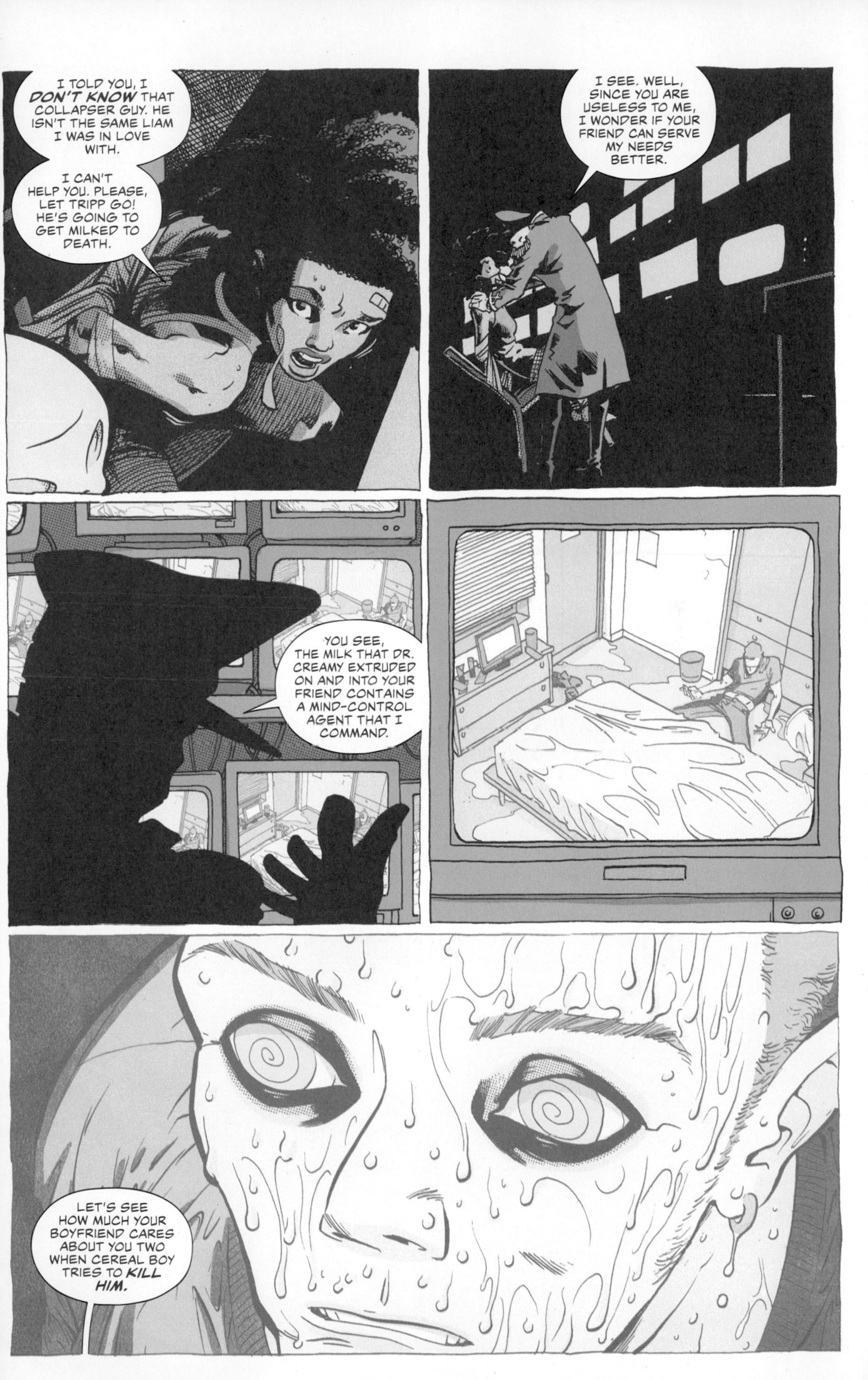
I TOLD YOU, I DON'T KNOW THAT COLLAPSER GUY. HE ISN'T THE SAME LIAM I WAS IN LOVE WITH.
I CAN'T HELP YOU. PLEASE, LET TRIPP GO! HE'S GOING TO GET MILKED TO DEATH.
I SEE. WELL, SINCE YOU ARE USELESS TO ME, I WONDER IF YOUR FRIEND CAN SERVE MY NEEDS BETTER.
YOU SEE, THE MILK THAT DR. CREAMY EXTRUDED ON AND INTO YOUR FRIEND CONTAINS A MIND-CONTROL AGENT THAT I COMMAND.
LET'S SEE HOW MUCH YOUR BOYFRIEND CARES ABOUT YOU TWO WHEN CEREAL BOY TRIES TO KILL HIM.

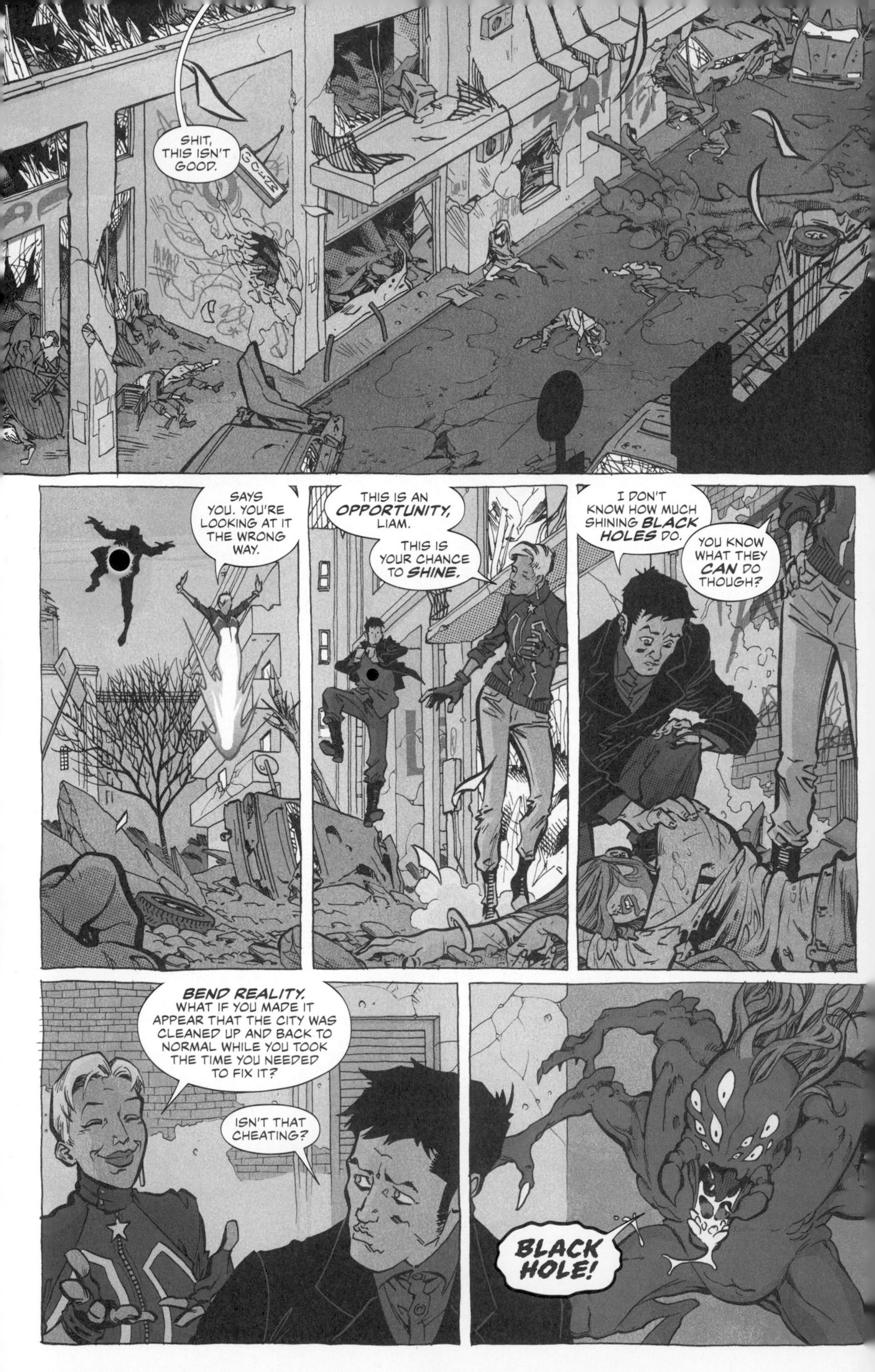
SHIT, THIS ISN'T GOOD.
SAYS YOU. YOU'RE LOOKING AT IT THE WRONG WAY.
THIS IS AN OPPORTUNITY, LIAM.
THIS IS YOUR CHANCE TO SHINE.
I DON'T KNOW HOW MUCH SHINING BLACK HOLES DO.
YOU KNOW WHAT THEY CAN DO THOUGH?
BEND REALITY. WHAT IF YOU MADE IT APPEAR THAT THE CITY WAS CLEANED UP AND BACK TO NORMAL WHILE YOU TOOK THE TIME YOU NEEDED TO FIX IT?
ISN'T THAT CHEATING?
BLACK HOLE!

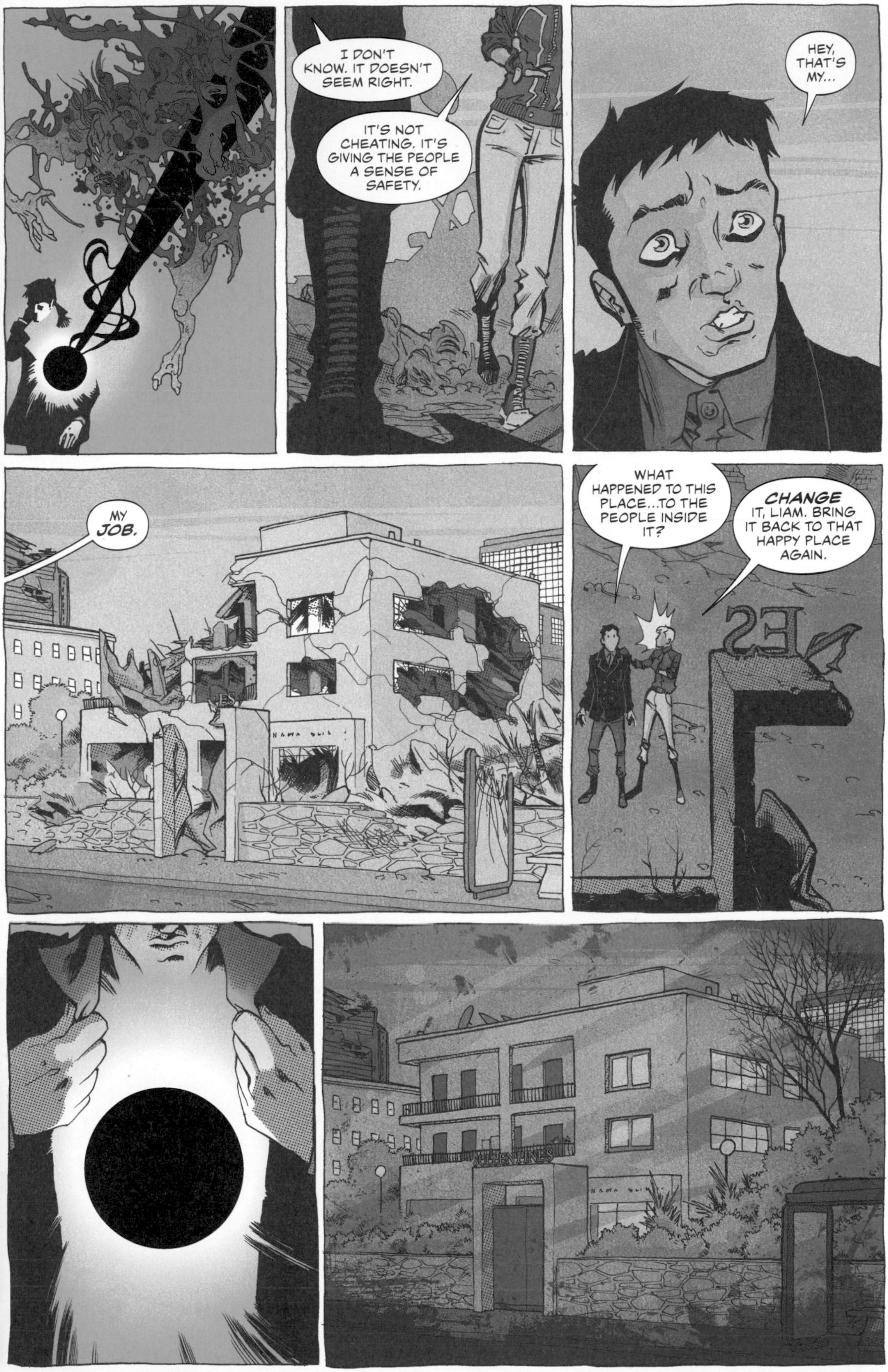

I DON'T KNOW. IT DOESN'T SEEM RIGHT.
IT'S NOT CHEATING. IT'S GIVING THE PEOPLE A SENSE OF SAFETY.
HEY, THAT'S MY...
MY *JOB.*
WHAT HAPPENED TO THIS PLACE...TO THE PEOPLE INSIDE IT?
CHANGE IT, LIAM. BRING IT BACK TO THAT HAPPY PLACE AGAIN.
ES

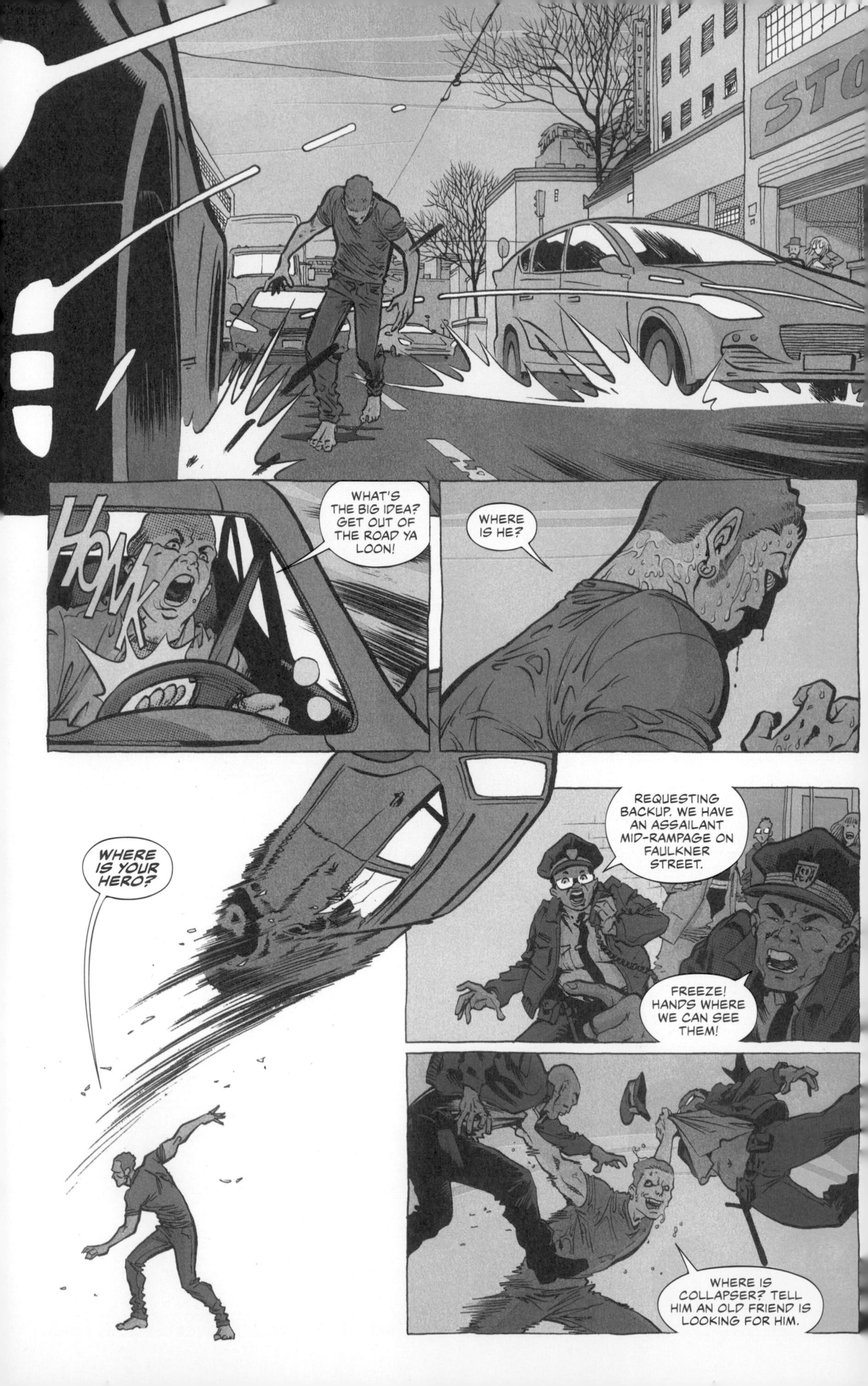
HOTEL LUX
STO
HONK
WHAT'S THE BIG IDEA? GET OUT OF THE ROAD YA LOON!
WHERE IS HE?
WHERE IS YOUR HERO?
REQUESTING BACKUP. WE HAVE AN ASSAILANT MID-RAMPAGE ON FAULKNER STREET.
FREEZE! HANDS WHERE WE CAN SEE THEM!
WHERE IS COLLAPSER? TELL HIM AN OLD FRIEND IS LOOKING FOR HIM.

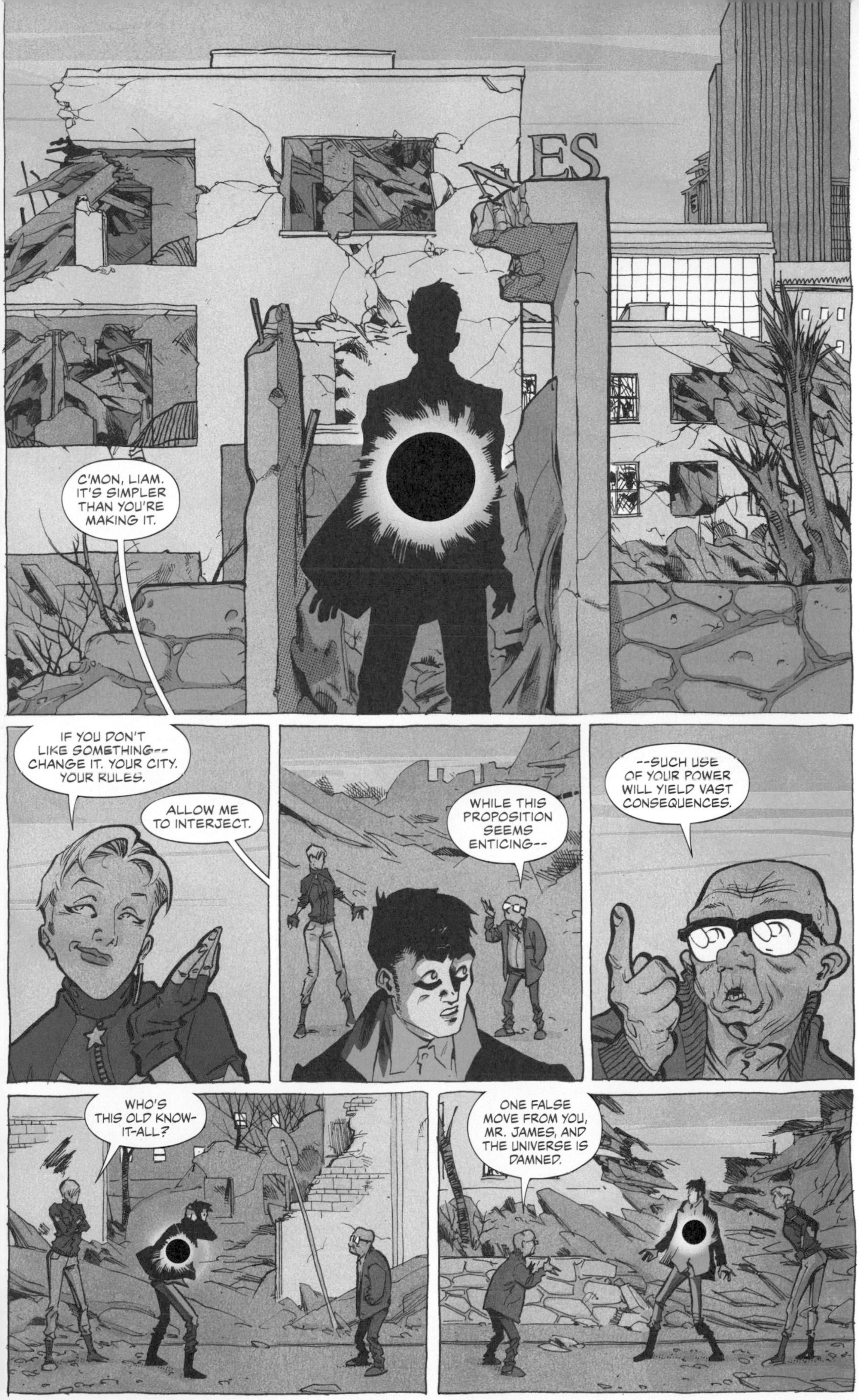
C'MON, LIAM. IT'S SIMPLER THAN YOU'RE MAKING IT.
IF YOU DON'T LIKE SOMETHING-- CHANGE IT. YOUR CITY. YOUR RULES.
ALLOW ME TO INTERJECT.
WHILE THIS PROPOSITION SEEMS ENTICING--
--SUCH USE OF YOUR POWER WILL YIELD VAST CONSEQUENCES.
WHO'S THIS OLD KNOW-IT-ALL?
ONE FALSE MOVE FROM YOU, MR. JAMES, AND THE UNIVERSE IS DAMNED.

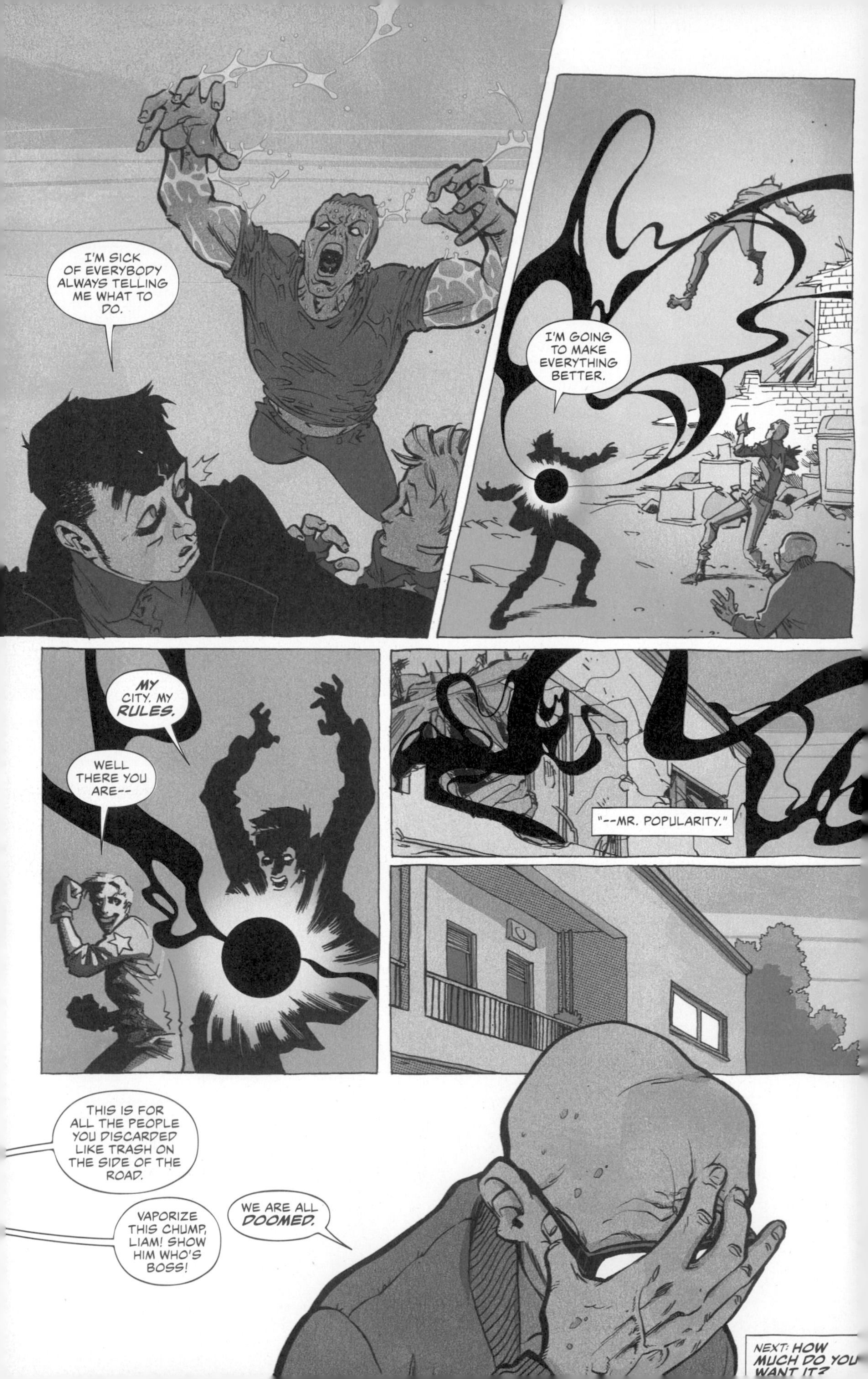
I'M SICK OF EVERYBODY ALWAYS TELLING ME WHAT TO DO.
I'M GOING TO MAKE EVERYTHING BETTER.
MY CITY. MY RULES.
WELL THERE YOU ARE--
"--MR. POPULARITY."
THIS IS FOR ALL THE PEOPLE YOU DISCARDED LIKE TRASH ON THE SIDE OF THE ROAD.
VAPORIZE THIS CHUMP, LIAM! SHOW HIM WHO'S BOSS!
WE ARE ALL DOOMED.
NEXT: HOW MUCH DO YOU WANT IT?

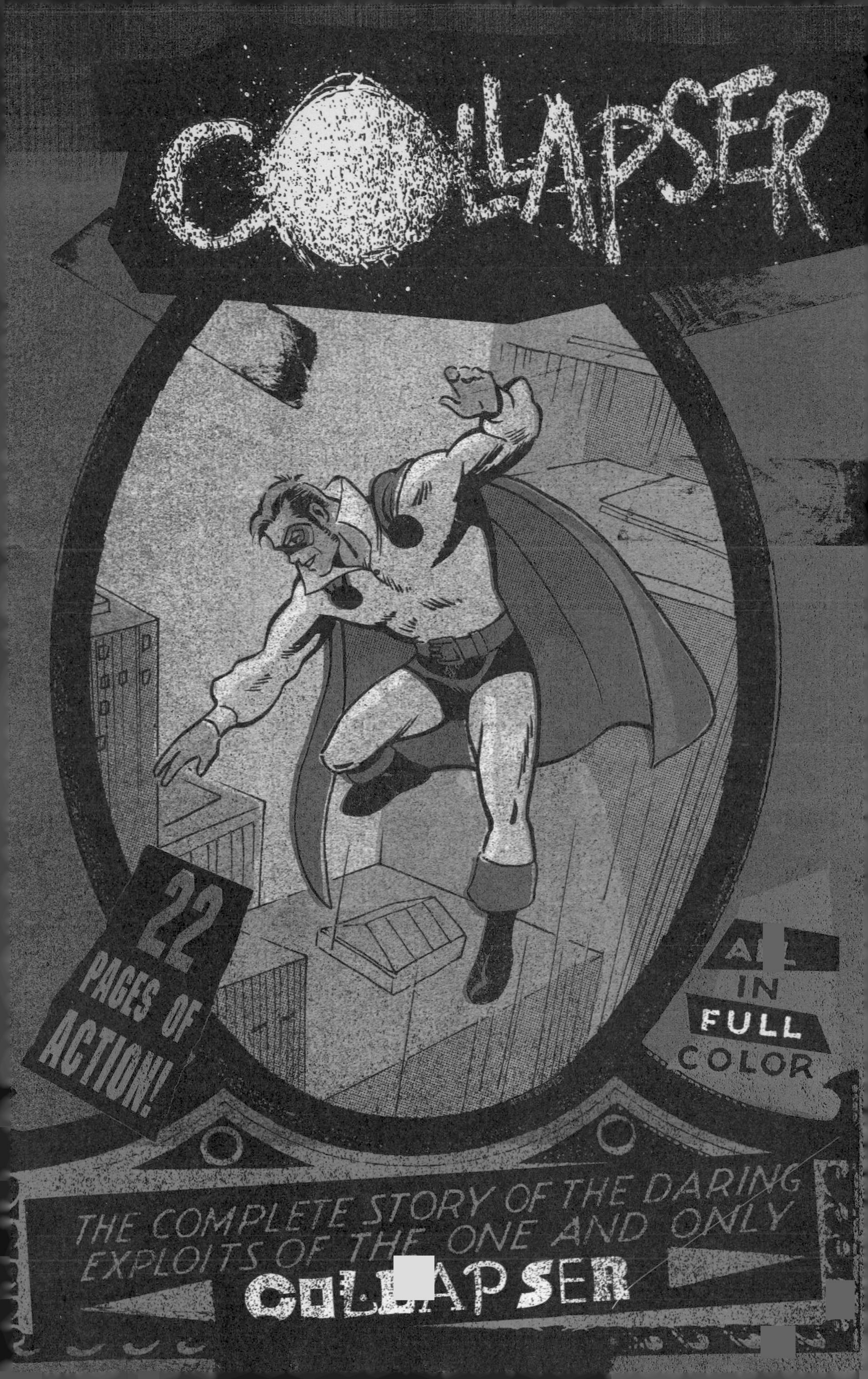

COLLAPSER
22
PAGES OF ACTION!
ALL IN FULL COLOR
THE COMPLETE STORY OF THE DARING EXPLOITS OF THE ONE AND ONLY
COLLAPSER

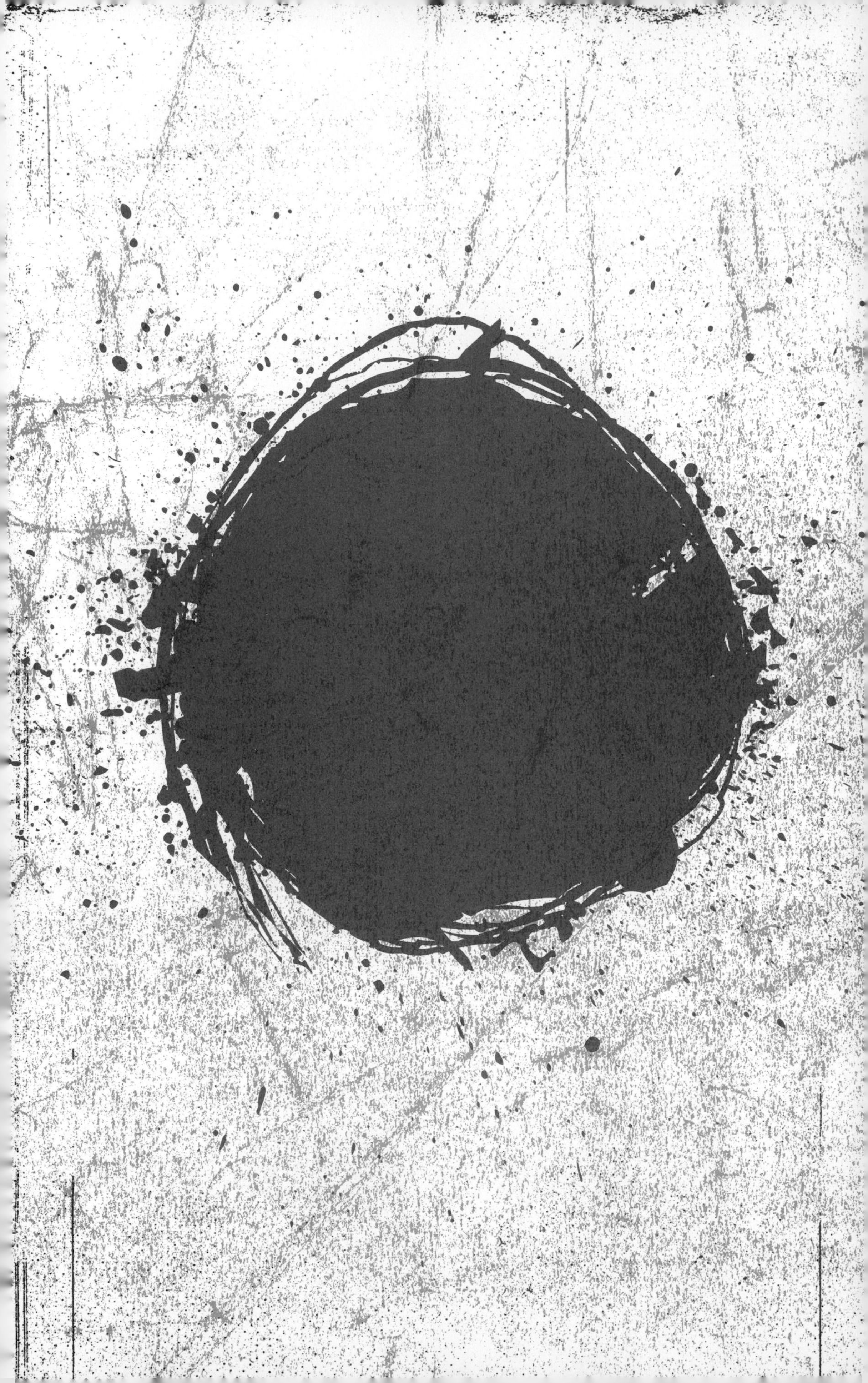

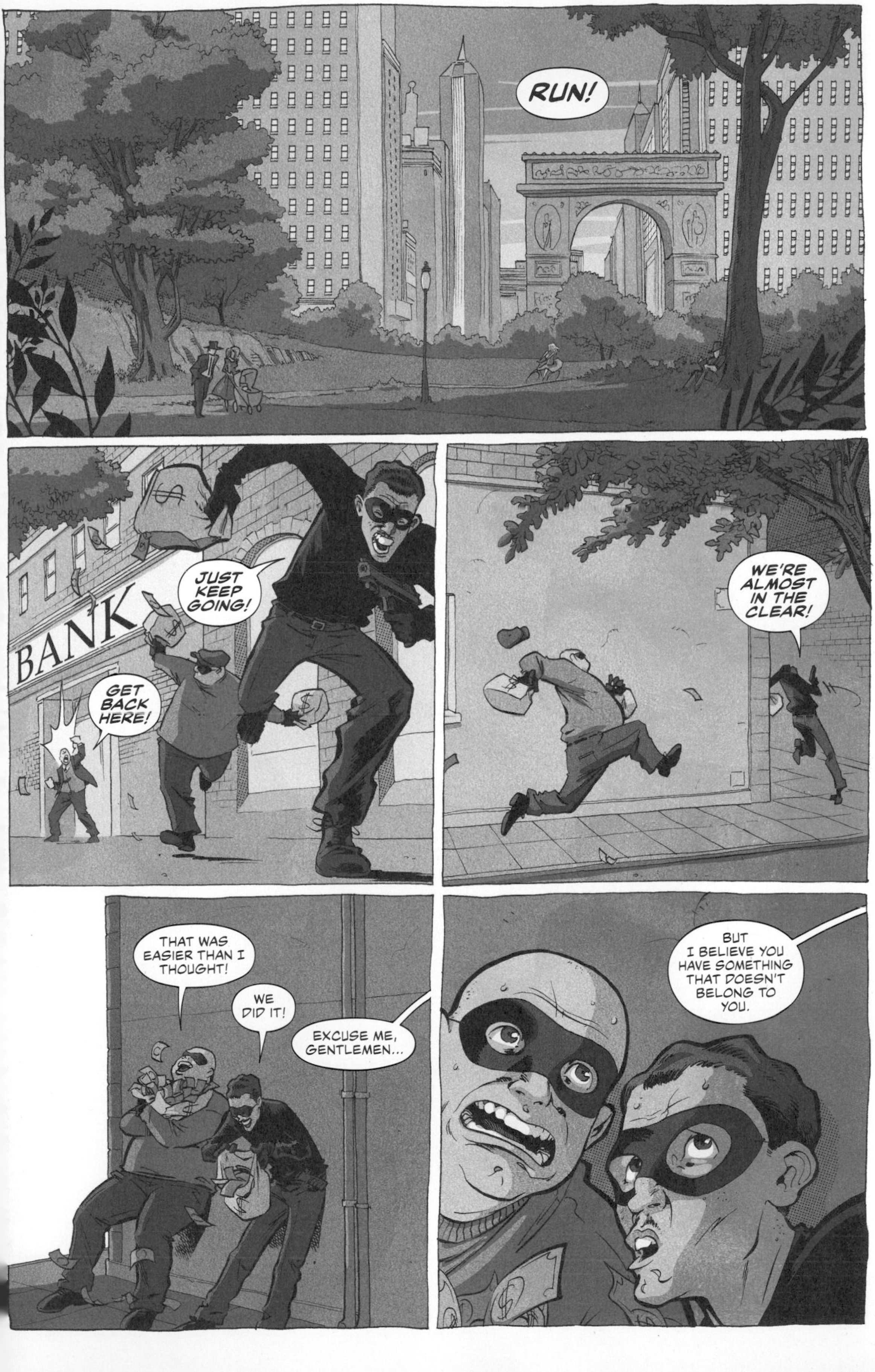
RUN!
BANK
JUST KEEP GOING!
GET BACK HERE!
WE'RE ALMOST IN THE CLEAR!
THAT WAS EASIER THAN I THOUGHT!
WE DID IT!
EXCUSE ME, GENTLEMEN...
BUT I BELIEVE YOU HAVE SOMETHING THAT DOESN'T BELONG TO YOU.

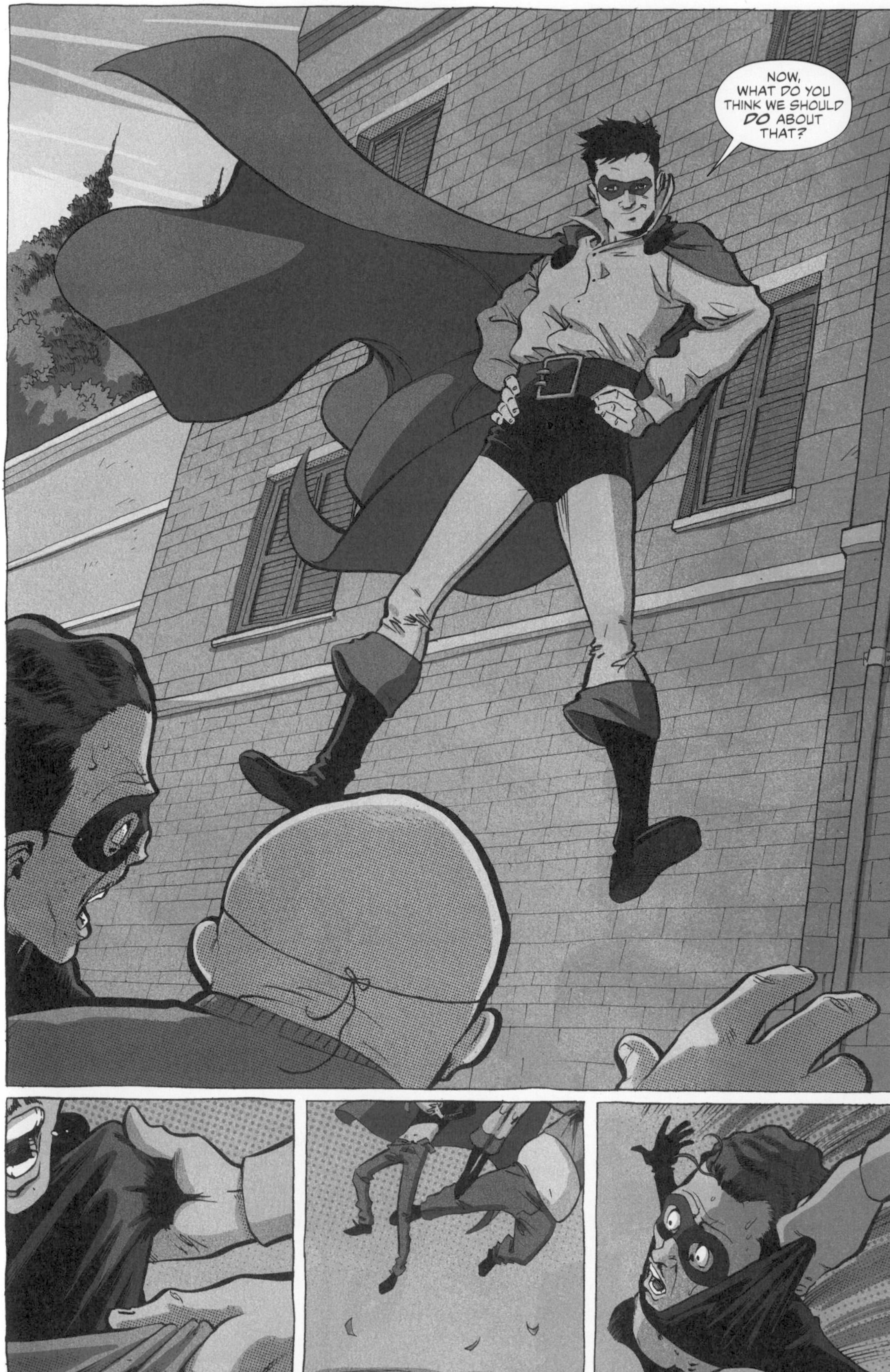
NOW, WHAT DO YOU THINK WE SHOULD DO ABOUT THAT?

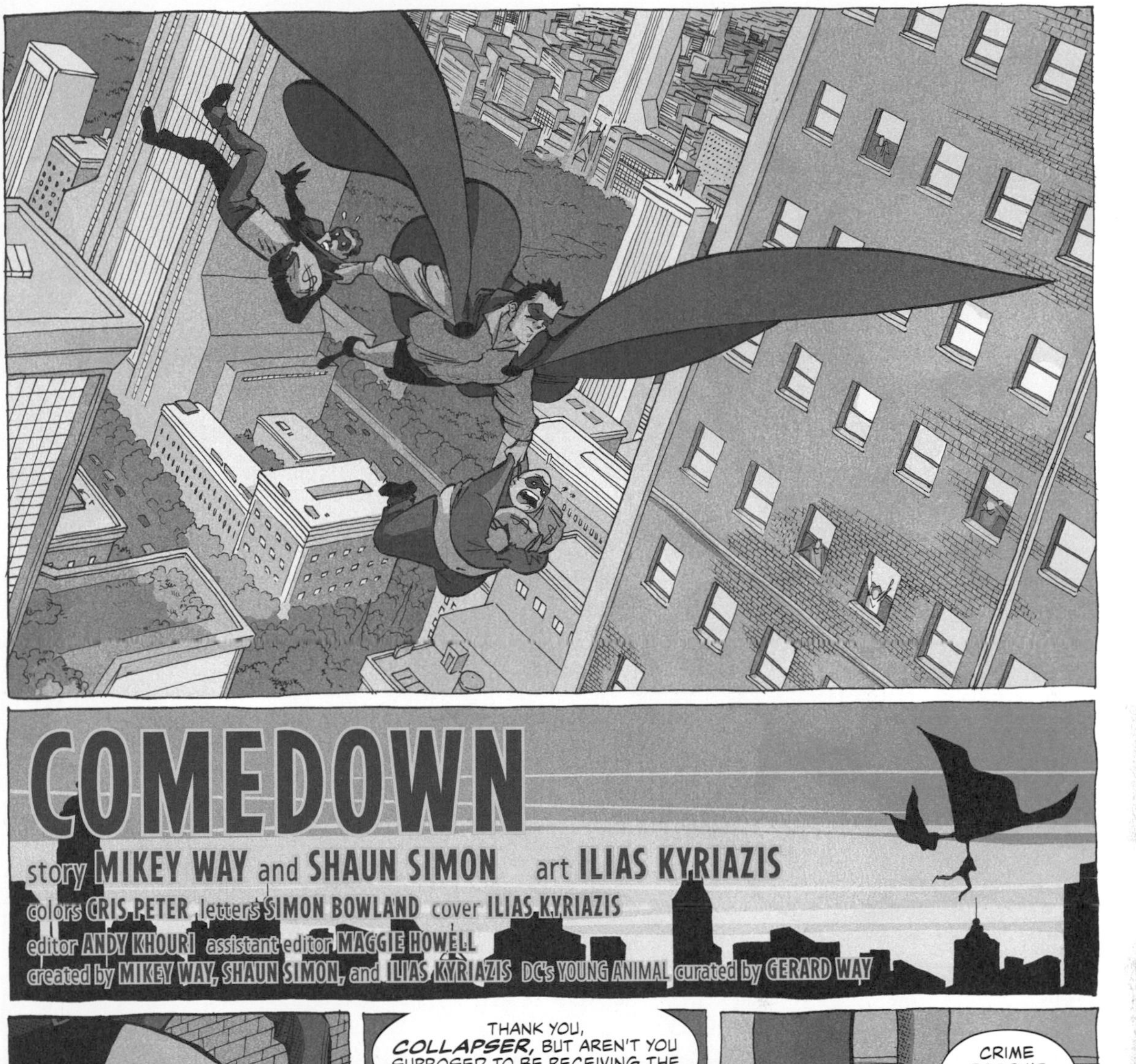
COMEDOWN
story MIKEY WAY and SHAUN SIMON art ILIAS KYRIAZIS
colors CRIS PETER letters SIMON BOWLAND cover ILIAS KYRIAZIS
editor ANDY KHOURI assistant editor MAGGIE HOWELL
created by MIKEY WAY, SHAUN SIMON, and ILIAS KYRIAZIS DC's YOUNG ANIMAL curated by GERARD WAY
POLICE
THANK YOU, COLLAPSER, BUT AREN'T YOU SUPPOSED TO BE RECEIVING THE KEY TO THE CITY RIGHT NOW?
CRIME DOESN'T TAKE A BREAK AND NEITHER DO I.

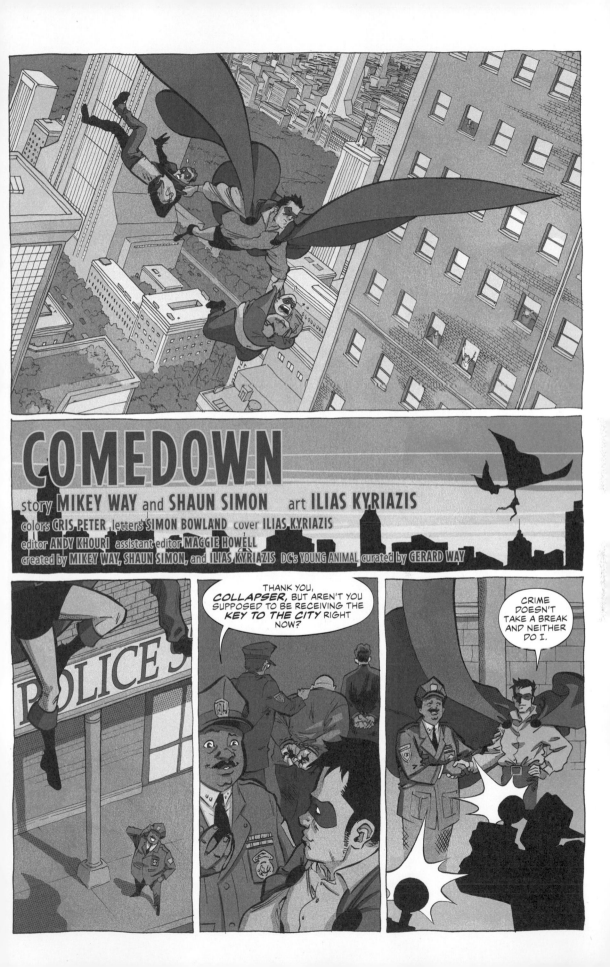

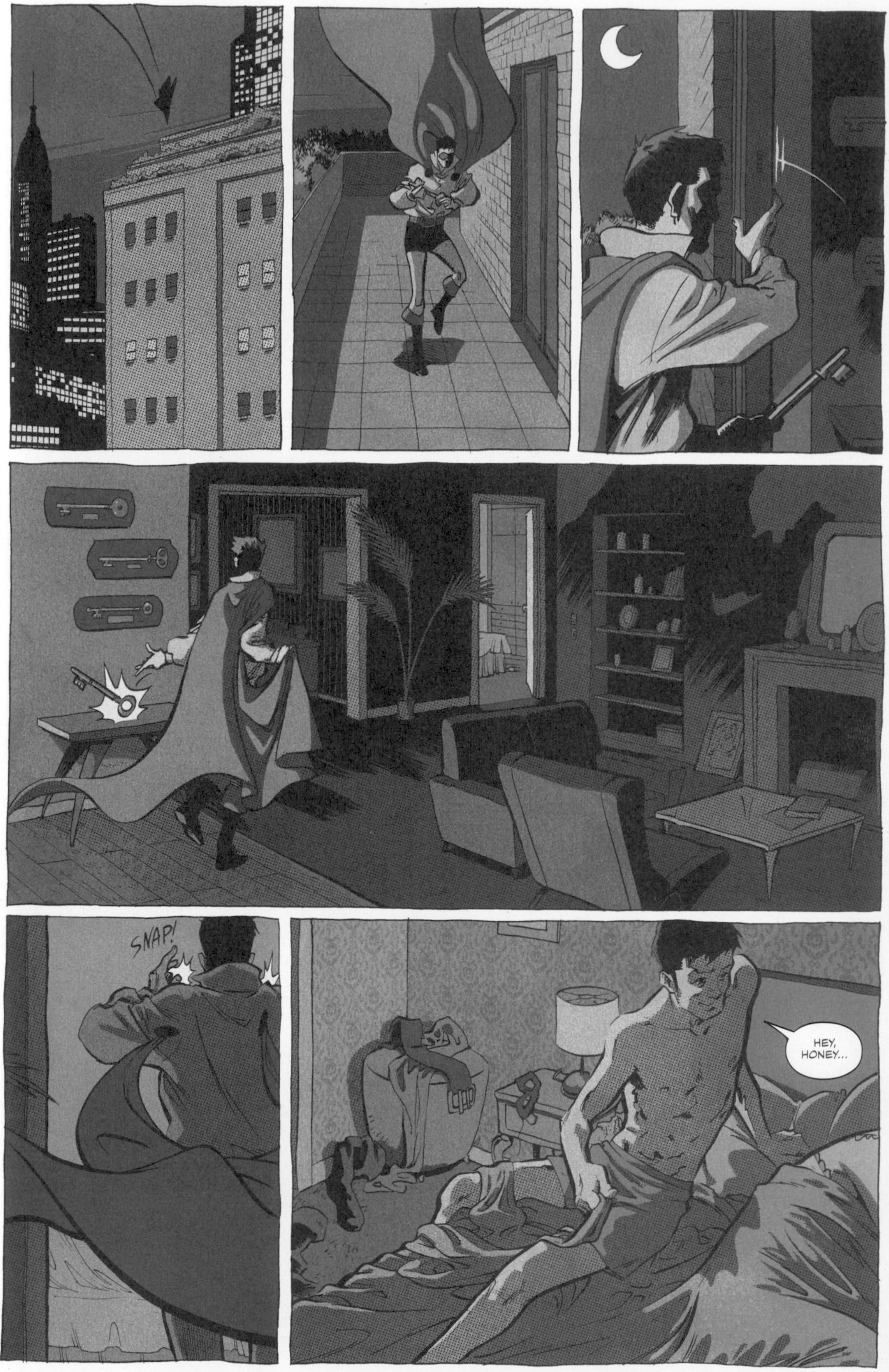
SNAP!
HEY, HONEY...

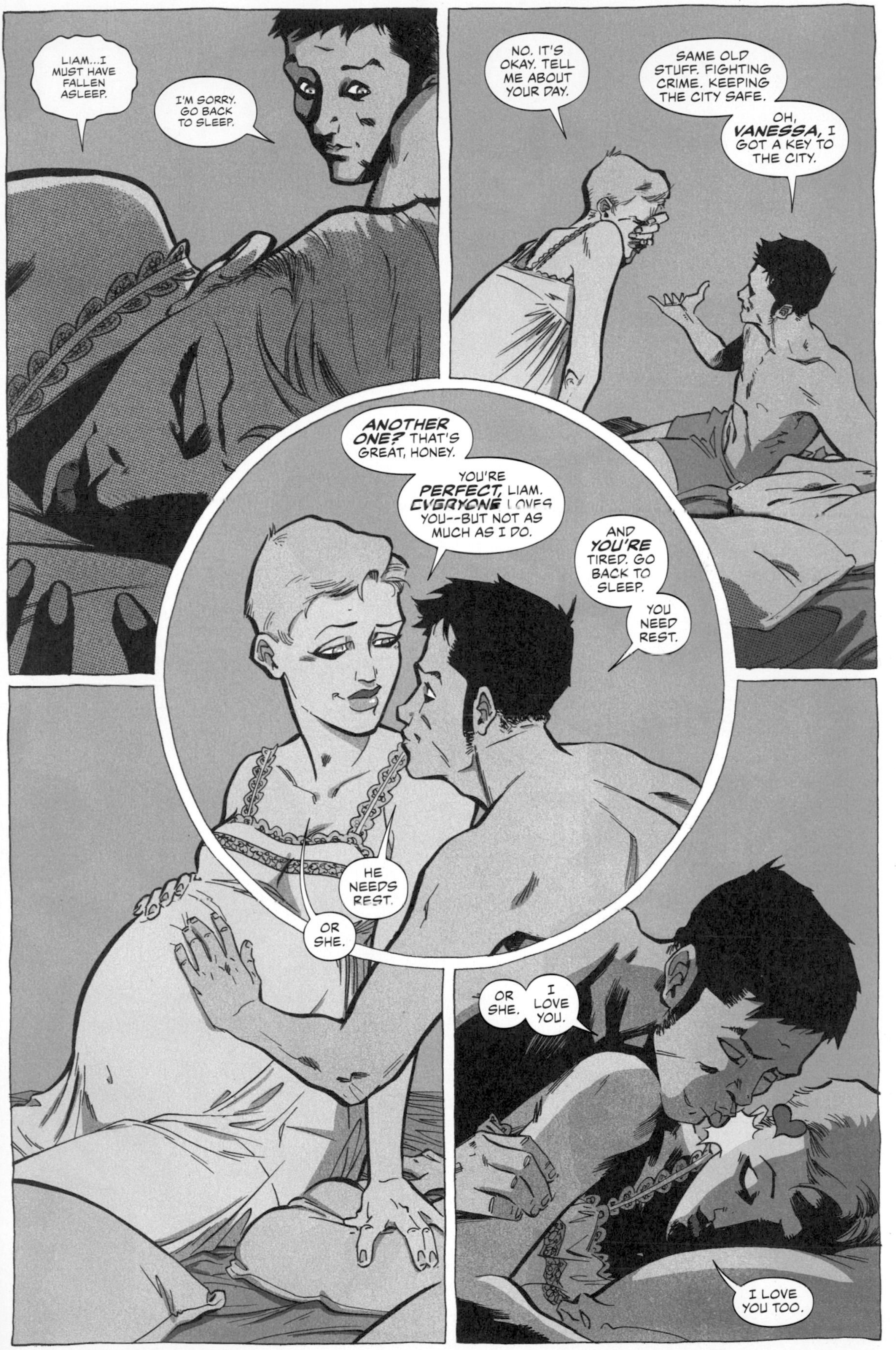

LIAM...I MUST HAVE FALLEN ASLEEP.
I'M SORRY. GO BACK TO SLEEP.
NO. IT'S OKAY. TELL ME ABOUT YOUR DAY.
SAME OLD STUFF. FIGHTING CRIME. KEEPING THE CITY SAFE.
OH, VANESSA, I GOT A KEY TO THE CITY.
ANOTHER ONE? THAT'S GREAT, HONEY.
YOU'RE PERFECT, LIAM. EVERYONE LOVES YOU--BUT NOT AS MUCH AS I DO.
AND YOU'RE TIRED. GO BACK TO SLEEP.
YOU NEED REST.
HE NEEDS REST.
OR SHE.
OR SHE.
I LOVE YOU.
I LOVE YOU TOO.

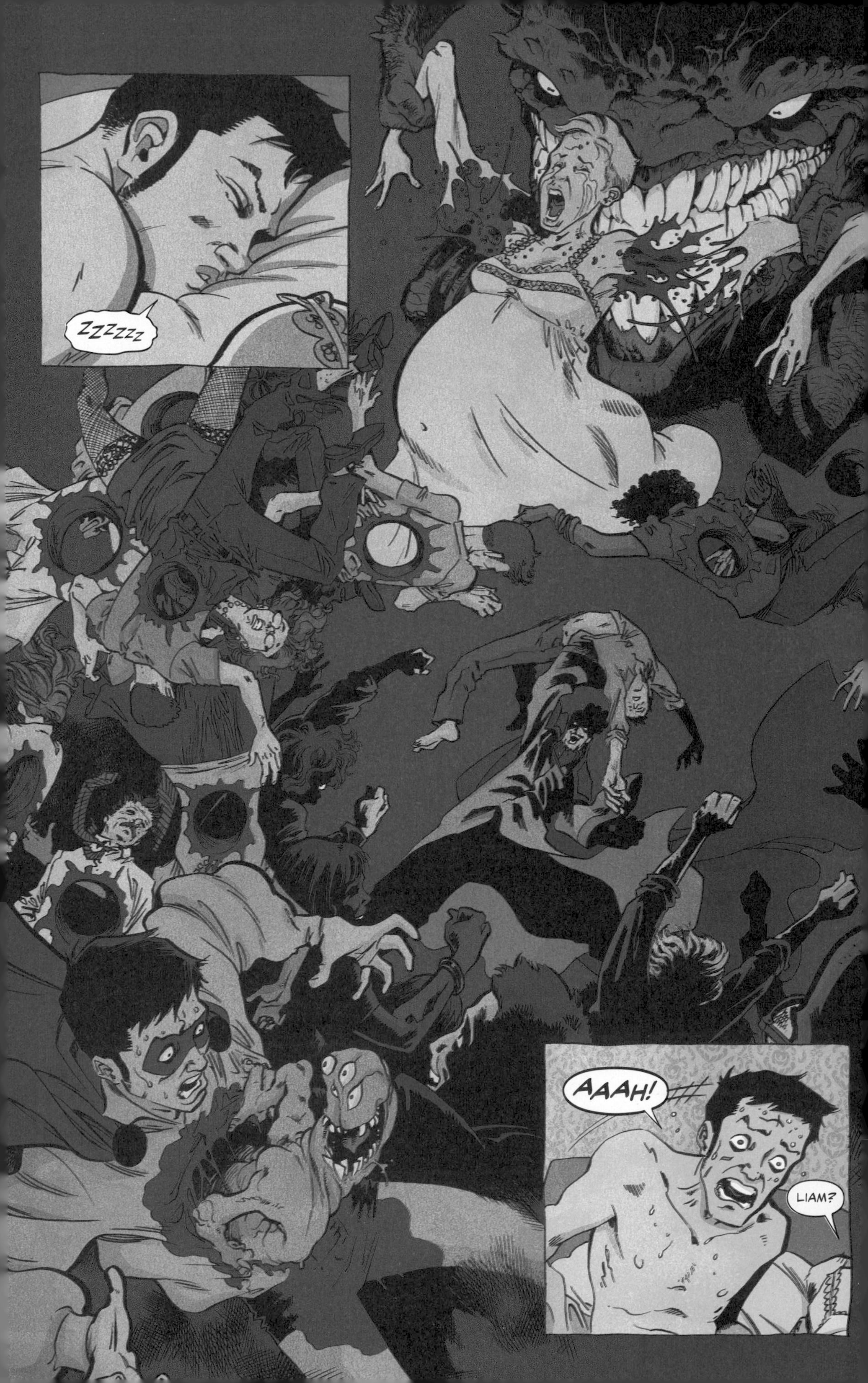
ZZZZZZ
AAAH!
LIAM?

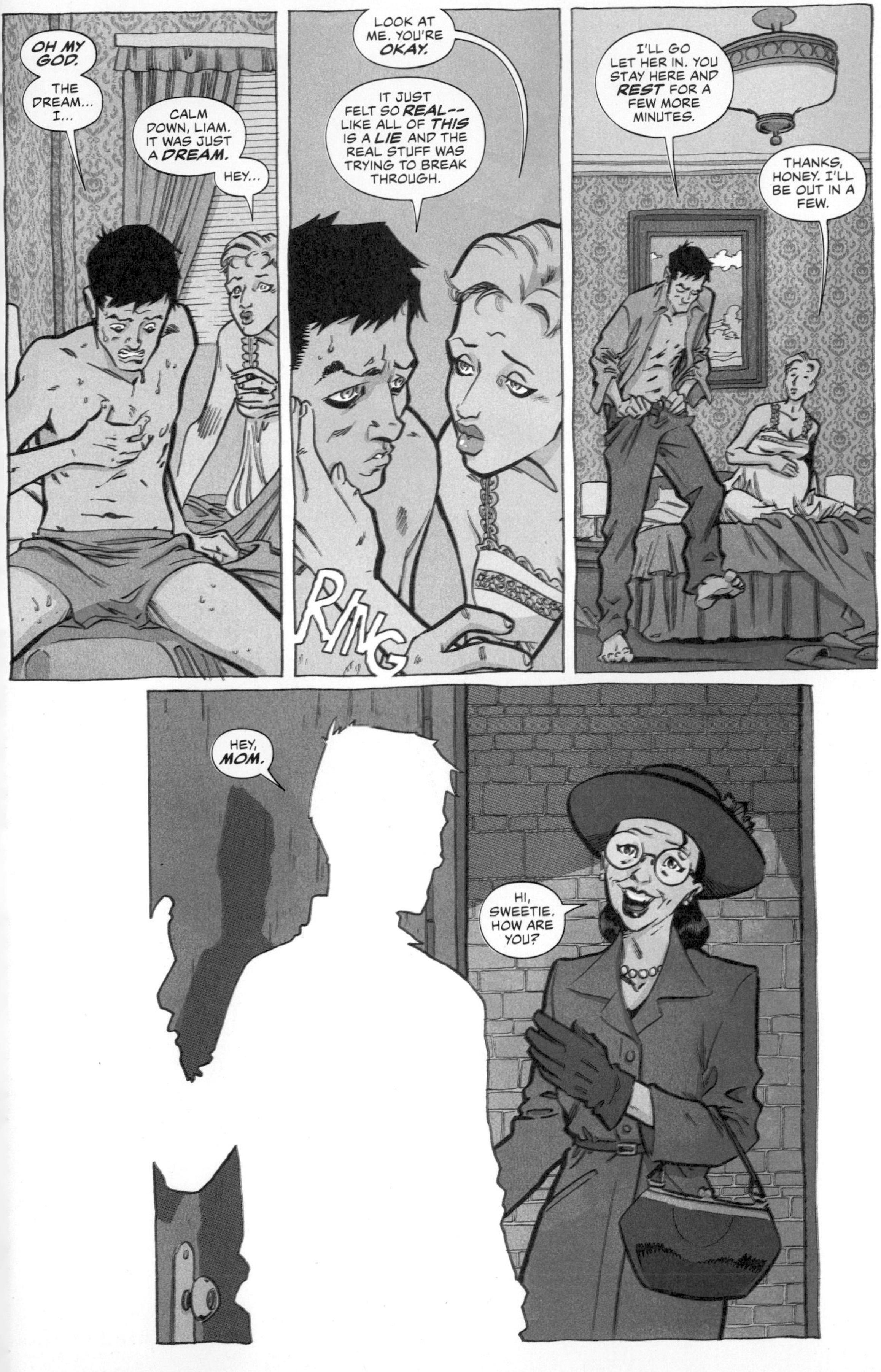
OH MY GOD.
THE DREAM... I...
CALM DOWN, LIAM. IT WAS JUST A DREAM.
HEY...
LOOK AT ME. YOU'RE OKAY.
IT JUST FELT SO REAL-- LIKE ALL OF THIS IS A LIE AND THE REAL STUFF WAS TRYING TO BREAK THROUGH.
RING
I'LL GO LET HER IN. YOU STAY HERE AND REST FOR A FEW MORE MINUTES.
THANKS, HONEY. I'LL BE OUT IN A FEW.
HEY, MOM.
HI, SWEETIE. HOW ARE YOU?

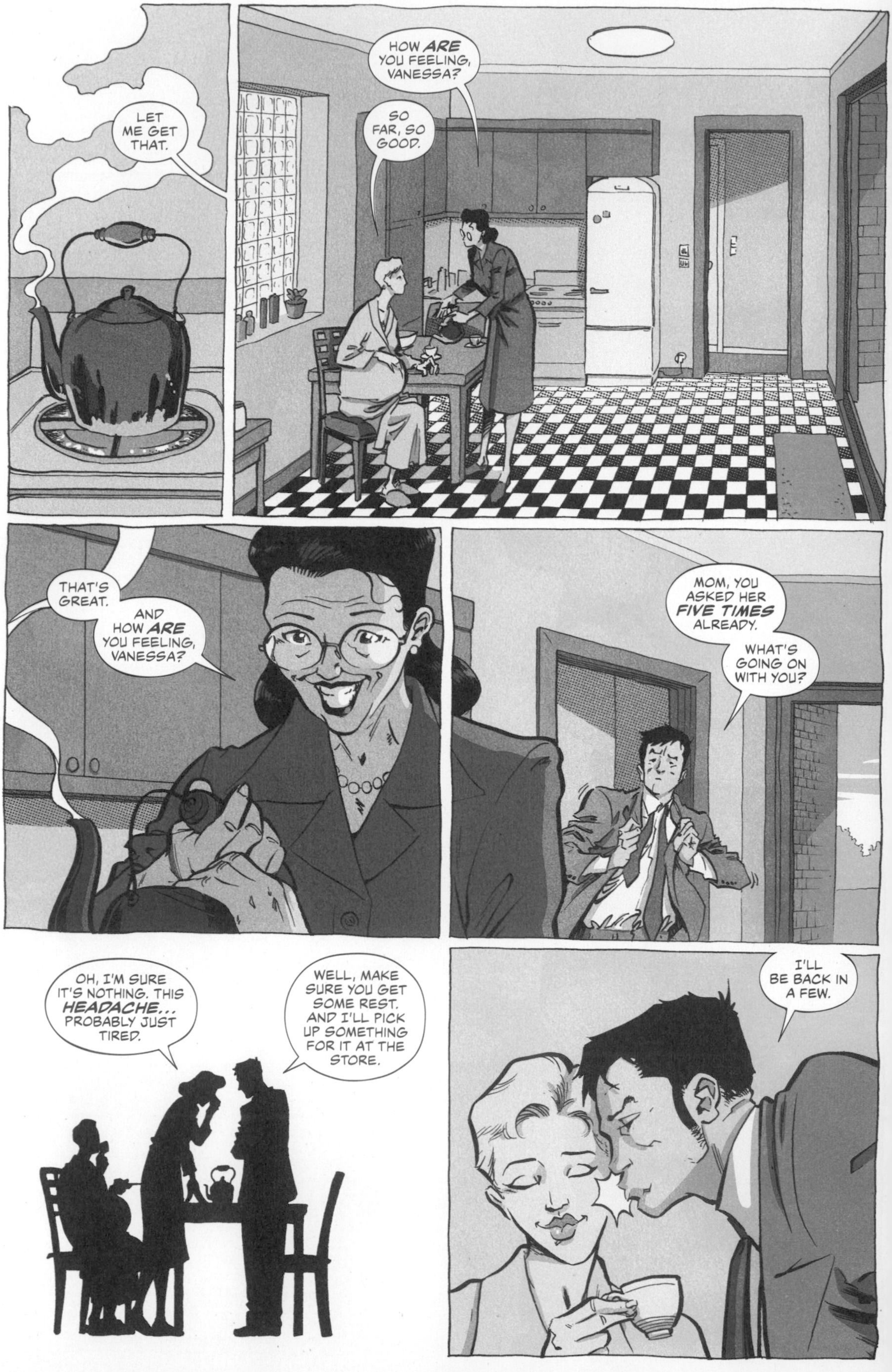
LET ME GET THAT.
HOW ARE YOU FEELING, VANESSA?
SO FAR, SO GOOD.
THAT'S GREAT.
AND HOW ARE YOU FEELING, VANESSA?
MOM, YOU ASKED HER FIVE TIMES ALREADY.
WHAT'S GOING ON WITH YOU?
OH, I'M SURE IT'S NOTHING. THIS HEADACHE... PROBABLY JUST TIRED.
WELL, MAKE SURE YOU GET SOME REST. AND I'LL PICK UP SOMETHING FOR IT AT THE STORE.
I'LL BE BACK IN A FEW.

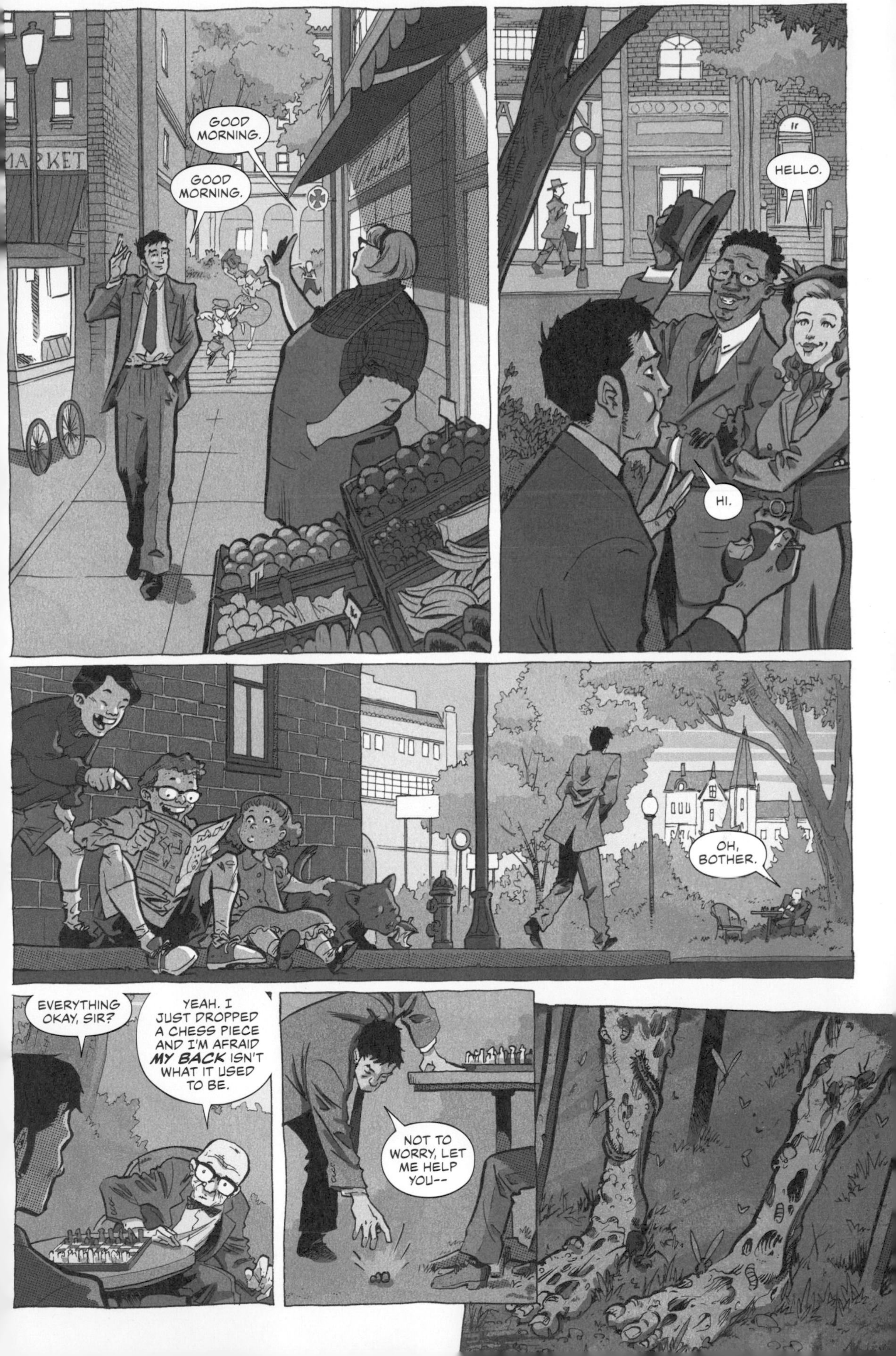
GOOD MORNING.
GOOD MORNING.
MARKET
HELLO.
HI.
OH, BOTHER.
EVERYTHING OKAY, SIR?
YEAH. I JUST DROPPED A CHESS PIECE AND I'M AFRAID **MY BACK** ISN'T WHAT IT USED TO BE.
NOT TO WORRY, LET ME HELP YOU--

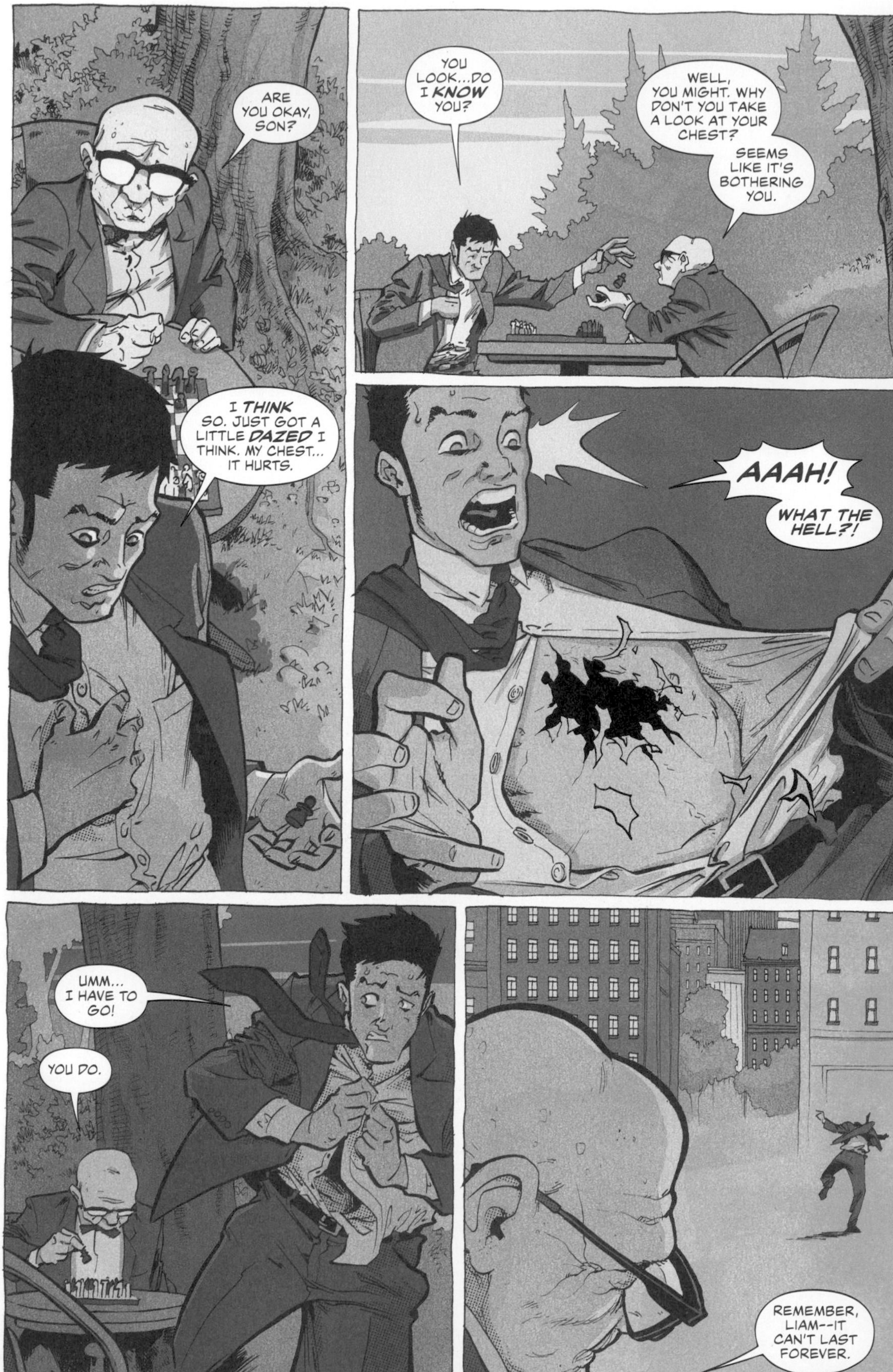
ARE YOU OKAY, SON?
YOU LOOK...DO I KNOW YOU?
WELL, YOU MIGHT. WHY DON'T YOU TAKE A LOOK AT YOUR CHEST?
SEEMS LIKE IT'S BOTHERING YOU.
I THINK SO. JUST GOT A LITTLE DAZED I THINK. MY CHEST... IT HURTS.
AAAH!
WHAT THE HELL?!
UMM... I HAVE TO GO!
YOU DO.
REMEMBER, LIAM--IT CAN'T LAST FOREVER.

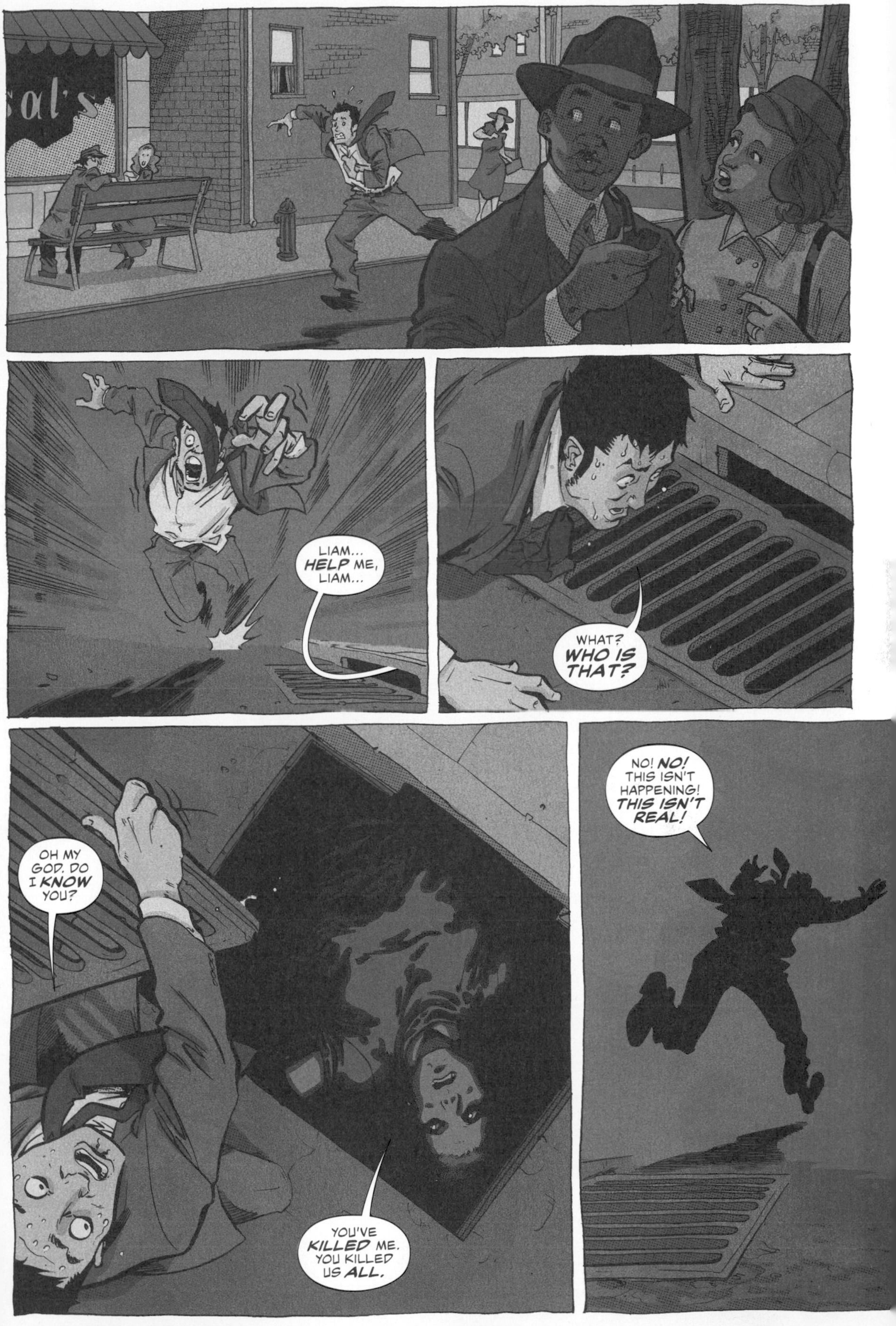
sal's
LIAM... HELP ME, LIAM...
WHAT? WHO IS THAT?
OH MY GOD. DO I KNOW YOU?
YOU'VE KILLED ME. YOU KILLED US ALL.
NO! NO! THIS ISN'T HAPPENING! THIS ISN'T REAL!

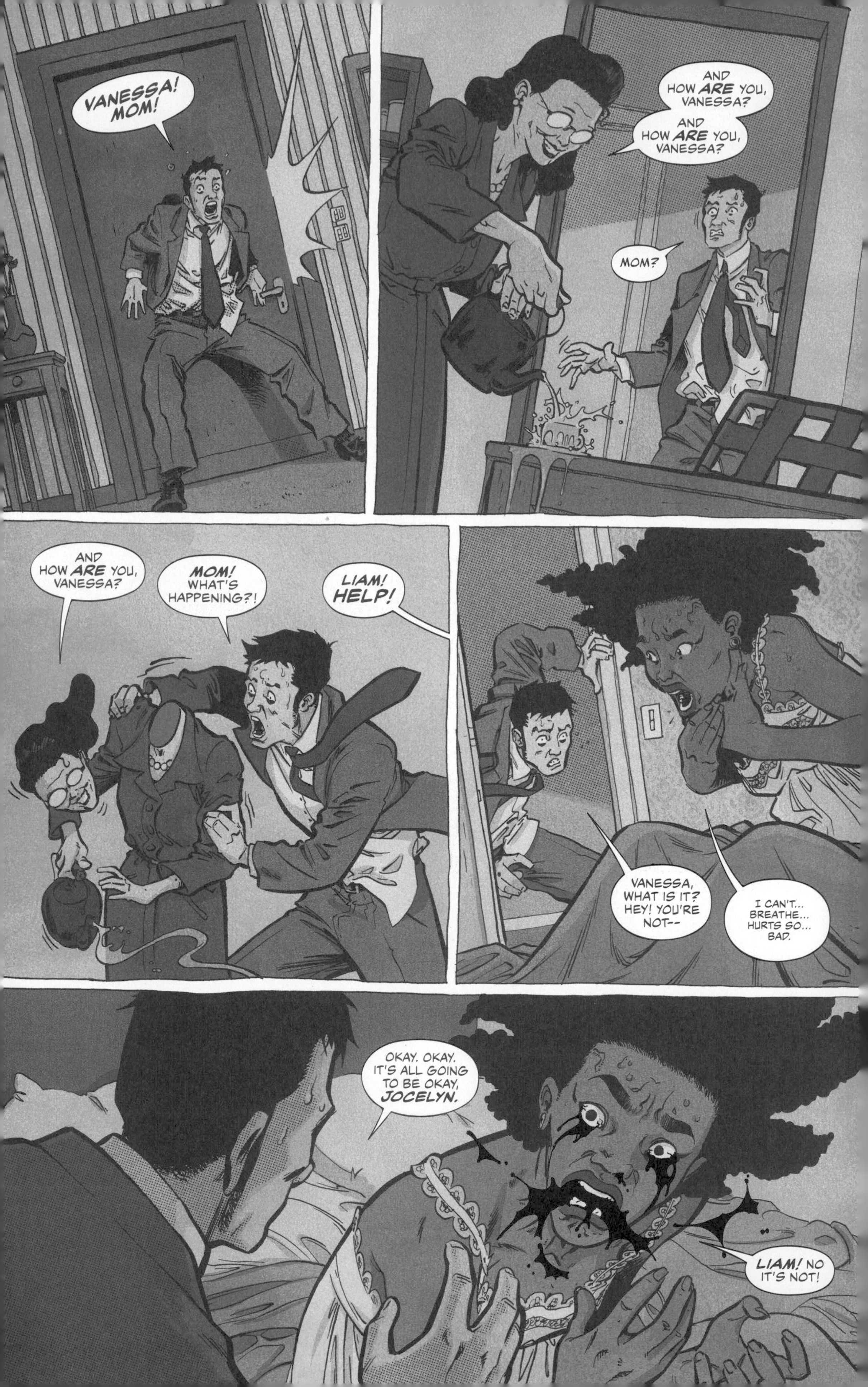
VANESSA! MOM!
AND HOW ARE YOU, VANESSA?
AND HOW ARE YOU, VANESSA?
MOM?
AND HOW ARE YOU, VANESSA?
MOM! WHAT'S HAPPENING?!
LIAM! HELP!
VANESSA, WHAT IS IT? HEY! YOU'RE NOT--
I CAN'T... BREATHE... HURTS SO... BAD.
OKAY. OKAY. IT'S ALL GOING TO BE OKAY, JOCELYN.
LIAM! NO IT'S NOT!

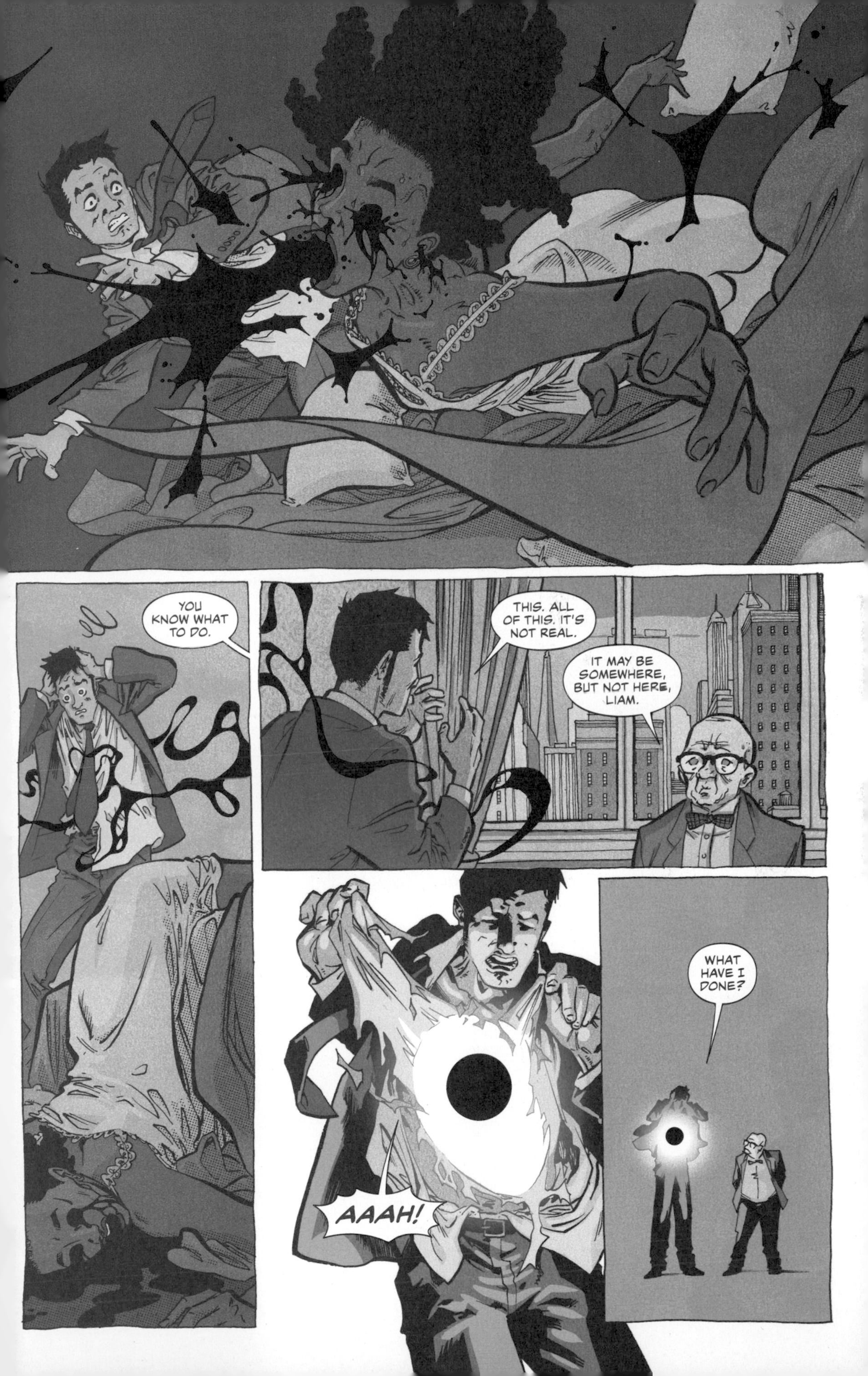
YOU KNOW WHAT TO DO.
THIS. ALL OF THIS. IT'S NOT REAL.
IT MAY BE SOMEWHERE, BUT NOT HERE, LIAM.
AAAH!
WHAT HAVE I DONE?

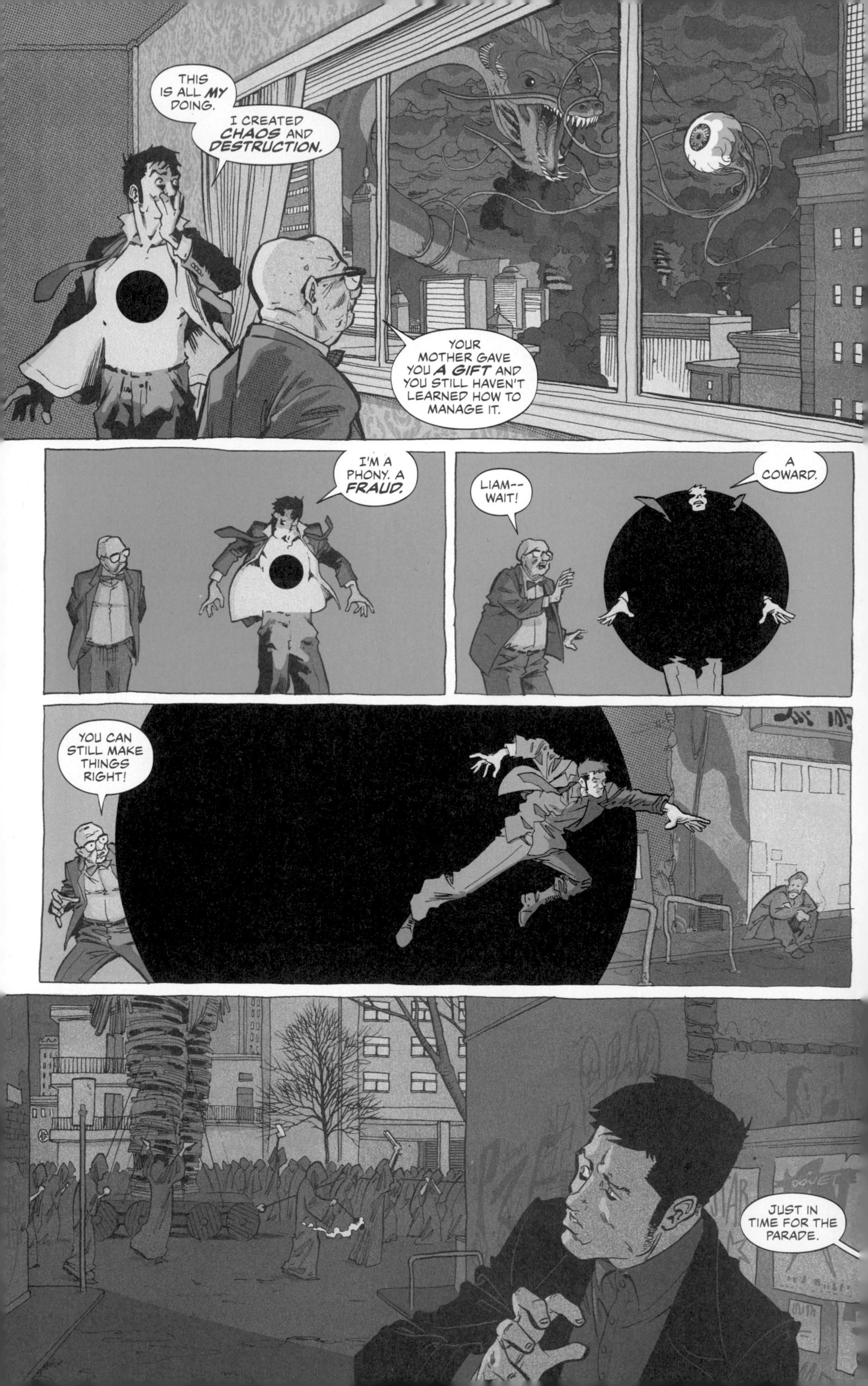
THIS IS ALL MY DOING.
I CREATED CHAOS AND DESTRUCTION.
YOUR MOTHER GAVE YOU A GIFT AND YOU STILL HAVEN'T LEARNED HOW TO MANAGE IT.
I'M A PHONY. A FRAUD.
LIAM-- WAIT!
A COWARD.
YOU CAN STILL MAKE THINGS RIGHT!
JUST IN TIME FOR THE PARADE.

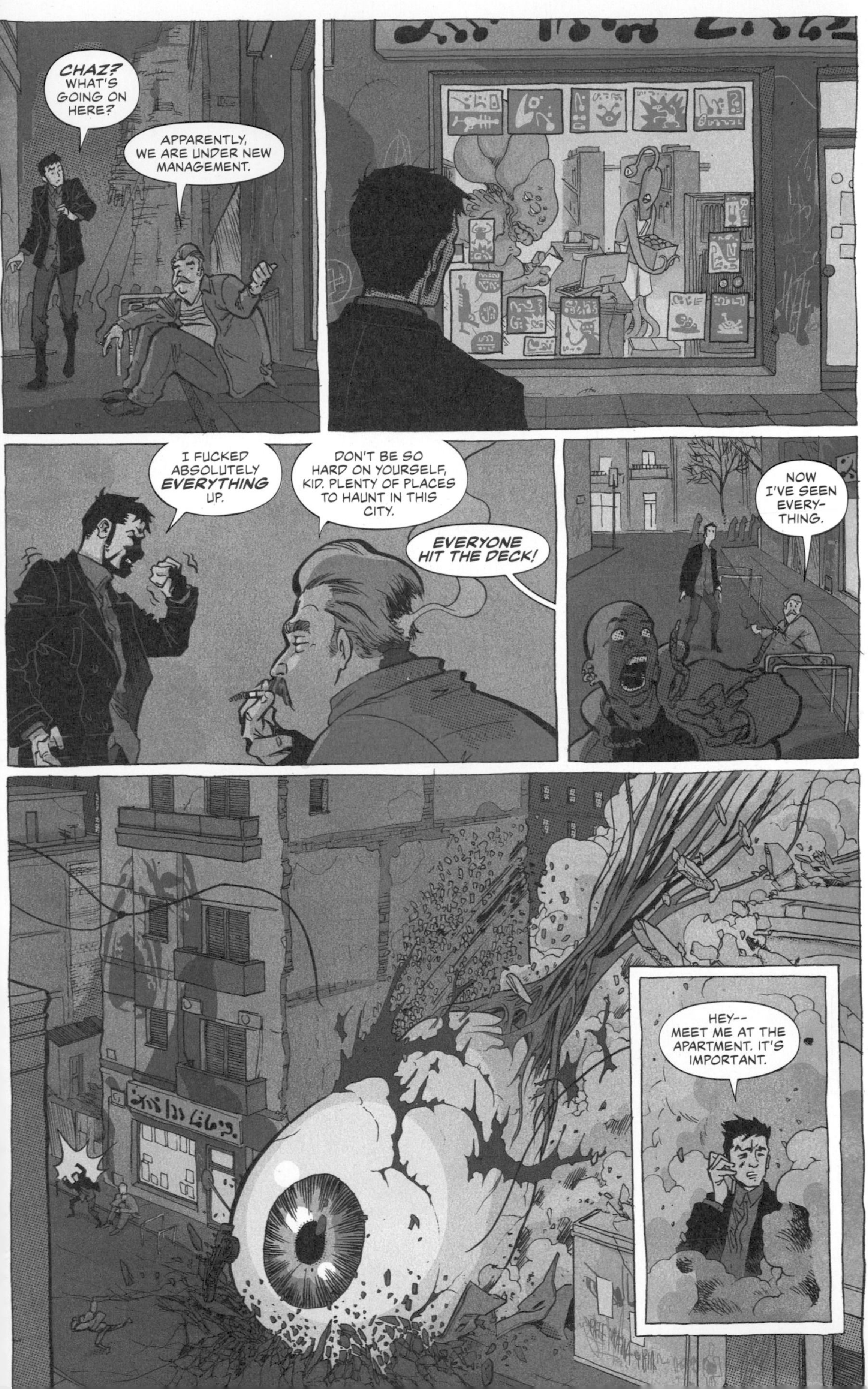
CHAZ? WHAT'S GOING ON HERE?
APPARENTLY, WE ARE UNDER NEW MANAGEMENT.
I FUCKED ABSOLUTELY EVERYTHING UP.
DON'T BE SO HARD ON YOURSELF, KID. PLENTY OF PLACES TO HAUNT IN THIS CITY.
EVERYONE HIT THE DECK!
NOW I'VE SEEN EVERY-THING.
HEY-- MEET ME AT THE APARTMENT. IT'S IMPORTANT.

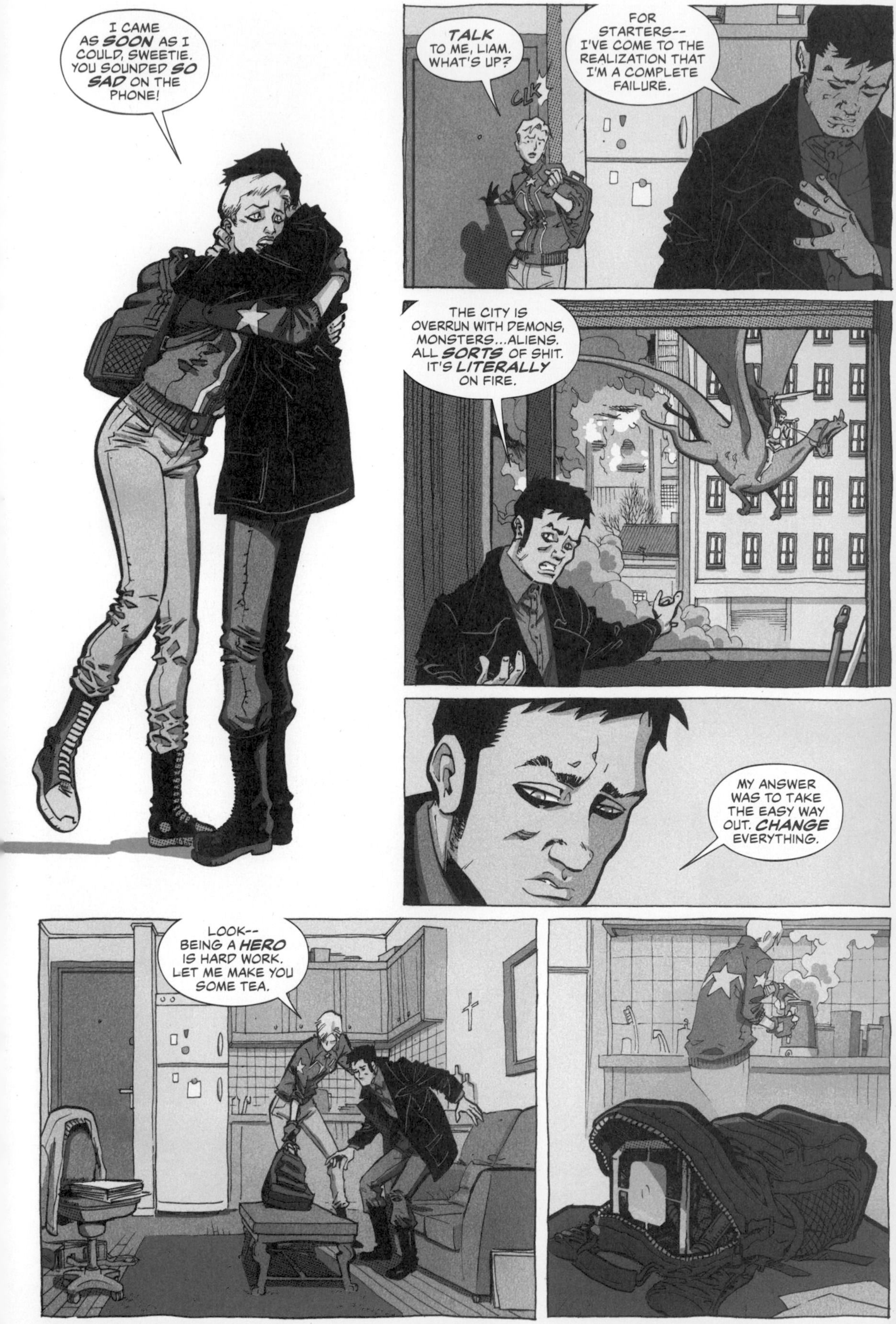
I CAME AS SOON AS I COULD, SWEETIE. YOU SOUNDED SO SAD ON THE PHONE!
TALK TO ME, LIAM. WHAT'S UP?
CLK
FOR STARTERS-- I'VE COME TO THE REALIZATION THAT I'M A COMPLETE FAILURE.
THE CITY IS OVERRUN WITH DEMONS, MONSTERS...ALIENS. ALL SORTS OF SHIT. IT'S LITERALLY ON FIRE.
MY ANSWER WAS TO TAKE THE EASY WAY OUT. CHANGE EVERYTHING.
LOOK-- BEING A HERO IS HARD WORK. LET ME MAKE YOU SOME TEA.

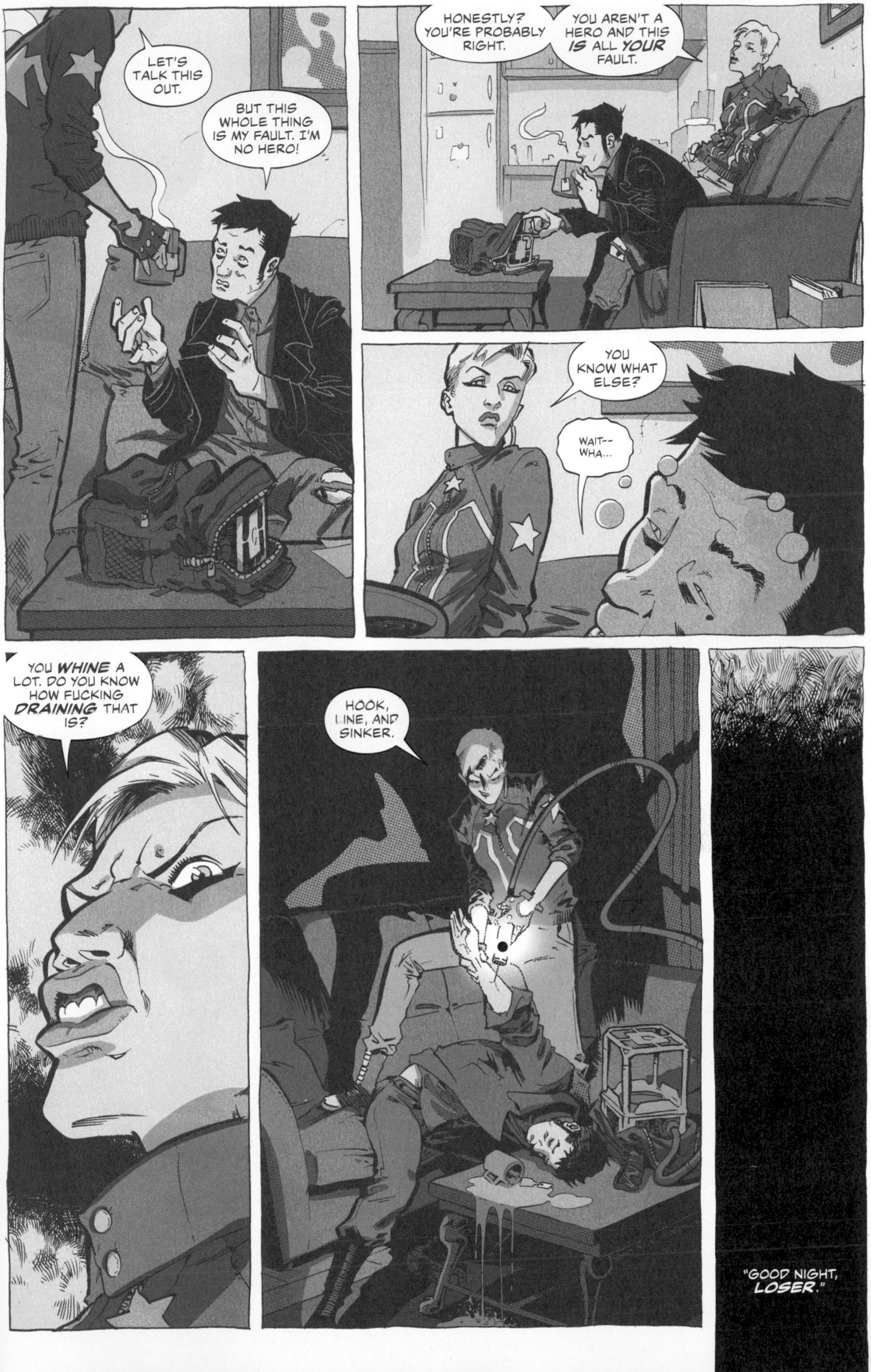
LET'S TALK THIS OUT.
BUT THIS WHOLE THING IS MY FAULT. I'M NO HERO!
HONESTLY? YOU'RE PROBABLY RIGHT.
YOU AREN'T A HERO AND THIS IS ALL YOUR FAULT.
YOU KNOW WHAT ELSE?
WAIT-- WHA...
YOU WHINE A LOT. DO YOU KNOW HOW FUCKING DRAINING THAT IS?
HOOK, LINE, AND SINKER.
"GOOD NIGHT, LOSER."

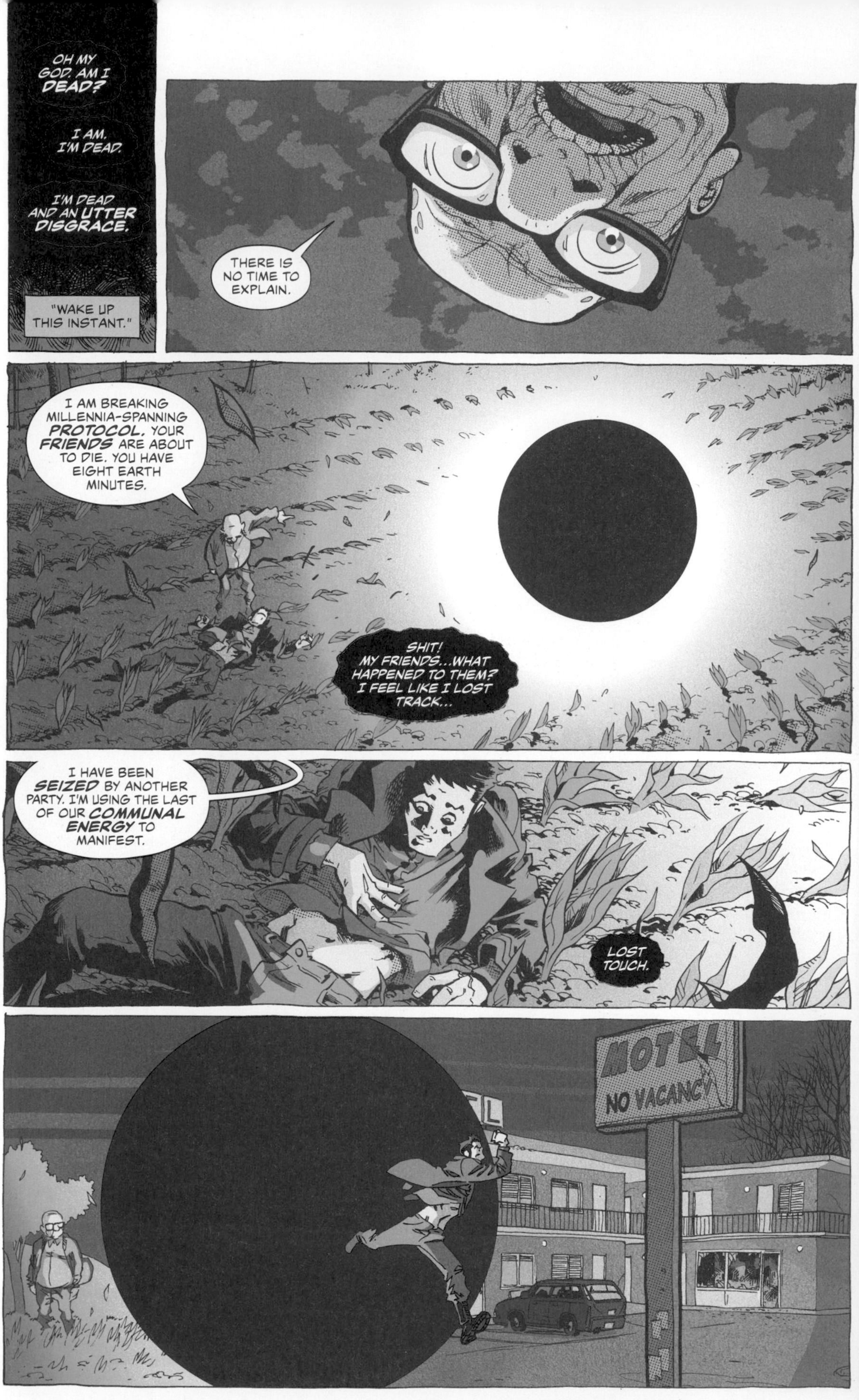
OH MY GOD, AM I DEAD?
I AM. I'M DEAD.
I'M DEAD AND AN UTTER DISGRACE.
"WAKE UP THIS INSTANT."
THERE IS NO TIME TO EXPLAIN.
I AM BREAKING MILLENNIA-SPANNING PROTOCOL. YOUR FRIENDS ARE ABOUT TO DIE. YOU HAVE EIGHT EARTH MINUTES.
SHIT! MY FRIENDS...WHAT HAPPENED TO THEM? I FEEL LIKE I LOST TRACK...
I HAVE BEEN SEIZED BY ANOTHER PARTY. I'M USING THE LAST OF OUR COMMUNAL ENERGY TO MANIFEST.
LOST TOUCH.
MOTEL
NO VACANCY

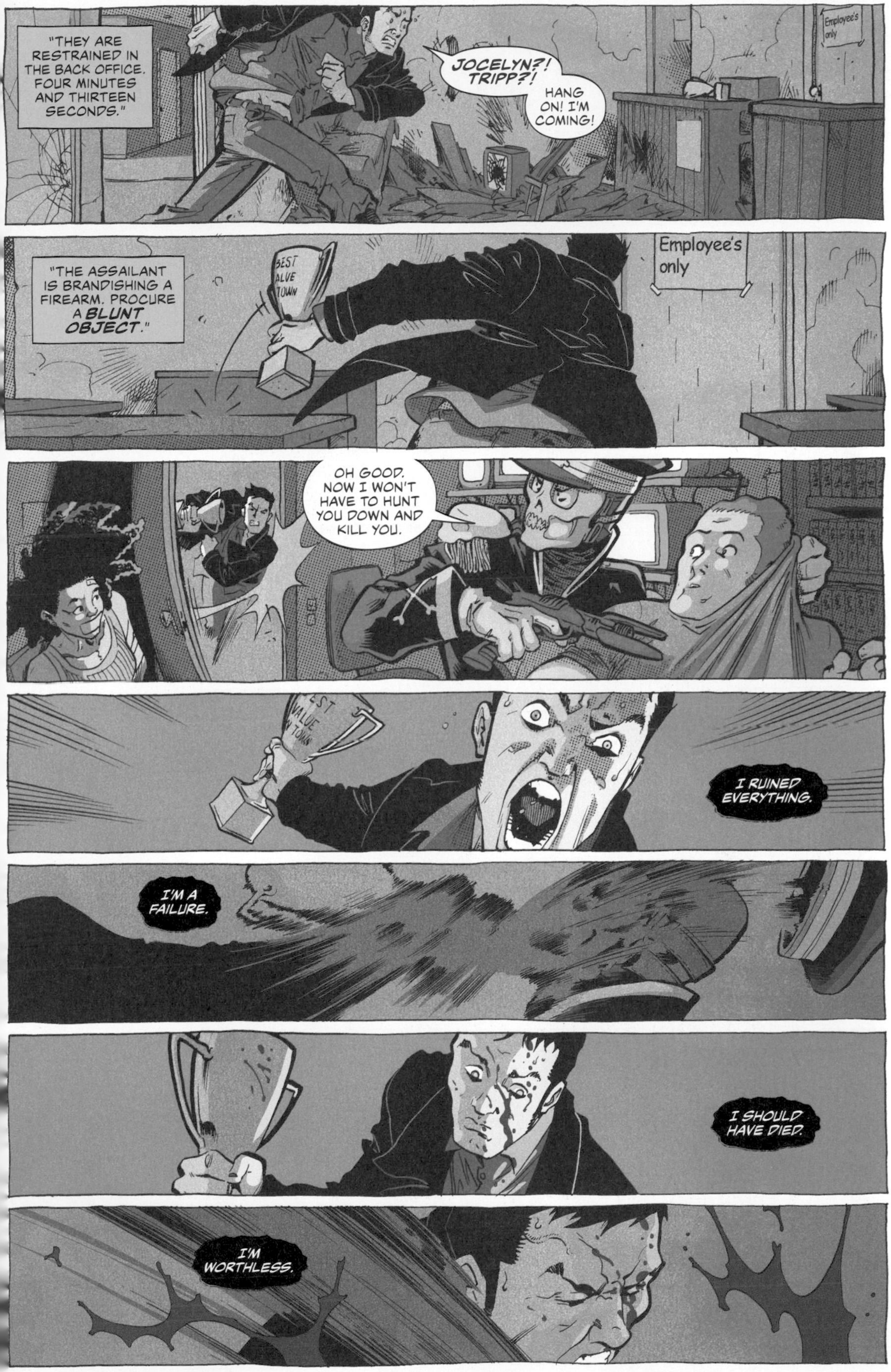
"THEY ARE RESTRAINED IN THE BACK OFFICE. FOUR MINUTES AND THIRTEEN SECONDS."
JOCELYN?! TRIPP?!
HANG ON! I'M COMING!
Employee's only
"THE ASSAILANT IS BRANDISHING A FIREARM. PROCURE A BLUNT OBJECT."
Employee's only
OH GOOD. NOW I WON'T HAVE TO HUNT YOU DOWN AND KILL YOU.
I RUINED EVERYTHING.
I'M A FAILURE.
I SHOULD HAVE DIED.
I'M WORTHLESS.

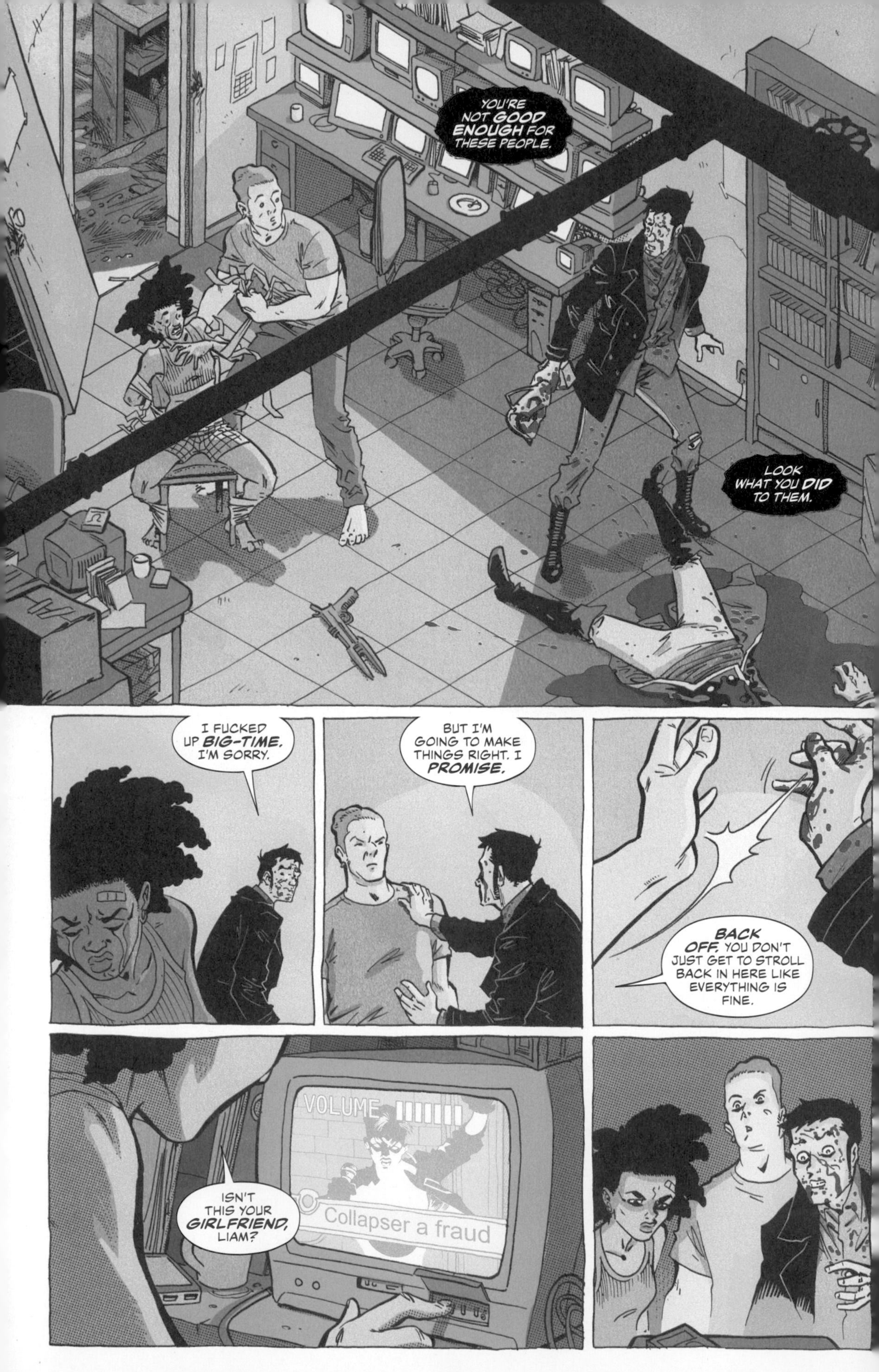
YOU'RE NOT GOOD ENOUGH FOR THESE PEOPLE.
LOOK WHAT YOU DID TO THEM.
I FUCKED UP BIG-TIME. I'M SORRY.
BUT I'M GOING TO MAKE THINGS RIGHT. I PROMISE.
BACK OFF. YOU DON'T JUST GET TO STROLL BACK IN HERE LIKE EVERYTHING IS FINE.
VOLUME
Collapser a fraud
ISN'T THIS YOUR GIRLFRIEND, LIAM?

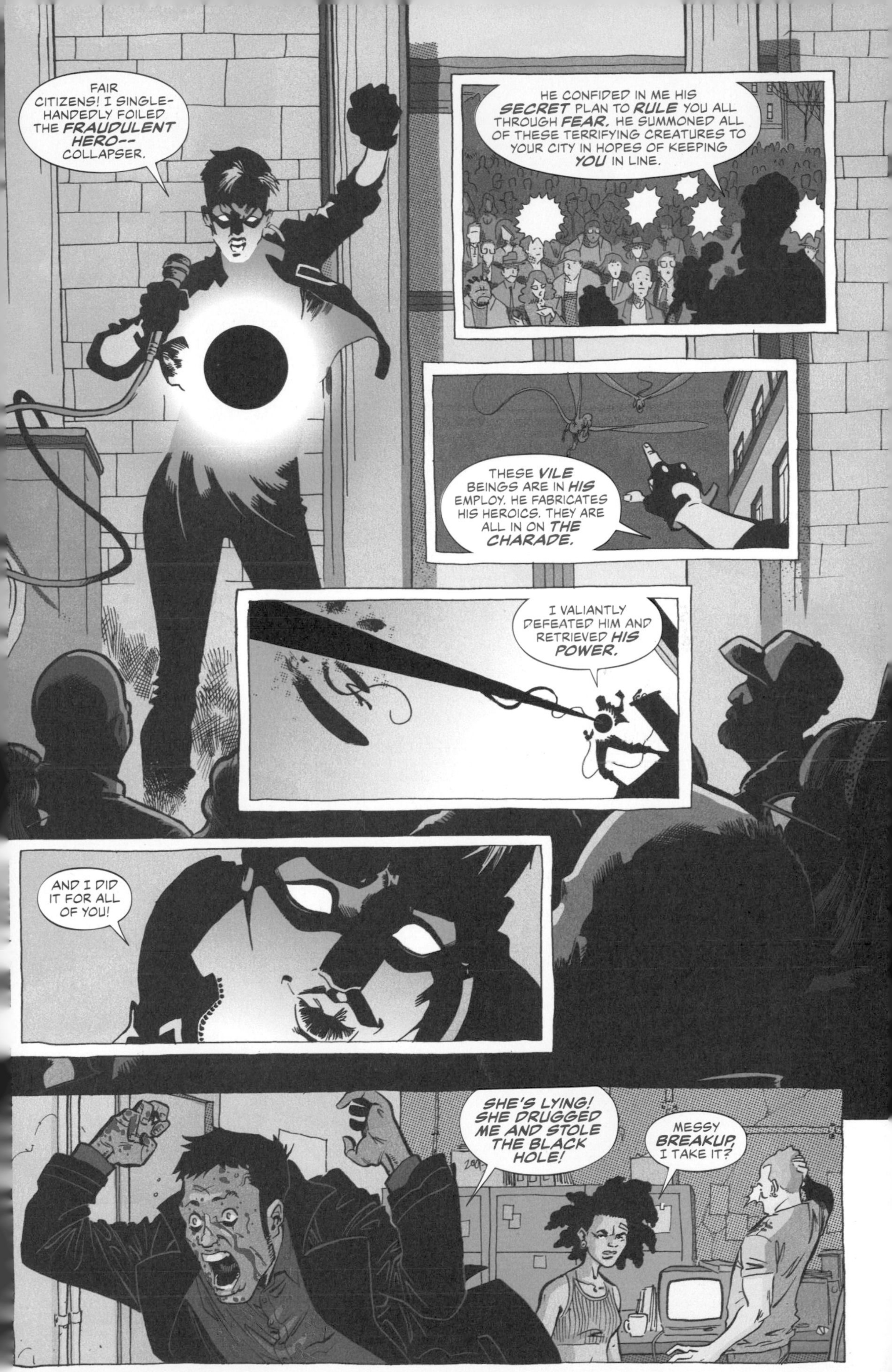
FAIR CITIZENS! I SINGLE-HANDEDLY FOILED THE FRAUDULENT HERO-- COLLAPSER.
HE CONFIDED IN ME HIS SECRET PLAN TO RULE YOU ALL THROUGH FEAR. HE SUMMONED ALL OF THESE TERRIFYING CREATURES TO YOUR CITY IN HOPES OF KEEPING YOU IN LINE.
THESE VILE BEINGS ARE IN HIS EMPLOY. HE FABRICATES HIS HEROICS. THEY ARE ALL IN ON THE CHARADE.
I VALIANTLY DEFEATED HIM AND RETRIEVED HIS POWER.
AND I DID IT FOR ALL OF YOU!
SHE'S LYING! SHE DRUGGED ME AND STOLE THE BLACK HOLE!
MESSY BREAKUP, I TAKE IT?

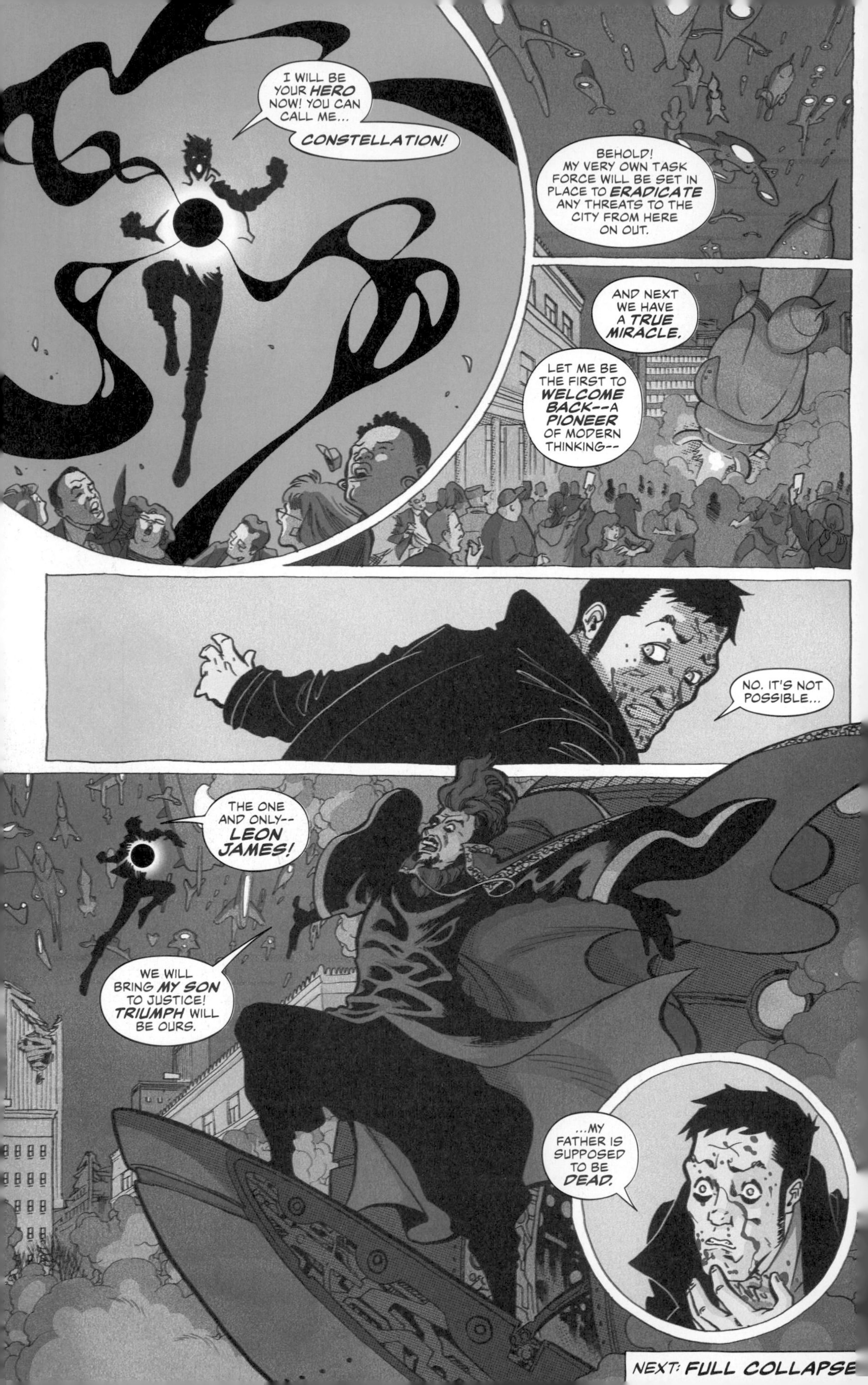
I WILL BE YOUR HERO NOW! YOU CAN CALL ME...
CONSTELLATION!
BEHOLD! MY VERY OWN TASK FORCE WILL BE SET IN PLACE TO ERADICATE ANY THREATS TO THE CITY FROM HERE ON OUT.
AND NEXT WE HAVE A TRUE MIRACLE.
LET ME BE THE FIRST TO WELCOME BACK--A PIONEER OF MODERN THINKING--
NO. IT'S NOT POSSIBLE...
THE ONE AND ONLY-- LEON JAMES!
WE WILL BRING MY SON TO JUSTICE! TRIUMPH WILL BE OURS.
...MY FATHER IS SUPPOSED TO BE DEAD.
NEXT: FULL COLLAPSE

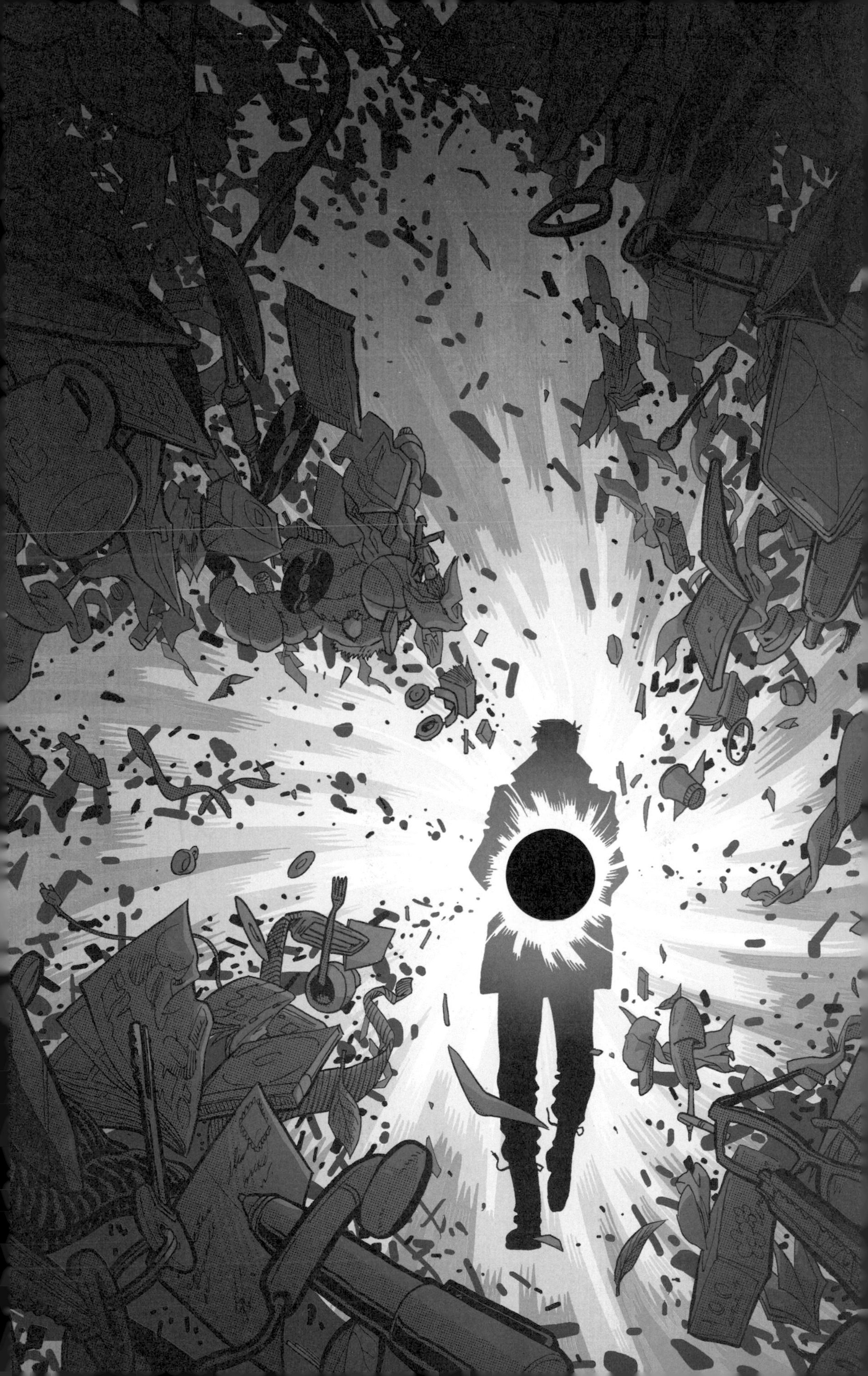

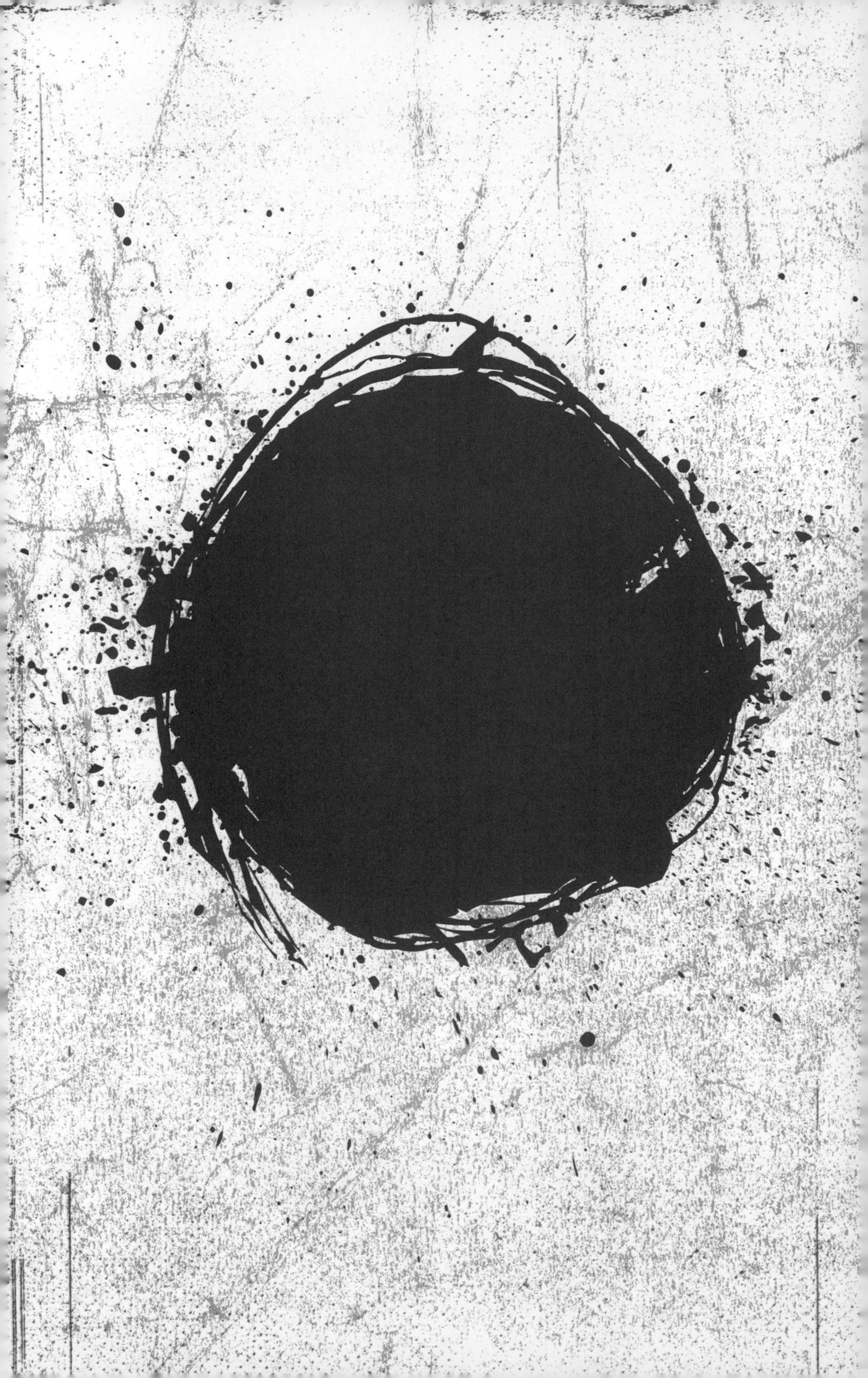

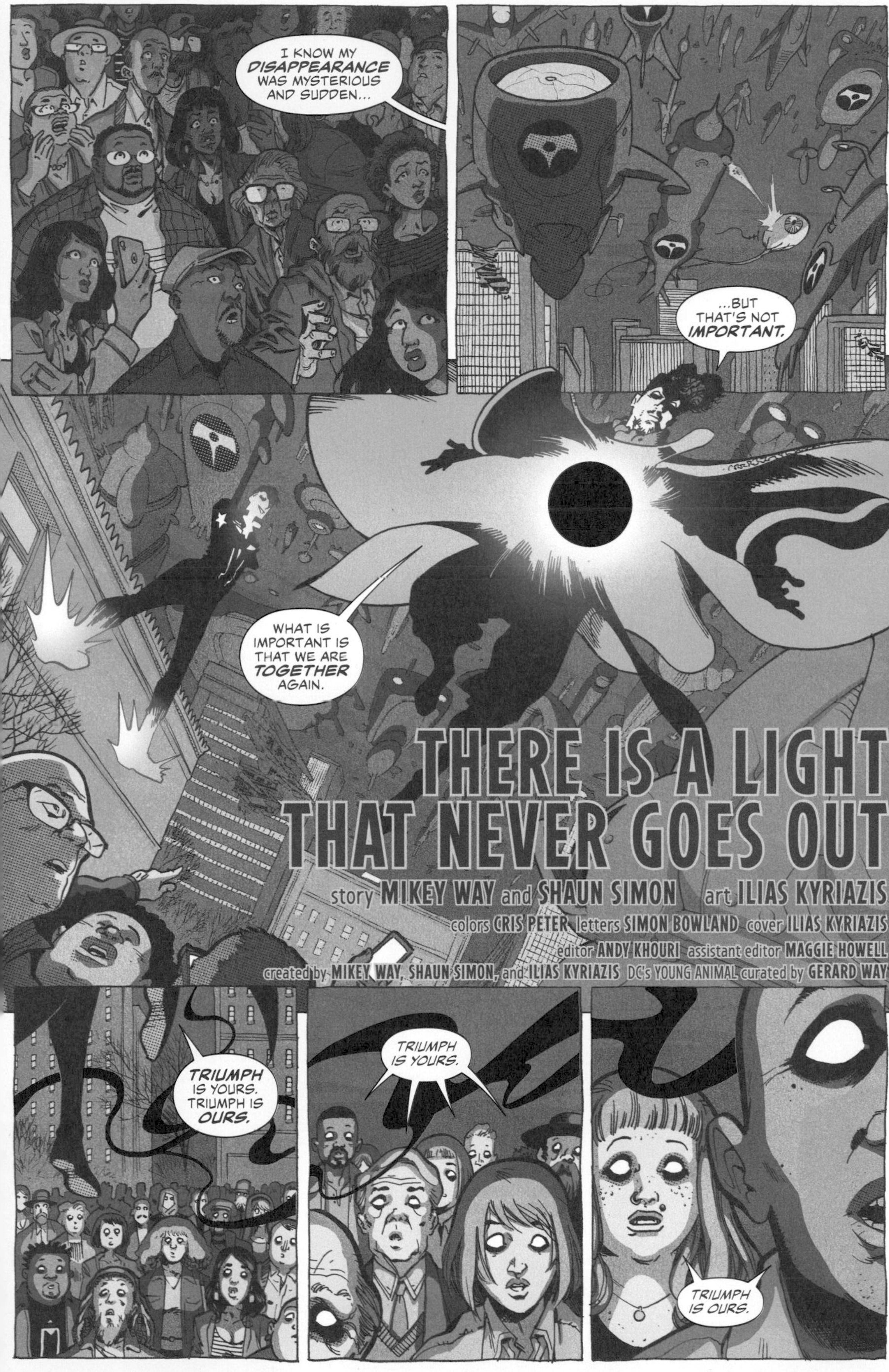

I KNOW MY DISAPPEARANCE WAS MYSTERIOUS AND SUDDEN...
...BUT THAT'S NOT IMPORTANT.
WHAT IS IMPORTANT IS THAT WE ARE TOGETHER AGAIN.
THERE IS A LIGHT THAT NEVER GOES OUT
story MIKEY WAY and SHAUN SIMON art ILIAS KYRIAZIS
colors CRIS PETER letters SIMON BOWLAND cover ILIAS KYRIAZIS
editor ANDY KHOURI assistant editor MAGGIE HOWELL
created by MIKEY WAY, SHAUN SIMON, and ILIAS KYRIAZIS DC's YOUNG ANIMAL curated by GERARD WAY
TRIUMPH IS YOURS. TRIUMPH IS OURS.
TRIUMPH IS YOURS.
TRIUMPH IS OURS.

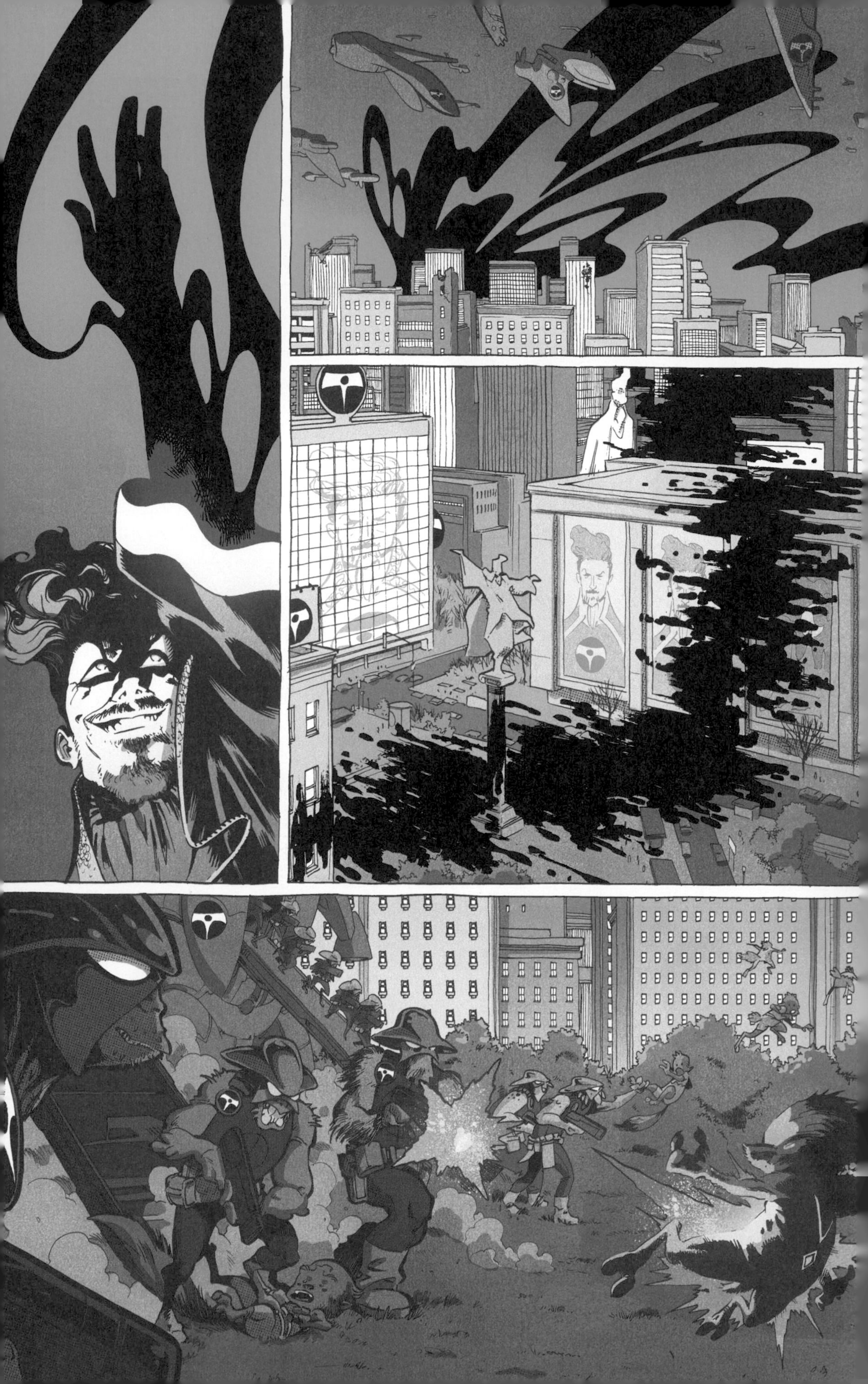

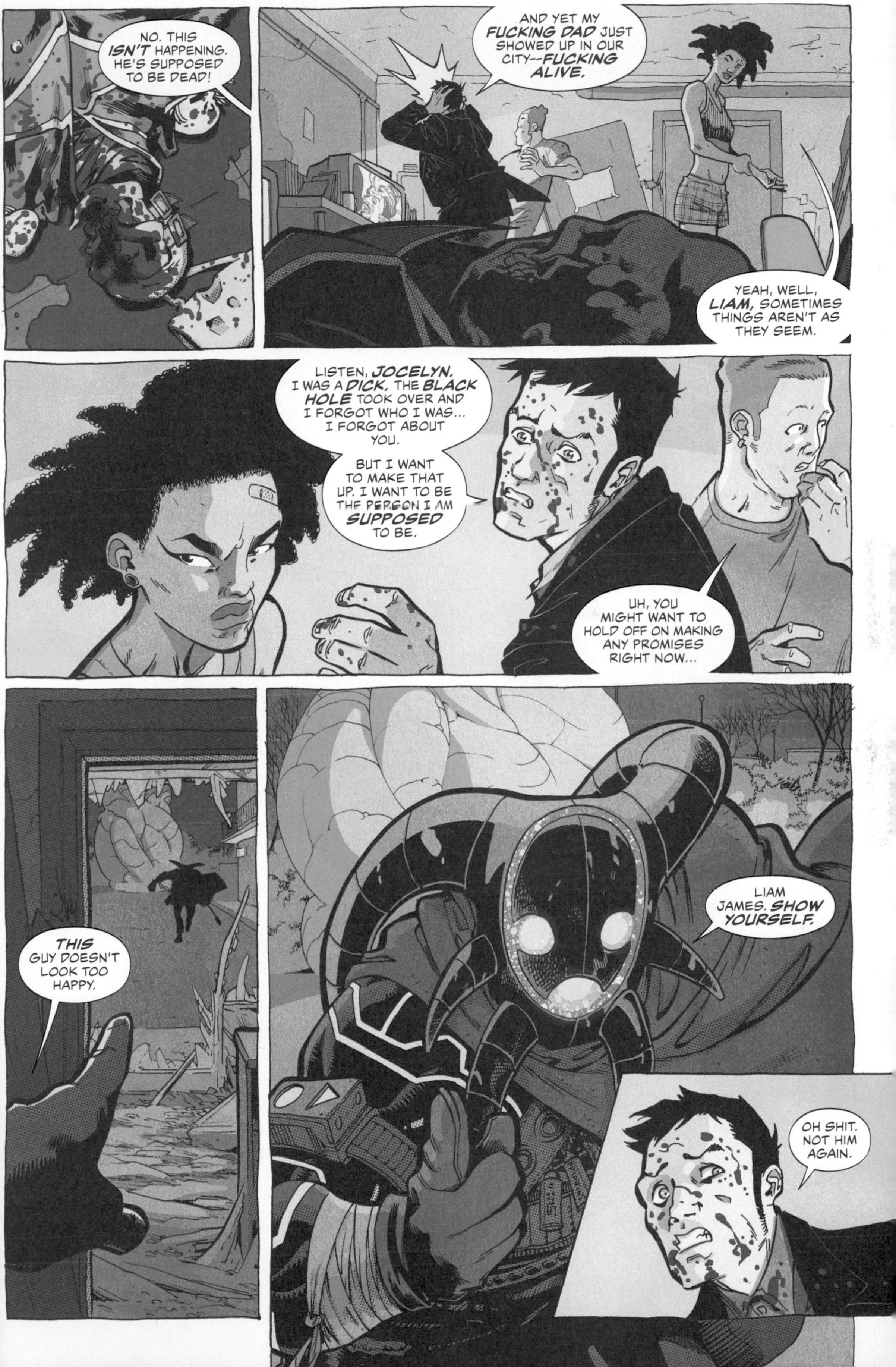
NO. THIS ISN'T HAPPENING. HE'S SUPPOSED TO BE DEAD!
AND YET MY FUCKING DAD JUST SHOWED UP IN OUR CITY--FUCKING ALIVE.
YEAH, WELL, LIAM, SOMETIMES THINGS AREN'T AS THEY SEEM.
LISTEN, JOCELYN. I WAS A DICK. THE BLACK HOLE TOOK OVER AND I FORGOT WHO I WAS... I FORGOT ABOUT YOU.
BUT I WANT TO MAKE THAT UP. I WANT TO BE THE PERSON I AM SUPPOSED TO BE.
UH, YOU MIGHT WANT TO HOLD OFF ON MAKING ANY PROMISES RIGHT NOW...
THIS GUY DOESN'T LOOK TOO HAPPY.
LIAM JAMES. SHOW YOURSELF.
OH SHIT. NOT HIM AGAIN.

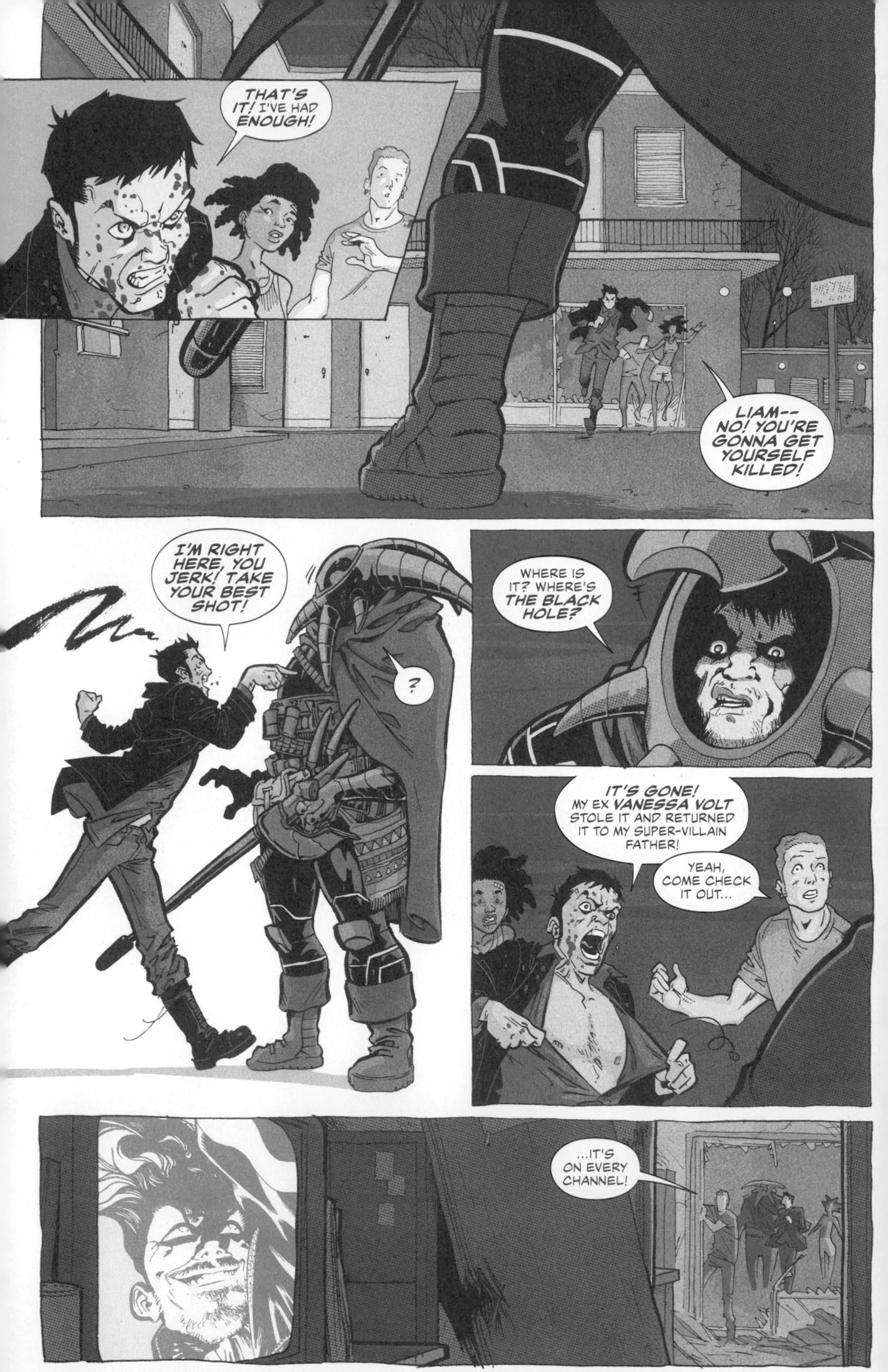
THAT'S IT! I'VE HAD ENOUGH!
LIAM-- NO! YOU'RE GONNA GET YOURSELF KILLED!
I'M RIGHT HERE, YOU JERK! TAKE YOUR BEST SHOT!
?
WHERE IS IT? WHERE'S THE BLACK HOLE?
IT'S GONE! MY EX VANESSA VOLT STOLE IT AND RETURNED IT TO MY SUPER-VILLAIN FATHER!
YEAH, COME CHECK IT OUT...
...IT'S ON EVERY CHANNEL!

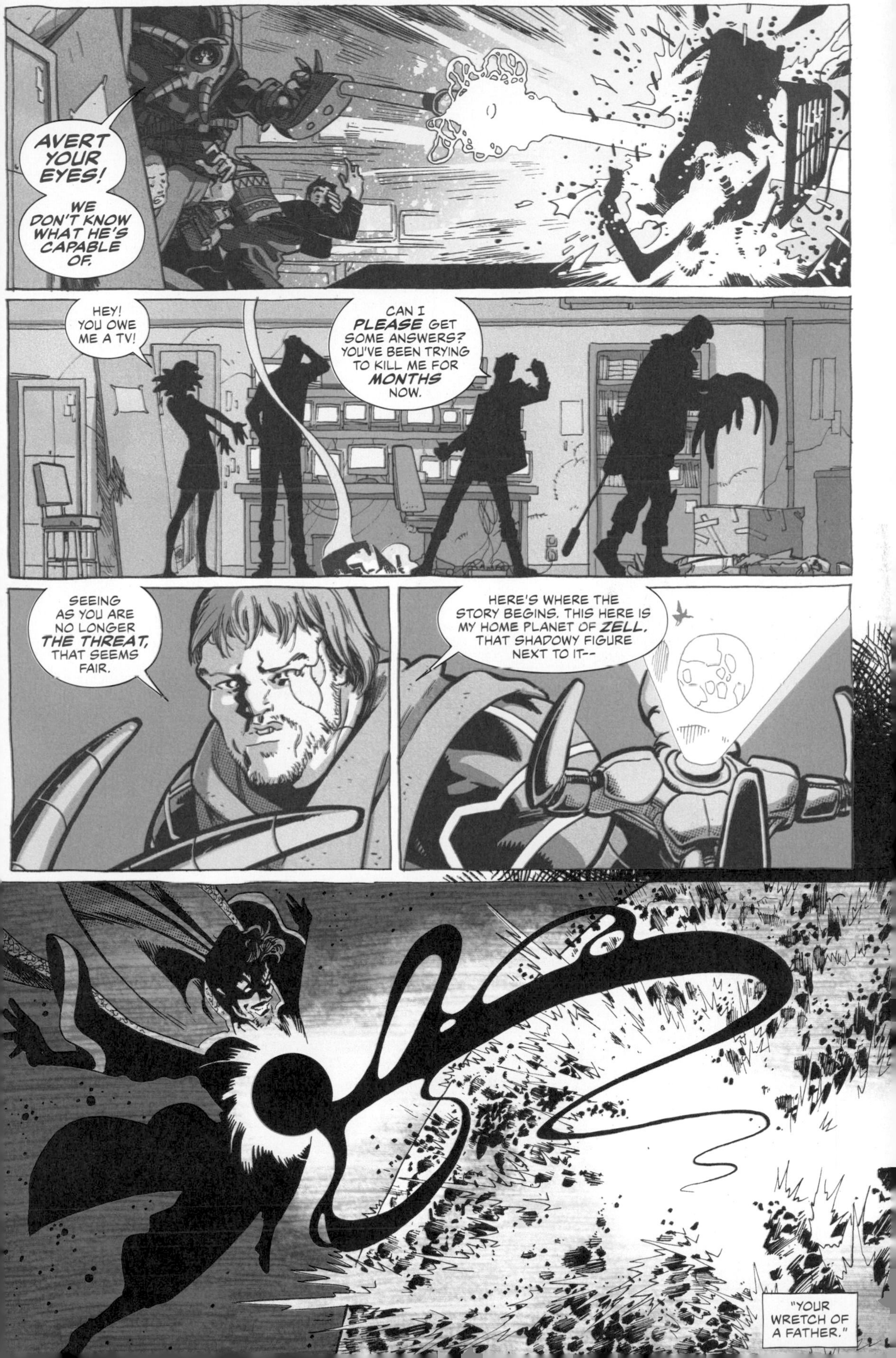

AVERT YOUR EYES!
WE DON'T KNOW WHAT HE'S CAPABLE OF.
HEY! YOU OWE ME A TV!
CAN I PLEASE GET SOME ANSWERS? YOU'VE BEEN TRYING TO KILL ME FOR MONTHS NOW.
SEEING AS YOU ARE NO LONGER THE THREAT, THAT SEEMS FAIR.
HERE'S WHERE THE STORY BEGINS. THIS HERE IS MY HOME PLANET OF ZELL. THAT SHADOWY FIGURE NEXT TO IT--
"YOUR WRETCH OF A FATHER."

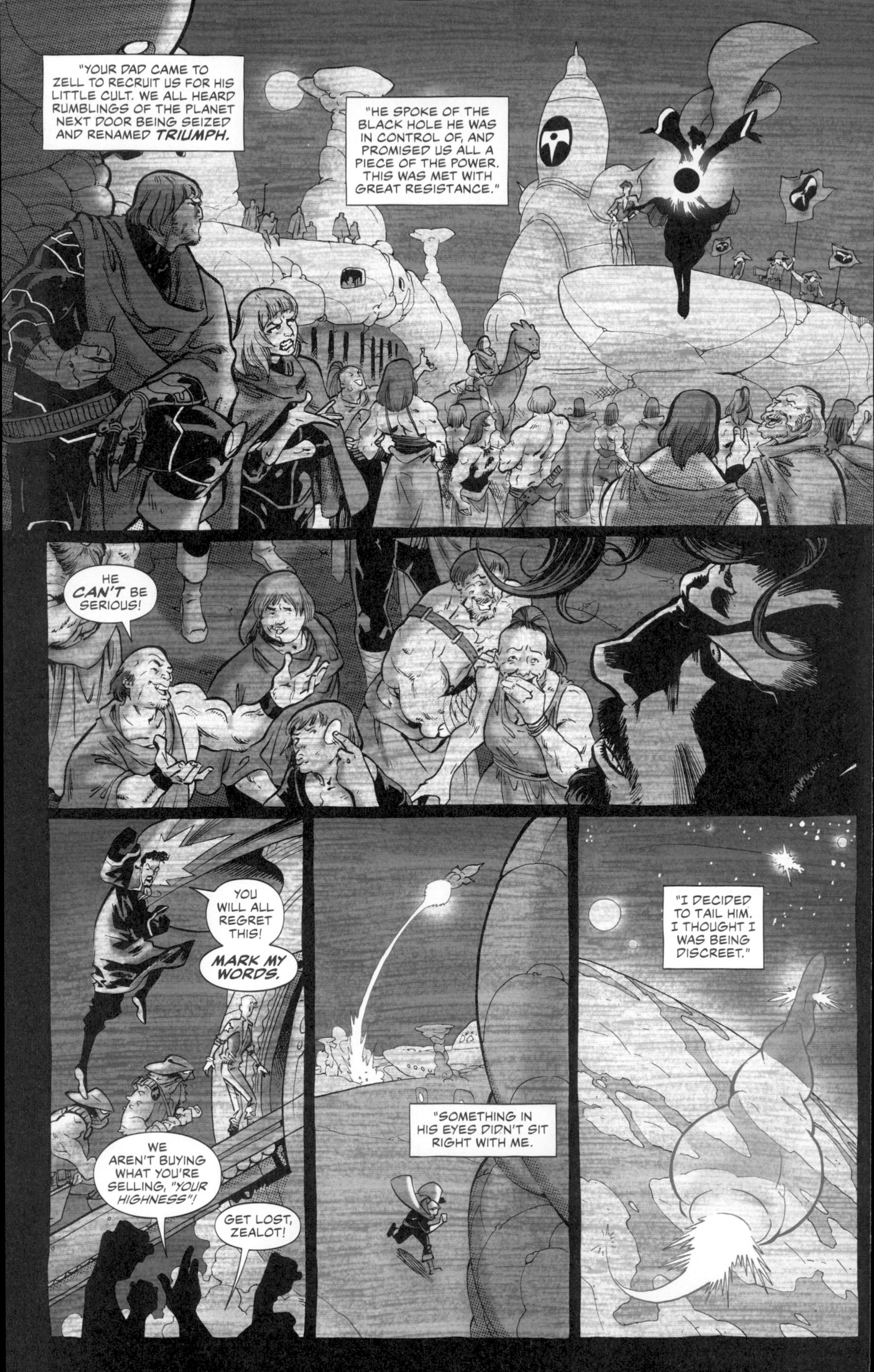
"YOUR DAD CAME TO ZELL TO RECRUIT US FOR HIS LITTLE CULT. WE ALL HEARD RUMBLINGS OF THE PLANET NEXT DOOR BEING SEIZED AND RENAMED TRIUMPH.
"HE SPOKE OF THE BLACK HOLE HE WAS IN CONTROL OF, AND PROMISED US ALL A PIECE OF THE POWER. THIS WAS MET WITH GREAT RESISTANCE."
HE CAN'T BE SERIOUS!
YOU WILL ALL REGRET THIS!
MARK MY WORDS.
WE AREN'T BUYING WHAT YOU'RE SELLING, "YOUR HIGHNESS"!
GET LOST, ZEALOT!
"SOMETHING IN HIS EYES DIDN'T SIT RIGHT WITH ME.
"I DECIDED TO TAIL HIM. I THOUGHT I WAS BEING DISCREET."

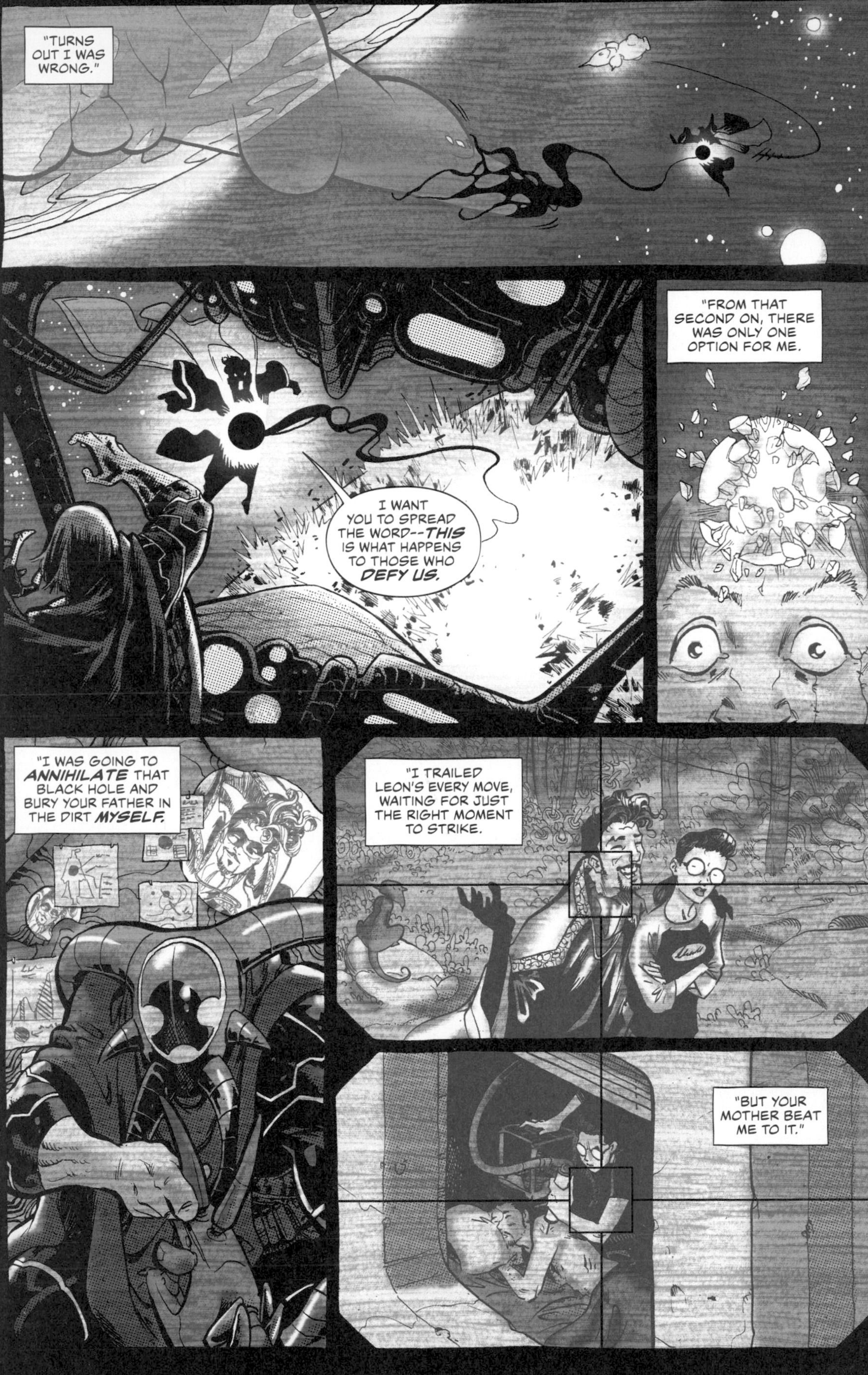
"TURNS OUT I WAS WRONG."
"FROM THAT SECOND ON, THERE WAS ONLY ONE OPTION FOR ME.
I WANT YOU TO SPREAD THE WORD--THIS IS WHAT HAPPENS TO THOSE WHO DEFY US.
"I WAS GOING TO ANNIHILATE THAT BLACK HOLE AND BURY YOUR FATHER IN THE DIRT MYSELF.
"I TRAILED LEON'S EVERY MOVE, WAITING FOR JUST THE RIGHT MOMENT TO STRIKE.
"BUT YOUR MOTHER BEAT ME TO IT."

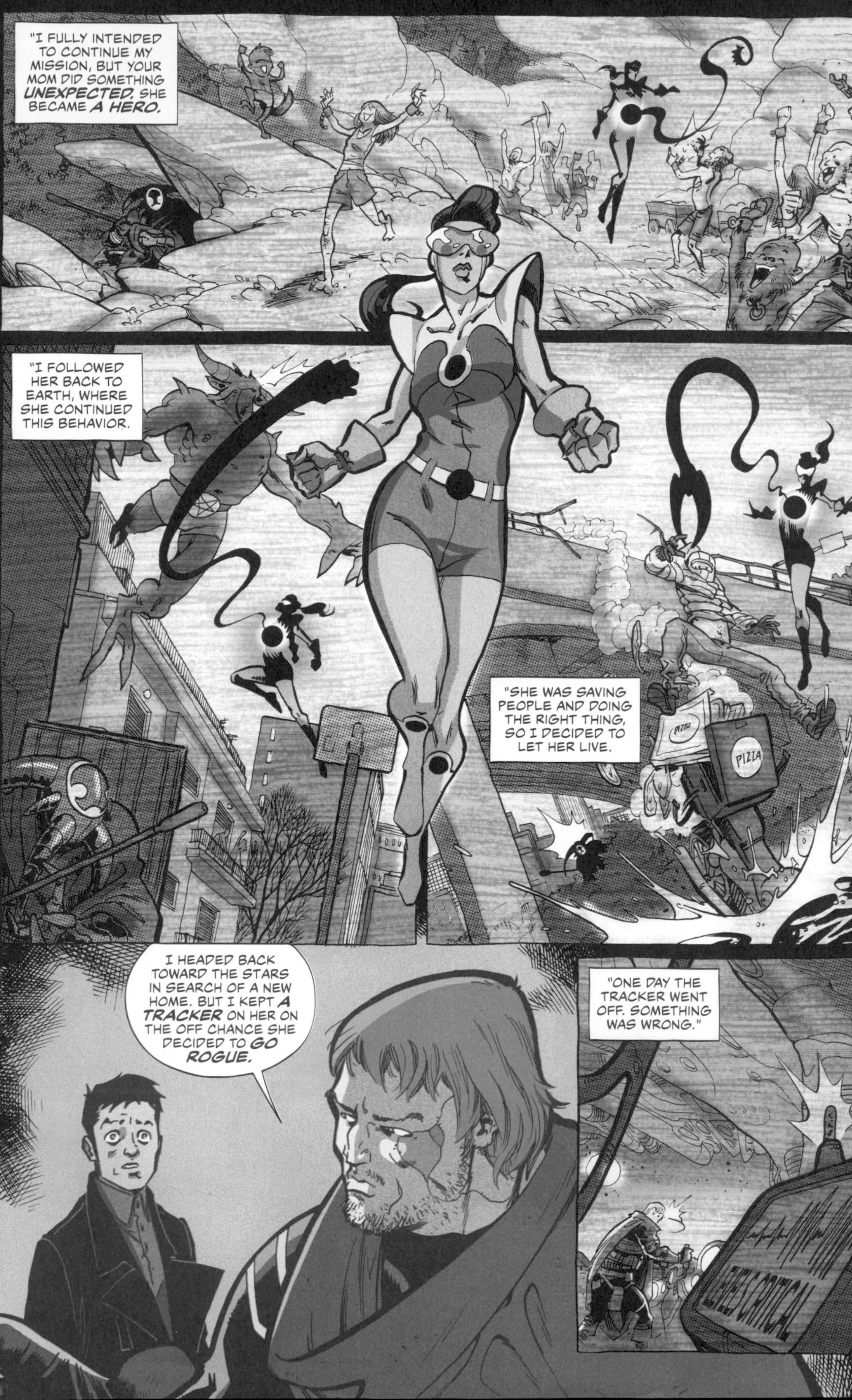
"I FULLY INTENDED TO CONTINUE MY MISSION, BUT YOUR MOM DID SOMETHING UNEXPECTED. SHE BECAME A HERO.
"I FOLLOWED HER BACK TO EARTH, WHERE SHE CONTINUED THIS BEHAVIOR.
"SHE WAS SAVING PEOPLE AND DOING THE RIGHT THING, SO I DECIDED TO LET HER LIVE.
PIZZA
PIZZA
I HEADED BACK TOWARD THE STARS IN SEARCH OF A NEW HOME. BUT I KEPT A TRACKER ON HER ON THE OFF CHANCE SHE DECIDED TO GO ROGUE.
"ONE DAY THE TRACKER WENT OFF. SOMETHING WAS WRONG."
LEVELS CRITICAL

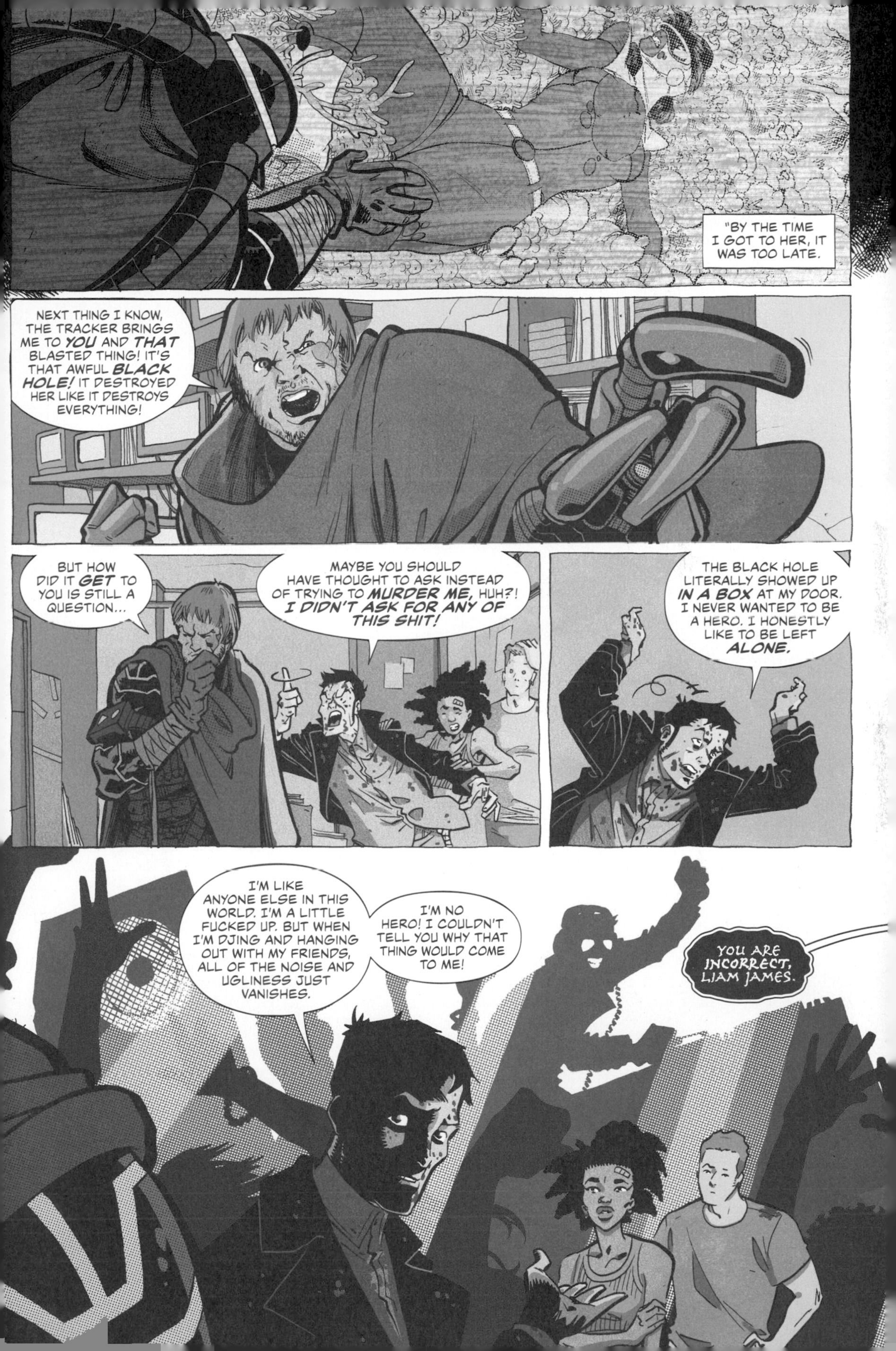
"BY THE TIME I GOT TO HER, IT WAS TOO LATE.
NEXT THING I KNOW, THE TRACKER BRINGS ME TO YOU AND THAT BLASTED THING! IT'S THAT AWFUL BLACK HOLE! IT DESTROYED HER LIKE IT DESTROYS EVERYTHING!
BUT HOW DID IT GET TO YOU IS STILL A QUESTION...
MAYBE YOU SHOULD HAVE THOUGHT TO ASK INSTEAD OF TRYING TO MURDER ME, HUH?! I DIDN'T ASK FOR ANY OF THIS SHIT!
THE BLACK HOLE LITERALLY SHOWED UP IN A BOX AT MY DOOR. I NEVER WANTED TO BE A HERO. I HONESTLY LIKE TO BE LEFT ALONE.
I'M LIKE ANYONE ELSE IN THIS WORLD. I'M A LITTLE FUCKED UP. BUT WHEN I'M DJING AND HANGING OUT WITH MY FRIENDS, ALL OF THE NOISE AND UGLINESS JUST VANISHES.
I'M NO HERO! I COULDN'T TELL YOU WHY THAT THING WOULD COME TO ME!
YOU ARE INCORRECT, LIAM JAMES.

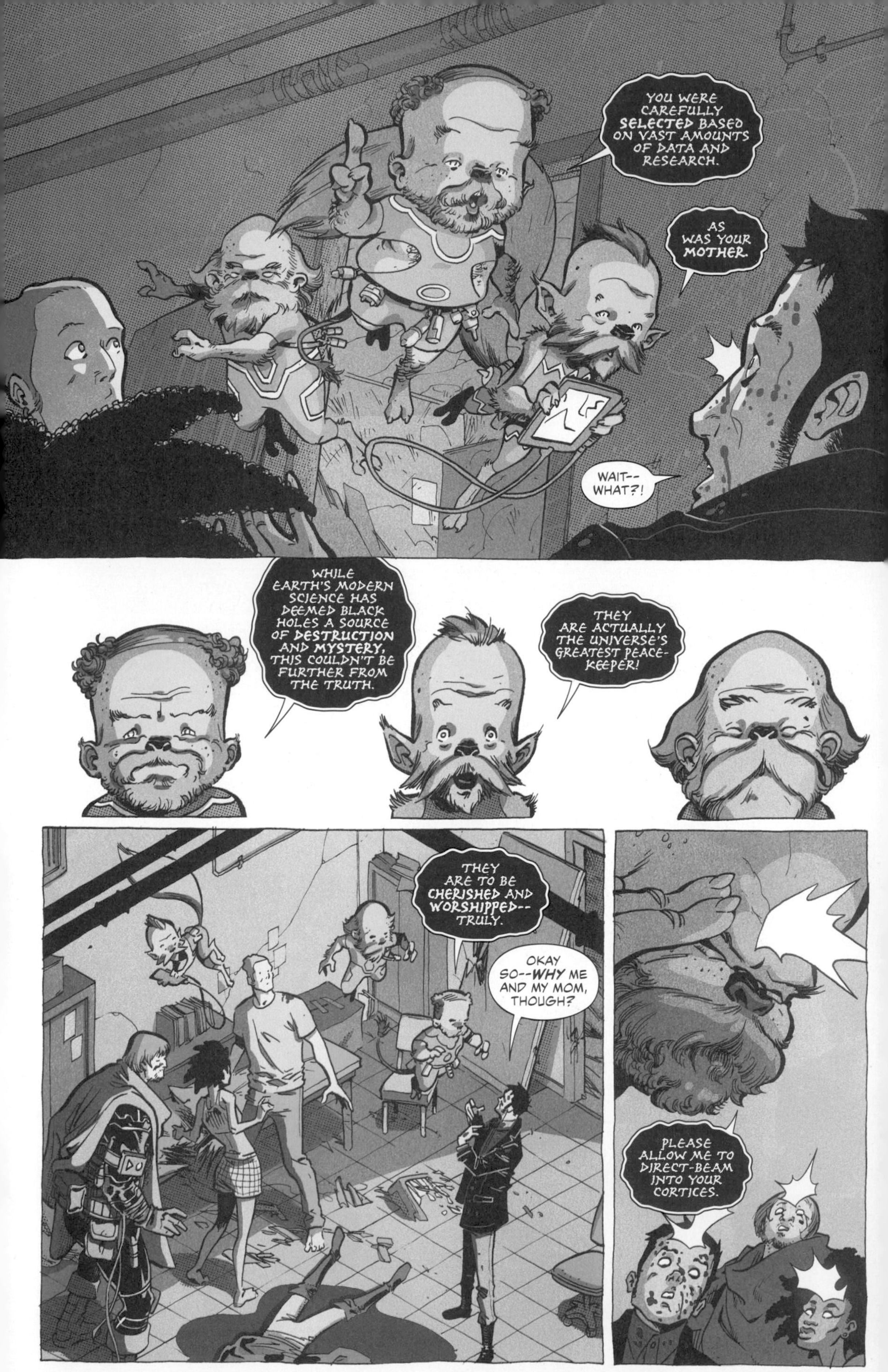
YOU WERE CAREFULLY SELECTED BASED ON VAST AMOUNTS OF DATA AND RESEARCH.
AS WAS YOUR MOTHER.
WAIT-- WHAT?!
WHILE EARTH'S MODERN SCIENCE HAS DEEMED BLACK HOLES A SOURCE OF DESTRUCTION AND MYSTERY, THIS COULDN'T BE FURTHER FROM THE TRUTH.
THEY ARE ACTUALLY THE UNIVERSE'S GREATEST PEACE-KEEPER!
THEY ARE TO BE CHERISHED AND WORSHIPPED-- TRULY.
OKAY SO--WHY ME AND MY MOM, THOUGH?
PLEASE ALLOW ME TO DIRECT-BEAM INTO YOUR CORTICES.

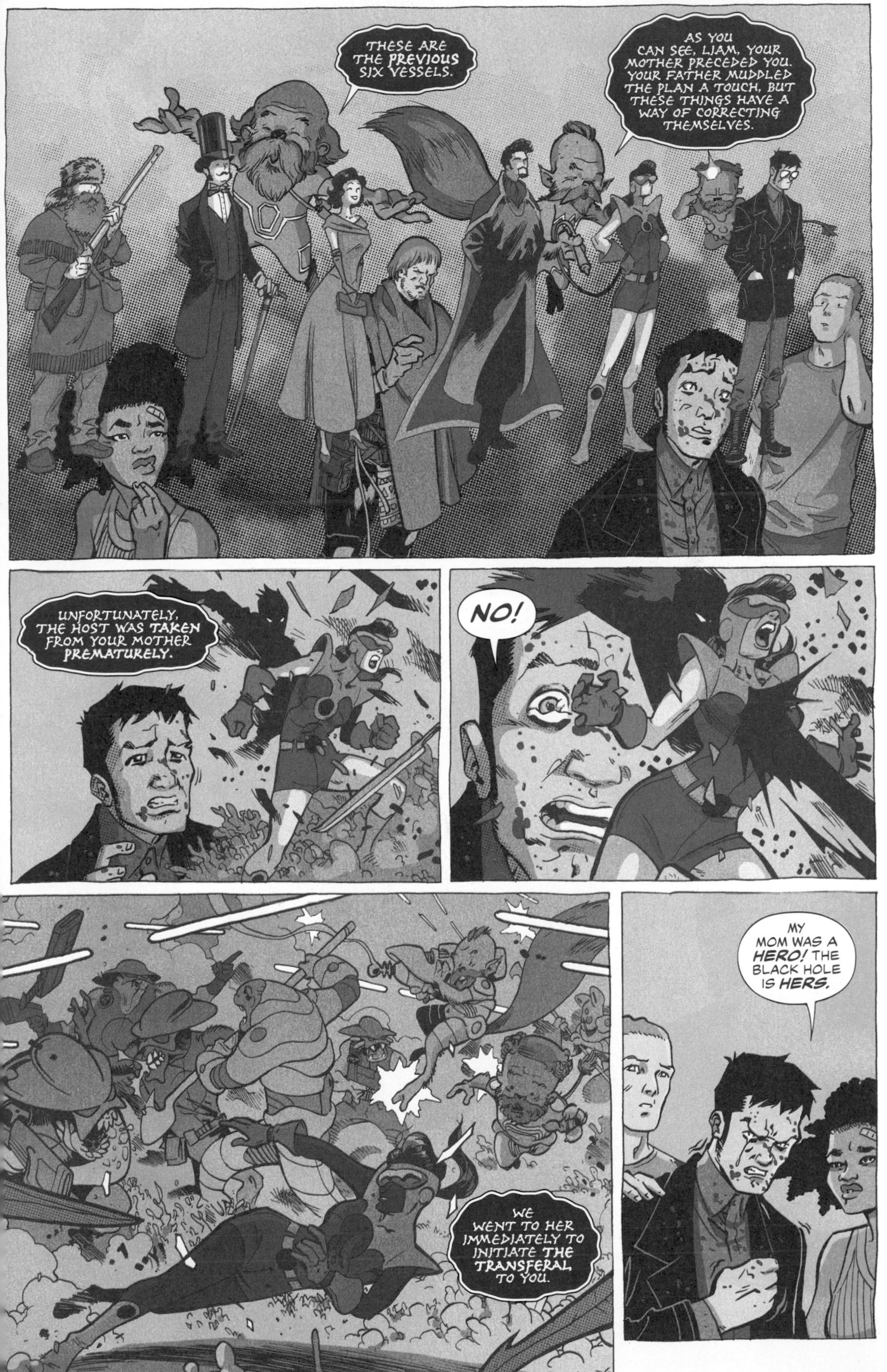
THESE ARE THE PREVIOUS SIX VESSELS.
AS YOU CAN SEE, LIAM, YOUR MOTHER PRECEDED YOU. YOUR FATHER MUDDLED THE PLAN A TOUCH, BUT THESE THINGS HAVE A WAY OF CORRECTING THEMSELVES.
UNFORTUNATELY, THE HOST WAS TAKEN FROM YOUR MOTHER PREMATURELY.
NO!
WE WENT TO HER IMMEDIATELY TO INITIATE THE TRANSFERAL TO YOU.
MY MOM WAS A HERO! THE BLACK HOLE IS HERS.

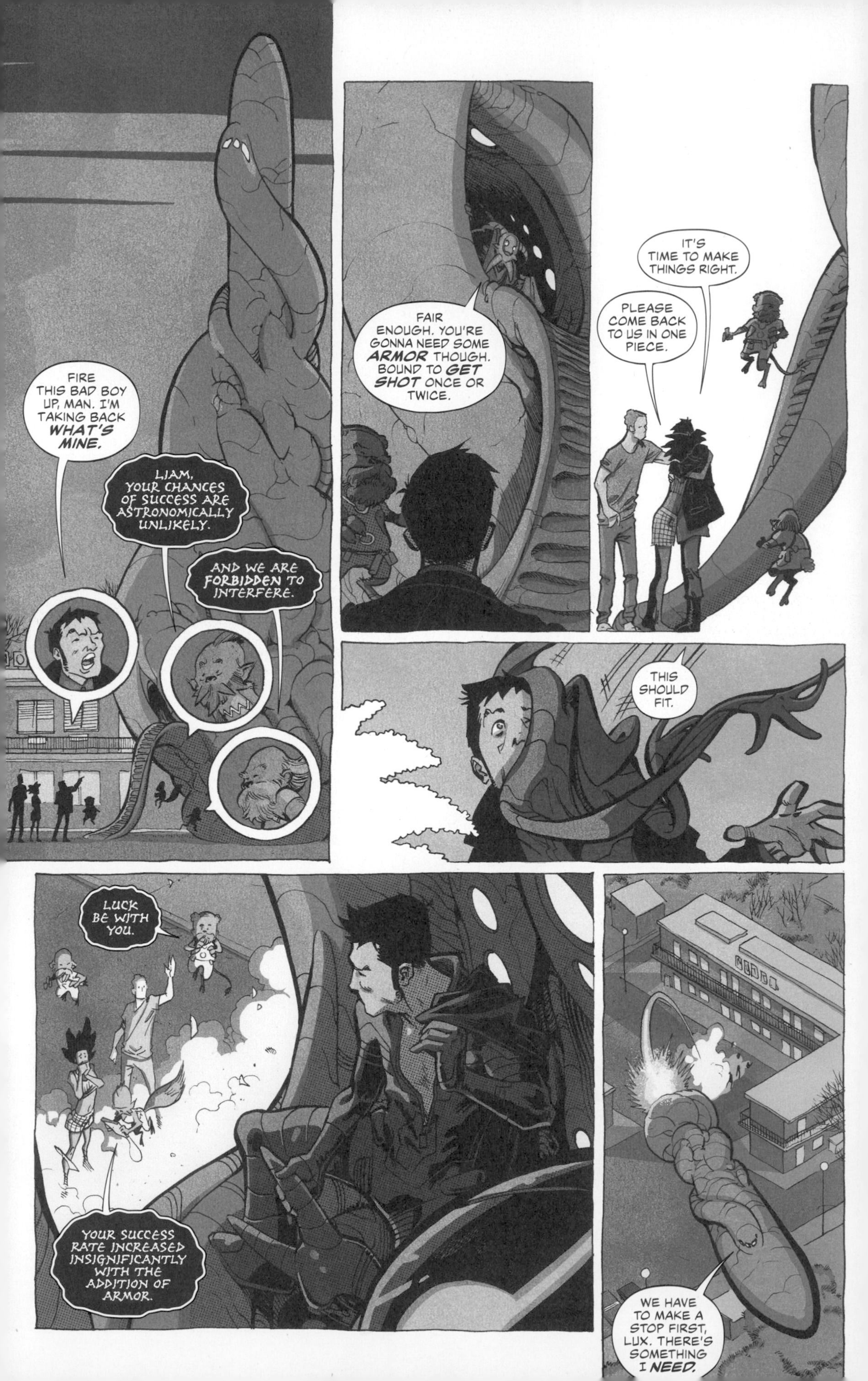
FIRE THIS BAD BOY UP, MAN. I'M TAKING BACK WHAT'S MINE.
LIAM, YOUR CHANCES OF SUCCESS ARE ASTRONOMICALLY UNLIKELY.
AND WE ARE FORBIDDEN TO INTERFERE.
FAIR ENOUGH. YOU'RE GONNA NEED SOME ARMOR THOUGH. BOUND TO GET SHOT ONCE OR TWICE.
IT'S TIME TO MAKE THINGS RIGHT.
PLEASE COME BACK TO US IN ONE PIECE.
THIS SHOULD FIT.
LUCK BE WITH YOU.
YOUR SUCCESS RATE INCREASED INSIGNIFICANTLY WITH THE ADDITION OF ARMOR.
WE HAVE TO MAKE A STOP FIRST, LUX. THERE'S SOMETHING I NEED.

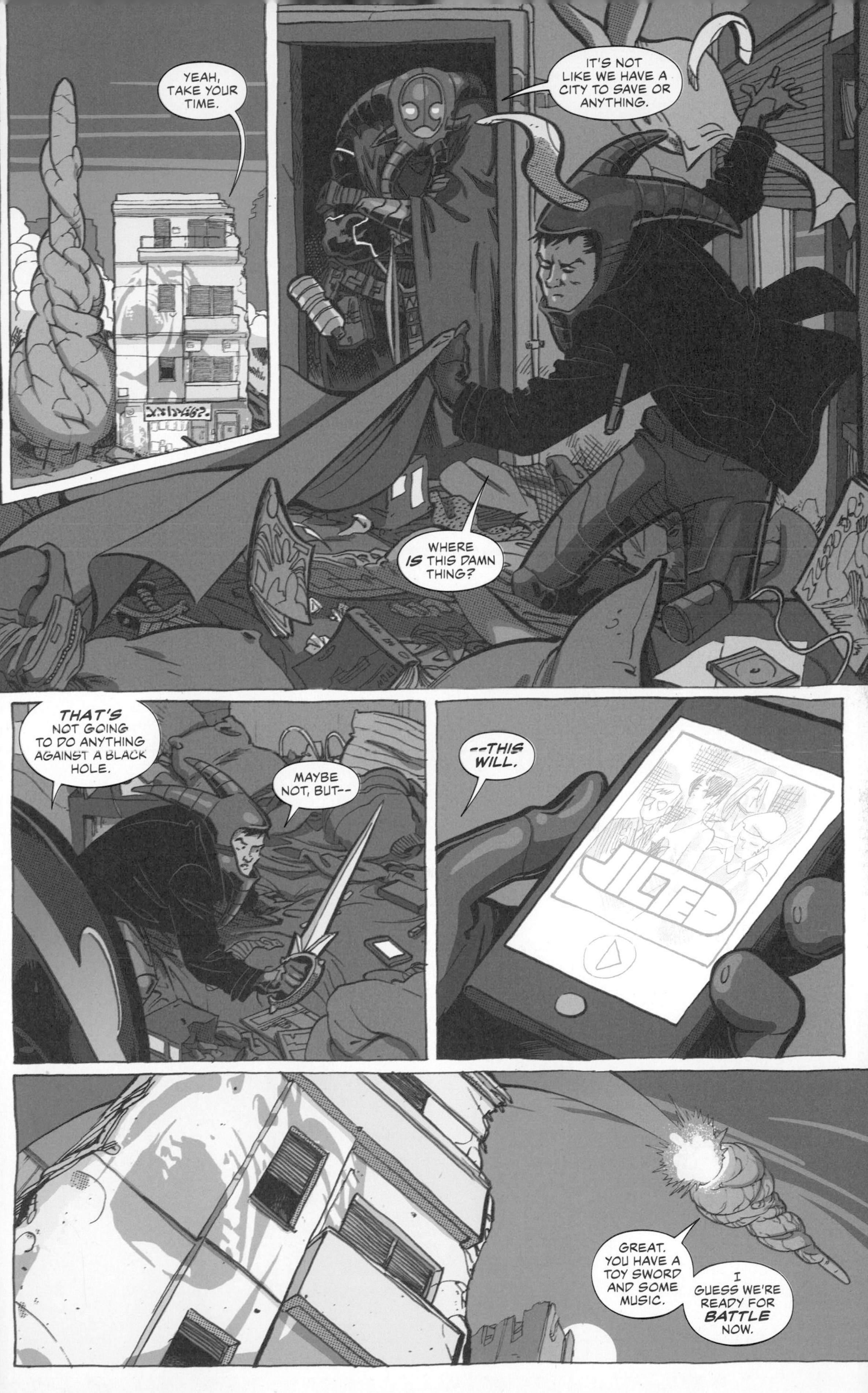
YEAH, TAKE YOUR TIME.
IT'S NOT LIKE WE HAVE A CITY TO SAVE OR ANYTHING.
WHERE *IS* THIS DAMN THING?
THAT'S NOT GOING TO DO ANYTHING AGAINST A BLACK HOLE.
MAYBE NOT, BUT--
--*THIS WILL.*
JILTED
GREAT. YOU HAVE A TOY SWORD AND SOME MUSIC.
I GUESS WE'RE READY FOR *BATTLE* NOW.

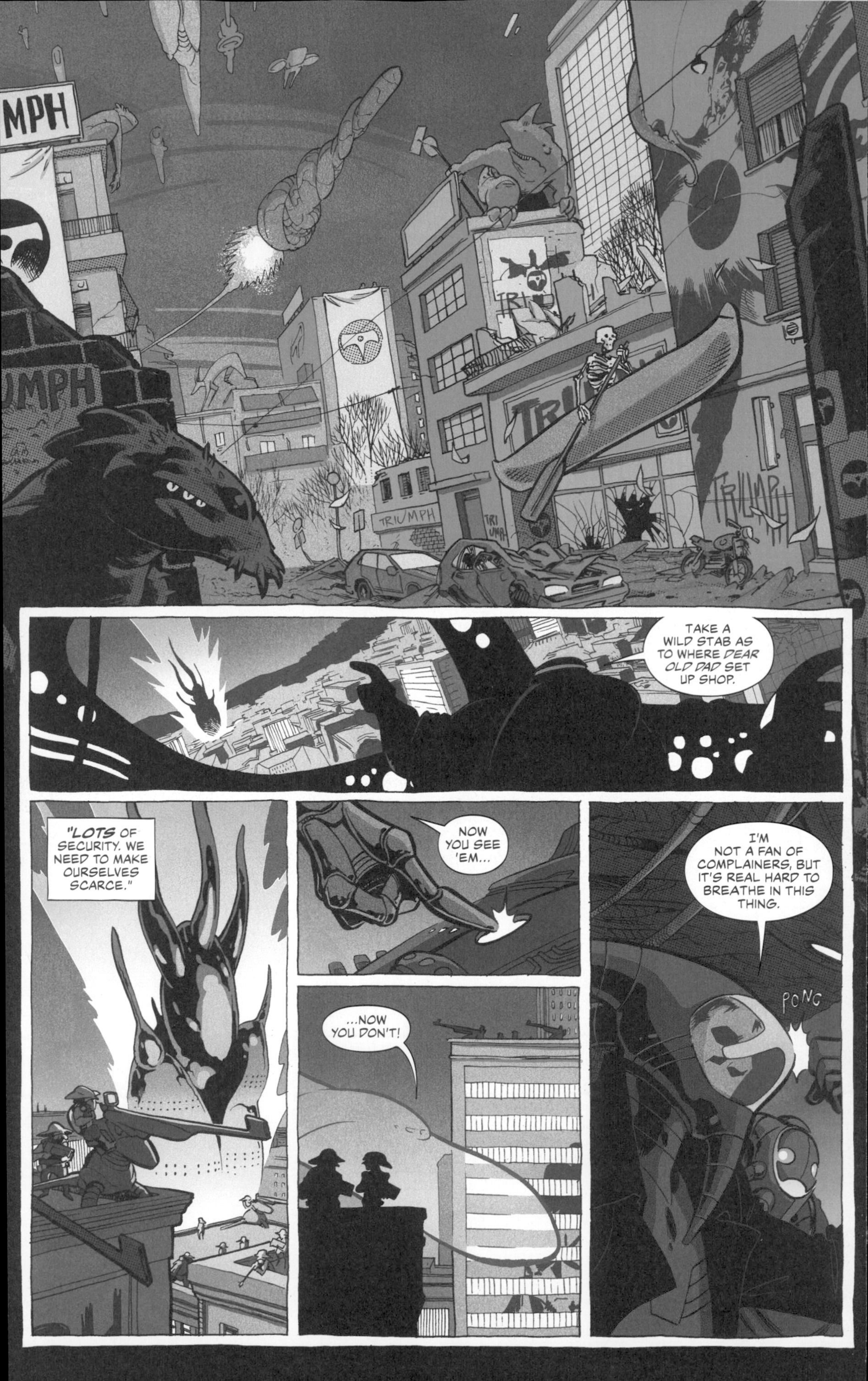
MPH
UMPH
TRIUMPH
TRI UMPH
TRIUMPH
TAKE A WILD STAB AS TO WHERE *DEAR OLD DAD* SET UP SHOP.
"*LOTS* OF SECURITY. WE NEED TO MAKE OURSELVES SCARCE."
NOW YOU SEE 'EM...
...NOW YOU DON'T!
I'M NOT A FAN OF COMPLAINERS, BUT IT'S REAL HARD TO BREATHE IN THIS THING.
PONG

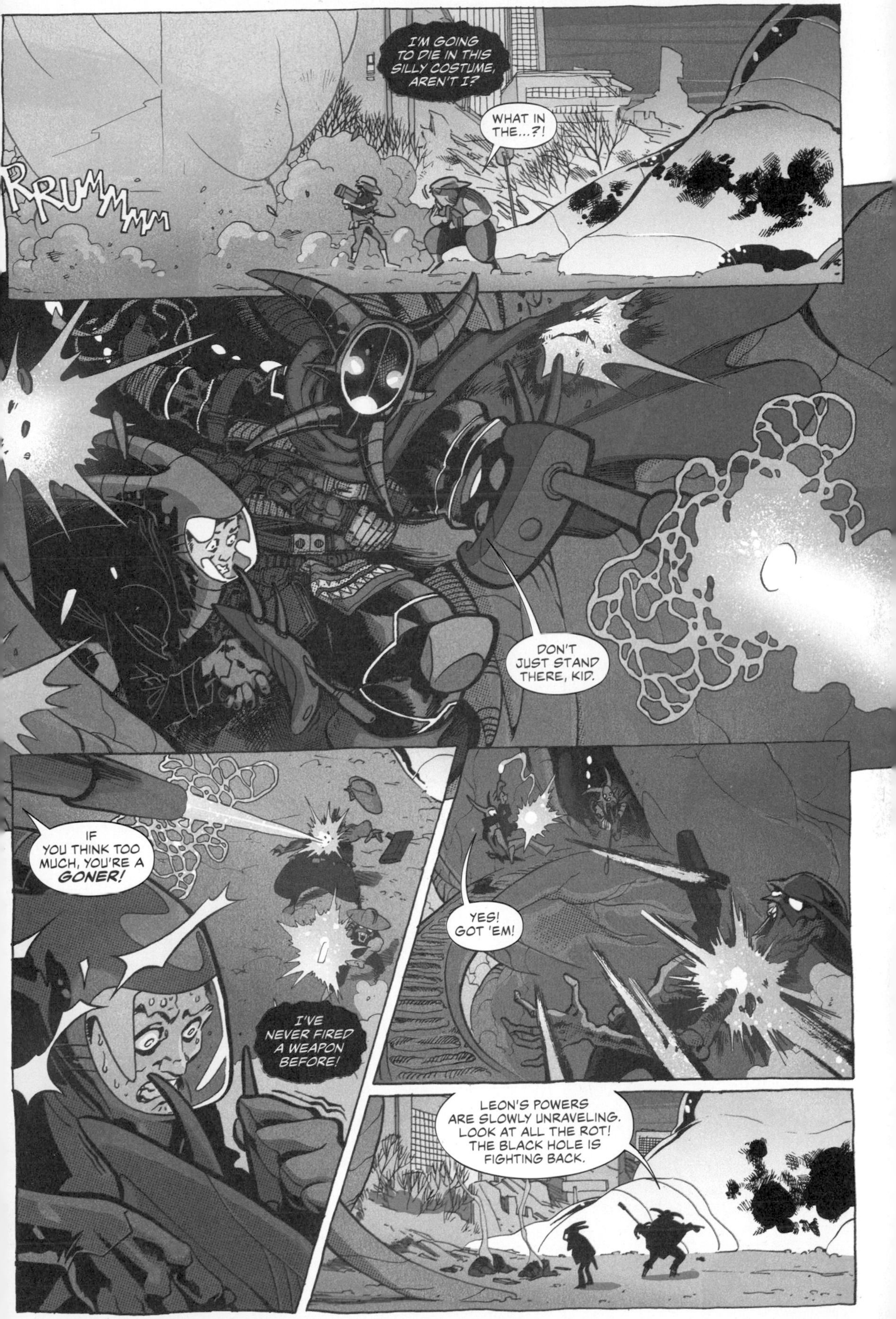
I'M GOING TO DIE IN THIS SILLY COSTUME, AREN'T I?
WHAT IN THE...?!
RRUMMMMM
DON'T JUST STAND THERE, KID.
IF YOU THINK TOO MUCH, YOU'RE A GONER!
I'VE NEVER FIRED A WEAPON BEFORE!
YES! GOT 'EM!
LEON'S POWERS ARE SLOWLY UNRAVELING. LOOK AT ALL THE ROT! THE BLACK HOLE IS FIGHTING BACK.

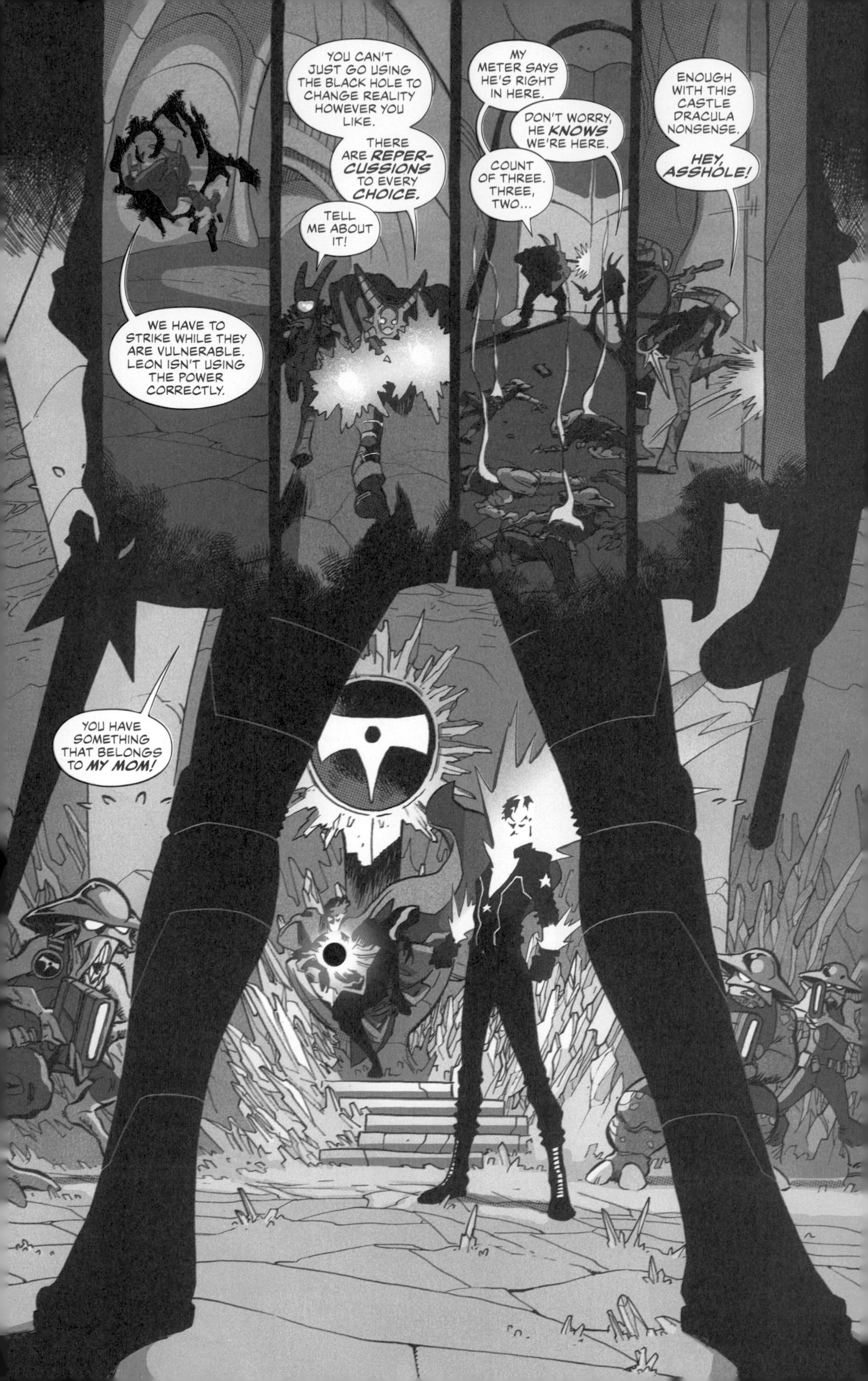

WE HAVE TO STRIKE WHILE THEY ARE VULNERABLE. LEON ISN'T USING THE POWER CORRECTLY.
YOU CAN'T JUST GO USING THE BLACK HOLE TO CHANGE REALITY HOWEVER YOU LIKE.
THERE ARE REPERCUSSIONS TO EVERY CHOICE.
TELL ME ABOUT IT!
MY METER SAYS HE'S RIGHT IN HERE.
DON'T WORRY, HE KNOWS WE'RE HERE.
COUNT OF THREE. THREE, TWO...
ENOUGH WITH THIS CASTLE DRACULA NONSENSE.
HEY, ASSHOLE!
YOU HAVE SOMETHING THAT BELONGS TO MY MOM!

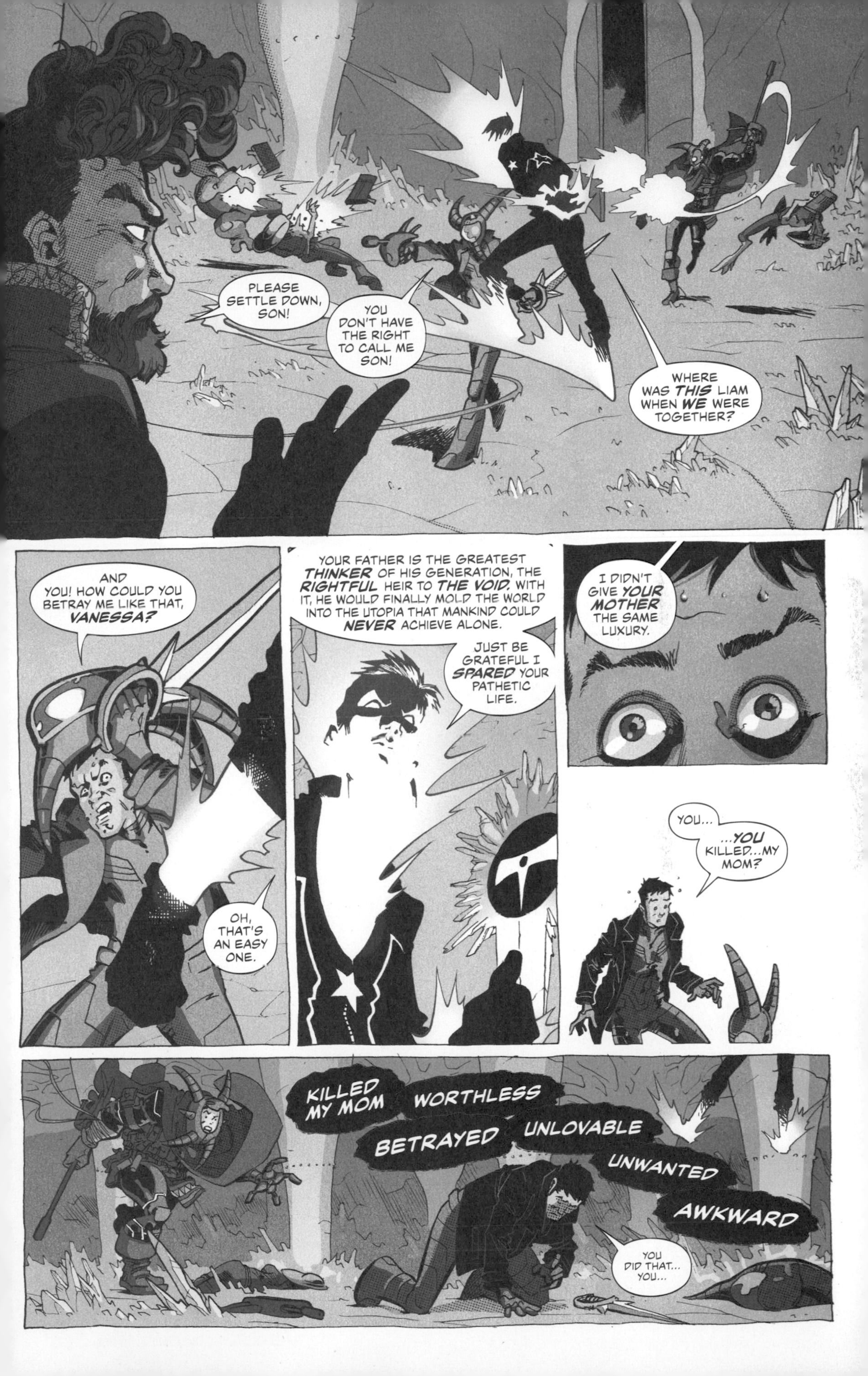
PLEASE SETTLE DOWN, SON!
YOU DON'T HAVE THE RIGHT TO CALL ME SON!
WHERE WAS THIS LIAM WHEN WE WERE TOGETHER?
AND YOU! HOW COULD YOU BETRAY ME LIKE THAT, VANESSA?
OH, THAT'S AN EASY ONE.
YOUR FATHER IS THE GREATEST THINKER OF HIS GENERATION, THE RIGHTFUL HEIR TO THE VOID. WITH IT, HE WOULD FINALLY MOLD THE WORLD INTO THE UTOPIA THAT MANKIND COULD NEVER ACHIEVE ALONE.
JUST BE GRATEFUL I SPARED YOUR PATHETIC LIFE.
I DIDN'T GIVE YOUR MOTHER THE SAME LUXURY.
YOU...
...YOU KILLED...MY MOM?
KILLED MY MOM
WORTHLESS
BETRAYED
UNLOVABLE
UNWANTED
AWKWARD
YOU DID THAT... YOU...

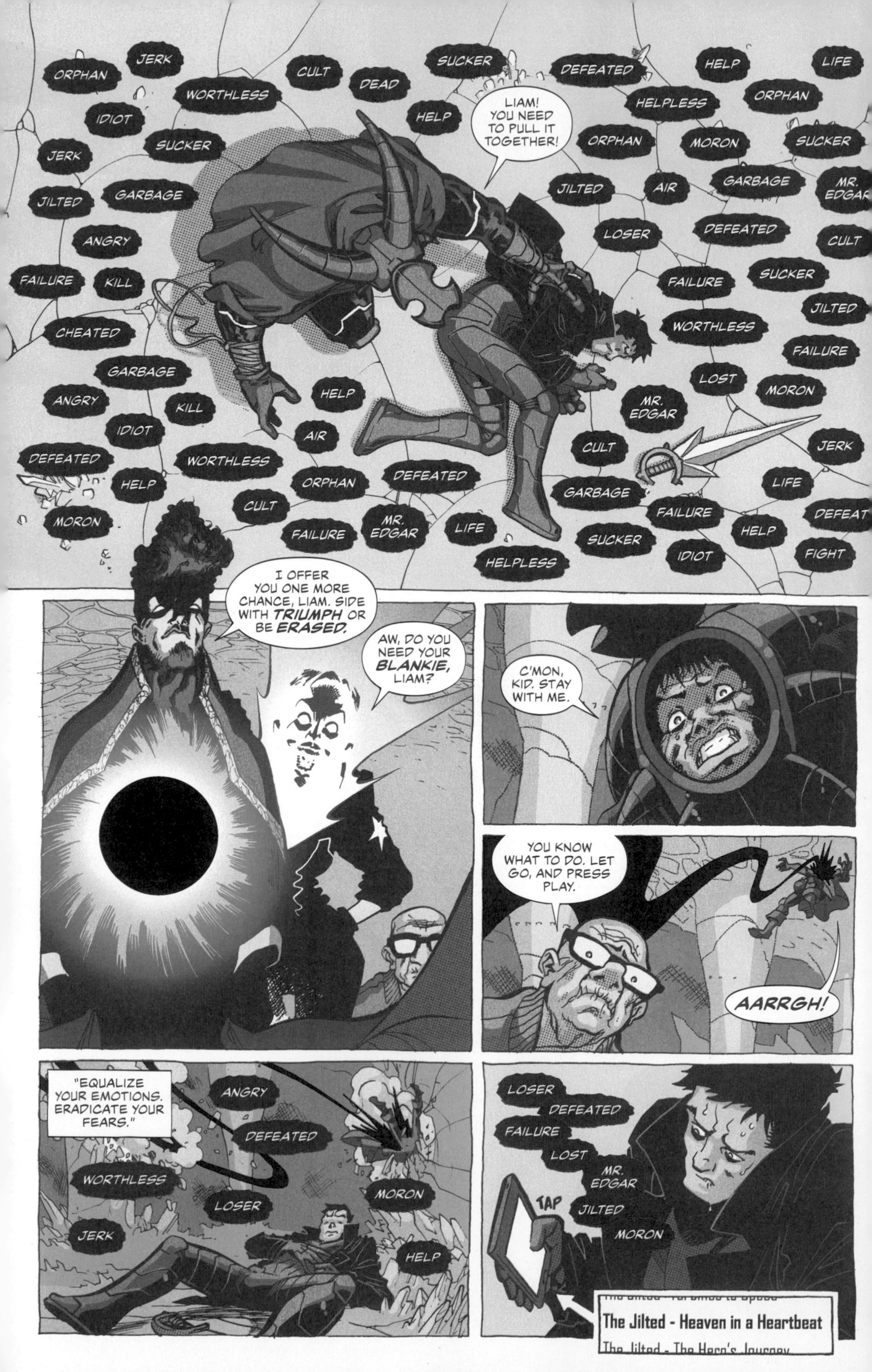
ORPHAN
JERK
CULT
DEAD
WORTHLESS
SUCKER
HELP
DEFEATED
HELP
LIFE
IDIOT
HELPLESS
ORPHAN
LIAM! YOU NEED TO PULL IT TOGETHER!
SUCKER
JERK
ORPHAN
MORON
SUCKER
JILTED
GARBAGE
JILTED
AIR
GARBAGE
MR. EDGAR
ANGRY
LOSER
DEFEATED
CULT
FAILURE
KILL
FAILURE
SUCKER
JILTED
CHEATED
WORTHLESS
FAILURE
GARBAGE
LOST
MORON
ANGRY
HELP
KILL
MR. EDGAR
IDIOT
AIR
DEFEATED
WORTHLESS
CULT
JERK
HELP
ORPHAN
DEFEATED
GARBAGE
LIFE
MORON
CULT
FAILURE
DEFEAT
FAILURE
MR. EDGAR
LIFE
SUCKER
HELP
IDIOT
FIGHT
HELPLESS
I OFFER YOU ONE MORE CHANCE, LIAM. SIDE WITH TRIUMPH OR BE ERASED.
AW, DO YOU NEED YOUR BLANKIE, LIAM?
C'MON, KID. STAY WITH ME.
YOU KNOW WHAT TO DO. LET GO, AND PRESS PLAY.
AARRGH!
"EQUALIZE YOUR EMOTIONS. ERADICATE YOUR FEARS."
ANGRY
DEFEATED
WORTHLESS
MORON
LOSER
JERK
HELP
LOSER
DEFEATED
FAILURE
LOST
MR. EDGAR
TAP
JILTED
MORON
The Jilted - Heaven in a Heartbeat

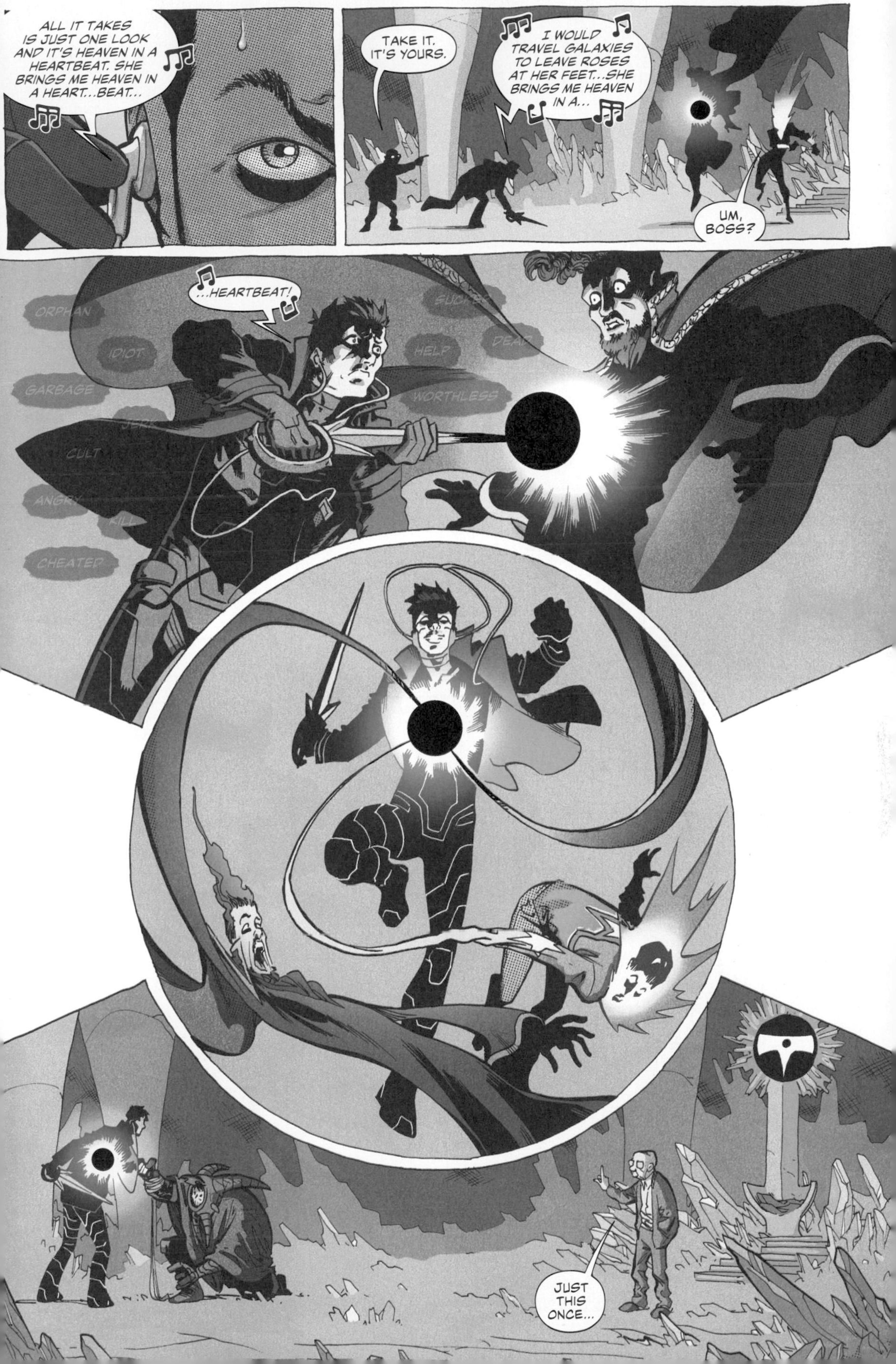
ALL IT TAKES IS JUST ONE LOOK AND IT'S HEAVEN IN A HEARTBEAT. SHE BRINGS ME HEAVEN IN A HEART...BEAT...
TAKE IT. IT'S YOURS.
I WOULD TRAVEL GALAXIES TO LEAVE ROSES AT HER FEET...SHE BRINGS ME HEAVEN IN A...
UM, BOSS?
...HEARTBEAT!
ORPHAN
IDIOT
GARBAGE
CULT
ANGRY
KILL
CHEATED
HELP
WORTHLESS
DEAD
JUST THIS ONCE...

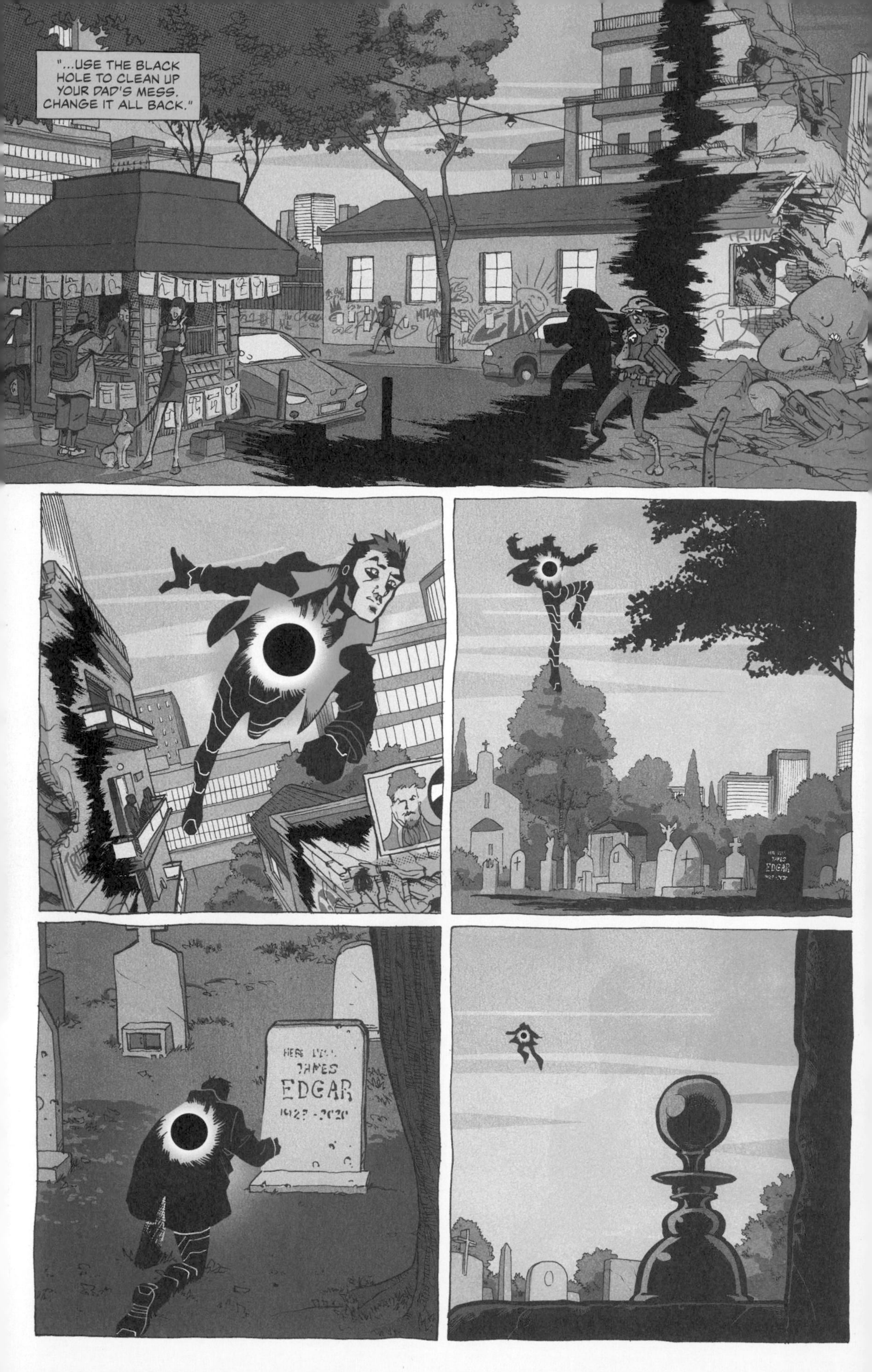
"...USE THE BLACK HOLE TO CLEAN UP YOUR DAD'S MESS. CHANGE IT ALL BACK."
EDGAR
EDGAR

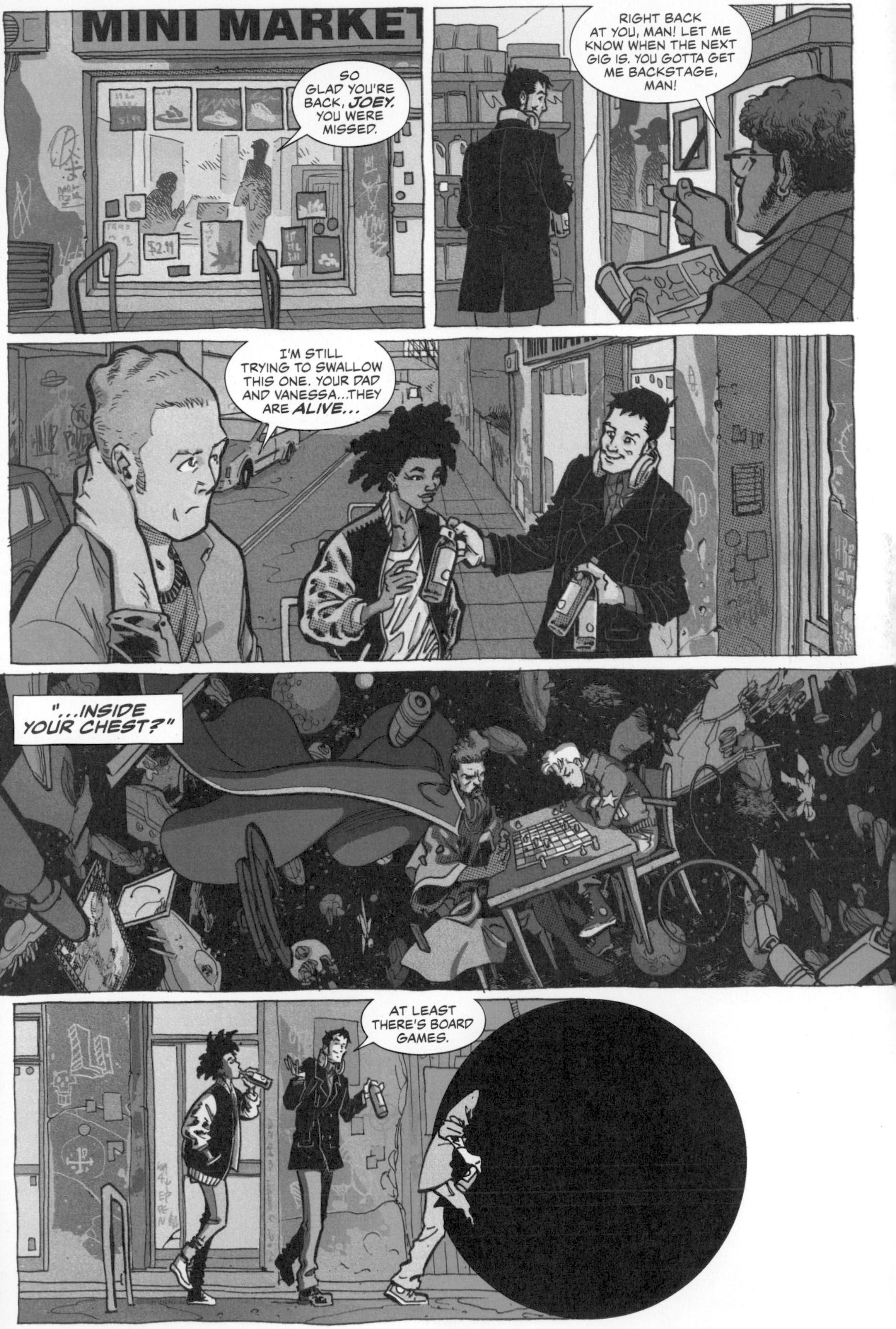
MINI MARKET
SO GLAD YOU'RE BACK, **JOEY.** YOU WERE MISSED.
RIGHT BACK AT YOU, MAN! LET ME KNOW WHEN THE NEXT GIG IS. YOU GOTTA GET ME BACKSTAGE, MAN!
I'M STILL TRYING TO SWALLOW THIS ONE. YOUR DAD AND VANESSA...THEY ARE ***ALIVE...***
"...INSIDE YOUR CHEST?"
AT LEAST THERE'S BOARD GAMES.

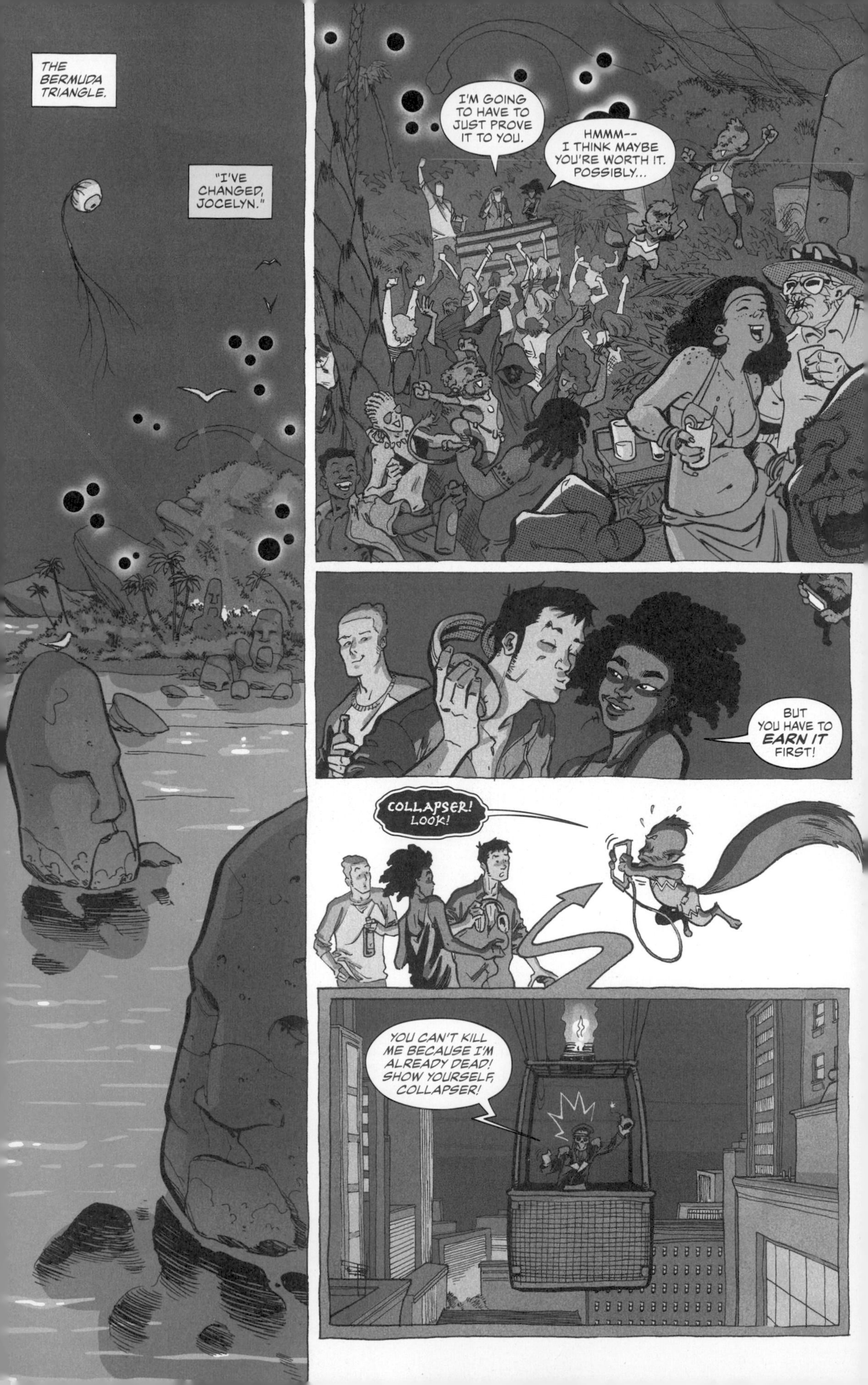
THE BERMUDA TRIANGLE.
"I'VE CHANGED, JOCELYN."
I'M GOING TO HAVE TO JUST PROVE IT TO YOU.
HMMM-- I THINK MAYBE YOU'RE WORTH IT. POSSIBLY...
BUT YOU HAVE TO EARN IT FIRST!
COLLAPSER! LOOK!
YOU CAN'T KILL ME BECAUSE I'M ALREADY DEAD! SHOW YOURSELF, COLLAPSER!

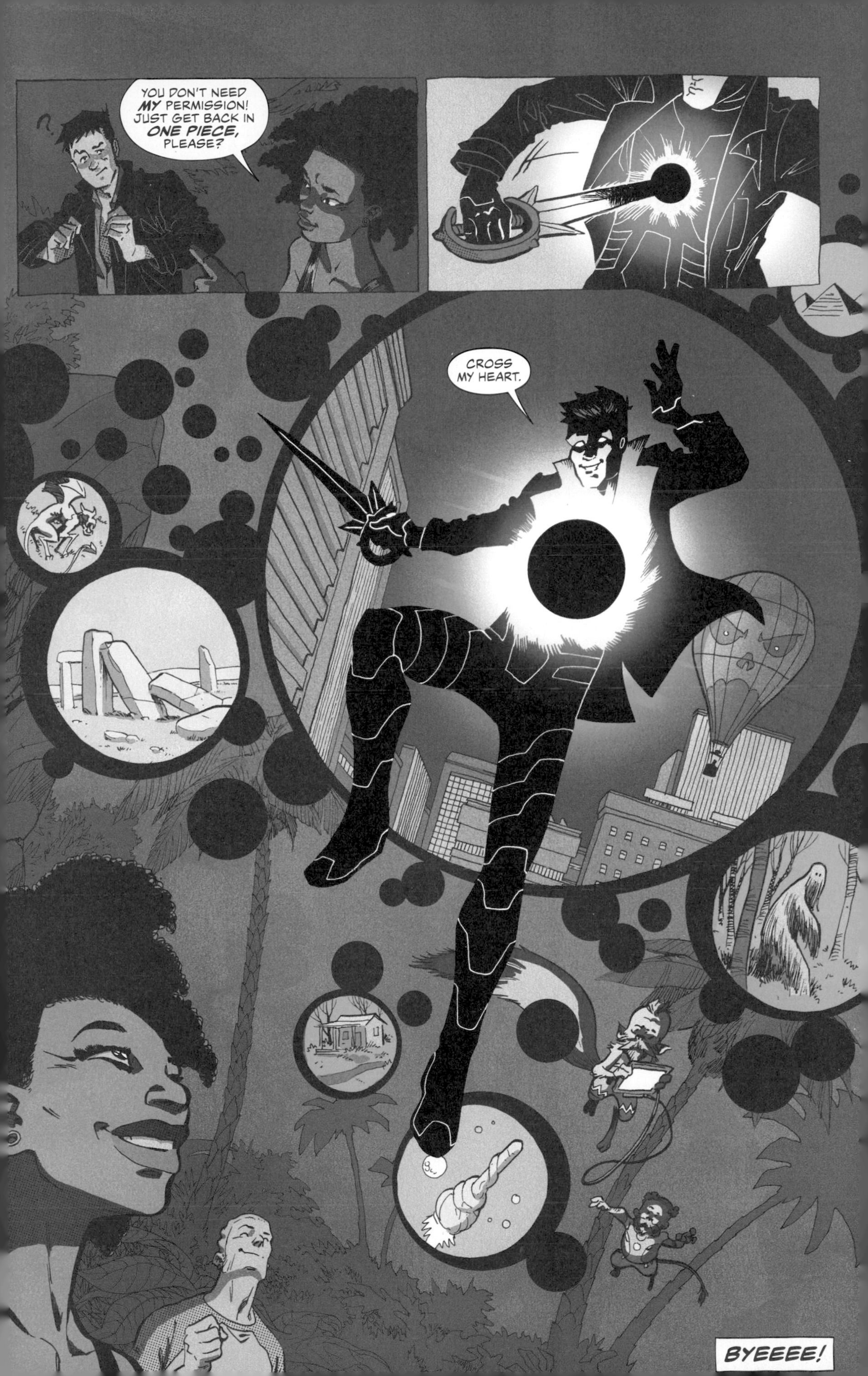
YOU DON'T NEED MY PERMISSION! JUST GET BACK IN ONE PIECE, PLEASE?
CROSS MY HEART.
BYEEEE!

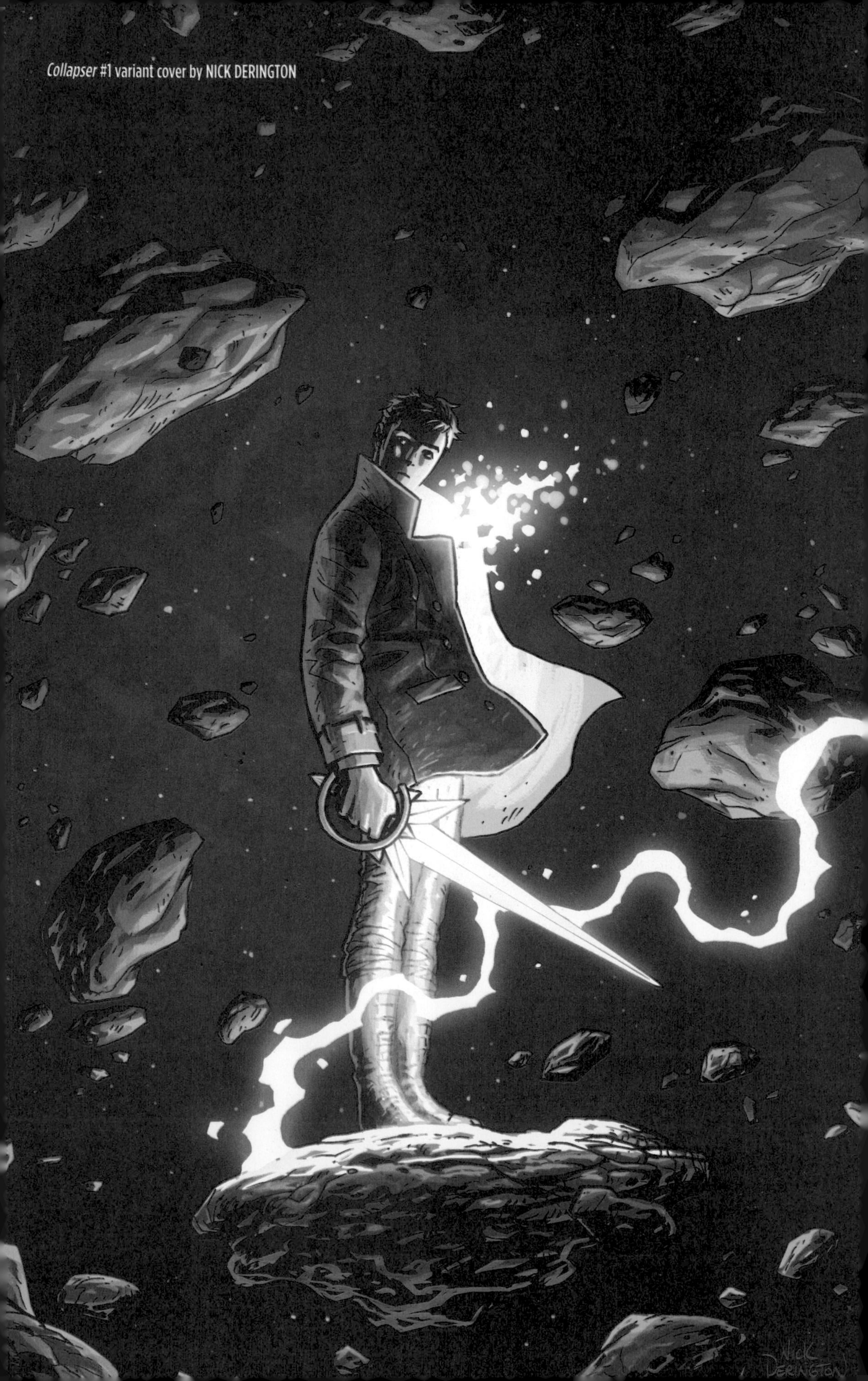

Collapser #1 variant cover by NICK DERINGTON

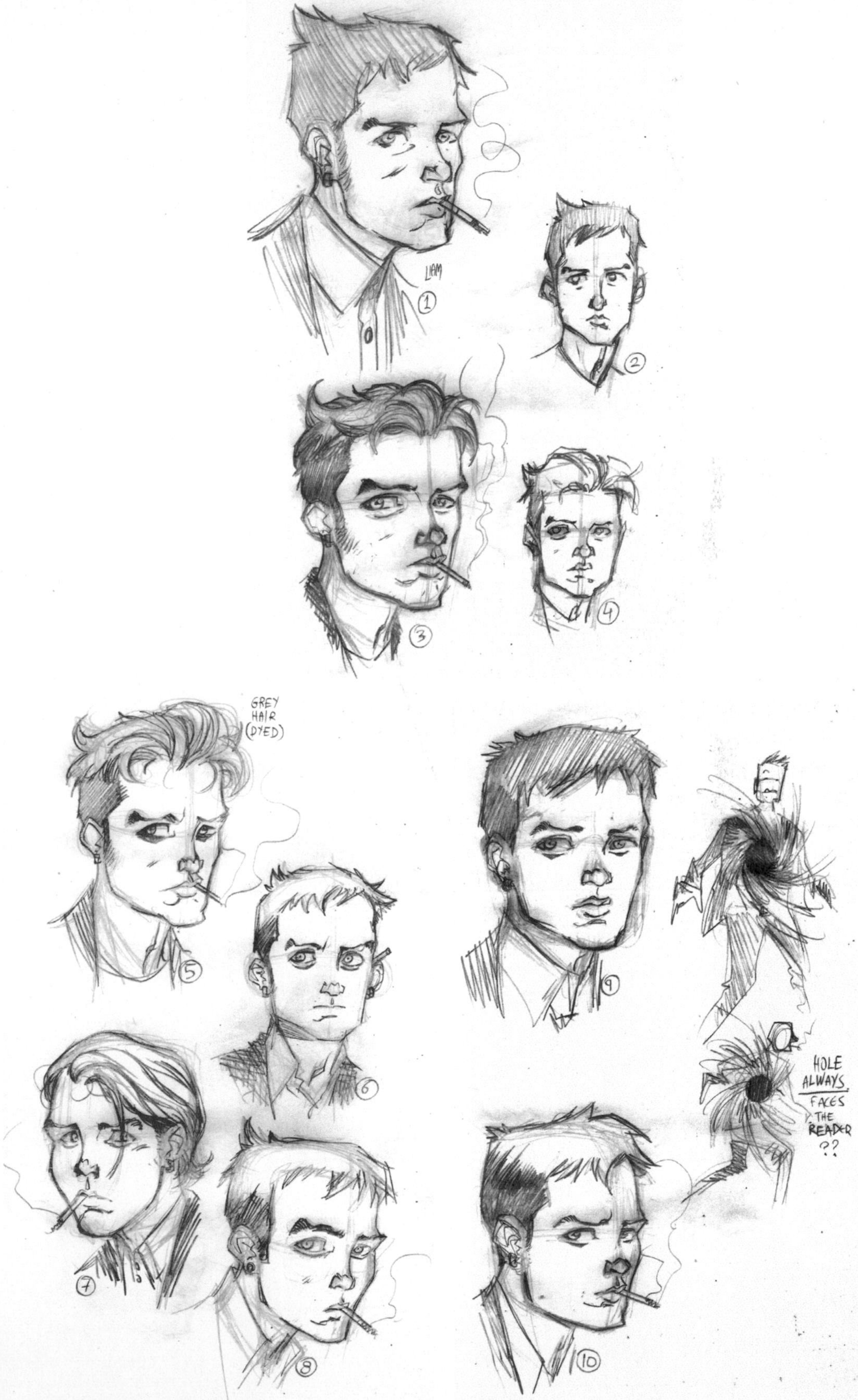
LIAM
1
2
3
4
GREY HAIR (DYED)
5
6
7
8
9
10
HOLE ALWAYS FACES THE READER ??

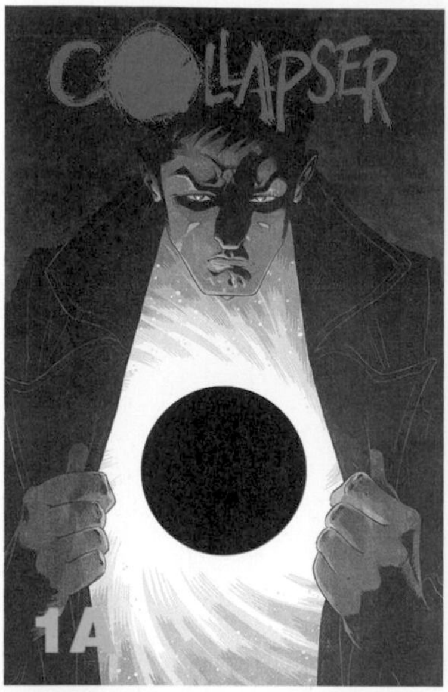
COLLAPSER
1A

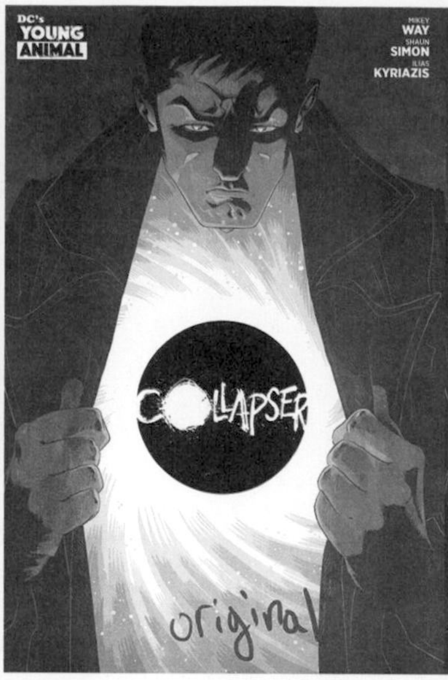
DC's YOUNG ANIMAL
MIKEY WAY
SHAUN SIMON
ILIAS KYRIAZIS
COLLAPSER
original

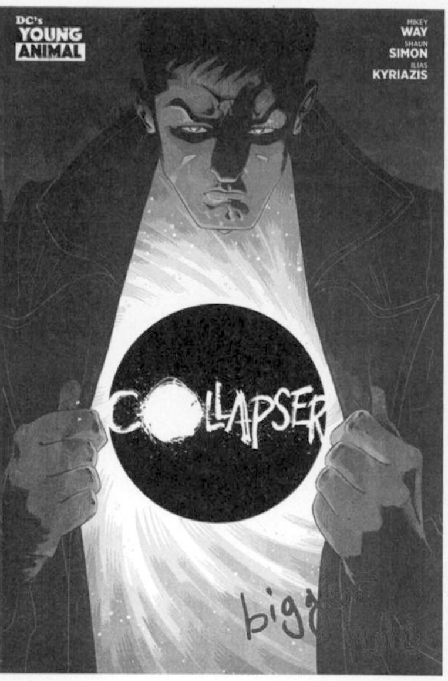
DC's YOUNG ANIMAL
MIKEY WAY
SHAUN SIMON
ILIAS KYRIAZIS
COLLAPSER

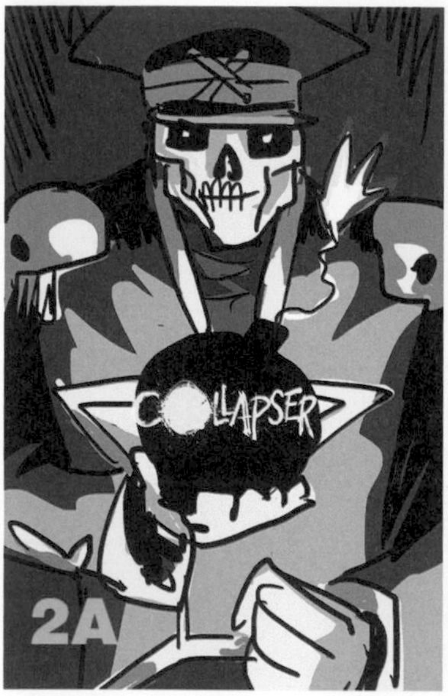
COLLAPSER
2A

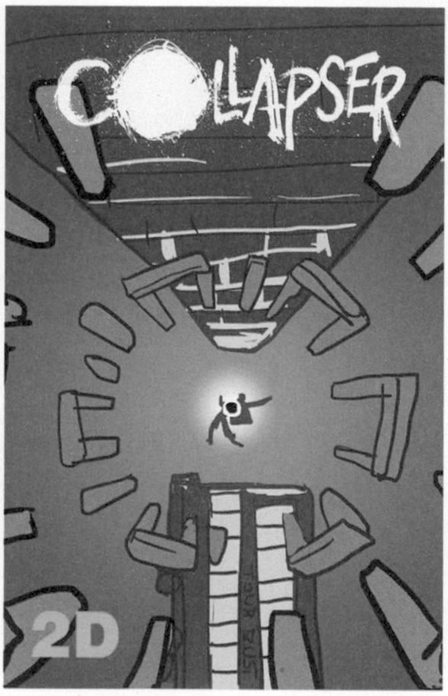
COLLAPSER
2D

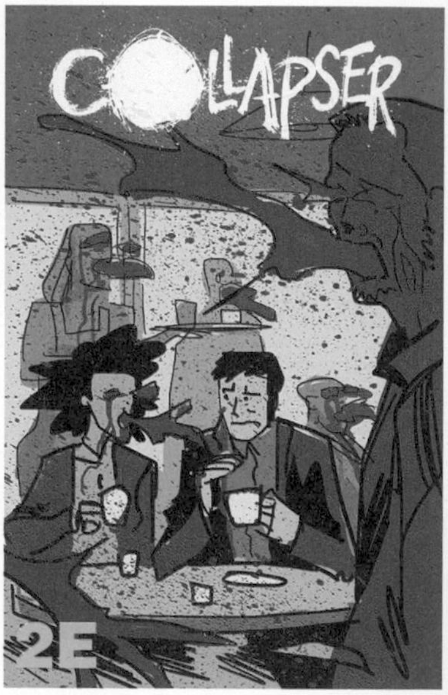
COLLAPSER
2E

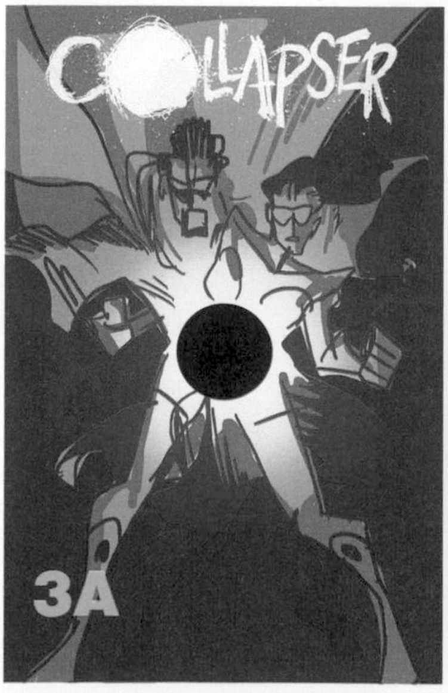
COLLAPSER
3A

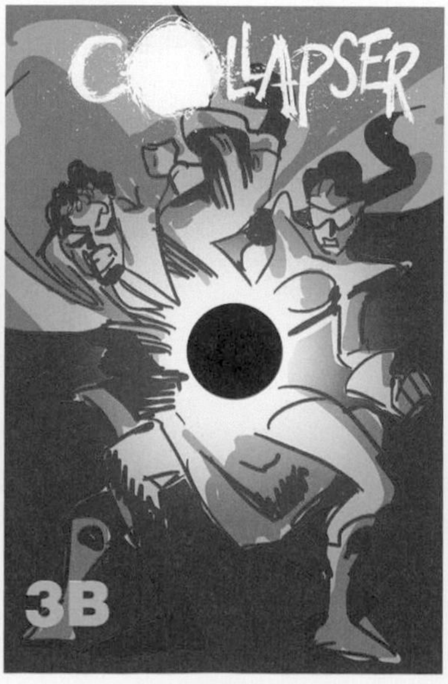
COLLAPSER
3B

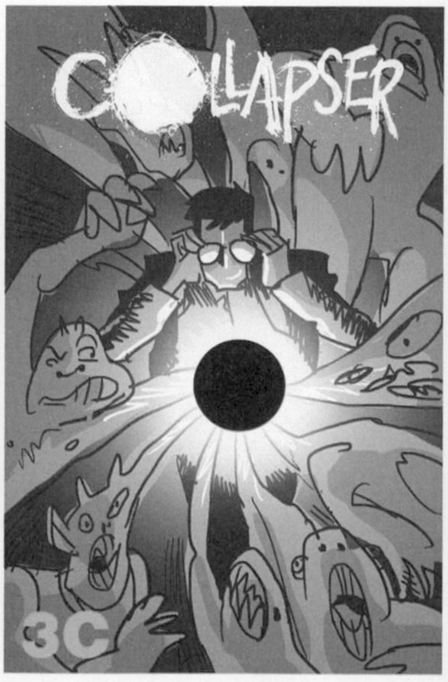
COLLAPSER
3C

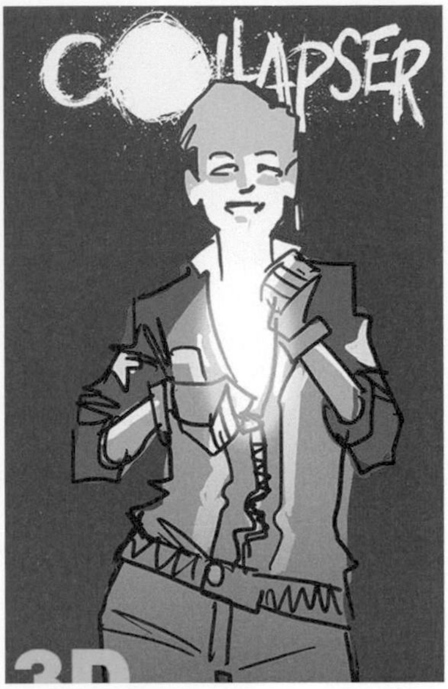
COLLAPSER
3D

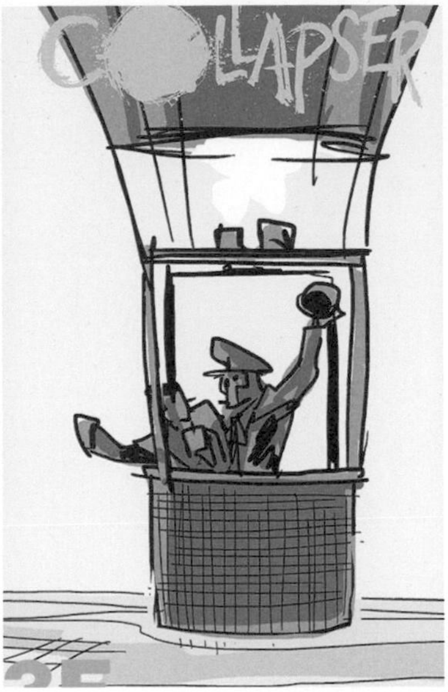
COLLAPSER

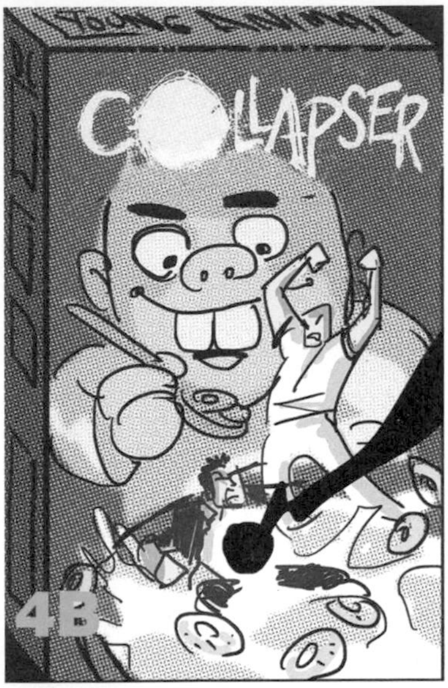
COLLAPSER
4B

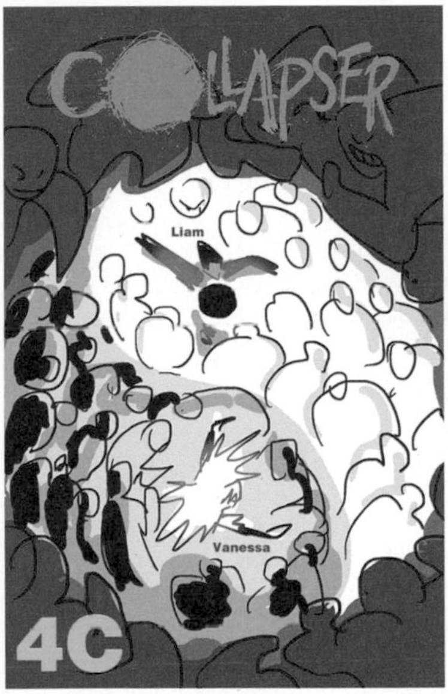
COLLAPSER
Liam
Vanessa
4C

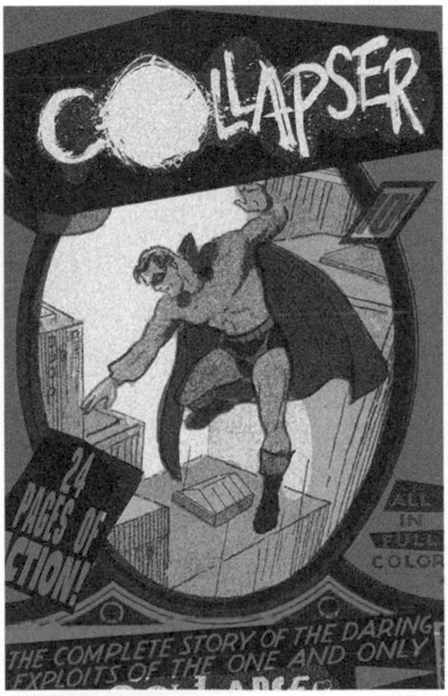
COLLAPSER
24 PAGES OF CTION!
ALL IN FULL COLOR
THE COMPLETE STORY OF THE DARING EXPLOITS OF THE ONE AND ONLY

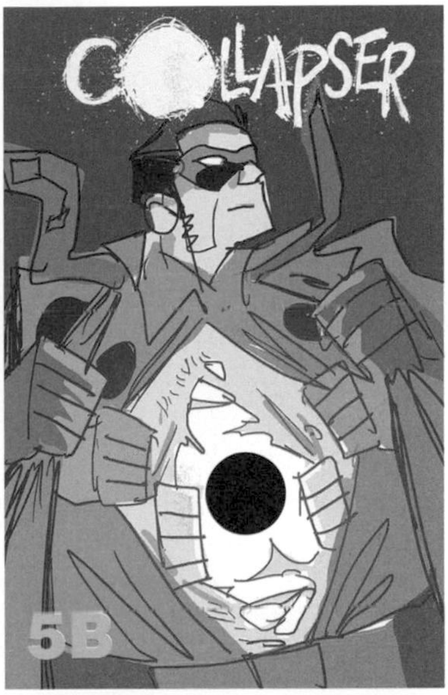
COLLAPSER
5B

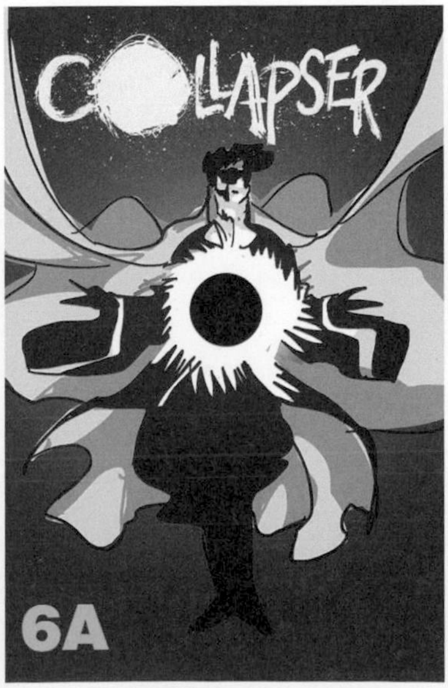
COLLAPSER
6A

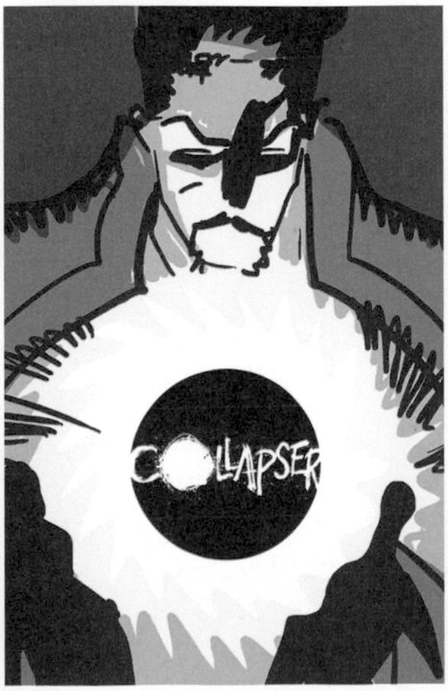
COLLAPSER

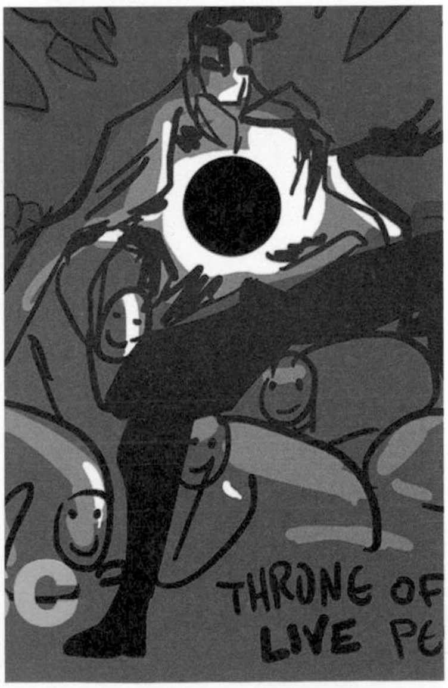
THRONE OF
LIVE PE

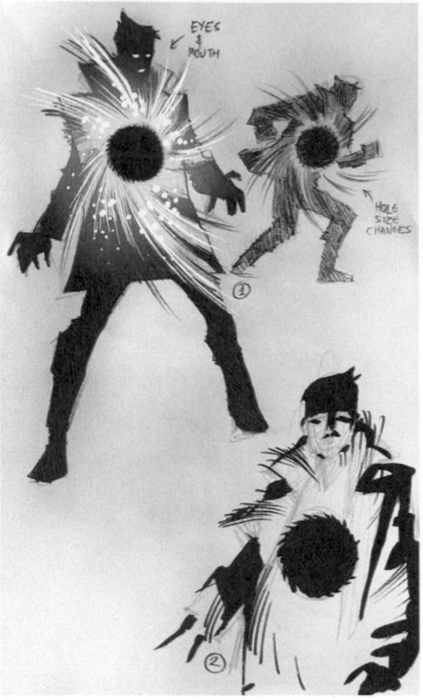
EYES & MOUTH
HOLE SIZE CHANGES
1
2

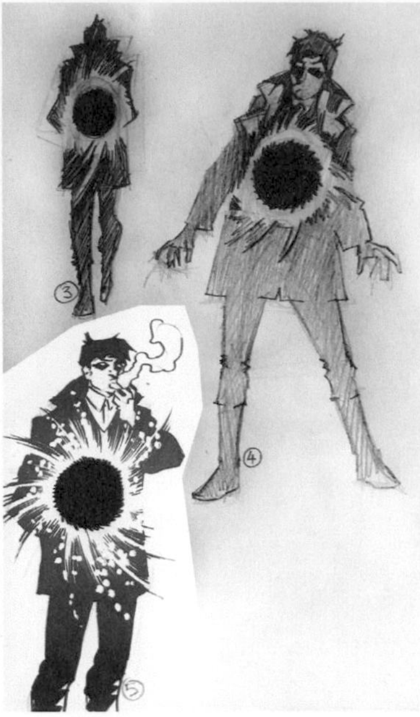
3
4
5

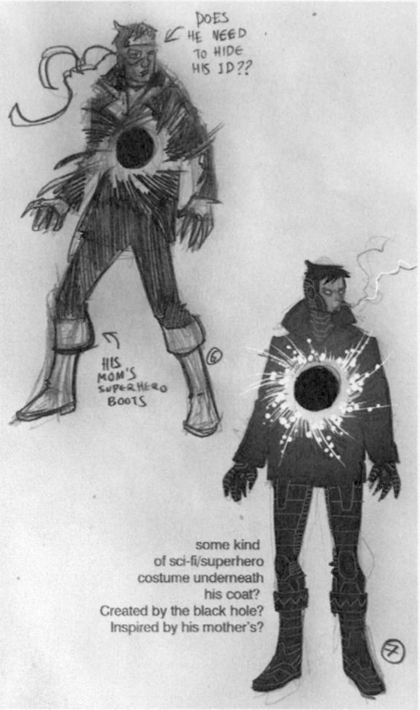
DOES HE NEED TO HIDE HIS ID??
HIS MOM'S SUPERHERO BOOTS
6
some kind of sci-fi/superhero costume underneath his coat? Created by the black hole? Inspired by his mother's?
7

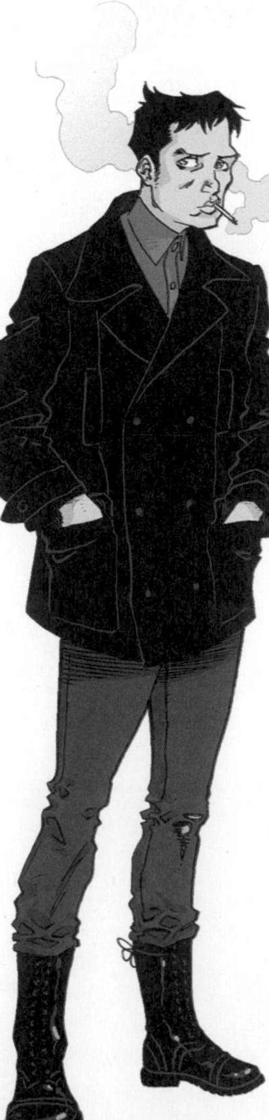

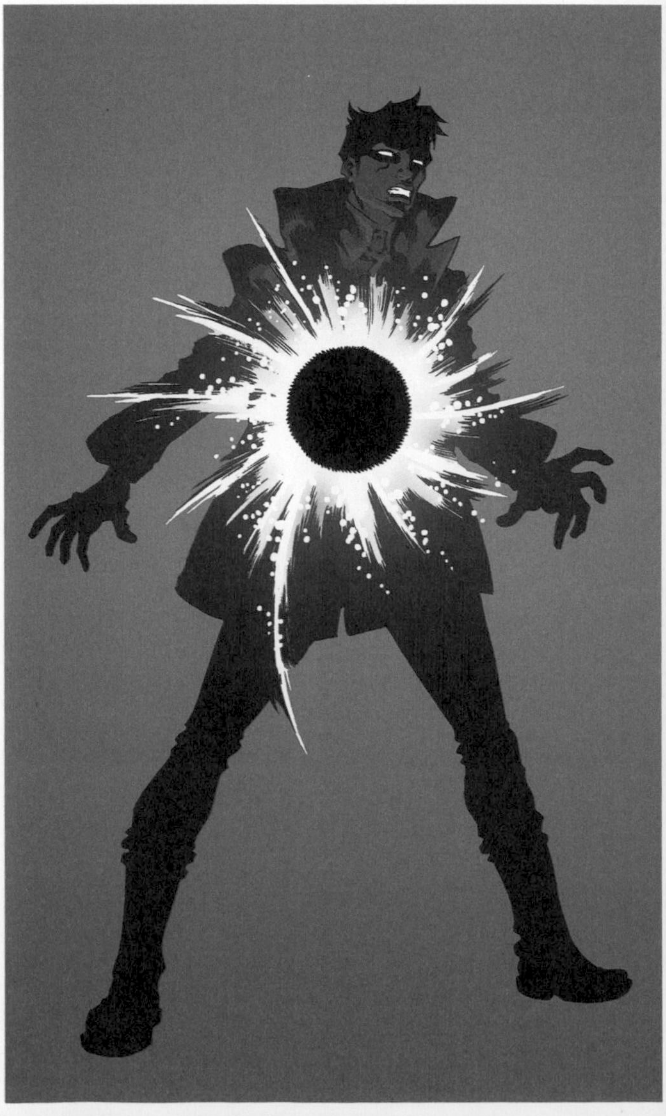

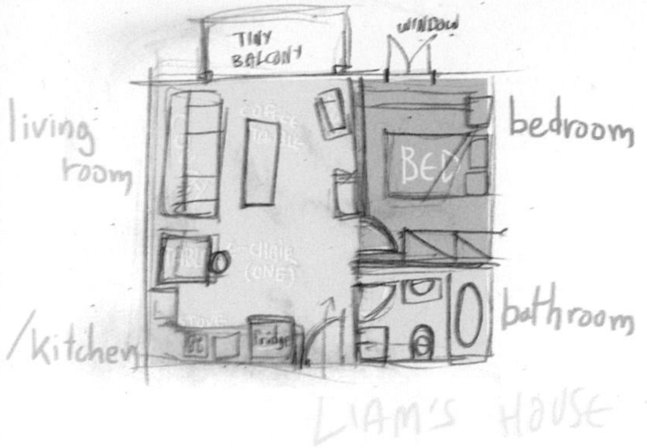
TINY BALCONY
WINDOW
living room
/kitchen
bedroom
BED
bathroom
fridge
LIAM'S HOUSE

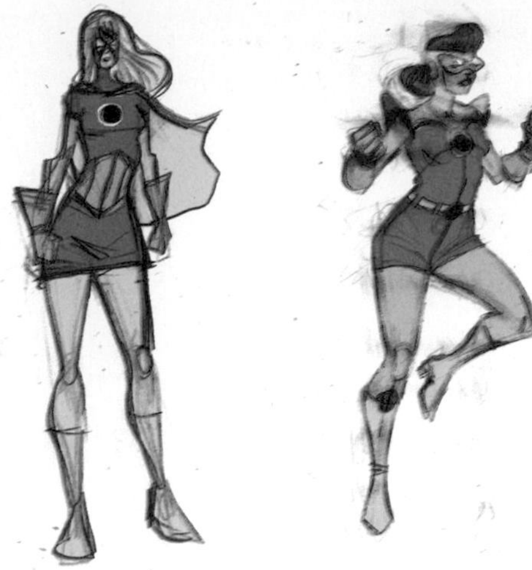

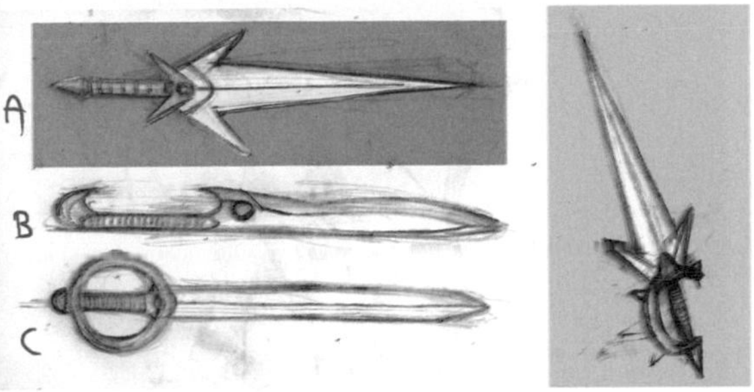
A
B
C

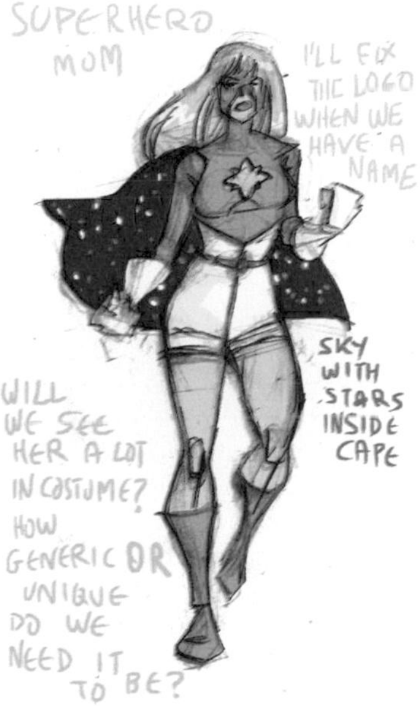
SUPERHERO MOM
I'LL FIX THE LOGO WHEN WE HAVE A NAME
SKY WITH STARS INSIDE CAPE
WILL WE SEE HER A LOT IN COSTUME? HOW GENERIC OR UNIQUE DO WE NEED IT TO BE?

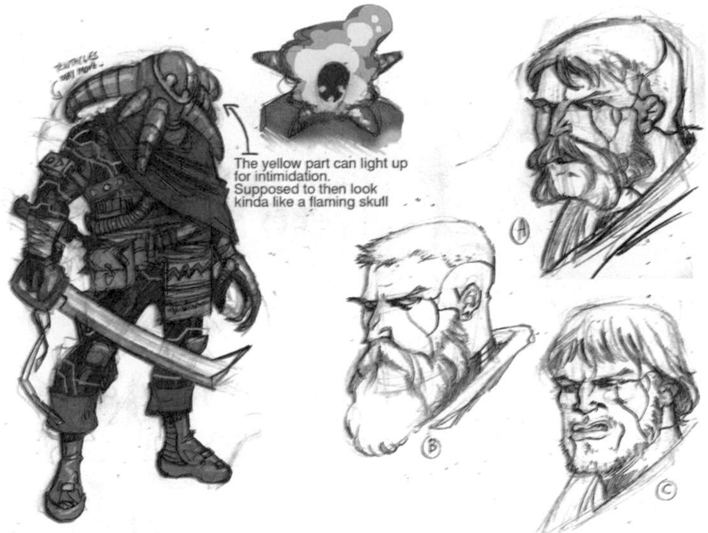
The yellow part can light up for intimidation. Supposed to then look kinda like a flaming skull
A
B
C

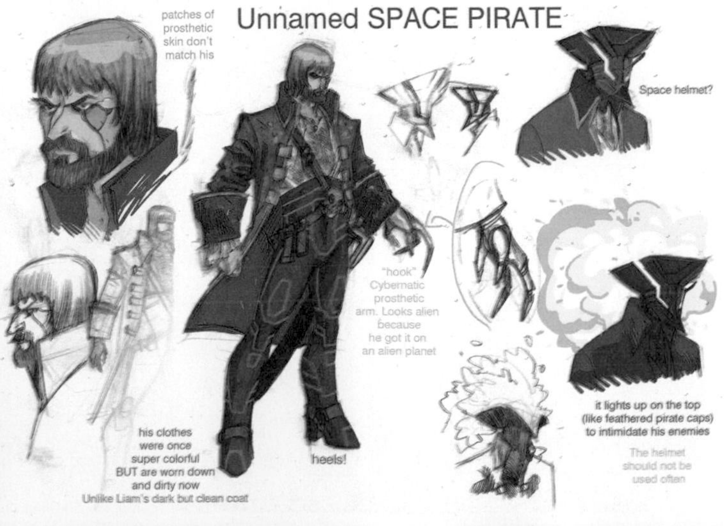
Unnamed SPACE PIRATE
patches of prosthetic skin don't match his
Space helmet?
"hook" Cybernatic prosthetic arm. Looks alien because he got it on an alien planet
it lights up on the top (like feathered pirate caps) to intimidate his enemies
The helmet should not be used oftan
heels!
his clothes were once super colorful BUT are worn down and dirty now Unlike Liam's dark but clean coat

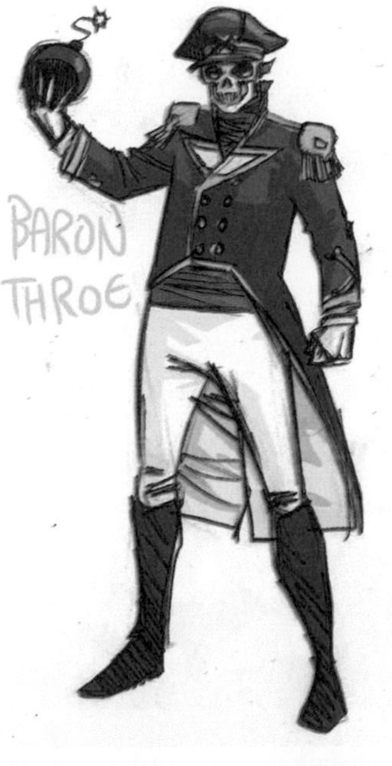
BARON THROE

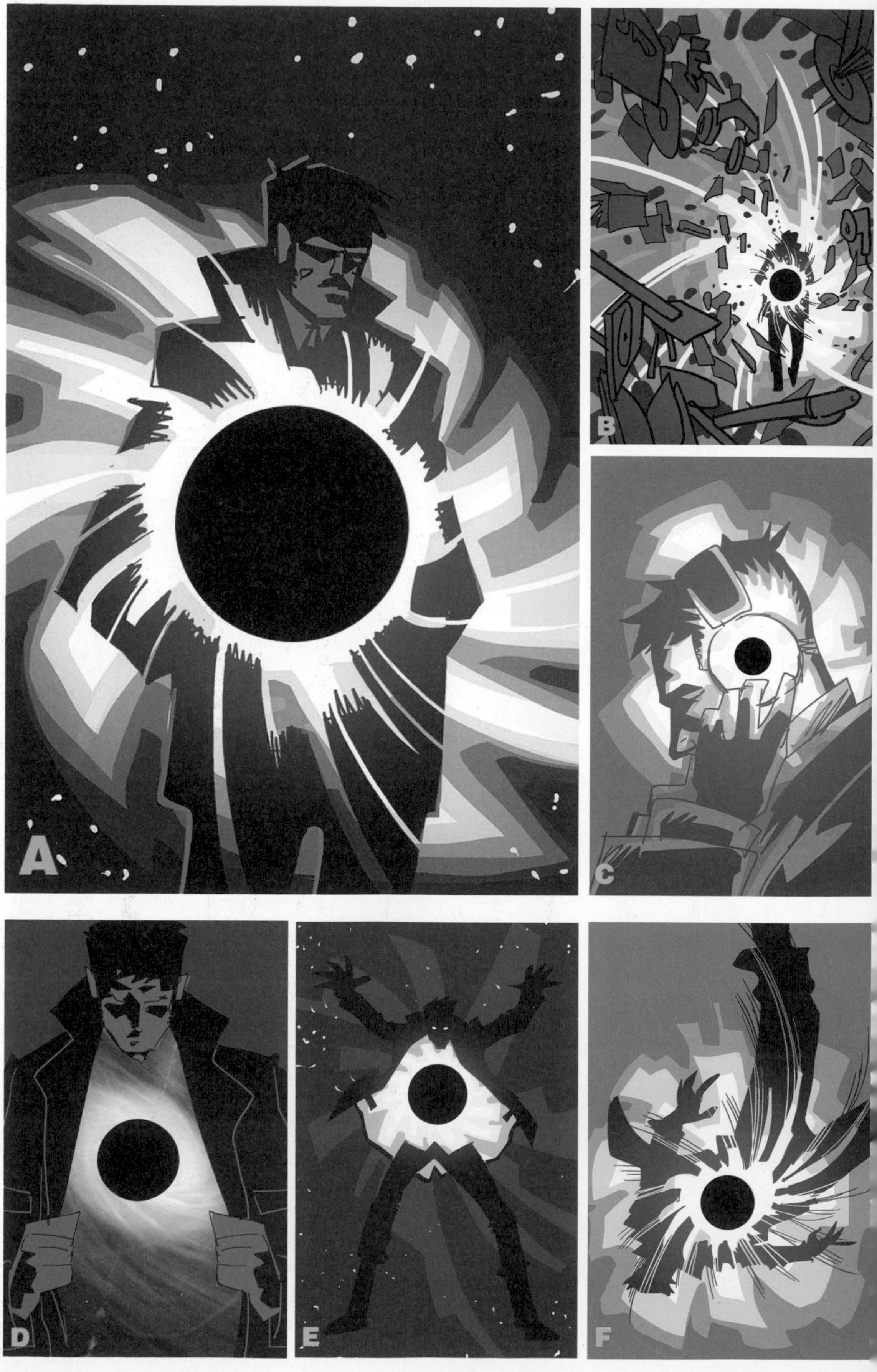
A
B
C
D
E
F